CHINA AND INTERNATIONAL INSTITUTIONS

In the post-cold war international system, the People's Republic of China (PRC) has shifted its foreign policy from one which eschews engagement in international organisations to one which embraces them and seeks to develop them. Beijing faces two unique barriers which prevent the country from taking the traditional paths of territorial expansion and political-economic domination in order to develop as a great power. The first is the United States and its inherent military and economic strength, the second the existence of nuclear weapons, which makes direct great power conflict unacceptably costly. China's response has been to opt for a different path, using institutions as stepping stones to great power status.

This book examines these new developments in Chinese foreign policy, and recommends a new approach to the study of great power development, using tools gathered from international institutional cooperation and development. In contrast to recent works on Chinese foreign policy, which have placed an emphasis on material goods and powers, this work will suggest an alternative approach to the 'rise of China' question, relevant not only to comparative politics but also the international relations of great powers.

This book will be of great interest to students of Chinese politics, Asian security studies and international relations in general, as well as to policymakers.

Marc Lanteigne is a lecturer, specialising in Chinese and Asian politics, at the Department of Political Science and International Development Studies Programme at McGill University in Montreal, Canada.

ASIAN SECURITY STUDIES
Edited by Sumit Ganguly
University of Indiana
and
Andrew Scobell
US Army War College

Few regions of the world are fraught with as many security questions as is Asia. Within this region it is possible to study great power rivalries, irredentist conflicts, nuclear and ballistic missile proliferation, secessionist movements, ethnoreligious conflicts and inter-state wars. This new book series will publish the best possible scholarship on the security issues affecting the region, and will include detailed empirical studies, theoretically oriented case studies and policy-relevant analyses as well as more general works.

CHINA AND INTERNATIONAL INSTITUTIONS
Alternate paths to global power
Marc Lanteigne

CHINESE NAVAL STRATEGY
Strategic implications of the PRC's tactical submarine fleet
Peter Howarth

CHINA AND INTERNATIONAL INSTITUTIONS

Alternate paths to global power

Marc Lanteigne

Routledge
Taylor & Francis Group

LONDON AND NEW YORK

First published 2005
by Routledge
2 Park Square, Milton Park, Abingdon, Oxon, OX14 4RN

Simultaneously published in the USA and Canada
by Routledge
270 Madison Ave, New York NY 10016

Routledge is an imprint of the Taylor & Francis Group

Transferred to Digital Printing 2007

© 2005 Marc Lanteigne

Typeset in Times by
HWA Text and Data Management Ltd, Tunbridge Wells

British Library Cataloguing in Publication Data
A catalogue record for this book is available from the British Library

Library of Congress Cataloging in Publication Data
Lanteigne, Marc.
China and international institutions : alternate paths to global power /
Marc Lanteigne.
p.   cm.
Includes bibliographical references and index.
1. China–Foreign relations–1976– 2. China–Foreign economic
relations. 3. International agencies. I. Title.
JZ1734.L36 2005
327.51–dc22   2005002009

ISBN10: 0–415–36584–8 (hbk)
ISBN10: 0–415–45956–7 (pbk)

ISBN13: 978–0–415–36584–0 (hbk)
ISBN13: 978–0–415–45956–3 (pbk)

CONTENTS

ACKNOWLEDGEMENTS

The writing of this book is the result of an abundance of new material available on the subject of China's foreign policy, and could not have been achieved without the assistance from a number of individuals and organisations. Thanks, first of all, to Professor T.V. Paul at McGill University, Montreal, who encouraged this project from its beginning. Earl Drake, Paul Evans, M. Taylor Fravel, Bernie Frolic, Dru Gladney, Wenran Jiang, Brian Job, André Laliberté, Pierre Lizée, Sam Noumoff, Jeremy Paltiel, Pitman Potter, Neil Renwick, Andrew Scobell, David Shambaugh, Jing-dong Yuan and David Zweig contributed invaluable insights and contributions to my research. Their cooperation and expertise in the politics of China and Asia were a source of continuous motivation for me. Encouragement and support during the initial researching for this book came from Nicole Baerg, Rex Brynen, Allen Chong, Jerome Davis, Xavier Furtado, Marc Lemieux, Saime Ozcurumez, Robin Ramcharan, Jim Storey, Flora Wan, and Bill Wieninger. I also gratefully acknowledge the contributions of the China and international relations scholars whose work has been cited in this book.

Many organisations also played a part in the research for this book via funding and other research assistance. The Research Group in International Security, based at McGill University and the Université de Montréal, was very helpful in providing assistance with fieldwork and the assisting with the presentation of previous research which helped build this book. The Canadian Consortium on Asia Pacific Security provided me with venues and opportunities to present my early research. The Centre for Foreign Policy Studies at Dalhousie University in Halifax provided both a sounding board and assistance for my fieldwork in Beijing in 2004.

The Asia Pacific Foundation of Canada also deserves many thanks, especially Yuen Pau Woo, Paul Irwin and Ron Richardson for their assistance and advice on matters related to Asian regional economic cooperation and trade policies. The APFC, along with providing a wonderful backdrop (Vancouver!) for me to conduct my initial research, made it possible for me to connect with China and Asia experts on both sides of the Pacific, assisted with fieldwork and helped support the development of early chapter drafts.

Many friends and colleagues at Foreign Affairs Canada, the Department of National Defence, and the Canadian International Development Agency provided assistance with data-gathering, research, and interviews. I would also like to thank the Canadian Embassy in Beijing, and especially Ambassador Joseph Caron, for their invaluable assistance and support during my travels to the city. Appreciation also must go to the various academics and officials in Beijing and Hong Kong who assisted with my fieldwork, granting interviews and providing me with material and data necessary to complete the case studies for this work, and for helping to make my trips to China such wonderful experiences.

Thanks must also go to Andrew Humphrys and Marjorie Francois at Routledge for their patience and assistance. Finally, I would like to thank my family for their unwavering faith, help and support for my first book. They have been my inspiration as I have negotiated the various twists and turns of further understanding the past, present and future of modern China.

ABBREVIATIONS

ABM	anti-ballistic missile
ACFTA	ASEAN-China Free Trade Association
AFC	Asian financial crisis
AMF	Asian Monetary Fund
ANZUS	Australia-New Zealand-United States Treaty
APEC	Asia-Pacific Economic Cooperation Forum
APT	ASEAN-Plus-Three
ARF	ASEAN Regional Forum
ASEAN	Association of Southeast Asian Nations
ASEM	Asia-Europe Meeting
ASPC	ARF Security Policy Conference
CASS	Chinese Academy of Social Studies
CBMs	confidence-building measures
CCP	Chinese Communist Party
CIS	Commonwealth of Independent States
CMC	Central Military Commission
CNNIC	China Internet Network Information Centre
CNPC	China National Petroleum Council
CSCAP	Council for Security Cooperation in Asia-Pacific
CSCE	Council for Security and Cooperation in Europe
DF-31	Dongfeng-31 (East Wind 31) missile
DPP	Democratic Progressive Party (Taiwan)
DPRK	Democratic People's Republic of Korea
EAC	East Asia Community
EAEC	East Asian Economic Caucus
Ecotech	economic and technical cooperation
ETIM	East Turkestan Islamic Movement
EVSL	early voluntary sectoral liberalisation
GATT	General Agreement on Tariffs and Trade
GCC	Gulf Cooperation Council
GLD	General Logistics Department (of the PLA)
HIODS	heavy industry-oriented development strategy
IAI	Initiative for Asian Integration

IAP	individual action plan
IMF	International Monetary Fund
IMU	Islamic Movement of Uzbekistan
KMT	Kuomintang (Nationalist) Party, Taiwan
MFN	most-favoured nation
MII	Ministry of Information Industry
MITI	Ministry of International Trade and Industry, Japan
MOFTEC	Ministry of Foreign Trade and Economic Cooperation
MTCR	Missile Technology Control Regime
NAFTA	North American Free Trade Association
NATO	North Atlantic Treaty Organisation
NGO	non-governmental organisation
NIE	newly industrialising economies
NIEO	New International Economic Order
NMD	national missile defence
NSC	New Security Concept
NSG	Nuclear Suppliers Group
NWFZ	nuclear weapons free zone
ODA	overseas development assistance
OSCE	Organisation for Security and Cooperation in Europe
PBEC	Pacific Basin Economic Council
PECC	Pacific Economic Cooperation Council
PfP	Partnership for Peace
PLA	People's Liberation Army
PLAN	People's Liberation Army Navy
PTA	preferential trade agreement
RATS	regional anti-terrorist structure
SARS	severe acute respiratory syndrome
SCO	Shanghai Cooperation Organisation
SDPC	State Development Planning Commission
SEA	Single European Act
SEATO	South East Asia Treaty Organisation
SETC	State Economic and Trade Commission
SEZ	special economic zone
SOE	state-owned enterprise
SPC	State Planning Commission
SPT	Six-Party Talks
TMD	theatre missile defence
TRIPS	trade-related intellectual property rights
UN	United Nations
UNCLOS	United Nations Convention on the Law of the Sea
UNDP	United Nations Development Programme
USSR	Union of Soviet Socialist Republics
WTO	World Trade Organisation
ZOPFAN	Zone of Peace, Freedom and Neutrality

INTRODUCTION

An emerging global power and international institutions reconsidered

> In a pond, no dragon's meant to lie;
> He'll ride the thunder to the sky!
> Luo Guanzhong, *Three Kingdoms*

Over the last twenty years, China has exhibited behaviour consistent with that of a great power, and a rising global power. Its foreign policy since the end of the cold war has included seeking to advance its stature within the international system, increasing its global interests and searching for a greater voice in its external environment. Unlike rising powers of the past, China faced two powerful barriers preventing the country from taking the traditional paths of territorial expansion and political-economic domination in order to develop as a global power. The first has been the presence of the United States, the world's remaining superpower after the cold war. China lacks the power to 'balance' American supremacy unilaterally and does not yet have the ability to gather allies together for balancing purposes, as the Soviet Union attempted in the last century. Beijing is unwilling to engage in direct competition with America, or indeed with other great powers, out of concern that such actions may lead to a downturn in China's security. The second barrier, closely related to the first, is the proliferation of nuclear weapons, which has made direct great power conflict, used in the past to change states' power positions in the global hierarchy, unacceptably costly to all sides. Faced with these barriers, China has chosen a different (and more indirect) path to greater power acquisition via an international system containing more institutions than had ever previously existed.

China's opening to international institutions since the late 1980s is a crucial component in its multilateral approach to foreign policy and to the advancement of state power. What separates China from other states, and indeed previous global powers, is that not only is it 'growing up' within a milieu of international institutions far more developed than ever before, but more importantly, it is doing so while making active use of these institutions to promote the country's development of global power status.

In examining these ideas, case studies of international institutions with which

1

China aligned itself will be conducted using six selected 'goods' to determine how Beijing's cooperation with selected institutions acted as a means for China to enhance its role within the international system, with the end being further development as a global power. These goods include state security, regime security, information acquisition, economic benefits, an improved position *vis-à-vis* other great powers, and prestige. Case studies chosen for this work were selected due to their different mandates and levels of formality. Two of these cases are primarily economic institutions, namely the World Trade Organisation, which China had been attempting to join for many years and only succeeded in doing in late 2001, and exclusive economic regimes, the Asia Pacific Economic Cooperation Forum (APEC), and other smaller trade regimes, including bilateral preferential trade agreements (PTAs) and the more elaborate ASEAN-Plus-Three (APT) grouping.

The other cases are primarily strategic organisations, including the ASEAN Regional Forum (ARF), which addresses security issues in east and southeast Asia, and the recent Six-Party Talks on security in the Korean Peninsula. The embryonic Shanghai Cooperation Organisation (SCO) was created, largely at China's initiative, to define mutual borders and to examine threats to state security in central Asia. These cases illustrate China's growing dependence upon international institutions as a means of creating a more effective foreign policy, while protecting valuable domestic interests.

The reasons for the choice of these case studies are threefold. First, these institutions well illustrate China's post-cold war economic and strategic policies at both regional and international levels. Second, each case study represents different degrees of mandates, norms and levels of formality. Third, these cases demonstrate a considerable spectrum of levels of Chinese engagement and influence. These cases will be used to suggest an evolving model of Chinese relations with international institutions and to explain why they are important tools for China in developing into a great power. They will also offer predictions as to how China's role in these regimes will shape international relations to come.

China abandoned its isolationist policies under Communist China's first leader, Mao Zedong, in favour of the foreign policy reforms of Deng Xiaoping in 1978–9, and especially following the 1990s with the end of the cold war and the dawn of economic globalisation. As a result of these foreign policy reforms, Beijing embarked on a policy of strengthening ties with other countries in the region and mending fences with past adversaries, such as Indonesia, South Korea, Singapore and Vietnam, attempting to improve relations with other great powers in the region (Russia and India), and forging ties with new states, (such as the former Soviet republics in central Asia).

These initiatives were designed to promote a greater atmosphere of confidence, as part of the Chinese government's *zhoubian*, or 'omni-directional' foreign policy initiatives. China's foreign policy of intensified diplomacy and forging new linkages with other states began in the 1990s as a means of mitigating the diplomatic damage created during the Tiananmen Square incident in 1989 and reaping the benefits of adopting a largely neutral stance during the 1991 Gulf War between American-led

United Nations forces and Iraq. On many fronts the initiative has been very successful.[1] Beijing's increasing foreign policy confidence and ability to project its ideas and policies within the international arena are clear signs of China's commitment to moving beyond pre-1979 isolationism and claiming the global power status to which it feels entitled. Beijing has focused on a number of specific goals, including maintaining the security of the state and ruling communist regime, greater wealth and economic power, and elevating China's position alongside other great powers, notably the United States. As well, at the turn of the new century China's 'charm offensive' in Asia appeared to be making considerable gains as more countries in the region view Beijing as an economic and political partner rather than a potential adversary.[2]

China's new leaders, led by President Hu Jintao and Premier Wen Jiabao, are now tasked with not only further developing China's power, but also determining the type of great power and possible global power the state will be. The Hu government presides over a China which has changed considerably from the time his predecessor took office in the wake of the Tiananmen tragedy. Beijing's level of respect, not only in Asia but around the world, is testing new heights. The security situation in the country is far more stable and the Chinese economy has boomed, despite many obstacles, to become an important component of the international market. The ideas of globalisation, an idea which previous Chinese governments had addressed only very gingerly, have been openly discussed by Hu and his inner circle.[3] At the same time, serious issues confront the new government, including the socio-economic effects of the country's market transition, as well as the still-unresolved issue of Taiwan, which Beijing has continued to maintain is a province of China.

One commonly used phrase in Chinese policy circles has been that of 'peaceful rise' (*heping jueqi*), a concept which was originally devised by Zheng Bijian, a former senior official in the Chinese government. By late 2003 the phrase was being used by senior officials of the new regime, including Hu and Wen. The phrase, which had been seen as a way of assuring the international community that Chinese growth would not lead to expansionism or threats to security, had nevertheless engendered much internal debate in Beijing.[4] According to the concept, while China is on the path to becoming powerful, it would do so only on the basis of its own strength, mindful of the need for world peace and international trade. Moreover, the country would develop its power in a gradual fashion and Beijing would continue its policies of not seeking hegemony over states.[5] In a speech to the Brazilian Parliament in November 2004, Hu explained that China would continue to focus on peaceful development and cordial relations with the international community in partnership with other states.[6]

International institutions have become increasingly important to China's growth and development. As Kim noted, inter-state institutions are hardly a new phenomenon in the international system, with such global organisations having their roots in the nineteenth century. What distinguishes the development of institutions, however, is the rapid growth in their numbers, following the Second World War.[7]

As well, institutions have expanded their areas of concentration, including strategic, economic, environmental, cultural, and so forth. The end of the cold war saw acceleration in the number of institutions being created, while at the same time new members were joining older institutions, occasionally altering their character or mandate. Another option for China has presented itself in the form of international institutions. Selective engagement and interaction with these institutions is essential to augmenting China's power in the international system and provides a means of expanding state power which was largely unavailable to great powers of the past.

Before launching into an explanation of the growing importance of international institutions and regimes to the rising power of China, it is useful to examine two themes: the concept of both 'great' and 'global' powers and, second, why China should be considered a great power and a rising global one. This introduction will include an examination of the definitions and functions of international institutions in the modern global system and how they have changed, and proliferated, subsequent to the end of the cold war.

China as a great power

An examination of the development of Chinese power (*liliang*) must include careful scrutiny of the various definitions of this concept. Barring any serious internal or external catastrophe that could bring about widespread social or economic disorder, China is a great power and will remain so for the foreseeable future. Using traditional measurements developed during the cold war period to determine the power level of a state, China fulfils or comes close to meeting most of the necessary criteria to attain the status of 'great power'. However, China has not yet reached the level of a 'global' power. The dividing line between great and global power has proven to be both thin and open to analytical interpretation. The end of the cold war and the rise of economic power as important factors in determining the international hierarchy of states have further blurred this distinction. Nevertheless, there are facets of global power status which distinguish this category. First, from a strictly realist viewpoint, global powers such as the United States have the ability to project military power to any part of the world, largely unilaterally, and possess a high level of superiority in their armed forces. Post-cold war American military operations in the Gulf War (1991), Kosovo (1999), Afghanistan (2001) and the Iraq conflict (2003–4), have underscored the far-reaching military capabilities of the United States. China, as will be noted, has worked to modernise its armed forces but has yet to achieve a reach beyond its immediate periphery.

Second, Keohane remarked that states at the topmost level of the international order are 'system-determining', having a pivotal role in shaping the overall international system.[8] This definition could be applied to global powers and at present the United States is arguably the only country with the ability to significantly affect the international system in so many dimensions, including political, strategic and economic. Third, in her assessment of American power, Strange moved beyond

4

the military sphere by describing the United States as being distinct in its possession of 'structural power', described as 'the power to choose and shape the structures of the global political economy within which other states, their political institutions, their economic enterprises, and (not least) their professional people have to operate'. The components of structural power, she added, include the ability to increase or decrease the security of others, to exercise control over production of goods and services, to determine the structure of finance and credit, and to have wide-ranging influence over ideas, information flows, and knowledge from many areas.[9]

Finally, an argument can be made that global powers are distinct in their ability to project a great deal of 'soft power', defined as 'the ability to get desired outcomes because others want what you want', and 'the ability to achieve goals through attraction rather than coercion'. States wielding soft power can transmit information abroad which carries attractive ideas and culture, thus increasing support for those states, without resorting to force.[10] Closely connected to this idea is that of 'sticky power', the ability to enmesh other actors within economic linkages to the point where any attempts to withdraw would carry large risks and costs.[11] The United States is currently the undisputed champion of both soft and sticky power projection. China, along with other current great powers, lags well behind.

Various instruments of measurement have been proposed by which to gauge Beijing's suitability to be considered of great power rank, drawing from capabilities in the military, economic, political, and cultural spheres. Keohane, in seeking to differentiate a small from a great power, describes the latter as 'a state whose leaders consider that it can, alone, exercise a large, perhaps decisive, impact on the international system'.[12] One useful set of prerequisites emanates from the cold-war era description of great power capabilities by realist analyst Kenneth Waltz. He argued that in order for a state to be placed in the top ranks of the global hierarchy, it must fare well in the following areas: territorial size and population, economic capability, resource endowment, military strength, political stability and 'competence'.[13] China at the dawn of the twenty-first century has made remarkable progress in fulfilling many of these criteria.

First, few would argue that China's size and population are not impressive and distinctive, giving the country a great deal of political and economic *gravitas* even before the development of the post-cold war international order. China's *presence gigantesque*, via its size and accompanying power, make the country difficult to ignore from either a political, economic, socio-cultural or strategic viewpoint. It has the largest population in the world, approximately 1.3 billion at the beginning of the twenty-first century. Geographically, China is not only a 'big country' (*daguo*) in terms of land size, (fourth largest in area after the Russian Federation, Canada, and the United States), but it also lies in a geographic region favourable to conducting multilateral foreign policy and trade. In addition, as Gray noted, unlike the former USSR, China has an extensive maritime coast, making any attempts at physical containment of the country extremely difficult.[14] However, China's size and location did not prevent the country from being subject to foreign domination from Asian and European actors at various times in China's Imperial era.

At the same time China shares extensive land and sea borders with countries in northeast Asia (Mongolia, North Korea, South Korea, Japan, Russia), southeast Asia (Laos, Myanmar/Burma, Vietnam), south Asia (Bhutan, India, Nepal, Pakistan), and central Asia (Afghanistan, Kazakhstan, Kyrgyzstan, Tajikistan). China also asserts a right of sovereignty over the province of Taiwan, as well as island chains in the South China Sea which are claimed by other southeast Asian countries. These many neighbours have prompted Beijing to remain vigilant of its borders, making China a *de facto* geopolitical nexus. The country's potential to tip the balance of power in the Asia-Pacific region is partially based on its proximity to key maritime shipping lanes, including the Taiwan Straits and the South China Sea, which service both northeast and southeast Asia. China's size and population are also factors when one considers international concerns such as energy availability, resource allocation, environmental protection, and the determination of standards of state-to-state conduct. Since China comprises a little more than one-sixth of the world's population, decisions on any of these issues cannot easily be made without Beijing's participation and acceptance of their outcomes.

Second, in terms of China's economic power, with the rise of market politics and globalisation over the past two decades and the increasing use of trade as a tool for international foreign policy, China's market has become a magnet for resources and investment, made even more tempting by its willingness to embrace economic, if not political, liberalisation in the wake of the Dengist reforms. These commenced in 1978–9 once Deng Xiaoping had secured the leadership of the Communist Party from Mao's chosen successor, Hua Guofeng, and accelerated after his subsequent 'Southern Tour' (*nanxun*) of 1992, which had been almost universally accepted as an official blessing for Chinese domestic openings to international markets.[15] Since that time, reform packages designed to optimise, or shut down, state-owned enterprises (SOEs), the scaling back of the 'iron-rice bowl' (or *danwei*, the lifetime support mechanism for Chinese workers and a central tenet of Maoist economics), taxation and financial reforms, attempts at legal restructuring, and attempts to join international economic regimes, have all contributed to China's economic growth and development.[16]

In addition, one of the major amendments to the Chinese constitution passed in March 2004 was a clause stating that 'citizens' legal private property is inviolable', further entrenching the right of the people to hold and benefit from private property.[17] The results of Beijing's economic opening over the past quarter-decade have been remarkable. Between 1978 and 2004, China's gross domestic product has quadrupled to approximately US$1.4 trillion, and in that time period the country's international trade levels rose from negligible to the third largest in the world after the United States and Germany.[18]

The partially closed nature of the national economy allowed Beijing to escape the worst of the damage created by the Asian Financial Crisis (AFC) of 1997–8, while the more economically open states surrounding it, especially Indonesia, Malaysia, Thailand and South Korea, and to a lesser degree the Philippines and Japan, suffered severe shocks. The perceived resiliency of the Chinese economy, as well as the 'big market' factor, kept foreign investment coming to China even during the worst of the crisis. In 1997, foreign investment in China stood at US\$62 billion, a 13 per cent increase from the previous year, with US\$43 billion comprised of direct foreign investment.[19] Clearly, few companies have been dissuaded by the crisis from enhancing their ties with China as that country continues to develop its economic power.

A different shock which created a great deal of socio-economic trauma was the outbreak of Severe Acute Respiratory Syndrome (SARS, or in Mandarin, *feidian*) within China. After reportedly originating in November 2002 in the southern province of Guangdong, the SARS virus spread to other parts of China, Hong Kong, Taiwan, parts of southeast Asia, and Toronto, Canada, and to a lesser degree Europe, Australia and the United States. By the time the virus abated in July 2003, there were approximately 8,000 cases reported and about 800 fatalities, 348 of these in China.[20] Beijing was harshly criticised abroad, and even to some degree domestically, for its initial reluctance to report the virus to international authorities and for its slow response in implementing quarantine procedures.[21] The crisis brought regional tourism to a halt and raised questions about a long-term economic downturn, should the virus persist. However, with no renewed outbreak of SARS in 2004 as was feared, the Chinese economy shook off the temporary setback and continued to grow at a strong clip.

Despite these successes, China's entry into the global economy has not been without occasional difficulties. Analysts have cited many factors, including corruption, a lack of transparency, a dearth of necessary infrastructure, and Beijing's convoluted restrictions on foreign direct investment. An erratic taxation system, and a legal apparatus which has yet to achieve a sufficient level of separation from the state, add to the roadblocks.[22] Legal reform remains one of the most crucial challenges of the Chinese state and is integral to future economic development and foreign investment. Indeed, one of the main reasons Beijing has endeavoured to create a stronger rule of law in the country is the recognition there is a link between stable, independent laws and economic development.[23]

China's resource capabilities are also important measurements in determining that country's global power potential. The country has shifted from pursuing self-sufficiency in its resource base and has begun to rely more heavily on international trade to fill its resource requirements. Even with more emphasis on manufacturing and services as part of its domestic modernisation process, large swathes of the Chinese interior still rely heavily on agriculture. Moreover, a majority of China's domestic energy needs are satisfied by coal, while in 1993 China became a net oil-importer as a result of surging demands.[24] As a result of China's rapid modernisation, oil has become a crucial commodity, as more citizens are able to afford private cars and demand for industrial and residential power skyrockets in both major cities and rural areas.[25] Not only has the need for increased access to petroleum supplies affected Beijing's foreign policy priorities, but predictions that China would become a nexus for energy imports have moved from speculation to reality.

China's military strength, it has been argued, is something the country already possesses in abundance, albeit on a regional scale. The Chinese People's Liberation Army (PLA) consists of active armed forces of just less than 2.5 million, and a defence budget estimated at approximately 185.3 billion RMB (US$22 billion) by 2003.[26] While that figure may be considered too conservative since many Chinese military developments are not publicly acknowledged, China's conventional military capabilities are not trivial. However, using conventional warfare, China is not currently in a favourable position to militarily engage the United States, or even some of its closer neighbours. The planes, ships and weaponry of the People's Liberation Army suffer from limited projection power, increasing obsolescence, and a widening technical gap with Western armaments. One tragic manifestation of these problems took place in May 2003 when Beijing announced that a PLA Navy submarine suffered an unspecified mechanical failure which killed 70 personnel.[27] Nevertheless, the country has benefited from a nuclear *force de frappe*, meaning an arsenal which does not rely on overwhelming force but is enough to cause great damage. Beijing conducted its first nuclear weapons test on 16 October 1964,[28] and since then has developed the means to deliver these warheads to faraway targets from either sea or land. This makes direct confrontation with China exceptionally risky and has provided Beijing with a great deal of breathing space to address its many shortcomings in waging conventional war.

In the 1990s, China began to develop its military force-projection capabilities, through the modernisation of its ballistic missile programmes and advancements in its naval and air forces. As well, Beijing has purchased a considerable amount of Russian-made weaponry, including fighter aircraft, naval vessels, submarines, and missiles.[29] Beijing's reliance on Moscow for much of its higher-end military equipment may explain much about the deficiencies of China's indigenous military research and development, but these acquisitions also illustrate China's acceptance of these shortcomings and its determination to rapidly overcome them.[30] In addition, during the past two decades, Beijing has been developing its own indigenous defences. For example, the PLA has been manufacturing attack submarines and in 2002 announced the unveiling of an advanced jet fighter purportedly capable of challenging fourth-generation Western jets.[31]

Finally, China's missile technology has evolved to where a small number of warheads can be launched at out-of-area targets. In 1999, China conducted a successful test of its *Dongfeng-* ('East-Wind') 31 (DF-31) intercontinental ballistic missile and an advanced version, the DF-41 with an estimated 12,000km range, is currently undergoing testing.[32] China moved its missile capabilities to a much different level in October 2003 when after a series of successful unmanned launches, the country sent its first astronaut, Lieutenant-Colonel Yang Liwei, into orbit aboard the *Shenzhou* ('Divine Vessel') *V* spacecraft. After 21 hours in space and 14 orbits, Yang's re-entry vehicle landed safely in Inner Mongolia and China became the third nation, after Russia and United States, to succeed in such an endeavour.[33]

The question of China's potential military capability, especially *vis-à-vis* other great powers, will likely continue to be a source of dispute among analysts.

However, it can be said that Beijing's defence policies are becoming increasingly oriented towards waging more modern warfare and developing a stronger conventional deterrence capability to a level matching the power of its nuclear weapons. In determining the course of military developments in the new century, China has positioned itself to where it can no longer be ignored by other great powers in the strategic arena.

Finally, there is Waltz's idea of state 'competence', an ambiguous and difficult term to measure effectively. Suffice it to say that Chinese foreign policy behaviour has been marked by a combination of conservatism, measured policies, and a great deal of caution, since the founding of the People's Republic in 1949. It must be remembered that China was one of the very few developing countries with the ability to walk a dangerous tightrope between the two superpowers for much of the cold war, breaking with the USSR in the early 1960s and then acting as an important lynchpin between Washington and Moscow until the Soviet Union's demise. There was even speculation China might go the same way, namely collapse due to mounting political chaos. A possible Chinese break-up, it was speculated, might be the result of Beijing being unable to handle the effects of centrifugal force from peripheral regions like Xiyang (Tibet) and Xinjiang, as well as the richer coastal states of Guangzhou and Fujian. The issue of government control could have been further exacerbated by Deng Xiaoping's passing and a resulting power struggle.[34] However, these conclusions were greatly coloured by the Soviet example and placed too much emphasis on historical patterns of rebellion in rebuilding during China's dynastic periods and not enough on the country's modern realities. The 1997 government transition in Beijing after the death of Deng proceeded reasonably smoothly, as has the handover of power from President Jiang Zemin to his successor, Hu Jintao, initiated at the 16th Party Congress in November 2002 and completed in September 2004 when Jiang stepped down from his final post as head of the Central Military Commission.[35]

Other factors may contribute to the question of what determines a great power. It has been hypothesised that great powers normally consider their interests on a regional and global scale rather than merely local (which China is increasingly doing, representing a considerable break with the past), and tend to defend their interests more vociferously, especially *vis-à-vis* other great powers, and with a larger set of tools. As well, great powers are often perceived as such by their 'peers', either through state-to-state contact, or through international constructions, such as treaties, alliances, and organisations.[36] China received one major trapping of a great power in 1971, when the country was granted a permanent seat with accompanying veto power on the United Nations Security Council. Since then, China has sought participation in other international institutions in order to solidify its status and enhance its legitimacy. This has been especially true on the regional level, where Beijing has evolved into a pivotal state in the Asia-Pacific region, and increasingly on a global scale.

The international system provided an impetus for China to evolve into the great power it is now, as it has for others in the past. First, since countries normally experience economic, political and technological growth at different rates, shifts are created in the distribution of state power.[37] The effects of this are threefold: rising powers may be more likely to advance their stature in the international system in keeping with their growth, such powers would want to enhance their security by increasing their capabilities and their control over their external environment, and rising states are likely to have increased international interests and commitments.[38] Second, despite impressive advances in international cooperation following the cold war, including new and enhanced formal international agreements, informal contact on many different levels, the growth of transnational actors, and increased overall economic contact, the international system is still very much anarchical. Both factors often compel states with the potential to become great powers to actually do so. To do otherwise creates an unacceptable risk of being at a disadvantage against present and future rivals.[39] Domestic and international factors have contributed to China's development as a great power, and may assist in Beijing's advancement towards global power status in this new century.

Defining institutions

The concept of an 'international institution' is one for which several definitions have been suggested. The term has very generally been applied to any sort of social construction with some degree of permanence. Beyond that, however, the concept is nebulous. For example, Keohane referred to institutions as 'a general pattern or organisation of an activity or to a particular human-constructed arrangement, formally or informally organised'.[40] International institutions differ from norms, which lack the level of framework required for a clear 'institution' to exist. Mearsheimer's definition of an institution is more concise and will be used for this volume: 'a set of rules that stipulate the ways in which states should cooperate and compete with each other. [International institutions] prescribe acceptable forms of state behaviour, and proscribe unacceptable kinds of behaviour'.[41] This definition is very close to that of an international 'regime' as described by Krasner.[42] In some cases, the concept of regime has been used to capture the idea of a larger set of political constructions of which institutions are a part. For our purposes, however, I will follow Martin's example,[43] and periodically use these terms interchangeably.

In addition to the definition of an institution, there has been a great deal of theoretical debate as to how strong a role they play in state interactions. For example, realism, one of the most long-lived and malleable of the international relations schools of thought, is an effective starting point in approaching the question of China's institutional relations. The major assumptions of realism are 1) the international system is anarchical, with states being the primary actors and no significant power existing above them; 2) state preferences are fixed and for the most part saturated with conflict; and 3) when states engage in bargaining, they do so while cognisant of the relative costs of threats and inducements, which are directly proportional to the distribution of material resources. Realism also surmises there is a significant distinction between international and domestic politics and those international relations are distinguished by struggles for power and the attainment of peace.[44] To apply this theory to the case of modern China, it would appear that Beijing would have a lot to lose by cooperating with institutions, since the country is developing global power status and wishes to retain it.

According to 'neo-realist' theories of cooperation, states which had previously ascended the international hierarchy towards global power status had traditionally followed a pattern of pursuing *relative* gains (gains measured against those of other states in the system) as well as *absolute* gains (those which are measured against what the state itself previously possessed) to enhance their power at the expense of cooperating with international institutions, largely out of concern that areas of vulnerability would be created.[45]

At first glance, this description may apply to China. For example, Ruggie noted in 1992 that after the Second World War, 'it was not possible to construct multilateral institutional frameworks' in the Asia-Pacific region and that 'the absence of such arrangements inhibits progressive adaptation to fundamental global shifts'. Thus, he concluded, unless some sort of 'Helsinki-like process' to create more formalised institutions in the region occurred, the Asia-Pacific was doomed to rely on bad old balance of power politics to keep the area from total destabilisation.[46] Granted, in comparison with Europe and North America, progress in developing formal institutions within the Asia-Pacific has been considerably slower. Such lethargy has occasionally been attributed to socio-cultural differences, a so-called 'Asian Way' theory which focuses on consensus-building, inclusiveness and equal veto power versus majority rules and exclusive memberships.[47]

Another rationale has been the negative effect of the cold war on regime-building in Asia, since many states, at that time, joined alignments based on ideology rather than shared regional interests. From a strategic view, there was much reliance in Asia on the so-called 'San Francisco System', a network of hub-and-spoke, American-dominated bilateral alliances which saturated the region beginning in the 1950s.[48] Nevertheless, limiting the definition of 'institutions' to formal constructions in both the Chinese and Asia-Pacific foreign policy milieu is both Western-centric and would result in an unacceptably incomplete view of regional interstate cooperation. There is a large number of regional bilateral arrangements, economic interactions, informal contacts, and groupings which operate beneath the level of formal government channels, such as business, bureaucratic, and academic contacts, (loosely defined as 'Track II' initiatives), which have arguably accomplished much in mitigating the anarchic nature of state relations in the Asia-Pacific region.[49]

The definitions of rising power and international institutions are also important when one considers how they are joined as in the case of China. According to Martin, looking at both numbers and complexity, the growth of institutions during the last century is incomparable to any other time period, and for every unsuccessful institution, many others thrive. One result, she adds, is that since the end of the cold war, states are valuing their institutional ties more than ever.[50] How does the existence of so many institutions affect a potential great power such as China? The provisional answer appears to be: as arguably the first great power to rise within a milieu of international institutions, China is more compelled, unlike great powers of the past, to make these regimes an important part of its goal to increase its power and maintain an enhanced role in the global order.

Risks and rewards of institutional engagement for China

In order to accurately measure the growth of Chinese power and emerging role in the international system, one should first question China's decision to more fully cooperate with the changing international system, including its growing number of institutions. Why would China, as a potential global power, wish to engage and participate in international institutions? Previous studies of Chinese interaction with various international regimes examined why institutions serve Chinese self-interests. Ostensibly, Beijing will only cooperate with institutions in a conservative fashion and under very select circumstances. For example, Christensen, who referred to China as the possible 'high church of *realpolitik*' noted in the same article that Chinese policymakers were highly suspicious of multilateral organisations of many stripes, economic, strategic, or otherwise, because they were largely perceived as being fronts for other great powers and their specific agendas. However, the author admits that although China was 'concerned and vigilant' in its approach to international regimes, it has not eschewed them,[51] an action which would have been more in keeping with realist perceptions.

One analyst, in summarising her own findings on Chinese institutional behaviour, concluded her observations in the form of three caveats. Specifically, any institutions with which China cooperates cannot hinder the country's economic development, infringe on its sovereignty through either external monitoring or outside determination of how Beijing should use its resources, or allow for the more industrialised states to widen the already considerable economic and technological gap between themselves and China.[52] However, general observations on state behaviour would suggest that these stipulations are hardly unique to Beijing. The first two caveats can be said to hold true of all states in the international system, since all states seek to avoid outside interference in domestic interests. The third is a common concern among many developing nations, including China, which are worried about their economic and political position *vis-à-vis* the developed world.

China is distinct, however, in that its size and growing international power permit Beijing to be more particular about the institutions it approaches and its degree of participation in them. As well, the international community has become more accommodating to China's wishes to join more institutions. Assuming great power competition, China's emergence does add concerns that other great powers would seek to halt or contain a future Chinese power. Oksenberg and Economy have suggested the structure of a given regime is also a determinant in China's level of cooperation. For example, they argue that Beijing prefers to enter institutions which are informal, lack a clear mandate, and evolve in such a way that is compatible to the country's domestic-level interests.[53] However, these various 'absolutes' are being continuously challenged by more recent Chinese behaviour towards international institutions.

On the surface, there would appear to be many reasons for it not to be in the interests of the country, or more specifically, the current regime, to interact with these institutions. First, China has many other outlets by which to engage the international system. These would involve fewer responsibilities and risks to the Chinese government. These alternatives take the form of bilateral agreements, which found favour during much of the cold war and remain a preferred foreign policy method.

In the strategic realm, Beijing has developed 'partnerships' with select states and organisations, including the United States, European Union, and Russia, as well as Canada, Egypt, France, Japan, Mexico and South Africa.[54] Economically, Beijing overcame its traditional wariness of bilateral preferential trade agreements and in the late 1990s began to actively seek PTAs with neighbouring economies. A PTA agreement with Hong Kong was completed in 2003 and other regional deals are currently under negotiation.[55] Bilateral agreements for China have, for the most part, been easier to construct and participate in, easier to alter when circumstances required, and provided China an acceptable level of control. Conversely, multilateral agreements involve more actors and thus more variables with which to contend, often proving more difficult for a single state to change unilaterally. Therefore, one might argue that other inducements prompted China to supplement its existing bilateral relationships with multilateral ones. Beijing's increasing confidence in incorporating larger numbers and types of multilateral and bilateral agreements has been correctly viewed as demonstrating 'a new flexibility and sophistication' in its foreign policy.[56]

In addition, engagement has been accomplished via sub-state actors and individuals, especially after the post-1979 Dengist reforms. Through education abroad, business transactions, joint ventures, and more recently, lower-level 'Track II' gatherings to discuss shared concerns on matters ranging from the environment to mutual trade matters, China has been able to gain insights into global interactions. Unlike China under Mao, the People's Republic, today, has far fewer restrictions on individual and business-level interactions, and these interactions have provided many small-scale but useful outlets for China to shape its foreign policy and understand the motivations of other global actors.[57] This process is further aided by the existence of an expansive overseas Chinese business network, connecting China with many Chinese minority populations in the Pacific Rim and providing Beijing with both information and outlets to developing and newly-industrialised countries. However, the effectiveness of this is limited since increased engagement on these levels has also brought foreign ideas and concepts into China which could pose future challenges to the Communist regime.

Second, unlike other great powers, China is a 'late-developer' in the international system,[58] a product of political isolationism and a failed attempt during the Maoist period to promote economic autarky, most recently in the wake of the Cultural Revolution, which resulted in massive socio-economic damage. As such, the Chinese state now participates in an international system dominated by established great powers and one superpower, the United States. According to realists such as Waltz, international institutions are created and dominated by the strongest states and are perpetuated as long as they serve or appear to serve the needs of their strongest members.[59] This was seen in institutions created after the Second World War, many of which were either created or guided by Washington as a means of reshaping the post-war international order.[60] Most of the institutions have remained intact, often with continued American domination. Following this logic, China's late arrival at the institutional 'party' could be considered seriously detrimental to Chinese interests. Neo-realist analysts suggest that states are concerned with their power levels not only singly in absolute terms, but also in relation to the power levels of other states and therefore institutions have a minimal impact on international relations, since cooperation under an anarchic system is very risky and problematic.[61]

Thus, according to this theory, engagement with international institutions has the potential to magnify China's deficiencies *vis-à-vis* the West and to place Beijing at a disadvantage. From an optimistic viewpoint, increased multilateralism would further Beijing's integration into the international system through increased socialisation, and institutions are important tools for achieving this goal.[62] However, in joining more institutions, China would be bound by rules created largely by great power competitors. Therefore, there is a considerable risk that China would find itself in a subservient position within these institutions with its options more limited than what would be deemed acceptable.

One solution to this problem would be for Beijing to attempt to balance American power, as the USSR attempted to do soon after the Second World War. However, post-cold war China is not in a strong enough position to balance against the West either unilaterally or within international fora. Segal's comment on this subject, that today's China is 'a beacon to no one – and indeed, an ally to no one'[63] uses a broad brush, but in a strategic sense China has few allies from which to balance the West either within institutions or via old-fashioned alliances. Despite initiatives over the past decade to engage its neighbours in east, southeast and central Asia, resulting in levels of peaceful dialogue unmatched during the cold war, most of these new relationships are not based on aligning against specific adversaries. In short, Beijing is still far from creating any 'balancing coalition' to counter Western dominance and therefore must make do with what's there, at least in the short term, and engage many Western-dominated international regimes.

Finally, any participation or engagement in international institutions entails added responsibilities and risks to both the regime and to the state itself. This issue is acute in the case of China, due to its history of (attempted) self-reliance, distrust of foreign influences, and direct interference by foreign powers in Chinese affairs during the nineteenth and twentieth centuries. Moreover, as the Chinese

Communist Party moves beyond the 2002–3 leadership transition, the last vestiges of traditional Maoism are being shed in favour of state-guided nationalism. Developing nationalistic ideas, while simultaneously seeking further ties to international institutions, may be seen as a contradiction, especially if signs appear that these institutions are hampering Chinese development in any way.

During China's ideological and socio-economic transition since the late 1970s, the potential for domestic instability is high both in the core and periphery of the country. Therefore, the degree to which China can engage various economic and strategic institutions without damaging what its government sees as a threshold state and regime integrity presents a constant dilemma for Beijing. Despite an increased understanding of the dynamics of multilateral cooperation and international-level institutions, the Chinese government is still very much dedicated to protecting state sovereignty, decrying 'hegemonistic' attempts by greater powers to subjugate weaker ones, and maintaining the 'neo-Westphalian' idea that states should remain the strongest units in the international system and should be free of external interventions. In short, these conditions are highly non-conducive to the level of institutional engagement which China has sought.

Yet, despite these formidable reasons for China to eschew international institutions, there are equally compelling explanations *for* China's engagement. Six 'goods' are being sought by China from its foreign relationships, all of which are integral not only to explain why the country has opted to enhance its relations with multilateral regimes, but also in constructing a blueprint for augmenting China's power in the international system. The order of these goods does not imply ranking, since all are important. However, different goods may take priority depending on the international context and which institutions are brought into play.

1) Promotion of external peace and stability

Since the 1970s, the underlying theme of Chinese foreign policy has been the need for peaceful coexistence and stability in China's large periphery, a stance developed after several centuries of internal strife and foreign invasion.[64] For this reason, China has behaved in a conservative fashion in conducting foreign policy, primarily out of the need to avoid distracting the country from important domestic level concerns. This has not meant, however, that China has shied away from the use of force as a foreign policy tool, as the twentieth-century conflicts in the Taiwan Strait, Korea, the Indian and Vietnamese borders and the South China Sea have demonstrated. Nevertheless, China has, over the last twenty years, demonstrated an aversion to using violence to solve external security issues, unless an unacceptable risk to Chinese territorial interests could be demonstrated or that China's perceived status in the international community was not sufficiently recognised by other states.[65]

The reasons for this conservative approach are many, including conventional interpretations of China's strategic traditions, dating back well into the imperial eras, of avoiding warfare unless absolutely necessary, and when required engaging in military activity only in a controlled and defensive fashion, ideas which have since become subjects of dispute.[66] However, modern China must also address several issues which would preclude marches into war. These include concerns over the socio-economic transition away from Maoist command economics, addressing rural poverty and underdevelopment, the need to develop modern infrastructure and technologies to improve standards of living, modernising domestic financial institutions and improving the ability to defend state interests through military upgrading. Since China underwent a complex transition following Deng's reformist policy, and is currently entering a second one as Beijing addresses the processes of globalisation and domestic reform, China would be unwilling to engage in the use of force against an external adversary unless core interests are threatened.

Today's China is in a most favourable strategic position. With increasingly warm relations with both Russia and southeast Asia, both areas of serious concern during the cold war, China's borders have rarely been more stable. However, in spite of the seemingly advantageous strategic position in which China finds itself, the country has become increasingly sensitive to perceived externally-based threats to both the state and its communist regime. The difference rests partially in the nature of the enemy. During the cold war the external challenges to China were primarily state-based, meaning that China viewed its serious challengers to be other states and especially the great powers. First, the United States and the West, in their support for the Republic of China on Taiwan in the 1950s, were a threat to Chinese interests. Also, China's firm placement in the communist camp indicated China's alignment against Western capitalist states. During the cold war, the 'revisionist' Soviet Union of the 1960s and 1970s, formerly an ally, became Beijing's primary adversary, prompting the initiative to warm relations with Washington. As well, China faced perceived threats from bordering small and medium neighbouring powers, primarily India and Vietnam.

By contrast, China's current security interests have shifted from traditional strategic concerns (namely state vs. state and ideology-based warfare) to more diverse issues more difficult to address and, therefore, take preventive measures against. Post-bipolarity warfare has become increasingly dominated not by the state-to-state conflicts of the past, but rather the so-called 'wars of the third kind', identified as wars of secession or factionalism and often involving non-state actors and taking place within the boundaries of a single state.[67] These forms of warfare often draw in other states, either in the form of support for one side, or due to 'spillover' effects, (refugee flows, smuggling of illegal goods, and transnational crime). Due to the greater diversity of these perceived threats, Beijing is behaving in a manner consistent with a perception that its security is more endangered today than it was during the previous 40 years. China's 'neo-strategic' concerns cover a wide spectrum of issues, including economic security, arms smuggling, drugs, ethnic unrest and separatism. As a result of the terrorist attacks of 11 September 2001 and the subsequent international war on terrorism, China along with many other states, has shifted its security priorities in order to combat terrorist networks. The need for interstate-cooperation to combat terrorist cells such as Al-Qaeda has added another dimension to Beijing's foreign policy.

Each of these strategic issues has the potential to create considerable problems for Beijing, and the sources of these threats are frequently based outside of Chinese borders and direct influence, making their addressing difficult. As such, China fears being caught up in such chaotic forces and, cognisant of the fact that it cannot effectively address these myriad issues unilaterally with the tools it possesses, has sought other means to attend to these sources of vulnerability. Only through cross-state cooperation with other actors sharing the same concerns can preventative action on these neo-strategic issues be effectively taken by China, at least in the short term.

In the past, the most visible method of addressing strategic vulnerabilities was to develop external territorial holdings, usually in the form of colonies, as with Britain, France, Germany, and Japan in the nineteenth and twentieth centuries, and/or create spheres of influence. This was accomplished either through direct military action, as exemplified by the Soviet Union's successful suppression of Eastern Europe and unsuccessful suppression of Afghanistan, or by the creation of alliances, as the US did with the creation of the North Atlantic Treaty Organisation (NATO) and the American partnership with Japan. These actions served to create buffer zones to enhance the stability of the home country by reducing vulnerabilities and deterring attacks on state interests.

None of these options is currently available to China, in large part due to the incorporation of nuclear weapons into the international power politics equation. China's military power is such that much of its strength lies in its nuclear deterrent rather than in its ability to fight conventional warfare. While being in possession of the bomb has helped to dissuade direct attacks on Chinese territory, it has not played a role in China's desire to bring stability to its borders. Even the breakaway province of Taiwan, which China has repeatedly stated would be subject to military invasion should it declare independence, is unlikely to be the subject of nuclear threats.

Beijing's adherence to the 'no first use' policy, (meaning that it would not be the first to use nuclear weapons in anger),[68] and its refusal to use the nuclear option when it fought wars over territories during the cold war, including skirmishes with the USSR, India, and Vietnam, indicates that like the other nuclear weapons states, China observes the so-called 'nuclear taboo'. This concept is an international norm which discourages the use of nuclear weapons in warfare on moral grounds because of the extreme scope of destruction and human suffering inherent in their use.[69] The development of nuclear weapons by other states has also served to limit the options of potential great powers seeking to change the international status quo through the use of force. The concept of 'mutual assured destruction', which suggests that an exchange of nuclear weapons between two states would simply produce two losers, has prevented China or any one of the other recognised or unrecognised nuclear powers from directly challenging others using nuclear arms.

This leaves conventional warfare, and on the surface, the large size of China's armed forces would suggest the country's ability to fight conventional wars is comparable to that of other great powers. However, as was previously mentioned, China lacks the capability to effectively engage in conventional warfare save for those within, or very close to, its borders. This is due to a military infrastructure left over from Maoist times which was well-suited to internal warfare but ill-equipped for power projection, especially against the more modern armed forces in the Pacific Rim and the West. During the early Maoist period, strategic thinking was dominated (in theory) by the concept of 'people's war', which stressed the supremacy of soldiers over weaponry, and the tactic of 'luring enemies in deep' to achieve victory. Although the people's war doctrine eroded as early as the 1950s, when Chinese forces were deployed in North Korea to stave off Western attack, it was not until after Mao's death in 1976 that serious steps towards alternative theories of modern warfare could be adopted.[70] Since the 1970s, the People's Liberation Army of China has needed to play catch-up both through the acquisition of modern conventional arms, (through both indigenous development and purchases abroad) and in the theories and realities of post-cold war combat which are dominated by the 'revolution in military affairs', with less stress on size and more on modern technology and information-gathering.

Another international norm, although less strong or visible than the nuclear taboo, may also be viewed as a deterrent against the forced creation of a strategic buffer zone. This is the 'territorial integrity norm', which refers to a growing understanding on the global level that the alteration of state borders through violence is an unacceptable practice. As Zacher noted, China has only resorted to the forcible seizure of another state's territory twice in its modern history, the absorption of the territories on Aksai Chin and the Northwest Frontier Agency in 1962, and the annexation of the Paracel Islands in 1974. During the 1990s, he adds, Beijing opted to use negotiations and legal accords to solve boundary issues in central Asia, Russia, and Vietnam. The author credited the overall visibility of this norm to the drop in importance of land as an economic 'good' in the modern era of globalisation, the risks and costs of retaining foreign land, and the disruption of economic flows.[71] Regardless of the explanation for this phenomenon, over the past two decades, China has opted to respect the concept of territorial integrity in its foreign policy dealings.

China has not followed this norm to the letter however, since in addition to the Indian borders conflict, Beijing fought brief border skirmishes with the Soviet Union in 1969 which had the potential for developing into full warfare between two nuclear-capable great powers.[72] In February 1979, Chinese forces attempted to 'punish' Vietnam for its invasion of ally Cambodia and to pacify the border region between the two long-time adversaries, in a short and chaotic conflict concluding with embarrassing losses for the PLA.[73] Two future 'exceptions' may be the cases of Taiwan and the disputed islands of South China Sea, both of which Beijing views as its own territory. As Johnston suggested in his study of China's interstate behaviour on addressing disputes during the cold war, China was prone to settling disputes with other states using violence to a greater degree than many other great powers, but a significant portion of those disputes involved cases where China's territorial integrity was perceived to be under threat, not as a result of Chinese attempts to extend power over other states.[74] Therefore, it can be inferred that China is very willing to use force to protect what it views as its core interests, including territory, but has not acted in an 'expansionist' manner, using force to extend its power over neighbouring states.

Due to the high level of risk involved in the use of force to solve strategic problems, coupled with an international system which for the most part discourages violence as a tool to unilaterally increase security, an alternative for China is to engage states with similar strategic issues in order to more effectively address them. On an international level, China has responded to concerns over nuclear proliferation by reversing its previous decision not to join nuclear weapons control regimes, and in the mid-1990s agreed to observe the Nuclear Non-proliferation Treaty. The 1990s also saw China agree to participate in other international arms control regimes, including the Chemical Weapons Convention and the Zangger Committee (which oversees nuclear export controls), while agreeing to adhere to the guidelines of the Missile Technology Control Regime (MTCR). In April 2004, China further altered its stance towards nuclear regimes and stated it would seek membership in the MTCR as well as the Nuclear Suppliers' Group (NSG), which regulates the export of nuclear weapons materials.[75] These decisions were important in light of American allegations during the past decade that Beijing engaged in repeated transfers of missile technologies to Iran, Pakistan and Saudi Arabia.[76]

Nonetheless, it is on the regional level where China has been most active in joining and participating in institutions developed to counter threats and preserve stability. In addressing modern security problems, China has called for a 'new security concept' (NSC) in its relations with neighbouring states, stressing the pursuit of common interests, peaceful dialogue, and a search for a means of creating common security for all regional actors and the discouragement of formal alliances or polarising unilateral policies. At the same time, China has recognised the need to undertake these policies in a phased process cognisant of the degree of political and economic diversity of the Pacific Rim.[77] The NSC, adapted from China's traditional foreign policy doctrine of the Five Principles of Peaceful Coexistence (mutual respect for sovereignty and territorial integrity, non-aggression, non-interference in each other's internal affairs, equality and mutual benefit, and peaceful co-existence),[78] has found favour among other east and southeast Asian states concerned about outside intervention in their domestic affairs.

2) Perpetuation of regime and domestic stability

The reasons for China opting to engage international institutions as a means of developing its global power can be found, in part, by examining international events and pressures on the Chinese state. Examining the issues within the Chinese state, and especially within the ruling Chinese Communist Party (CCP), provides a clearer understanding of China's policies towards institutions evolving as they did. In many cases of Chinese institutional cooperation, such engagement was undertaken to strengthen domestic stability, further enrich the state and perpetuate the leading role of the CCP as the sole actor governing the Chinese state.

At the close of 2004, China entered into a new phase of government after Hu Jintao assumed most major offices of power, save for the influential position as head of the Central Military Commission, which Jiang retained. The so-called 'fourth generation' of potential Chinese leaders has been marked by more heterogeneous backgrounds and higher levels of education and professionalism.[79] Since the death of Deng in 1997, the successor regimes of Jiang and Hu have been far less monolithic than their predecessors, relying on many different factions to maintain coherence. Added to these is the politically powerful People's Liberation Army, which continues to view the international system with varying degrees of suspicion. According to Shambaugh, this unease is largely based on a lack of experience with, and exposure to, foreign actors among the PLA's upper echelons. As a result, the organisation has expressed reluctance about multilateral security cooperation and alliances and is wary of potential security threats on a regional and international level.[80]

In the current transition period, Beijing remains concerned about maintaining regime security and stability and continues to guard against any domestic influences which may damage or weaken its hold on power. Communications, including the internet, are still heavily regulated, and safeguards remain in place to prevent the development of domestic organisations which challenge the legitimacy of the communist party. This concern was exemplified by the harsh government crackdown on members of the Falungong spiritual movement, created in 1992 and officially banned in China seven years later following a protest of approximately 10,000 members near the Chinese governmental compound, Zhongnanhai, in Beijing. Falungong was declared an illegal cult by China's government, which has accused the group of perpetuating falsehoods and damaging the state's social fabric.[81] The hard line taken against the group is indicative of the degree to which the central government will go in order to avoid perceived challenges to its regime. Beijing has sought greater institutional engagement in order to pursue a means of augmenting the legitimacy of the CCP government and to discourage large-scale extra-governmental groups which may form a possible opposition.

China is also very concerned about enhancing its role in ensuring economic growth and increasing the standard of living of its citizens. As was demonstrated during the Asian Financial Crisis of 1997–8, a sudden downturn in economic fortunes can be detrimental to non-pluralist governments, such as the Suharto regime in Indonesia, which stake their legitimacy upon providing continuous economic gains to their people. Participation in economic multilateral institutions can shift some of the onus from the Chinese government, since such engagement often implies *de facto* international acceptance of a state's domestic development policies. For example, China's engagement with the World Trade Organisation as well as various exclusive economic regimes has served as an extra 'lock' on the government's policy of liberalising trade with the international community. Membership in the WTO, achieved in December 2001 after 13 often rancorous years of negotiations, may make it more difficult for detractors of liberalisation to attempt to overturn reform policies despite the hardships such reforms may bring about, such as increased sector-specific unemployment, potential closures of banks and other financial institutions, and possible labour unrest.

In addition to protection of the Chinese regime, the country's leaders are concerned with maintaining Chinese sovereignty by withstanding various international pressures. Indeed, the issue of sovereignty has become an important component in Chinese strategic thinking. As one analyst wrote, 'China's foreign policy is based on an outmoded Westphalian notion in a world where state sovereignty is being eroded and the traditional notion of national interests is under increasing challenge, thanks to unprecedented "dense interdependence".'[82] As Kent noted, one of the major contributions in the study of China's evolving interactions with international organisations has been that it provides needed insights into 'the tension between interdependence and sovereignty' within Chinese policies.[83] In short, China is facing a post-cold war international system where sovereignty is not as absolute.

One of the most discussed features of the post-cold war system has been a reinterpretation of the traditional Westphalian view of the near-absoluteness of state sovereignty. The fall of the Soviet Union and the end of its 'spheres of influence' provided conditions more favourable to international intervention in crises which had previously been considered domestic in nature. As then-Secretary General of the United Nations Boutros Boutros-Ghali noted in 1992, soon after the victory of US-led United Nations forces against Iraq to liberate Kuwait, 'the time of absolute and exclusive sovereignty ... has passed; its theory was never matched by reality'.[84] Since the early 1990s there has been less international support for UN-sponsored intervention within state boundaries, largely as a result of difficulties experienced in Somalia, Rwanda, and Congo-Kinshasa. Yet, this has not led to a halt in international interventions.

American-led military actions in Yugoslavia in 1999 to counter forced expulsions of Albanians in the contested province of Kosovo were a strong indicator that the world's superpower perceived a right to direct intervention within state borders on humanitarian grounds. Western-led military actions in Afghanistan in late 2001 also proved that state governments could be held accountable for harbouring violent non-state actors, in this case terrorist organisations, and be punished for that transgression. Finally, in March 2003 the United States and a small group of allies circumvented the United Nations, launching an attack on Iraq, to remove that country's alleged weapons of mass destruction. This unseated the government of Saddam Hussein and placed Baghdad under *de facto* American-led trusteeship.[85] As a result of these events, China has grown concerned that such interventionist trends could potentially adversely affect their foreign and domestic affairs and has fallen back on the Five Principles to express their opposition.

As China expands its relationships with international institutions, it has maintained that states should remain the most important actors in the international system and that institutions should not seek to engage in domestic intervention or the undermining of state sovereignty. Therefore, China has shown the strongest support towards those international institutions which observe and respect the ideals of state sovereignty and non-intervention in other states' domestic affairs. At the same time, China has used its membership in some institutions to discourage separatism within China, for example by refusing to permit Taiwanese membership in some organisations (primarily political) while cautiously accepting Taipei's role in others (primarily economic), under specific conditions. However, it is unclear whether China will be able to reconcile its newfound policy orientation towards increased institutional engagement with its desire to maintain a threshold level of sovereignty and regime stability.

3) Reduction of the risks and costs of information gathering

In the area of state-to-state relations, the axiom 'information is power' takes on additional relevance in the post-cold war system. Asymmetries in the level of information between countries can be a source of vulnerability and greatly hamper peaceful international relations. Although information gaps can create difficulties in many areas, including trade and financial issues, insufficient information in matters relating to security can be even more problematic since that may threaten the integrity of the state itself. As Keohane noted, one of the most significant advantages of participating in international regimes is that they reduce the costs of transactions between actors during legitimate bargaining, but increase the costs of bargaining in bad faith. One reason for this phenomenon is that institutions facilitate the exchange of information amongst members, thus reducing the risks of bargaining.[86] This was certainly an asset to an emerging China being forced to play catch-up in its understanding of the international system. Information gathering was a primary reason for China's post-1970s policy of institutional engagement, and has played an important role in Chinese power acquisition.

The platform of the Dengist reforms was the understanding amongst the Party elite that China's policy of isolation, which reached a fevered pitch after the 1960s as a result of the Sino-Soviet split and the Cultural Revolution, was no longer viable. The damage created by the Cultural Revolution, and the Great Leap Forward which preceded it, had soured many in the Communist Party on the concept of 'going it alone' while facing two superpowers and an increasingly uncertain security situation. However, entering into the international system belatedly, after many great and medium-powers had established themselves and were already helping to shape international institutions, left China with a serious dearth of information as to the rules, norms, and practices of many state actors. This was especially true regarding Western nations, which China needed to engage in order to construct a foreign policy reflecting the country's opening to the outside. Moreover, this information was required in order to avoid costly errors which might delay the engagement process, or worse, place China at a greater disadvantage within the international system.

As Krasner explained, in situations where there are both coordination problems between actors and disparities in power, the atmosphere is conducive to the creation of regimes to address these asymmetries. The key to achieving this is the improved flow of information concerning the rules and norms required for all actors to be satisfied with the relationship. This raises confidence and lessens concerns over cheating and having one actor take unfair advantage of others.[87] At the same time, once a state is within an institution, larger amounts of information are normally demanded by that institution as a requisite for continued membership. While this does involve sovereignty costs, the advantage is that other states will also need to provide additional information.[88] China has been prompted to provide economic and strategic information, to varying degrees, to other states as a means to remain within certain institutions. However, Beijing in turn gains greatly from the data provided by the other regime members. This is particularly important within regimes which include other Pacific Rim states, since Beijing wishes to avoid losing strategic or economic ground to its neighbours, including other great powers.

As previously noted, international institutions are not the only means by which China can gain the information and expertise it requires to effectively enhance its foreign policy and its role in the international system. China's pattern of fostering bilateral agreements, which began well before the Dengist reforms, was the result of a growing number of countries switching recognition from Taipei to Beijing. They provided a great deal of information to China on the policies of countries in which it is most interested, including the United States. During the 1990s, the number of bilateral agreements rose significantly as Beijing moved to repair relations with cold war rivals. However, because of the increasing number of decisions being made in international fora over the past three decades, and the need for China to understand the art of policymaking within multilateral constructs, China increasingly opts to participate in international institutions rather than relying exclusively on bilateral agreements. In other words, while China can learn a lot about state *A* from engaging it alone, engaging state *A* within an institutional framework also provides added data on how states *A*, *B*, *C*, *D*, engage each other.

4) Attainment of effective relations with other great powers

One potential problem facing emergent great powers is the issue of how to maximise relations with other great powers. As history has shown, mismanagement of such relations has the potential to bring about great conflict on a regional or even international scale. China is no exception, and indeed must overcome the added obstacle of its previous isolationist foreign policies and lack of relative experience with great-power interactions. Although, a considerable amount of Chinese concern about strategic threats has shifted to less traditional security issues, this does not imply that state-to-state issues have completely vanished from Beijing's thinking.

Rather, China's modern-day concerns about state behaviour are focused less on the ramifications of direct attack on China from another state, and more on the continued actions of great powers and the detrimental effects of ongoing power asymmetries in the current global order. As China's 2002 National Defence White Paper noted, great powers still competed with each other, despite a rise in cooperation after September 2001, and economic and military inequalities still threatened peace and security.[89]

The end of the cold war prompted much soul-searching within the Chinese government on the subject of future great power relations. The most visible change produced by the fall of the Soviet Union was that China's position as a 'balancer' with the United States on one side and the USSR on the other was gone. The United States, since the beginning of the 1990s, was widely perceived as the world's sole remaining superpower,[90] and this development changed many of the rules and options available to China as it attempted to define its new role in the international system. This evolving global order began to produce conditions for which China was ill-prepared: the ongoing development of unipolarity with the United States at the apex, the appearance of other Asian power centres in Japan, Korea, India and southeast Asia and, not insignificantly, the realisation that communist ideology and closed markets were becoming anachronistic in many parts of the world. All of these changes required a rapid evolution in Chinese thinking.

Washington has developed into the lynchpin of Chinese foreign policy thinking. The fall of the Soviet Union was closely followed by the erosion of the businesslike Sino-American relations which marked the 1970s and early 1980s. International anger in the wake of the Tiananmen Square incident in 1989, largely spearheaded by Washington, resulted in a brief suspension of relations. Yet, even after links resumed between the two countries, the perception of China as a reformist American ally against Soviet expansion was steadily being replaced by one of China as a non-democratic, dissatisfied and revisionist power during the 1990s.

Various incidents contributed to strains in the Sino-American relationship. In July 1993, American forces boarded the Chinese freighter *Yinhe* (*The Galaxy*) on the erroneous suspicion that it was smuggling weapons parts to Iran, eliciting strident protests from Beijing.[91] Then in March 1996, China began conducting missile tests in the Taiwan Strait as a thinly-veiled protest against Taipei's elections that month. However, the effectiveness of the tests was muted when a United States carrier group moved through the Strait. In May of 1999, an American jet engaged in the bombing campaign against Yugoslavia, destroyed the Chinese Embassy in Belgrade, killing three Chinese nationals.[92] Beijing vigorously protested and was sceptical of American claims that the bombing was accidental and a result of faulty intelligence information. In April 2001, an American EP-3E surveillance plane flying near the Chinese island province of Hainan was challenged by two PLA Air Force J-8 jets. A collision occurred between one of the J-8s and the American plane, sending the Chinese fighter into the South China Sea and forcing the EP-3E to land on Hainan, where its crew of twenty-four was temporarily taken into custody.[93] As China continues to develop its regional interests and modernise its military, chances of other direct brushes with American armed forces remain high.

Other actions taken by the United States and its allies at the turn of the century added to fears of containment of China by foreign influences, or to use the more diplomatic term, 'strategic encirclement', using the same means advocated a half-century ago to control the growth and influence of the Soviet Union by surrounding it with states and other actors hostile to it.[94] Another concern is that of 'peaceful evolution', a euphemism for diluting Chinese power by encouraging domestic challenges to the regime.[95] These include augmented military ties between the United States and Japan after 1996, a *rapprochement* between America and Chinese rivals, Vietnam and India during the latter part of the decade, weapons transfers and other low-level support to Taiwan in 2001, cordial (for the most part) American strategic relations with Australia and South Korea, and an increased American military presence in Central Asia and the Caspian region as part of the post-9/11 war on terrorism.[96]

In addition, the controversial decision by the administration of George W. Bush to further develop anti-missile defence systems to protect American territory and allies from long-range missile attacks created a serious concern in China over the effectiveness of its own missile deterrent. The United States has insisted that any developing national missile defence (NMD) – to protect North America – or theatre missile defence (TMD) to protect American interests and friends in a particular conflict zone – would only be used to counter missiles from 'rogue states' with only a handful of missiles. However, China fears these systems, once operational, could counter China's small arsenal of intercontinental ballistic missiles, thus removing the country's most important offensive capability.[97]

There is ongoing concern in Chinese policy circles that although the past decade brought about significant change in the international system, the shaking-out process from the cold war's end is not over. Thus, without sufficient caution, China could find its growing power cut off by outside players, particularly the United States. The overall relationship between China and America has been shown to have disturbing parallels with other cases of an unsatisfied rising power challenging the authority of a satisfied, dominant one. Power transition theories revolve around the scenario of what happens when a challenger power comes close to overtaking a dominant one, and whether or not the result would be warfare between the two. Much depends on the challenger power's level of satisfaction with the international system, and the degree of cooperation between the two actors.

Thus, the question with which many China-watchers have grappled is to what degree is Beijing dissatisfied with the present international order, and what is Beijing willing to risk in attempts to change it, especially through the possible use of force. The situation becomes more tenuous when the challenger state in question obtains power very rapidly, (as China has done), since swift growth often leads to internal strains which the government attempts to deflect by engaging in more aggressive behaviour towards the outside world. Moreover, Kennedy notes that very often, when a state expands economically, it is often prompted to expand its military and political power to better protect its interests.[98] This can be observed in the case of China.

Some analysts have painted a picture of the next power transition being between that of a Chinese challenger and an American hegemon. Tammen *et al.* noted that China's growing power stems from three fundamentals: population, productivity, and political capacity. Once these three are properly combined, China will overcome its current power projection deficiencies and become a true challenger.[99] Mearsheimer pointed more specifically to China's economic growth as the determining factor in China's development into a challenger power, noting that by continuing to develop as a financial powerhouse, ('a giant Hong Kong'), neither the country's neighbours nor the United States would easily be able to check its overreaching power. According to this argument, after a sufficient threshold of wealth is achieved, China would wish to pursue its own version of the Monroe Doctrine, designating a sphere of influence where American interference would not be permitted.[100] The stage would then be set for, at least, a new cold war or, even more troubling, open military competition in Asia causing the oft-discussed 'China threat' scenario to become fact. Because both actors possess nuclear weapons, such an outcome would be dangerous not only to both great powers, but to the global arena as a whole. However, through international institutions, Beijing has been able to air its views on important political and strategic issues both with neighbours and other great powers to ensure that other great powers will not seek to contain or marginalize growing Chinese power.

5) Economic development and security

Economic development has become one of the crucial elements of Beijing's domestic and international policies. Since the late 1970s, when Deng Xiaoping instituted sweeping changes to the Chinese economic system, permitting private ownership and trade liberalisation, China has benefited from one of the largest sustained economic growth rates in the world, even taking into account an upward bias in Chinese statistics.[101] Considering that China was one of the poorest countries in the region when the People's Republic was founded, and considering the socio-economic disasters China faced in the Maoist period as a result of the Great Leap Forward (1958–60) and the Cultural Revolution (1966–76), the country's development since the beginning of the Dengist period is impressive. Beijing remains very anxious to maintain that economic momentum.

Arguably the most serious obstacle to China's continuing rise in great power status would occur if its current transition from command to market economy is derailed by the oftentimes painful side-effects of reform. In spite of its impressive economic growth, there is a host of issues having the potential to bring chaos to Chinese development. The country still must contend with state-owned enterprises which are unprofitable drains on the economy, an unwieldy banking system, rising unemployment and labour migration, transparency issues, cumbersome administrative bureaucracy, and general problems of corruption in many sectors.[102]

26

As Pei noted, four features which contribute to an increase of state predatory activity, as well as the decentralisation of such predatory practices, can be found in today's modernising China. These four are the decentralisation of property rights, declining ability of the state to effectively monitor its various apparatuses and prevent abuses, an increasing number of 'exit options' which allow state officials more freedom to attain and hide wealth, and the erosion of ideological and institutional norms, which in the case of China, means a steady drop in popular support for Communist doctrine.[103] Poverty remains a serious issue for the country despite economic advances, as exemplified by a July 2004 report released by the Chinese government's Poverty Alleviation Office which suggested that during the previous year the number of people living on less than RMB637 (US$77) a year jumped by 800,000 people to more than 85 million, the first such rise recorded since the 1978 reforms.[104]

Attempts at resolving these problems have proven slow and unwieldy, leading to concerns that the country remains unprepared for the realities of twenty-first century global economics. Although China was successful in opening itself to the World Bank and the International Monetary Fund (IMF) in the 1980s, it continues to undergo a learning process in global economics and the role institutions play in it. In fact, Beijing has yet to implement a coherent policy on the subject of economic globalisation (*quanqiuhua*), although the government has recognised it as imperative to continue the process of opening up to global markets in order to better compete in world trade.[105] China's adaptation to economic globalisation will depend on how skilfully the country completes the difficult transition to economic liberalisation and the Chinese government is well aware of the linkage between state and economic security on the domestic level as a result of increased economic interdependence and the accompanying vulnerabilities.[106]

However, as with other countries which have made the transition to more liberalised economics, China faces increased vulnerability as more economic sectors shift from direct governmental control to the unpredictability of the free market. For this reason the reform process has been very slow and measured, with much financial control remaining in the hands of the government and the SOEs. The example of the post-Soviet Russian economy during the past decade, marked by chronic instability and corruption, is one which Beijing is determined to avoid.

The impact of the regional economic slowdowns which dominated the Asian Financial and SARS crises were clear indicators that what goes up can go down, rapidly and unforeseeably. The AFC, which in reality was a series of smaller economic shocks causing a contagion effect, left China's economy one of the few unscathed, largely due to restrictions on the yuan's convertibility, favourable trade balances, and large foreign exchange reserves.[107] In addition, China was able to win the respect of its crisis-hit neighbours by assuring them that the yuan would not be devalued despite strains on China's exports. At the same time, Beijing feared lower Asian currencies would erode its regional economic competitiveness and spotlight its own internal financial shortcomings. Adding to this were the financial tribulations of Hong Kong, which had reverted to Chinese rule mere months before the Asian contagion struck the former colony's markets in October 1997.[108] After the SARS crisis and Beijing's belated response, the Chinese government had to work diligently to restore regional trust and ensure that such lapses would not recur.

Specific economic sectors are of special concern to China. For example, Beijing's energy needs have grown considerably over the past few decades due to increased demand from a growing economy and an expanding middle class. For this reason the country has needed to develop indigenous supplies, for example through the Tarim Basin petroleum development project and the controversial Sanxia (Three Gorges) hydroelectric project. In addition, Beijing has been seeking external sources of energy through oil exploration in the South China Sea, which is also claimed by other Southeast Asian states, and via deals with Central Asia and other regions of the world.[109] China has made use of two regimes largely created to address security issues, the ASEAN Regional Forum and Shanghai Cooperation Organisation, in order to pursue its external energy policies.

As a growing country, both in population and in power, China requires greater resources, natural and manufactured, human and technological. These needs have spearheaded China's increased foreign trade (*duiwai maoyi*) as well as the development of increased external business interests, partnerships and joint ventures. As international trade falls increasingly under institutional jurisdiction, it is in China's interests to play a larger role in developing the rules and norms to avoid losing out to other trading powers. Since 1986, China lobbied hard to rejoin the General Agreement on Tariffs and Trade, only to experience many delays over rules and procedures.[110] When the World Trade Organisation (WTO) was founded at the end of the Uruguay Round in 1993–4, China requested membership, only to once again be subject to delays over the proper implementation of international trade guidelines. In the intervening years before China gained WTO membership in December 2001, Beijing was more successful in pursuing its trading agendas through regional groupings such as the Asia-Pacific Economic Cooperation forum and exclusive bodies such as the ASEAN-Plus-Three regime. Through these smaller institutions, China has been able to address its specific trading needs more effectively than by relying on traditional bilateral diplomacy.

6) Acquisition of greater prestige

Within its current foreign policy, Beijing has sought to gain a level of global prestige which it feels it is due as a once and future great power. International institutions have acted as effective theatres-in-the-round for China to demonstrate its developing greatness. As the cold war ended, China faced difficult decisions as to how best to redefine itself in the international system, both for a domestic audience (the Chinese people) and an international (other states and global actors) one. As Wendt explained, the identity of a given country can be a crucial component of its international relations. Perceptions of how a given actor attains and utilises power are coloured by how that actor is identified by others.[111] China has made use of institutions not only to advertise its *presence gigantesque* for domestic and international consumption, but also to emphasise its desire to be a participant in international discourse rather than a spoiler or a possible international threat.

One of the key components of China's ideological shift has been from Maoism to nationalism. This change has been reflected in attempts by the Chinese government to improve the country's prestige in the international order, thus leading to an increase in Chinese power. Although nationalism has been part of the Chinese political landscape since well before the communist era, the concept has taken on new meaning with the erosion of Maoist doctrine since the onset of the Dengist era and Beijing's opening to the international system. The post-Dengist strains of Chinese nationalism have been reflected not only within the CCP, but also in intellectual discourse and on the societal level. These changes have had a considerable effect on Chinese foreign policy thinking not only from the government but also the governed.[112] Modern Chinese in its international relations, described by Oksenberg as 'confident nationalism', is based not only on the long history of the Chinese people, but also through the adaptation of modern economics and technologies to stimulate Chinese growth and return the country to its rightful high perch in the international order.[113]

The ongoing growth of the Chinese economy and infrastructure has certainly contributed to a higher comfort level in dealing with international issues. Although economic problems remain, there is a growing sense among economists that China is poised to become the next economic giant.[114] These ideas were reflected in Jiang Zemin's 'Three Represents' paradigm, which explained the new mission of the Communist Party: a call for the Chinese citizenry to represent the development of 'China's advanced productive forces', the orientation of China's 'advanced culture', and the interests of the great majority of the Chinese people.[115] This doctrine adds strong evidence that nationalism is playing an increasing role in Chinese politics, including foreign policy.

Since the 1990s, other forms of nationalism have arisen in China, many of them directed against an international order seen as excessively Western, and specifically American-dominated. Elite-level frustrations in China have risen over perceived US efforts to check Chinese power through human rights protests, interference in the Taiwan question, and delays in China's WTO membership due to American objections.[116] As well, more recent incidents such as the May 1999 bombing of the Chinese embassy in Belgrade, which led to widespread anti-American protests across China, tolerated and in some cases facilitated by Communist authorities, and the April 2001 spy plane incident in Hainan have fed feelings of anti-US sentiment among Chinese citizenry and have provided Chinese nationalism with a more specific focus.[117] This type of nationalism, which Xiao referred to as 'reactive-defensive' (*yingji-zhiwei*), may be considered an heir to previous frustrations aimed at the West since the mid-nineteenth century Opium Wars,[118] and has the potential to be troublesome not only for Chinese foreign policy but also for its efforts to continue the process of rejoining the international system. Since the end of the cold war, Beijing has tried to keep such opinions controlled, but not curtailed, since they do serve as a means of defining Chinese interests independent of the perceived American-led status quo.

In the past, great powers seeking to develop as global powers resorted to improving their prestige *vis-à-vis* other states either by military means through the direct use of force or, more often, by 'swaggering' (demonstrating the power to deter attacks and compel other actors to take actions they would not ordinarily do),[119] or by economic power. A less costly and risky choice for China today, however, is the institutional route. China has already been granted a strong voice (with veto power) on the United Nations Security Council after regaining its seat from Taipei in 1971, and is now demonstrating its determination to play a larger role in the world by joining or engaging other key institutions. To use the terminology of Hirschman, since 1949 China had largely opted to pursue its foreign policy goals through the use of 'exit', withdrawing from an international order that went against China's domestic ideologies.[120] Since 1979, and especially since the 1990s, China has increasingly turned to the opposite technique of using 'voice', making the international system more congenial for its present and future policies by participating in a growing number of institutional bodies. This represents a remarkable departure from previous great power behaviour.

Even the most apolitical of international regimes has been shown to have a galvanising effect on Chinese prestige. For example, after losing their bid to host the Olympics in 2000 to Sydney, Australia, Chinese citizens were overjoyed during the summer of 2001 when Beijing was awarded the 2008 Games. More than being granted the opportunity to host an international event, the right to hold the Olympics can be seen as a rite of passage, as the 1964 Tokyo Games and the 1988 Games in Seoul were for their respective host countries. Clearly, in spite of misgivings about the role of Western-led regimes in international relations, Beijing is willing to make use of them as mirrors reflecting China's developing great power status and enthusiasm to play a major role in international activities.

Why institutions matter for China

Weighing the assets and liabilities of institutional engagement, China has opted for a measured approach, but as Chinese power is growing, the number of institutions being engaged is also on the rise. It will be argued that these initiatives are an important part of Beijing's goal to promote stable borders to allow for continuing Chinese development. China is more willing than ever before to use its status as a rising global power to assert greater influence in shaping the international order. At present, both politicians and international relations scholars in China see a present-day international system beset by contradictions (*maodun*) which, if left unchecked, could escalate to crisis (*chongtu*). The most serious of these contradictions is economic exploitation of the poor by the rich, the attempt to force ideologies or systems on others against their will, the violation of state sovereignty and the persistence of hegemonism. Chinese study in international relations has recently centred on the concept of international patterns (*guoji geju*), which is a subset of the international systems with the actors being only the great powers.[121] The concern is that the current state of the *geju* has not only shifted away from bipolarity but is on the way to becoming unipolar, dominated by the United States.

China has in many ways exhibited behaviour which, under realist theory, is consistent with rising power behaviour, including its current policies of seeking to advance its stature in the international system, increasing its global interests and desiring a greater voice in its external environment. However, it is in the area of institutional engagement where China deviates significantly from traditional realist theory, which has not viewed 'institutions' as being significant to rising powers. China's approach to international institutions is a crucial component in that country's evolving multilateralist foreign policy orientation.

However, what sets China apart from previous rising powers is a) it is 'growing up' within a milieu of international institutions far more developed than ever before; b) China's turn towards international institutions was a sharp departure from the isolationist policies seen within the first few decades of the People's Republic; c) China is a potentially dissatisfied power which may challenge the dominant player in the system, namely the United States; and d) most importantly, it is developing its power while making active use of these institutions as stepping stones to greater power status. In opposition to traditional realist assumptions about rising potential great powers, engagement with international institutions has been a crucial component for China to enhance and develop its power in the current international order.

China's status as a great power and developing global power has allowed it to interact with these institutions more selectively, without the same level of concern which other developing states have about the costs or consequences of partial compliance or 'misbehaviour'. Since the end of the cold war, Beijing has developed an increasing ability to shape the mandate and direction of certain international bodies. The present degree of cooperation and/or interaction with international regimes of many stripes lies in marked contrast to Maoist China's limited foreign policy between 1949 and the 1970s, and despite China having less time than other potential great powers to adapt to the 'rules' of state cooperation, Beijing has managed to greatly enhance its power through international institutions, more so than by developing traditional military power, an expensive and risky venture in today's international order. Since China is growing increasingly concerned about its stature and level of vulnerability in the emerging post-cold war international order, one that is arguably still very much anarchical, it is in China's interest to expand its power within the shortest timeframe possible to address these issues.

However, taking the traditional paths to great power status (economic and military expansion) would be an extensive endeavour with a long timetable and obvious risk, especially with two considerable obstacles present: the United States, a great power with which China has many policy differences, and the addition of nuclear weapons into the international security equation greatly inhibiting direct conflict between great powers. Therefore, it is necessary for China to utilise other options, specifically international institutions, as a supplement, a means of expanding power unavailable to rising powers in the past.

This study will be of significance on three fronts. First, it will explore an important facet of Chinese foreign policy, moving beyond the limitations of analysing the country's material resources and capabilities, which has dominated post-cold war discourse on China's foreign relations. Material-based examinations of Chinese power have, in much literature since the early 1990s, led to conclusions representing extreme ends of various spectrums: China may collapse, or it may become an undisputed economic powerhouse; China is an imminent threat to international stability and American power, or it may be unable to mount such a challenge. The real answers to determining China's future role in the global order will very likely not be found at these extremes and new variables should be introduced in order to better understand the ramifications of China's growing power. The method to be examined is the opening up of the country's institutional relations as another important measuring tool for determining the evolution of Chinese power.

Second, the study aims to provide insights into international relations theory as they relate to the activities of great powers, including adding an extra dimension to the definition of great power in terms of how these actors evolve within an international system saturated with institutions. International relations schools of realism and institutionalism, which have been at odds over the question of state priorities, can complement each other when determining how emerging great powers and global powers may interact with regimes and institutions in an international system so heavily dominated by them. Such relationships are crucial to the understanding of great power growth in the post-cold war system.

At the same time, as Chinese power approaches that of the United States, it will be useful to investigate the effect this will have on the distribution of international power. Will China's growth within a regime-intensive international system have any bearing on relations between the largest and the fastest-growing great power? Will the outcome of China's development as a global power involve the creation of another bipolar international system? Can China's increased integration, politically and economically, into the international system create sufficient disincentives for China to act in a disruptive manner in international interactions? What effect will the added variable of international institutions, a larger global presence than ever before, have on these above scenarios? It is the hope that these analyses will provide insights into the changing political landscape of China itself, as the country undergoes its third major change in leadership and policy orientation since the founding of the People's Republic more than 50 years ago. As we begin a new century, these questions will be of importance not only to analysts but also to those with an academic, business, or political interest in the rise of the next global power.

1

RED LIGHT, GREEN LIGHT
China and the World Trade Organisation

Only when you know why you have hit the target, can you truly
say you have learned archery.
Guan Yinzi, Warring States Period

Introduction: the closed door

China's evolving relationship with the World Trade Organisation (WTO), as well
as its predecessor, the General Agreement on Tariffs and Trade (GATT), has
represented one of the most complicated cases of Chinese institutional engagement.
Unlike many other institutions with which China has opted to engage, the WTO is
international, formal and requires a great deal of policy reorientation on behalf of
its members. Nevertheless, China actively lobbied for sixteen years to enter this
complex regime, resulting in painful and often frustrating bilateral and multilateral
negotiations until membership was formally granted. On 11 December 2001, China
officially became the 143rd member of the World Trade Organisation,[1] allowing
Beijing to send both a delegation and an ambassador to WTO headquarters in
Geneva, Switzerland. China had finally been granted a much greater voice in the
developing international trade regime, one befitting its growing economic power.

A comprehensive examination of the Chinese relationship with the WTO and
the GATT would be beyond the scope of this chapter, and indeed has been the
subject of entire studies. However, an explanation can be offered of the evolving
relationship between Beijing and the World Trade Organisation with an eye to
understanding the domestic and international-level factors which led China, a
country experiencing an as-yet-unfinished transition from a communist command
economy to economic liberalism, to pursue admission to the largest international
trading regime. At first sight, such a move would tend to run against previous
perceptions of China's economic development policies, which have been affected
by the country's ideological turn from communism to greater nationalism. It can
be argued, however, that China's admission to the WTO has permitted Beijing to
pursue nationalist economic policies by framing the organisation as an important

component in China's maturing economic power, rather than as a Western-dominated obstacle to China's growth. Such framing goes far in explaining why China tolerated a protracted negotiation process in bringing the country into the WTO regime, and will now be forced to endure considerable economic sacrifices in order to fulfil the responsibilities for membership.

An examination of the WTO through the lens of Chinese power considerations will demonstrate that this regime is doing much to alter Chinese perceptions of institutional cooperation, and is contributing a great deal to the enhancement of China's economic abilities while at the same time promoting the legitimacy and integrity of the government in Beijing. China's admission to the WTO will provide much-needed support for economic reforms which the country had been developing since the late 1970s, ensuring that these reforms cannot be easily brought down by reactionary forces. As well, China's push towards WTO membership illustrates well the new-found importance which Beijing has placed upon international institutions as tools permitting the government to demonstrate China's increasing importance in the world, as well as to better understand the rigours of the international economic system. The main question, however, remains. How will this new institutional relationship play out for China, the WTO, and the other economic powers concerned with accelerating Chinese economic growth and power?

The long road back

The turbulent political situation in China following the communist revolution of 1949 and the expulsion of the nationalist regime necessitated a withdrawal from existing organisations created before that year, the most visible of these being the General Agreement on Tariffs and Trade. The GATT, created after the Second World War and dominated by Western economies, was one of many new institutions formed to address the massive financial traumas after that conflict. It was to become the main instrument for developing international trade guidelines, and encouraging the development of more liberal and equitable global trade practices on an international level.[2] The Maoist government, like other communist regimes in Europe and Asia, wanted no part of what it saw as little more than a tool to enhance the grip of capitalist forces.

The nationalist government of Chiang Kai-shek had enlisted as a founding member of the GATT in October of 1947, two years before being forced to flee to Taiwan, and was ratifying its role in that organisation when the communists took power. Upon settling in Taiwan, the Kuomintang regime determined that it was unable to continue abiding by GATT guidelines and opted to withdraw from the organisation in March 1950, removing both rival governments from the Agreement until Taiwan requested and received observer status from 1965 to 1971.[3] As the Taiwanese political system began to liberalise in the 1980s, the question of full GATT membership was revisited. Following an internal review in 1987 of Taiwan's relationship to the GATT a formal bid to re-enter the regime was submitted three years later.[4] After driving the nationalist forces from mainland China, the new Maoist regime was determined to pursue economic self-sufficiency and was highly distrustful of multilateral economic regimes and their motives.

Mao Zedong wished to void any international agreements or treaties struck by the nationalists and just before the People's Republic was declared, he called upon the people to refuse to recognise the legal status of any 'foreign diplomatic establishments', 'treasonable treaties' of the Kuomintang period, and to 'take immediate control of foreign trade and reform the customs system'.[5] After consolidating power, Mao shaped China's foreign policy as being defined by the three axioms of 'making a fresh start' (redefining China and its political system and creating a clear separation from diplomatic practices of the past), 'cleaning the house before entertaining guests' (fortifying the revolution before returning to external matters), and 'leaning to one side' (establishing China as a member of the communist world and solidifying linkages with the Soviet Union).[6] All ties to the GATT, along with international institutional commitments, were severed by the communists after October 1949.

During most of the Maoist period, the Chinese economy was based on what Lin termed the inward-looking, heavy-industry-oriented development strategy (HIODS), a common model for socialist states and some developing nations during the mid-twentieth century. Despite the evolving realisation that the HIODS system in China was doing little to improve standards of living, only after the end of the Cultural Revolution and the death of Mao Zedong in 1976 could change be brought about.[7] Mao's successor, Hua Guofeng, attempted to reverse the disastrous economic effects of the Great Leap Forward period by introducing his own version of the 'four modernisations' programme, which involved raising production, productivity and efficiency, and augmenting China's role in the global economy.[8] While these goals were ambitious, their execution proved less than satisfactory, since they involved massive investment (more than a trillion yuan (US$121 billion)) in grandiose heavy industrial projects.

The programme was scrapped after a year, and when Hua was pushed aside by Deng Xiaoping after December 1978, the reform initiative turned to more area-specific programmes, including the phasing-out of collective farming in favour of a new contract responsibility system, the permitting of private and individual businesses in urban areas, greater authority granted to state-owned enterprises (SOEs), and a reform of the pricing system, which under Maoist economics had become distorted and unworkable.[9] The command economy which Mao had instituted was now under the full scrutiny by the Dengist regime.

As one study noted, the many events which took place during this time necessitated a bolder stance on Chinese economic reform.[10] The reform process included the acknowledged failure of concentrating on heavy industry development, the economic takeoff of some of China's neighbours who started out on the same developmental level but grew to become 'little dragons', such as Singapore, South Korea and Taiwan, and the convictions of the post-Maoist leadership that an improvement in Chinese living standards would solidify their political position.

The authors also stated that post-Mao reformers acknowledged the 'trinity' of the Maoist economic system, namely the distorted macro-policy environment which favoured heavy industry, planned resource-allocation systems which frequently led to shortages, and the inefficient state micro-management of industries, had to be scrapped for true restructuring to take place. Although much of the economic reform process in China after Mao took place on the domestic level, the international community and its institutions would play an increasingly important role.

In addition to changes on the domestic level, there were other factors on the international level which prompted a change in direction for China's relations with the global economic system. In short, the opening to market forces was not as daunting an option in the late 1970s as it would have been at an earlier time. As one analyst noted, China's position in the international order was stronger due to Beijing's representation in the United Nations, formidable armed forces backed by nuclear weapons capability, and a warming of relations between the superpowers resulting from détente.[11] As well, direct colonialist tendencies in the West, a bane to China for more than a century, had almost completely eroded, lessening concerns China would face economic subjugation if it opened its economy to international markets. These perceptions within the Chinese government suggested the country would increasingly be able to address economic and political issues with developed nations, not necessarily as equals, but at least from a stronger bargaining position.

The period after 1978 has been described as the launch pad of China's economic 'takeoff', a sharp rise in growth and productivity which resulted in an average annual increase in gross domestic product between 1978 and 1995 of 6–8 per cent, depending on the source of the figures.[12] The results stood in marked contrast to the economic chaos which ensued with the Maoist regime's attempt to implement the Great Leap Forward (1958–60), which, as Rostow noted, represented a reasonably successful attempt to improve production rates and forcibly institute a planned economic takeoff,[13] but nevertheless created massive socio-economic damage. Other sweeping changes included the encouragement of Chinese firms to export abroad, and for Chinese students to obtain advanced degrees by studying outside the country. The formation of a legal system to accommodate foreign investment was undertaken and the production of goods began to be based on consumer demand rather than quotas.[14] After decades of being one of the most underdeveloped economies in Asia, a distinction which was becoming more obvious as many of China's neighbours, including Taiwan, South Korea and Singapore, were abandoning closed economic practices and adapting export-oriented industrialisation, China was ready to re-define its approaches to the international economic system.

The opening process also necessitated that China adjust its stance toward the economic institutions which were Western-dominated. This policy was a significant reversal from previous years, when Beijing tended to side with other developing countries in exerting pressure against what they saw as neo-mercantilist regimes, including the GATT as well as the World Bank and the International Monetary Fund (IMF). For example, although Beijing had declined to formally join the

'Group of 77' developing states, it did support their initiative to redress what they perceived as stark inequalities between developed and developing nations through such initiatives as the 'New International Economic Order' (NIEO) declaration.[15] The NIEO, affirmed in 1974, called for non-discrimination of states based on their governmental or social system, compensation for damages suffered under colonialism, the sovereign right of states to control their own resources, and more favourable conditions for funding transfers to developing nations.[16] In 1978, when China decided to approach the United Nations Development Program (UNDP) for technical assistance, Beijing began to take a more conciliatory stance on the subject of engaging international financial institutions.[17]

Between the late-1970s Dengist economic reforms and July 1986, when the Chinese government announced its intention to 'recover' its membership in the GATT, Beijing began a series of steps designed to both educate and prepare itself for re-entry into international economic discourse. The year 1980 was a watershed for these efforts, largely due to China's official recognition by the United States. This, plus Beijing's membership of the United Nations in 1971, replacing Taipei, provided a much larger array of diplomatic avenues and opportunities by which China could better its domestic economic situation and strengthen its policy, advocated by Deng Xiaoping, of 'socialism with Chinese characteristics'. Beijing was able to take advantage of regaining its UN seat by resuming its position on the United Nations Interim Commission for the International Trade Organisation, a body given the mandate of making appointments to the GATT Secretariat.[18]

This period also marked the launch of China's experiment in controlled market reforms and measured foreign investment in the form of the special economic zones (SEZs). Four such zones were approved in 1979 and created the following year: three in Guangdong province (Shantou, Shenzhen and Zhuhai), and one in Fujian, (Xiamen, across the strait from Taiwan). The goal of the SEZs was to attract foreign investment through a series of incentives, including tax exemptions and a favourable business climate. It was hoped the zones, located in southern China and thus closer to economic centres in Hong Kong, Taiwan and Singapore, would attract overseas Chinese business interests anxious to tap into promising mainland markets.

Despite detractors from the conservative echelons of the Communist Party, the original four zones proved sufficiently successful with central and provincial leaders that pressure was applied to expand the SEZs into other parts of China. In 1984, SEZs were declared for Hainan Island as well as fourteen cities on the Chinese coast, including Beihai, Dalian, Guangzhou, Shanghai and Tianjin, and four years later these privileges were extended by reform-minded General Secretary Zhao Ziyang to encompass the entire Chinese coastal area.[19] The SEZ idea originated both from the pre-communist Chinese treaty ports operated by Western powers along the coast (which was of major concern to reactionaries in the party), and the success enjoyed by other parts of Asia, particularly Taiwan, after they had instituted reforms allowing for expanded trade and foreign investment.[20] The SEZs were the first serious step taken by post-Maoist China to demonstrate its desire to open up to the global economic system, representing a remarkable departure from the orthodox views of Maoist command economics.

Before announcing its intention to explore GATT membership, China tested the waters by engaging market economies as well as lower-tier economic institutions and agreements for their educational value and contributions to China's reform policies. In 1979, China reversed its long-standing aversion to receiving overseas development assistance (ODA) in favour of a more outward-looking policy. Many market economies began sending financial assistance to China, with Japan the largest contributor (providing US$92 billion between 1979 and 1985, or 42 per cent of total ODA to China during that period), followed by western Europe, Canada, and Australia.[21] In 1980, Beijing took giant steps towards re-integration with international economic institutions when diplomatic relationships with the United States were made official, granting China most favoured nation (MFN) trading status by America on a conditional basis.[22] During the same year, China was granted membership of the World Bank and the International Monetary Fund, making the country eligible for international loans from these organisations. Beijing responded to its new position with the World Bank by creating a new institution the following year, the China Investment Bank, designed for better distribution of World Bank donations.[23] In 1983, China joined the Multi-fibre Agreement, created a decade earlier to regulate textile exports.

China's announcement in 1986 that it would seek membership in the General Agreement on Tariffs and Trade came with the anticipation that admission would provide the country with many economic benefits previously unavailable. China sought GATT membership as a means of attaining international support for its economic reforms, improving trade relations with the United States and making it more difficult for Washington to engage in protectionist policies without violating GATT rules. This assisted in China's discouragement of protectionist policies in the global economy as a whole, and provided Beijing with the use of the GATT's dispute-settlement mechanism, allowing China to address trade disputes more effectively than relying on bilateral means.[24] However, China's request for GATT membership raised difficult issues within that body, especially the question of how an organisation dedicated to the facilitation of trade between market economies could admit a state which had taken only very preliminary steps towards trade and market reform. Beijing's insistence that the nationalist government in Taiwan acted illegally when it withdrew 'China' from the GATT in 1950, making the People's Republic a *de facto* member of the organisation, was not accepted by the GATT.[25] Therefore, China had to apply for membership of that body without special consideration given to history.

The remainder of the decade saw a torpid negotiation process begin with the United States and other key economic actors determining the conditions for China to enter into the GATT. However, it was not long into the discussions that political factors began to insinuate themselves. The Tiananmen tragedy in June 1989 created a massive international outcry and resulted in a considerable setback in the negotiation process. GATT negotiations with China were also sidelined due to mounting frustrations over members' inability to bring the intricate Uruguay Round of trade talks to a successful close. It was not until March 1994 when the working group on GATT membership, which China established six years earlier, could revive its efforts.[26] Despite global condemnation and damage to China's external relations, the reforms of its foreign trade policies were not halted. Neither did the incident result in a turn towards greater isolationism.[27]

Nevertheless, the resulting downturn in Sino-American relations as a result of the Tiananmen incident served to further politicise the question of China's GATT membership and to further complicate the annual debate concerning China's MFN status. It was not until 1991 that the issue of China's GATT membership was again seriously considered by Washington.[28] However, as another election year in the United States loomed, the China issue became the subject of increased interest to the administration of George H. W. Bush, especially after the president vetoed attempts by the rival Democratic Party to attach further conditions to China's annual MFN renewal in early 1991.[29] Thus, domestic infighting within the United States dashed Chinese hopes for American-approved fast-track acceptance into the GATT.

China's GATT efforts during this period were further hampered when the attention of the organisation was diverted to eastern Europe's breaking away from Soviet hegemony, followed by the break-up of the USSR itself, creating several new 'transition economies' also seeking to join GATT. Lardy suggested that China, itself a transitional economy, was perceived as a template for negotiations between the GATT and former Soviet republics and allies. Therefore, Western governments wished to negotiate China's entrance on more rigorous terms as a sign to other hopefuls. Nevertheless, the progress of China's admission fell behind many other emerging markets. Slovenia gained admission before the GATT transformed into the WTO, and 11 others, including Georgia, Hungary, Kyrgyzstan, Mongolia and Poland, entered the WTO before China.[30] Rather than being perceived as distinct amongst GATT applicants, during the 1990s China became one among many economies seeking to codify their desire to adapt to the free market by joining one of the world's largest economic associations.

Additional pressures on Beijing were created when Taipei announced its intention in January 1990 to join the GATT under Article 33 of the General Agreement, which allows for territories with autonomous customs laws to apply for membership separately.[31] Taipei submitted its application under the heading of the 'Customs Territory of Taiwan, Penghu, Kinmen (Quemoy) and Matsu'. Beijing reacted to this news by repeatedly insisting that Taipei, regardless of qualifications, could not join the GATT ahead of the People's Republic.[32] Despite the fact that Taiwan's negotiations with the regime were faster and easier than Beijing's, the GATT was unwilling to defy the latter's wishes and admit Taipei first. This meant that Taiwan's own GATT ambitions became directly tied to the results of Beijing's talks, an unwelcome development for Taipei, which was seeking to increase its international stature through participation in multilateral institutions.

In December 1990, China's economic modernisation reached another defining moment with the opening of the country's first stock exchanges in Shanghai and Shenzhen.[33] The following year, China, along with Hong Kong and Taiwan, was granted membership in the Asia Pacific Economic Cooperation forum (APEC), which had been created two years earlier. During the 1990s, APEC grew to encompass many major regional economies, including Australia, Japan, southeast Asia, Russia, and the United States. China made use of annual APEC meetings to promote its desire to enter the GATT and the advantages of China's further opening to foreign trade for the global economy. APEC was also useful as a smaller-scale tutorial, enabling China to learn about the intricacies of international trading rules and norms. During the first few years of APEC's existence, the forum pressed for a satisfactory resolution to the faltering Uruguay Round of international trade negotiations under the GATT, a position China supported.

Another significant event within China which not only radically transformed Chinese thinking about capitalism and the free market, but also mentally prepared the citizenry for further engagement with the international economy and its institutions was the 'Southern Tour' which Deng Xiaoping undertook in 1992.[34] Although having formally given up the last of his government positions two years earlier, and officially retired, Deng remained the most powerful figure within the Chinese government, and was still very much able to unilaterally shape the country's policies. During his tour of the south, he praised economic reform efforts in Guangdong province and the Shenzhen stock exchange, while expressing hope that more areas of China could emulate Hong Kong and other Asian 'tigers'. He insisted the state was powerful enough to withstand the negative effects of further market openings, and that market development and the pursuit of socialism were not mutually exclusive. Finally, he created a major stir within party ranks with his warning that 'China must watch out for the right, but mainly defend against the left', meaning that although China still needed to be vigilant against imperialist and bourgeois influences, a greater threat could be found from those opposing reform and preaching isolationism.[35] This declaration was a dramatic reversal of longstanding Maoist doctrine in China, and did much to influence the public perceptions of the reform process.

Deng's call for economic transformation, and the revival of the axiom, 'black cat or white cat; if it catches mice, it is a good cat', he used in 1962, signalled to the Chinese people and to their government that an official blessing had been given to embrace further economic reform and the private acquisition of further wealth. The phrase *xia hai*, literally 'to jump into the sea' became a catch phase during the 1990s for going into business and joining the rapidly growing Chinese private sector.[36] Another term, *jiegui*, (literally, 'to get on track') was now liberally used by Chinese business interests to describe the country's intensifying efforts to link up with the international economy through the reform of domestic institutions.[37] Although China's early attempts to gain entrance to the GATT proved unsuccessful, on the domestic level the preparations for membership, both to the institution and to the more general international economy, were well underway by the early 1990s.

'Jumping into the sea'

The seven-year Uruguay Round of the GATT finally concluded in December 1993, and the Final Act of the Round was signed in Marrakesh, Morocco, four months later. The Marrakesh Agreement was a considerable achievement not only due to the size of the final treaty, (about 22,000 pages) but also because of the new sectors which were brought under the institution's aegis, including services, agriculture, intellectual property, textiles, and product standards, as well as a new unified code for the resolution of trade conflicts between members.[38]

The most far-reaching agreement signed at Marrakesh, however, was the charter of the World Trade Organisation, which was to be launched in 1995 as the successor body to the GATT. The WTO's genesis was primarily a response to the perceived weaknesses of the GATT. These included ambiguities in defining the powers of the contracting parties (the signatories of the GATT agreement) as well as the authority to issue waivers, deficiencies in the dispute-settlement process, and its nebulous legal and institutional status.[39] In addressing these problems, the WTO mandate would provide codes of conduct for reducing tariff and non-tariff barriers while ending discrimination, establishing an institutional framework to support these codes, providing the means to enforce the codes through economic surveillance and supplying a dispute-settlement mechanism. Additionally, it would act as an agency for facilitating economic relations between states and supporting greater liberalisation of the overall global trading network.[40]

Once the creation of the new body was confirmed, China shifted its negotiation efforts to ensure that it could enter the WTO as a founding member by joining GATT first. However, the primary obstacle to China's admission to the new WTO, in addition to the organisation's own rules, remained the United States, the largest economy of the group and thus the major voice in deciding on new admissions. To further complicate the issue, in order for a Sino-American trade agreement to succeed, Washington had to be convinced to waive the annual vote on whether China should retain most favoured nation status under the rules of the Jackson-Vanik amendment to the 1974 Trade Act. This amendment stipulated that American trade with a 'non-market economy', (a euphemism for 'communist nation'), required the president to notify Congress of such trade every year.[41] Predictably, voting over renewing China's MFN status often resulted in heated political debate within American government and society, especially when foreign relations with Beijing ran into political troubles.

Removing the MFN vote in the United States was therefore a key goal for Chinese negotiators, who were anxious to ensure uninterrupted linkages with the American economy. However, as Sino-American relations remained unstable after Tiananmen, support for revoking China's MFN status developed within sectors of the American government concerned about China's human rights record. Former American President Richard Nixon, who was greatly responsible for America's opening to China in the 1970s, warned in 1994 against any alteration of Beijing's MFN status, noting that such a move would not only undercut reformist elements within the country but also damage the economic integrity of China, and by association Hong Kong.[42] However, during the 1990s, various political incidents between Washington and Beijing kept the question of China's MFN status open for most of the decade, and the deadline for becoming a founding member of the WTO came and went with no American deal.

China's failure to join the WTO as a founding member was not only a blow to the country's prestige, but since the rules of admission were more stringent for the new organisation than for its predecessor, the GATT, concerns were raised that future negotiations would be considerably more difficult. As well, there was considerable resentment towards the United States for refusing China's latest trade offerings and for seemingly not being serious about seeing Beijing join the organisation. The rejection also contributed to Chinese concerns that American mule-headedness on the WTO issue was part of a larger policy of containing China's growing power, politically and economically. Anti-American sentiment, not helped by Washington's refusal to support Beijing's bid to hold the summer Olympics in 2000, was coupled with growing debate from Chinese policymakers as to whether WTO admission was truly necessary or desirable.[43] The United States was willing to continue negotiations. During his campaign for re-election in autumn 1996, President Clinton sent a team of negotiators to China hoping to re-start the negotiation process.[44] However, the talks failed to produce an agreement in time for either the Clinton–Jiang summit in Washington in October 1997 or Clinton's visit to Beijing the following June. The American side insisted that Chinese conditions and trade concessions remained insufficient for an agreement to be struck.

While China continued to try and negotiate terms that would be most favourable to its economic and trade needs, the US concerns included China's slow response to the reform or elimination of state-owned enterprises, many of which were unprofitable and archaic, ongoing government price controls, high tariffs, and a lack of transparency in the country's trade regulations.[45] An additional issue between the two was a disagreement over whether China should be admitted to the organisation as a 'developed' or 'developing' country. The United States insisted on the former designation, while China pushed very hard for the latter, or at the very least wanted a trade deal which reflected developing status, since being classified as such would result in more lax conditions and deadlines in meeting WTO requirements. More specifically, under WTO rules developing nations are permitted to protect infant industries, restrict imports, and have their governments issue development subsidies. In this, China presented a very awkward case. Although China was one of the top ten trading nations during the 1990s, it was also the only one of the group which could be considered a developing state.[46] While China had adopted the characteristics of both types of state, the lack of any kind of official middle ground meant that the country's classification remained highly subjective.

In addition to classification issues, there were other areas of contention between Washington and Beijing complicating the process, including American concerns over China's lax regulation of intellectual property rights (IPR). During the 1990s, revelations that China was becoming a hub for counterfeit electronics goods, computer software, and videocassettes led to sanctions followed by agreements designed to strengthen China's IPR laws.[47] Nevertheless, the scope of the problem indicates this issue will remain an area of contention in China and elsewhere. For example, it was estimated in 2002 by the Development Research Centre of China's State Council that about US$16 billion worth of counterfeit material was being released into the Chinese market annually. In 2001, during a three-month campaign, the State Council attempted to crack down on these counterfeits. However, resistance at the local and regional level to such initiatives, especially because of the loss of revenue for counterfeiting agents and the heavy bureaucratisation and jurisdictional disputes among copyright law-enforcement bodies, continued to hamper the process.[48] This issue will likely remain a divisive one, especially since those countries suffering economic harm from counterfeit items now have the option of making use of the regime's dispute-settlement mechanism to take Beijing to task.

The result of these many areas of contention between China and the United States was a protracted game of 'red light, green light' in the search to find sufficient middle ground acceptable to both sides, as an agreement with America was essential to the WTO membership process. However, when the world's largest economy sat down with the world's largest market, tensions and conflicts were the inevitable outcome. As Pearson noted, several factors contributed to the complexity of the Sino-American negotiations, including China's acceptance that sweeping changes in their economic system would be required, the realisation that admitting a China which was unwilling to follow WTO rules would be detrimental to all sides, the growing understanding among Chinese policymakers as to what level of concession was required to attain membership and, a factor always flitting in the background, the difficult political relationship between Washington and Beijing which frequently interfered in the negotiations.[49] Despite conventional thinking that non-market related issues should best be left outside WTO-related organisations, in practice many economic, as well as political, factors outside strict WTO interests are often included as peripheral issues in the sidelines of various negotiation processes.[50] The US–China talks were one of the clearest examples of that phenomenon.

During the latter stages of the Sino-American negotiations, Chinese negotiators had to endure not only a difficult American stance but also widely differing views from various domestic Chinese political actors. The governmental body most in favour of WTO admission was the Ministry of Foreign Trade and Economic Cooperation (MOFTEC), led by Wu Yi and, after 1998, by Shi Guangsheng. In explaining China's need to enter the organisation, Shi made note that membership would prompt an acceleration of Chinese economic reforms and also lead to an overall improvement in the development of the global economy. He added that in the two decades since China had embarked on its reforms, Beijing had been supporting a policy of 'leading in', or encouraging foreign investment in China, while more recently advocating a 'walking out' strategy, supporting Chinese enterprises in their quest to tap international markets, as a result of China's drive to join the WTO.[51] During the years of negotiation with the WTO, MOFTEC had been granted the leading role in carrying out the negotiations, largely because it was sufficiently isolated from the more protectionist ministries. Consequently, MOFTEC members became known for their international exposure and experience as well as their willingness to align China with global norms and institutions.[52] Thus MOFTEC, along with the inner circle of the Chinese government represented the strongest support base for the WTO negotiations.

However, both the Chinese negotiators and the WTO supporters within the Chinese government had to contend with the intransigence of domestic political actors within China seeking to protect their interests from perceived international competition. One major detractor was the State Planning Commission (SPC), which acted as a bastion for those supporting the perpetuation of the Chinese planned economy.[53] American negotiators were also critical of the fact that the Chinese government was unable to prevent certain ministries such as the State Planning Commission and the Labour Ministry from adding new trade barriers as preventive measures against future competition. For example, it was reported in 1997 that the Ministry of Labour issued new rules requiring foreign firms operating in China to pay local inspectors (including their travel costs) to visit their plants and determine the safety of imported parts used for power generators and textile mills.[54] These sorts of 'non-tariff barriers' were responsible for greatly complicating the negotiating process.

There were also many differences of opinion on this divisive issue at the provincial and local level. Geography was a major factor, as those coastal provinces which had already begun to benefit considerably from China's opening to international trade were heavily in favour of admission both to improve their economic abilities via increased competition, and in some cases to open up new trading possibilities with Taiwan. Shanghai, however, was split on the issue. While it housed the Pudong development zone, which stood to benefit from further foreign investment, the city contained many state-owned enterprises which would certainly suffer from foreign competition.[55] Equally, China's 'rust belt', the heavily industrialised provinces of the northeast, could face extreme pressures after becoming exposed to foreign competition. The northeastern provinces of Heilongjiang, Jilin and Liaoning have already suffered from mass closures of inefficient SOEs and resulting unemployment.[56] One of the most serious issues China will have to address as it adjusts to WTO membership is how, and to what degree, economic disparities, which have already developed over the last two decades between the rich coastal regions and elsewhere, will evolve as a result of membership and the associated jump in foreign investment.

In addition to opposition forces within the Chinese government aligned against the WTO was an increasing number of concerned voices from scholars and intellectuals, who not only faced greater marginalization and lower standards of living in comparison with China's growing business class, but also expressed fears that political stability and order was being sacrificed by the sudden rush towards market reforms. These dissenters would form the basis of the 'neo-conservative' movement within the Chinese elite.[57] Opposition to the WTO also came from another elite quarter, namely the 'postmodernist' or 'new left' wing of Chinese thinkers. Adherents to that school of thought expressed concern that Chinese policymakers were too willing to make concessions to American and Western demands in their pursuit of WTO membership, and that admission would result in considerable costs with uncertain benefits for China. Some postmodernists, taking a page from previous eras of communist doctrine, viewed economic organisations such as the WTO as American-led tools to subjugate lesser-developed countries.[58] Arguments between postmodernists and the more liberal schools over the merits of WTO membership marked much intellectual discourse during the 1990s.

The upper echelons of the Chinese government, however, remained focused on their WTO goals. Reform initiatives accelerated under Premier Zhu Rongji, who had been appointed to the position in March 1998, replacing arch-conservative Li Peng. The removal of Li from the premier's position was instrumental not only to China's plans to join the WTO but also to the success of China's economic reform process as a whole. Li had been the most visible member of the communist old guard within the Chinese politburo, as well as the voice of the factions representing the country's planned economy.[59] Zhu, a strong supporter of China's WTO admission as a means to further codify the country's economic reforms, oversaw the streamlining of both government and bureaucracy in the wake of recommendations made following the Fifteenth Party Congress in 1997 requiring drastic measures to trim bureaucratic excess and bolster the economic reform process.

Among these measures was a reduction in the number of government ministries to 29 from 40. Several ministries were also absorbed by the State Economic and Trade Commission (SETC), which was directly overseen by Zhu Rongji himself. Such diverse sectors as electric power, textiles, internal trade, machine-building, and forestry became subordinate to the SETC, which as Yang noted, began to take on a predominant role within the Chinese economy, similar in stature to the then-powerful (now-defunct) Ministry of International Trade and Industry (MITI) in Japan.[60] The creation of the SETC, he added, also served to marginalise the reactionary State Planning Commission, which was renamed the State Development Planning Commission (SDPC) after March 1998 and given the reduced mandate of economic forecasting.[61] What was especially noteworthy, however, was the fact that many ministries slated for elimination or restructuring were those representing the more reactionary elements of the Chinese economy, including the Ministry of Metallurgical Industry and Ministry of Machine Building Industry.[62]

The most visible example of this new bureaucratic centralisation was the creation of the Ministry of Information Industry (MII),[63] which was created via the merger of the Ministry of Posts and Telecommunications and the Ministry of Electronics Industry. The MII was designed to address China's interests in the 'new economy', dominated by computer technology and electronic commerce. However, since the leadership of the MII was assumed by members of the notably conservative Ministry of Posts, and regulation of China's internet-based industries has been hampered by other ministries either seeking a voice in the development of electronic commerce and high-technology networks, or expressing concern about the possible dangers these new technologies may present to state security, this industry still has a long way to go before achieving maturity.[64] In September 1999, when MII minister Wu Jichuan declared that Chinese internet content providers were to be considered telecommunications firms and therefore forbidden to accept foreign investment, content providers such as Sina.com and Sohu.com who sought to become public offerings were temporarily hamstrung until a compromise could be found.[65] Wu had been well-known for his opposition to China's WTO negotiations, expressing the opinion that the country would have to cede too much of its sovereignty in order to join.[66]

The information technology sector has been viewed as an essential resource to ensure continued economic growth in the coming years, and has embarked upon a series of ambitious initiatives, such as projects designed to provide officials with access to government information, to create information linkages for all provinces, and to allow authorities easier access to the sales records of various firms.[67] While China has been a strong supporter of Asian regional information technology initiatives, the country struggles with its desire to become a hub for high technology communications and concern that the internet (*hulian wang*) and other electronic media could be used as a medium by which to spread anti-government materials. In 1997 strict regulations concerning internet usage in China were implemented, forbidding the transmission of materials considered to be incitements to 'overthrow the government or the socialist system', as well as advocating falsehoods or 'destroying the order of society'. To protect against misuse, internet service providers and net businesses were required to accept governmental regulation and supervision.[68] Government-sanctioned blocking of Western news and entertainment websites is a routine occurrence in the country and in July 2004 Beijing announced the regulation and filtration of phone text messaging. This was seen as a response to the use of cell phones in 2003 to transmit news relating the SARS epidemic, revealing initial attempts by Beijing to suppress the health crisis, as well as cases involving state corruption and abuses of power.[69]

The erratic approach of the Chinese government towards electronic communications has the potential to be extremely problematic, not only for Chinese plans to integrate further into the high-tech-heavy 'new economy' but also for foreign investors seeking to tap into China's large potential telecommunications markets. While the number of internet users in China had reached an estimated 94 million by January 2005, according to data sampling taken by the China Internet Network Information Centre (CNNIC),[70] there remains considerable potential for the expansion of both high-technology users and industries in the country. Despite American attempts to reach a deal with Beijing on investment in Chinese internet firms, Chinese officials insisted that even after WTO admission was achieved, there would be prohibitions placed on foreign investment in Chinese internet service providers. The labyrinth of rules governing internet activities and ventures in China will be extremely difficult for foreign interests to navigate and it is unclear that even WTO membership would convince the Chinese government to liberalise these rules.[71] As such, questions of internet regulation within China will likely remain problematic in the short term.

Another feature of the 1998 reforms was the groundbreaking initiative by President Jiang to openly call for the People's Liberation Army to divest itself of all its business interests, reversing a trend which had been in development since the beginning of the Dengist reforms. The July announcement reportedly stemmed from concerns that burgeoning corruption within PLA ranks represented a growing threat to economic stability in the country. A new auditing system, unveiled in 1995, concluded that some PLA members were engaged in myriad types of corrupt activities, including misappropriation or misallocation of funds, bribery, smuggling, establishing shell enterprises, and so forth.[72] Continued illegal activities by sections of the armed forces threatened to become both an embarrassment and a liability for Beijing's reform initiatives.

After the announcement was made, however, the actual divestiture process took several more months of negotiations and planning, with PLA-owned businesses being asked to register with the government, and owners being given the choice of remaining within the armed forces or retaining their enterprises. Those choosing to divest would be eligible for compensation packages from the government. Some areas were more adversely affected than others; for example, the General Logistics Department (GLD) of the PLA was forced to close or transfer more than 84 per cent of its business holdings, while telecommunications firms owned or overseen by the PLA were reportedly given frequent exemptions due to their role in maintaining Chinese security as well as developing the armed forces' high-technology capabilities.[73]

These moves were risky for both the Chinese government and the PLA, since it has been estimated that the official state military budget normally supplies only about 70 per cent of the armed forces' annual financial requirements,[74] and after 1998 there was a question of how to address the shortfall. Moreover, the sheer scope of PLA activities, covering everything from commodities to services to arms trading, calls into question the ability of the state to separate the PLA from its business interests to an acceptable degree. There was reportedly a great deal of bitterness from the PLA over what they saw as insufficient compensation and the tarnishing of its reputation, especially since it was suggested that Jiang's decision may have been one of political expediency. After Zhu Rongji accused a PLA front company, Tiancheng Group, of carrying out massive smuggling operations, Jiang was reportedly forced to admit to financial irregularities within the armed forces and issue the divestiture directive to protect Zhu from a PLA backlash.[75] Both the Jiang and Hu governments have tried to offset these PLA financial losses through budget increases for the military. As of 2004, the PLA's budget stands at approximately US$25 billion in the wake of an announced 11.8 per cent budget increase in March of that year.[76] Despite these funding increases, it remains to be seen what kind of longer-term political and economic effects the party's reforms of the PLA in the name of economic modernisation will create.

Endgame

By the end of the 1990s, the domestic economic landscape of China was drama-tically transformed as a result of economic liberalisation and a more concentrated effort to remove political obstacles to further growth and development. None of these internal changes, however, were having the desired effect on the negotiations with Washington. Attempts to strike a final trade deal between America and China ran into serious problems by the beginning of 1999. Premier Zhu came to Washington hopeful that an agreement for Chinese WTO admission could be struck, but, despite much progress, the proposed final deal was rejected by President Clinton over the objections of his national security advisors and his own trade negotiator, Charlene Barshefsky. Clinton's rejection of the accord stemmed from his conviction that the American Congress would refuse to endorse the deal unless more protection was guaranteed for American industries and labour unions, stipulations which were unacceptable to Zhu.[77]

There were larger political issues involved in Clinton's decision. The president was cognisant of an anti-Beijing backlash within the American Congress following the May 1999 release of a congressional survey, later known as the Cox Report, detailing alleged Chinese theft of US missile and weaponry technology and lax American security procedures. There were also claims of China illicitly obtaining information on the designs of intercontinental and submarine-launched ballistic missiles, the W-88 tapered nuclear warhead and a neutron bomb.[78] Although Beijing vehemently denied any such espionage, the report dampened American enthusiasm for a trade deal. At the same time, there remained a lingering distrust on the part of the Americans of Chinese motives as a result of the 1996–7 'Donorgate' scandal, when President Clinton and the Democratic National Committee were accused of accepting illegal campaign funds through sources connected to Beijing.[79] Clinton was also cognisant of protests by both the American labour unions concerned about the loss of domestic industries to China, and human rights organisations which claimed that a WTO deal with China would be inadvisable in light of the country's poor record in this area.[80]

The debacle of the April 1999 meeting proved costly for the prestige of Zhu as well as President Jiang Zemin. When Zhu returned from the United States after presenting China's most generous offer on trade concessions to date, only to have the offer refused, elements within the government opposed to the WTO negotiations questioned Zhu's credibility. Adding insult to injury was the decision to post a list of proposed Chinese concessions on the United State Trade Representative's website without first informing the Chinese government. MII Minister Wu was especially incensed after reading of the rejected concessions, arguing that Zhu had attempted to give away far too much for the sake of a deal.[81] Dissent also came from the Chinese media and intellectuals, including an article which accused the United States of attempting to coerce China into the WTO while demanding repeated concessions in the hopes of eroding Beijing's position. The piece also noted that America was anxious to bring China into the organisation in hopes of 'globalising' the People's Republic, which in reality was no different from expanding American hegemony over the Chinese economy.[82] In response to the overwhelming barrage of criticism, Zhu offered to resign on three separate occasions, but Jiang would not hear of it, and instead called upon other members of the Politburo to maintain support for the premier.[83]

Shielding Zhu became more difficult after May 1999 following the diplomatic fallout from the bombing of the Chinese embassy in the Yugoslavian capital of Belgrade that month by an American fighter jet. NATO forces had sought to compel the government of Yugoslavia to halt human rights abuses in the province of Kosovo. Three Chinese journalists were killed in the embassy attack, which according to the United States, took place after the embassy had been misidentified as a viable military target.[84] The bombing touched off anti-American protests across China, including the torching of the American consulate in the city of Chengdu. The protests were tacitly condoned on a limited scale by the Chinese government, a reversal of longstanding government policy of discouraging mass protests, especially those with nationalistic overtones.[85] One of the legacies of these protests was further questioning of the wisdom of engaging the American government over the WTO. However, Jiang and his ministers refused to dash any hopes of reviving trade talks after the incident, despite lingering questions as to whether the embassy bombing had been deliberate or a careless accident.[86]

There was ongoing pressure from both sides to conclude a Sino-American trade deal before the WTO summit in Seattle in late 1999, after which it was hoped that a 'Millennium Round' of trade talks would commence, with China participating as a full member. Following six days of intense negotiations, a deal was signed on 15 November 1999, an agreement almost identical to the one rejected by the United States in April.[87] One exception was a change which favoured the Chinese side, a provision that foreign firms could own 50 per cent of Chinese telecommunications firms, rather than 51 per cent presented for the April agreement. However, China had to make its own considerable concessions in order to facilitate the deal, including the dropping of tariffs on imported industrial products from an average of 24.6 per cent to 9.4 per cent, removing quotas on textiles by 2005, permitting foreign banks to provide services using Chinese currency for Chinese enterprises, and for Chinese individuals at a later date, and the lowering of tariffs on American farm goods.[88] After so many years of talks, Chinese hopes grew that it would soon take part in the next global round of trade negotiations as a full partner.

Although the hoped-for 'Millennium Round' of the WTO failed to materialise when talks fell apart in December 1999 amid intractable policy differences between developed and developing nations inside and unprecedented street protests outside, China remained hopeful that it would be playing a strong role when the round finally got underway. That month, MOFTEC minister Shi issued proposals for the next global set of trade negotiations which reflected China's evolving policy towards multilateral economic engagement. The proposals included respect for the developing countries' methods of market opening, a call for developed countries to meet their Uruguay Round commitments and facilitate market access for developing countries, the creation of new trade rules with the input of developing nations, and a stipulation that the next round focus squarely on trade and avoid other issues unrelated to WTO functions, specifically labour standards.[89]

These recommendations were further evidence that China perceived itself as a potential spokesperson for the developing world, in the same tradition as its views on the NIEO decades earlier. It is unclear, however, that Beijing will continue to hold that position as its economic power increases, narrowing the gap between itself and developed nations. As China furthers its integration with the global economy, Beijing may very well find itself unable to reconcile its attempts to portray itself as a white knight for developing nation interests while at the same time seeking to bolster its economic power to levels consistent with the richest states.

The Sino-American trade deal was presented to the US Congress for a vote. A bill to grant China permanent normal trade relations, a precursor to American acceptance of China's WTO bid, was passed by the US House of Representatives in May 2000 after months of political arguments, and the American Senate approved the bill that September.[90] In June 2001, American and Chinese negotiators met in Shanghai to seek agreements on various outstanding issues, including agriculture, a longstanding staple of the Chinese economy. Although China's agricultural output had improved in the 1980s due to increased foreign trade, the sector was nevertheless seen as vulnerable to international price fluctuations and increased imports.[91] Other items included services, notably the thorny issue of insurance, and trading rights. The June deal also reportedly included a consensus on the question of whether China would enter the WTO as a developed or developing country, but neither side was willing to provide specifics as to what kind of compromise was reached.[92]

However, China still needed to continue its campaign to secure trade deals with the remaining key economies, while demonstrating to the WTO that it was prepared to assume the many responsibilities of membership. Only a few months before the final deal with the WTO in November 2001, a small bombshell was dropped when Jiang stated in his 1 July speech commemorating the 80th anniversary of the Chinese Communist Party that private businesspeople and entrepreneurs would be permitted to join the Chinese Communist Party.[93] This concession marked an official confirmation of a trend which had been growing in China from the beginning of the Dengist reforms: that private sector workers and independent entrepreneurs would be considered integral political and economic actors able to join the party. This invitation to the private sector was part of a broader explanation of Jiang's 'Three Represents' theory of the new role of the CCP. There was little doubt that both the announced opening of the party to the private sector and the 'Three Represents' doctrine as a whole were meant to signal China's readiness for the WTO and the international economy.[94]

However, while the change in thinking on behalf of the party is, on the surface, revolutionary, and has certainly been the subject of much controversy within the Chinese government, there remain unanswered questions. What will be the reaction of the more conservative elements within the party to the expansion and what will be the real benefits to both the party and the growing number of entrepreneurs? As one scholar noted, bringing entrepreneurs into the CCP may provide the government with a means to address corruption more effectively, but at the same time this closer relationship will provide Beijing with a higher level of direct control over the private sector, potentially a serious problem for domestic and international business interests alike. The same scholar also noted that although the Chinese government has been trying to further integrate private economy actors for some time (indeed, one of the five stars on the Chinese flag stands for the 'patriotic capitalist' class), in practice the relationship between party and private business is still a thorny one.[95]

The move towards accepting private sector workers and entrepreneurs in and of itself was revolutionary, but the constitutional groundwork had begun many years earlier. As part of the reform process, while preparing China for entering the WTO, Jiang, and Deng before him, attempted to continue the process of setting the stage for gradual acceptance of the private sector. Among the amendments to the Chinese constitution which were implemented in April 1988 were additions to Article 11, describing the composition and limits to the 'individual economy', which could exist with acceptable government guidelines. The article was amended to include the assertion that:

> the state permits the private sector of the economy to exist, and develop within the limits prescribed by law. The private sector of the economy is a complement to the socialist public economy. The state protects the lawful rights and interests of the private sector of the economy, and exercises guidance, supervision and control over the private sector of the economy.

The article was further altered in March 1999 to stipulate that

> the non-public sector of the economy comprising self-employed and private businesses within the domain stipulated by law is an important component of the country's socialist market economy.

and that the state protects the rights and interests of, as well as providing guidance to, said self-employed and private businesses.[96]

The formal admission of China to the WTO took place during the organisation's conference in Doha, Qatar, on 11 November 2001,[97] during the second day of larger international talks designed to launch a new round of multilateral trade negotiations, picking up where the failed 1999 Seattle talks had left off. For the Chinese delegation, their new membership was an event on the same level as China's return to the United Nations in 1971.[98] China appointed Sun Zhenyu, former vice-minister for MOFTEC, as Beijing's first ambassador to the WTO and he promised Beijing would 'strictly abide by WTO rules and earnestly honour its commitments so as to make positive contributions to the improvement and strengthening of the multilateral trade regime'.[99] The news of China's admission also benefited Taipei, which was informed a day after Beijing's announcement that the island had also been granted membership. Taiwan officially joined the WTO as that body's 144th member on 1 January 2002.[100]

Following the signing ceremony in Doha, the head of the Chinese delegation to the conference, Minister Shi, stated that the resolution of China's WTO ambitions demonstrated three factors: that 'positive' participation in multilateral trading institutions was the only way for countries to share in the overall benefits of economic globalisation; that countries must build these regimes in accordance with their own specific economic and foreign policy practices; and that these regimes will only succeed if they continuously adapt to changing global economic conditions and reflect the interests of all participants, including those held by developing countries.[101] The implications of these conclusions were that although China viewed economic institutional participation as an indispensable means of benefiting from globalisation, the country would continue to insist such participation must take into account China's distinct position as a large but still developing economy, and that these regimes must not condone exploitation of poorer members by the richer.

Premier Zhu retired after the November 2002 16th Party Congress, and Zhu successfully pushed for his protégé, Vice-Premier Wen Jiabao, to assume the premiership as part of the new leadership's inner circle.[102] Although originally a specialist in geography, his political and economic skills and his ties to both Zhu and Jiang Zemin helped elevate Wen within the Communist Party to the vice-premier position in March 1998. In that capacity, Wen served as an advisor to Zhu on China's agricultural and financial sectors, two key targets of the current reform process.[103] Premier Wen has continued to support the reforms begun by Zhu, while showing signs of paying more attention to rural development, a nod to his previous role as manager of Western Development Strategy, assisting the territory of Xinjiang in catching up to other parts of China.[104] The question of whether China's long negotiations to enter the WTO can be considered truly successful will depend on how effectively the state's economic sectors are opened to international competition.

Risks and contradictions

'Political development', noted Gourevitch, 'is shaped by war and trade'. China is certainly no exception to this rule, and provides a compelling case study of his 'second image reversed' argument, describing how the international system can greatly affect developments in a country's domestic politics.[105] As explained, the long negotiation process between China and various WTO actors did much to shape Chinese domestic economic foreign policy, while complementing the country's larger plans of completing its ambitious economic reform policies. China's drive to join the World Trade Organisation was originally undertaken to add a perceived missing piece to the state's embryonic reform process, but the long negotiation period, marked by politics and frequent great power disagreements, caused the admission process to assume an expanded shape. Acceptance by the

WTO became one of the most important litmus tests for the country's ability to integrate into the modern international economy and in creating this linkage the Chinese government was tying its own legitimacy, or at the very least the legitimacy of the post-1978 Dengist economic reforms, to the success of these negotiations.

The challenges facing China as it attempted to enter the WTO were many, especially after it became clear that Western actors, particularly America, would refuse to separate politics and foreign policy issues from their discourses with China. On more than one occasion, stalls in the talks might have resulted in serious setbacks for the reformist elements in the Chinese government and possibly even a grand scaling-back of free-market reforms. The history of China's negotiations in joining the GATT/WTO thus represents a clear case example of Putnam's 'two-level game' theory, as Chinese negotiators not only had to contend with the demands of their foreign counterparts, but also the often conflicting influences within the Chinese government itself.[106] Those 'players' who did not succeed either on the international or the domestic level ran the risk of being ejected from the game altogether, and indeed there were signs that Chinese negotiators, especially Zhu, were faced with that risk at the later stages of the talks as frustration set in within the Chinese government and the WTO's detractors made their voices heard. Moreover, the 'game' was made riskier by the fact that the Chinese government made little secret of the fact that WTO membership was sought in order to force the less reform-minded elements of the government to accept the economic restructuring doctrines.[107] Therefore, Zhu and his negotiators had small margins for error in their interactions both with the international actors and with members of their own party.

Now that China is a member, many risks remain to both China and its government as the country adapts to the rules of this international regime. First and foremost, many of China's most important economic sectors will be adversely affected by the opening up of Chinese markets to foreign competition. One local economist suggested that some 3,000,000 employees of state-owned enterprises will face layoffs in the short term as a result of WTO membership, and sectors such as agriculture, automobiles, metallurgy, machinery and communications equipment will also suffer from foreign competition and will shed jobs as a result.[108] As noted, many of these job losses will be region-specific, and have a great impact on the more underdeveloped regions within China. As Fewsmith stated, WTO admission could result in an even greater exacerbation of regional differences within China, especially those between the country's relatively prosperous coastline and the more necessitous interior. He added it may be more difficult in the future for the two sides to forge links with each other because of the growing income disparities.[109] The social impact of these effects within a country which was founded on the principles of communism may be considerable.

Since 2001, Beijing has taken a conservative approach to its membership in the organisation, but by no means an inactive one. In its first few years the Doha Round found itself besieged by many of the issues which complicated its predecessor, especially those dealing with specific issues facing developing economy members. Doha's problems assumed a new sense of urgency in the wake of the backlash from the failed trade talks in Cancun of September 2003. Although analysts differed on the exact causes of the failure at Cancun, many have pointed to irreconcilable differences in two traditionally thorny areas of trade reform, namely agriculture and 'trade-related aspects of intellectual property rights' (TRIPS). Other contentious issues inundated WTO negotiations since 2002, including cotton trading and the so-called 'Singapore issues', namely the regulation of investment, competition, trade facilitation and transparency.[110]

The three major bloc players within the talks, the United States, the European Union, and a coalition of emerging markets known colloquially as the Group of 22 (G-22), could not reach significant common ground on these matters. Membership of the G-22, which represents slightly over half the world's population and 63 per cent of the world's agricultural output, included China and other developing economies such as Brazil, Chile, Egypt, India and Indonesia. The missteps at Cancun raised concerns that the hoped-for goal of completing the Doha Round by early 2005 would prove untenable.[111] Despite China's membership of the G-22, the country did receive some plaudits from observers for its restrained approach in advocating developing-area issues, a further indication that Beijing has adjusted very quickly to its role within the WTO.

Lardy also pointed out the potential impact on Chinese financial services, including banking, insurance and securities, from WTO-mandated competition. He noted foreign banking institutions will benefit from lower operating costs since they will be more likely to service large cities and firms. National banks oversee a larger number of locations and individual clients and thus have higher costs.[112] In addition, many of China's domestic institutions will have to undergo considerably more reconstruction before the country can become more competitive within the WTO. Informal banking and grey- and black-market financial institutions still litter the Chinese landscape, a legacy of lingering ties between formal banks and state-owned institutions. In many cases, these ties have hampered private entrepreneurial initiatives.[113] As well, other Chinese industries had not been directed by specific laws to address foreign investment by December 2001, laws which would regulate joint venture fund management companies as permitted under WTO rules.[114] In short, the Chinese legal system has a considerable distance to cover in order to more effectively address its post-WTO membership responsibilities.

In his very pessimistic assessment of whether the Chinese government will be able to withstand the political and economic pressures of WTO membership, Chang asserted the main battleground for the organisation's acceptance will be within government ministries and state-owned enterprises, but that both groups are still unprepared for the shocks of membership. He blames the ossification of China's economic structure, and its tendency to resort to protectionist measures, for the government's inability to bring an unprepared economic system into the world's largest trade regime.[115] Undoubtedly the short-term transition will be difficult, but the current Chinese government accepts that such high risks are necessary to achieve the levels of economic modernity which China needs to survive and flourish as an evolving great power. One question which will be the focus of many future studies is whether Beijing can succeed in producing the reforms necessary to survive and prosper within the WTO.

This question can be linked to the problem of whether China's push to join the WTO was in line with a so-called policy of 'economic nationalism'. According to Ross, China has practised its economic and trading policies in keeping with Gilpin's description of economic nationalism, which stresses that all economic activities should be subordinated to state building and the interests of the state. He adds that in this view, economic resources are sources of struggle between states, and that countries have the option of pursuing both wealth and power rather than being forced to choose one over the other.[116] In the case of China, Ross cited Beijing's preference for keeping 'close control over foreign economic relations to ensure that they maximise state interests', adding that despite the country's considerable progress towards liberalising its economy, bureaucrats hold more sway over Chinese trade than the free market, and that the interests of the state in this area are still more powerful than those of consumers.[117] It is unclear whether this degree of party control will be compatible with China's WTO obligations, and it is very possible that Beijing's desire to be a member of the organisation and to maintain strong party control over the country's economic activity will result in an unworkable contradiction.

From these viewpoints, the question challenging many both within China and elsewhere was whether it made sense for China to voluntarily cede a significant degree of control over its domestic markets over to an international body, especially one which has been dominated by advanced Western economies. The answers to this require a closer examination of the goods which the Chinese government hopes to accrue via WTO participation. Despite the considerable gamble which China's leaders are taking with the country's economic and political future, the party has worked to convince itself and the Chinese people that this institution is an essential part of the country's economic future.

Rewards and gains

The question of why China chose to engage the GATT/WTO is linked to the question of why the Chinese government opted to pursue sweeping economic reforms in the first place. The most obvious answer to both is that the costs of not acting were perceived as excessively high compared to the risks involved. On the domestic level, Chinese economic power was becoming increasingly threatened by a torpid reform process and the GATT/WTO negotiations became an added incentive for the government to continue the complicated process. More crucially, the WTO was considered by Beijing to be an essential step both to ensure the continued economic growth of the country and to help China regain its place as a great power within the international system. Therefore, any costs accrued in the process of making its trade deals had to be interpreted by the Chinese people as necessary steps towards a beneficial goal. The economic and political restructuring under Jiang Zemin required pressure to be applied to those resisting reform, especially during the watershed years of 1998–2001 when changes affecting almost all ministries, the armed forces, and even the party were pushed through by the government. The WTO was thus transformed by the reformers into a source of international-level pressure to be added to their own domestic-level rationales for continuing and strengthening the reforms begun by Deng Xiaoping.

The importance to the CCP of maintaining China's strong economic performance cannot be overstated. Economic growth has been tied to the stability and longevity of the communist leadership. As Xiang noted, Deng Xiaoping's philosophy of the black cat and the white cat, meaning that economic development could, and should, be separated from ideological preferences, could also be reversed. In other words, the Communist Party can endure as long as it continues to deliver the financial goods, but increased economic problems may serve to threaten party stability and its dominant role in governing China.[118] The Asian financial crisis could be seen as a warning emphasising the connection between economic performance and regime stability.[119] The chaos of the crisis, in addition to creating great economic instability was a major cause of both the May 1998 ousting of the Suharto regime in Indonesia and strong opposition pressures placed on the Mahathir government in Malaysia. In each case, the people were willing to accept a lesser say in government policy provided the benefits of the 'Asian miracle' continued indefinitely.

Beijing is very anxious to avoid a similar fate, especially during a process of such delicate economic restructuring which has produced losers (larger numbers of unemployed as well as closed state-owned enterprises) as well as winners (the private sector). It can be argued, however, that the Asian financial crisis provided evidence to support both the pro- and anti-WTO factions within the Chinese government. One Chinese scholar noted that the country's financial markets would be further exposed as a result of WTO admission, and therefore China would be less able to protect itself in case the same conditions which prompted the financial crisis were to recur.[120] However, Lardy argues the crisis also had a galvanising effect on supporters of the WTO since the same vulnerabilities within crisis-affected economies, especially large bank loans to inefficient institutions, many of which were non-performing, could be found in China as well.[121] Thus the crisis accomplished much in convincing Beijing to speed up financial reforms, a task facilitated by presenting the need to join the WTO as a justification. What remains to be seen, however, are the effects on China, should another economic downturn on a regional scale occur in Asia.

At the same time, the WTO has a considerable domestic-level impact on both the Chinese government and the people. Beijing is hopeful the WTO will act as a powerful tool in the party's current campaign against another potentially crippling economic problem, namely corruption. During much of the country's history, open discussion of the subject was largely unacceptable, and it was only recently that scholars have spoken of the problem of 'systematic corruption' within the Chinese hierarchy.[122] As Huang explained, the corruption problem in China had become worse by the 1990s due to many factors, including the growing number of corruption cases involving larger amounts of capital, the rising number of high-level officials involved, the emergence of organised groups engaging in illegal activities, and the development of corrupt networks reaching across many economic sectors. All of these developments, he noted, have contributed to serious economic losses and public disillusionment. The government began to respond through policies of more supervision and transparency, separating commercial interests from government departments, and experimenting with public tenders rather than using a closed purchasing system.[123] As well, in the months before the leadership transition the question of corruption was publicly woven into talk of the economic challenges China must face in order to continue its developing process. Addressing corruption through increased competition has acted as another rationale for China's WTO participation.

For example, in the months leading to the 16th Party Congress, the problem of corruption had been increasingly illuminated by the Chinese government as a serious obstacle to Chinese economic growth. During a speech to China's legislature, the National People's Congress, in March 2002, Premier Zhu pointed to 'deception, extravagance, and waste' as having potentially crippling effects on the Chinese economy, and pointed to increased regulation as the only method of ensuring the success of the country's modernisation programmes. Zhu remarked as well that China's admission to the World Trade Organisation four months earlier served to benefit Chinese reforms, but that less competitive industries faced greater challenges because of WTO membership.[124] The fight against corruption has been gaining momentum within Chinese policy circles, partially as a result of the push to join the WTO, and now that the country is a member, the state may continue to frame the organisation as another spotlight on Chinese economic activity, designed to discourage illicit activities which may damage China's standing within the global economy. Nevertheless, should a greater proportion of the CCP be comprised of entrepreneurs, it is likely these representatives will play a strong role in shaping China's post-WTO admission policies as well as its ongoing integration with the global economy.

A second domestic-level factor can be identified by mounting evidence that the economic reforms carried out both before and after WTO admission are compatible with a private sector within China which was growing and diversifying at the turn of the twenty-first century. WTO membership has equally acted as a method for the Chinese government to force itself to 'catch up' to the new economic realities faced by the people it governs. A study released by the Chinese Academy of Social Studies (CASS) in January 2002 suggested that although the agricultural sector which has made up the bulk of the Chinese workforce was still strong, its proportion of the total labour force had dropped from 84.2 per cent in 1952 to 44 per cent in 1999, while the number of private-sector employees, including owners of private enterprises, technicians and specialists, and business and service workers, climbed steadily during that period. More importantly, the survey concluded that the 'middle stratum' (the term 'middle class' was deemed too politically sensitive) comprised

15 per cent of the country's workforce, a small percentage but one which nonetheless comprises about 110 million people.[125]

As Barmé noted, the economic boom within China during the 1990s not only forced changes in economic thinking, but also in how increasing affluence and the development of consumerism will affect domestic-level political discourse. In fact, he added, these economic changes on their own could be considered a revolution, since although representative democracy was not yet ripe in China, thanks to the economic opening, 'the free-range republic of shopping could be realised immediately'.[126] With China now in the WTO, citizens have increased access to global markets and goods, and analyses of the political impact of increased market exposure on the Chinese political system will be the subject of many future studies.

The belated acceptance of the private sector by the Chinese government, especially the invitation to entrepreneurs to officially join the Communist Party, reflects this group's growing political influence, which will do much to shape China's future foreign economic policy as well as Beijing's relations with the WTO post-admission. However, it is unclear whether this sweeping reform of the party will be carried forward, now that WTO membership has been achieved. Nevertheless, should a greater proportion of the CCP be comprised of the entrepreneurial sector, it is likely these representatives will play a strong role in shaping China's post-admission policies towards further integration with the global economy. As China continues the adjustment process of operating within the WTO, that organisation will likely continue to influence China's economic sectors, both in carrying out the reforms and restructuring required to continue Chinese economic growth and to tolerate the short-term losses to various industries forced to compete in international markets and the accompanying inevitable spike in national unemployment as a result of sector losses due to foreign competition.

There are further explanations for Beijing's turn towards the WTO when one examines China's economic relations with foreign actors. First, China's engagement with the WTO has served to assist in Beijing's understanding of the nebulous yet increasingly important trend towards 'globalisation'. The concept is still very new to official Chinese politics, and was only publicly detailed in official documentation at China's Fifteenth Party Congress in 1997, when President Jiang made note of the phenomenon to explain why the country needed to intensify its policies of improving the openness and quality of the nation's economy.[127] However, as one analyst explained, this foreign policy directive, like many others, is of a top-down nature and therefore it is the government's responsibility to make sure that it is properly accepted by the Chinese populace. Since admission will require many financial changes on the domestic level, as well as short-term costs to various sectors, should the government fail to properly explain the benefits of globalisation to the Chinese citizenry, he argued, the result will be greater difficulty in implementing reformist polices, since additional time, effort and funding will be spent on countering opposition pressures.[128] In a time of both economic and governmental transition, the risks of policy missteps are considerably higher than at any point since the Dengist reforms began.

It is in this area that the question of 'framing' a particular issue or problem comes into play. Although the Deng regime and the successor government under Jiang saw many advantages to attaining membership in the GATT/WTO, the question of whether China was trying to avoid the negative effects of non-membership also needs to be addressed. It is possible to examine the question of China's WTO choices in the context of the 'loss avoidance' model described by Stein, which asserts that leaders tend to cooperate when they perceive immediate and definite losses from non-cooperation, even when there may be larger but less-defined costs by cooperating.[129] In the case of China, the immediate losses would have meant attempting to carry out delicate economic reforms with less international institutional support and assistance. Even though the Chinese leadership would have to endure varying degrees of economic dislocation as a result of complying with WTO rules and norms, those risks certainly appeared less formidable than navigating openings into international markets without an institutional platform as a guideline.

Second, China wishes to ensure the international trading system remains as congenial as possible to Chinese economic and trading interests. By entering the WTO as a large, albeit still developing, economy, Beijing is hopeful its presence will encourage the development of the organisation on terms which are sufficiently fair to Chinese trade and development. Early signs suggest that Beijing will not hesitate in utilising the WTO to protect its trading interests. In March 2002, China filed its first complaint with the WTO after Washington temporarily levied tariffs on foreign steel exports.[130] Then, in March 2004, Washington brought its first complaint against Beijing to the organisation over China's heavy subsidisation of indigenous computer chips, a dispute resolved in July of that year when Beijing backed down and promised to halt tax breaks to local semiconductor producers.[131] Such activities suggest that China will be in the thick of future WTO negotiations, disputes and settlements, and much will ultimately depend on whether the Doha Round will come to a satisfactory conclusion.

Third, WTO membership has also been defined by the Chinese government as both a source of prestige and a rite of passage to underscore to the international community the country's rapidly developing economy and desire to be perceived as a maturing economic actor. As China increases its economic activities both on a regional level, within the Asia-Pacific region, and internationally, many will be watching to see whether China will succeed in its market transition, and the WTO will provide a highly visible yardstick for that measurement.

Conclusions: to whom the good?

Consensus, within both China and elsewhere, has remained elusive as to what degree both the WTO and the international system as a whole will be changed with the addition of a country boasting a population of almost 1.3 billion people and an economy only partially converted to the free market system but still boasting strong growth and burgeoning international trade. The long process of attaining

GATT/WTO admission has greatly coloured the processes and results of the post-1978 Dengist economic reforms which were designed to end a nonviable doctrine of self-sufficiency and command economics in favour of allowing the free market to bring sorely-needed improvements to the standard of living for Chinese citizens while also improving China's economic power, which to Beijing has become as important as military or political power. After deciding to make the arrangements and pay the prices to join the organisation, the government portrayed the GATT/WTO at various times as a carrot, a future reward for present sacrifices, and as a rightful place for China to be, in order to properly reclaim its title as a great power in fact as well as in name.

Many questions remain unanswered, however. First, will the next Chinese government be able to properly walk the line between fulfilling its WTO commitments and ensuring continuous economic growth, social stability, and the continuing longevity of the Communist Party? As the obligations of membership begin to assert themselves, there may have to be sacrifices to some degree in all of these areas. Second, what kind of actor will China be within the WTO? The country may find itself with a number of cases being brought against it via the WTO's dispute-settlement mechanism in the near future for past and present grievances. How then will China react? Third, how will China's WTO membership affect its neighbours and trading partners, including the United States?

While these economies will certainly benefit from potential new opportunities in the Chinese market as a result of Beijing's membership in the WTO, there is also the question of whether they can adjust to engaging an economically-powerful China which has now been given addition tools via that organisation to increase this power. In the short-term, there will be an acceleration of efforts among various countries to improve their economic status within the Chinese market, and as such more winners and losers will be produced, with the former comprised of those who are able to best understand the often labyrinthine dynamics of the Chinese economy.

2

FLYING GEESE AND RISING PHOENIX

China, APEC and exclusive trade regimes

> Pioneers plant trees, but the latecomers rest in the shade.
>
> Traditional Chinese proverb

Introduction: large clubs, small clubs

The founding of the World Trade Organisation in 1995 did little to stop the spread of regional-level trade agreements designed to address more localised trading and economic cooperation issues. The Pacific Rim has proven no exception to this phenomenon and indeed the number of bilateral and regional preferential trade agreements (PTAs) in that region has actually increased since the mid-1990s. The development of exclusive economic regimes designed to address region- or area-specific issues and for a select membership, has continued to experience growth over the past two decades. Beijing, seeking to increase international trade in order to continue its economic reform process, has found these organisations invaluable. These PTAs, large and small, have been crucial to China's expanding knowledge of modern international trade, and the enhancement of its economic power. In joining smaller-scale economic organisations within Asia, with their less formal and non-hierarchical format than their counterparts in the West, China has been striving to overcome the obstacles inherent in joining the international trading system so 'late', well after the rules of economic interactions have become so entrenched, and largely dominated by Western powers and regimes.

China's participation in one of the most prominent of these regional trade bodies has demonstrated how such groups have become necessary tools in the development of Beijing's economic power and political growth, both on a regional and on an international level. The Asia-Pacific Economic Cooperation forum (APEC), created in 1989, is designed to create a free trade regime in the Pacific Rim by 2020. Membership in this forum has provided China with several foreign policy advantages, as it could provide a means to discuss trade liberalisation on a regional level without the strict rules and mechanisms of the other major 'trade blocs', namely the European Union and the North American Free Trade Agreement (NAFTA). China also made use of APEC in the 1990s to demonstrate its determination to join the WTO by advertising its own unilateral trade liberalisation initiatives. As well, the 1991 agreement bestowing APEC membership upon China, Hong Kong and Taiwan as strictly economic entities, rather than as 'states', provided valuable cross-Strait ties which were unavailable via other regimes. Although the relationship between Beijing and Taipei within APEC has been far from cordial, the forum has provided a more congenial atmosphere than previous erratic, acrimonious bilateral talks between the two sides. Beijing has also made use of APEC to trumpet its status as an emerging market and potential great economic power, finding its efforts rewarded in November 2001 with China's first APEC leaders' meeting in Shanghai. Today, China's power has allowed the country to challenge Japan for the role of economic nexus within the Asia-Pacific region, while requiring APEC to accommodate a rising China into its evolving trade liberalisation policies.

Regional enthusiasm for the APEC process was dampened by the ravages of the Asian financial crisis (AFC) in 1997–98, which began in Thailand with a sudden currency devaluation and then spread to much of southeast Asia, South Korea, and Russia. It also adversely affected Japan, which had been trying to pull itself out of recession when this crisis hit. Although China was spared the economic brunt of the crisis, its increasing economic ties to the rest of east Asia prevented Beijing from remaining completely aloof. One of the major after-shocks of the AFC was a rise in regional enthusiasm for bilateral and small-multilateral free trade agreements and Beijing found itself courting, and being courted by, other Asian economies seeking exclusive trade agreements.[1] That China is at the centre of the 'PTA proliferation' in the Pacific Rim is a clear sign of that country's growing economic weight.

One of the largest and most notable of the post-crisis PTAs was the ASEAN-Plus-Three (APT) group, based upon economic meetings between the ten ASEAN members and the north Asian economies of China, Japan, and South Korea. While economic ties between north and southeast Asia had grown well before the development of the APT, the regional trauma created by the crisis prompted both regions to look to each other to ensure that such an extensive degree of economic contagion would not recur. Although the APT has yet to show signs of developing into a formal regional economic community, the agreements made within that institution have begun to define trading norms and it has been an incubator for promising new regional economic initiatives. It is unclear if the APT will develop as a challenger to APEC, or act as a supplement, but during its short history China has grown to recognise its importance in developing a regional trade policy which advances its interests. However, with its major economic rival, Japan, attempting to recover from a vicious cycle of recession which has lasted since the early 1990s, will Beijing grow to become first among equals in the APT, and what would that mean for the regional and international economic landscape of the future?

China and APEC

The Asia-Pacific Economic Cooperation forum was assembled in 1989 and represented an ambitious attempt to create a regional institution by which to address issues relating to Asia's rapidly evolving economies and trade. Its membership has expanded over the past decade to include not only representatives from Asia, but also the south Pacific and the Americas as well as two entities which are not considered states, namely the Hong Kong Special Administrative Region and 'Chinese Taipei' (Taiwan).[2] China joined the APEC forum two years after its inception, and although it has refrained from assuming a paramount role in its development, the country's growing importance to the regional economic milieu has greatly impacted on APEC and the process of Chinese integration within the Pacific Rim and global economies.

The development of regional economic institutions in Asia, along with other forms of institutions, lagged in development behind the West. With the exception of the Association of Southeast Asian Nations (ASEAN), economic cooperation between Pacific Rim actors was largely restricted to bilateral and informal exchanges. As Yamazawa noted, economic interdependence in Asia was created not through institutional ties but rather the methodical transfers of industries, mostly in the manufacturing sector from early developers to late developers.[3] This method was also known as the 'flying geese' effect, a term first coined by Japanese economist Kaname Akamatsu in the 1930s. Using this model, a country develops industries which were discarded by a country further ahead in the technological development area. For example, after Japan developed its electronics industries, its former dominance in textiles was taken up by the 'newly industrialised economies' (NIEs) of Hong Kong, Singapore, South Korea and Taiwan. Once they began to develop their electronics sector, textile manufacturing was assumed by the next level down the chain, in Indonesia, Thailand, and so forth.[4] Japan was therefore considered the lead goose, followed by the NIEs, and then the 'little tigers' in southeast Asia.

The reasons for Asian economies being traditionally unwilling to explore institutionalised economic cooperation before the 1980s have been the subject of debate. Among various rationales are the extensive economic ties between Asia and the West negating the requirement for regional institutions, historical/cultural aversions to economic ties, a legacy of colonialism and Japanese imperialism during the Second World War, and the heterogeneity of political systems in the region (with different levels of democratisation and state economic control).[5] After the Second World War, cooperation in east Asia was sharply defined along cold war lines and dominated by the 'San Francisco System' of American-dominated, hub-and-spoke strategic cooperation,[6] with little room for economic ties based on geography or market compatibility.

Nevertheless, low-level talks on the subject of creating greater liberalised trade in Asia began as early as the 1960s, with business interests from almost all Asia-Pacific countries instituting informal meetings in 1967 as the Pacific Basin

Economic Council (PBEC), designed to facilitate the exchange of views and information and to provide economic advice to home governments.[7] The APEC forum has its origins in the Pacific Economic Cooperation Council (PECC), a nongovernmental forum designed to explore methods of regional cooperation. PECC, consisting of low-level government interests as well as businesspeople and academics, was created in 1980 (Beijing and Taipei became members of this group at PECC's Vancouver conference in 1986).[8] Beijing was slow to react to those fledging attempts at Asian economic coordination. China, during the 1970s and early 1980s was still economically underdeveloped and was attempting to overcome the damage created by the Cultural Revolution. Therefore Beijing did not figure prominently into regional perceptions of economic cooperation. Also, many of the initial proposals for Asian economic cooperation, including the first proposal for an Asia-Pacific free trade area in 1968, came from Japanese sources. China was concerned that Japan's calls for regional economic cooperation, while emanating mostly from private initiatives rather than governmental, were actually tacit strategic plans designed to improve Japan's, and possibly America's, stature in Asia. Equally, China was anxious to demonstrate to its Asian neighbours that it had no plans to join with Japan and the United States to create a hegemonic troika in the region.[9]

Despite Chinese ambivalence, the idea of Asian economic cooperation began to solidify during the 1980s. The catalysts which transformed Asian economic regime-building from low-level cooperation to the APEC idea were developments in the European Community and North America, as well as the serious problems facing the Uruguay Round of the General Agreement on Tariffs and Trade (GATT), begun in September 1986. From the start, the Round became hamstrung over disagreements between the United States and Europe regarding the methods of bringing the sensitive agricultural sector into the Agreement.[10] The negotiations proved to be long and contentious, with the 1980s drawing to a close amongst concerns that failure of the Round to reach a final agreement might cause severe damage to the global economy. Coinciding with the deadlock of the GATT talks were renewed discussions in North America and Europe to develop region-specific free trade agreements to better suit their more specialised economic needs. With the 1987 signing of the Single European Act,[11] the EC had taken positive steps toward a single market culminating in the Maastricht Agreement of 1992, the founding of the European Union that year, and the development of a common European currency, the euro, by the end of the decade. Coinciding with the Single European Act, 1985 (SEA) negotiations, the United States and Canada prepared to lower trade barriers as a first step towards a North American free trade pact which would later expand to include Mexico.[12]

Such developments created much concern within regions, including the Pacific Rim, left out of these economic agreements. As one analyst noted, concerns in the Asia-Pacific region about the development of exclusive economic regimes elsewhere were far from baseless and his critical analysis of how a post-1992 European Community would affect trade in the Asia-Pacific region argued the latter would be negatively affected by being placed very low on a perceived hierarchy of the Community's preferential trade areas. Asian countries would then be queuing behind European non-EC members and those developing countries which had economic ties to Europe. In response to the enthusiasm from Europe and North America for creating free trade areas, east Asia would be left with three options: to continue to try to circumvent the export barriers, to invest in Europe and North America behind these barriers, or to establish a free trade area of Pacific Rim nations.[13] By the end of the 1980s, Asia strongly supported the third option. East Asian economies were well aware that since they had only just begun to play a strong role in the global market, the failure of the Round would be especially disastrous for them. It was also acknowledged that the level of 'clout' they possessed before the opening of the Uruguay Round was negligible at best, making it difficult for any one Asia-Pacific state to influence the Round's final agreement by acting unilaterally.[14]

Another theorist noted the convergence of other issues which contributed to the development of the APEC idea. The first was that growing economies in Asia began to be treated as a group with greater relevance, by outside actors, including Western economic organisations. The second was that during the 1980s, security and economic concerns which would accompany a decline in the American presence in Asia, led to discussion of how to keep the United States sufficiently engaged in the region.[15] China was certainly not on the sidelines on this issue. Although it was not satisfied with an extended US presence in the Pacific after the cold war, an American pullout was feared as a precursor to Japan taking a more independent and active military role in the region, which Beijing strongly opposed.

These external factors, coupled with domestic reactions to them, played their parts in convincing many east Asian regional heads of governments that Pacific economic integration required a greater priority. The Australian government invited delegations from Pacific states to meet in the capital of Canberra in November 1989 to discuss the possibility of creating a multilateral trading system in the Pacific Rim. Delegations from nine countries (Australia, Brunei, Canada, Indonesia, Japan, Malaysia, South Korea, Thailand and the United States) attended what would become the first official APEC summit. The Canberra meetings produced an agenda that would eventually provide ongoing support for a satisfactory resolution of the Uruguay Round. This would, in turn, create an international environment conducive to further free trade agreements and economic growth in the Pacific Rim, while continuing to address any trade impediments left out of the Round's agreements, most notably in the areas of services, the protection of intellectual property and investment measures. APEC also called for the promotion of economic interactions between regions, using non-discriminatory trading policies with outside actors, and the accommodation of 'heterogeneous' sub-regional groups, assisting their development in accordance with accepted GATT standards.[16]

The admission of China to APEC was the result of many months of diplomatic manoeuvring among Beijing's neighbours. Chinese representatives were not invited to the November 1989 APEC meeting in Canberra, largely due to the diplomatic fallout caused by the Tiananmen Square incident five months earlier. Further complicating China's desire to join APEC was the question of how to include both Beijing and Taipei as members, since both were important economic actors within the Asia-Pacific region. Despite regional outrage following Tiananmen, Australian Prime Minster Robert Hawke voiced an opinion that APEC would not function effectively without Chinese participation.[17] There was less enthusiasm from some members of ASEAN who feared China would assume a central role within APEC should it receive early admission.[18] However, since both Beijing and Taipei were members of APEC's predecessor, PECC, and considering China's rapidly opening markets, many observers doubted China would be left out of the organisation for very long.[19]

In the early 1990s, China began to indicate it would welcome the opportunity to join APEC. This decision reflected the growing importance of regional trade in developing the Chinese economy. The coming together of APEC coincided with the Chinese government providing support for engaging economics-based multilateral institutions, albeit stressing that Beijing would not tolerate a loss of economic sovereignty. For example, during an interview in 1990, Chinese Foreign Minister Qian Qichen noted growing economic dynamism in the Asia-Pacific had spurred increased talk of regional institutions and that Beijing not only supported such movement but furthermore regional political and economic institution would be 'incomplete' without China's participation. He added, however, that any regional body must not be exclusive in nature, and that 'protectionist measures' must be avoided.[20]

A year later, Chinese Premier Li Peng went further by stating China supported the efforts of different regions to increase economic and political ties, on the condition that the final goal was cooperation, not military expansion or economic protectionism. The premier specified ASEAN, the Organisation for African Unity, and the Gulf Cooperation Council as examples of regimes designed to improve peace and cooperation on a regional level. Citing the NAFTA case, Li noted such a mechanism should be used to further enhance the overall global economic system. He stressed, however, that regional trade regimes should not serve as a means of excluding certain countries from the benefits of liberalised trade.[21] Such statements suggest that China's strong level of confidence in its economic abilities must not blind it to the negative effects of a regional economic regime being built up around it, especially one which could echo the perceived 'closed' trade practices of Western-based institutions such as the European Community. At this time, China wanted to break free of what remained of its Maoist-era isolation, and participation in open regional economic regimes was seen as an efficacious way of achieving that goal.

In striking a deal for admission, Beijing (and by association, Taipei and Hong Kong) found a powerful ally in South Korea, as Seoul was instrumental in creating the framework within which all three entities would become APEC members. During the spring of 1990, Beijing and Seoul developed communication links including the opening of trade offices and China removing its objections to South Korea joining the United Nations. The warmed relations benefited both, as Beijing was anxious to break free of its post-1989 regional isolation and establish solid ties with South Korea's burgeoning economy. The South Korean government of Roh Tae Woo sought to build upon Seoul's opening to the region after successfully hosting the 1988 Summer Olympics.[22] After Seoul was awarded the hosting duties of the 1991 APEC conference, the Roh government began to seek a deal by which both Beijing and Taipei would join the organisation, in the process, altering Beijing's Korean policy from exclusive support of North Korea to the tacit development of a Chinese 'two Korea' policy.[23]

Beijing agreed to Taiwanese admission to APEC under the name of 'Chinese Taipei' to ensure there would be no implied support for the breakaway province's independence.[24] At the same time, those within APEC became known as member 'economies' rather than states, since neither Taiwan nor Hong Kong were to be considered 'states' actors within that body. Taiwan and Hong Kong each would agree to send lower-level officials to APEC meetings to further stress their distinct status within the organisation. Chinese admission to APEC was greatly desired by Beijing since it wanted to be seen as improving the regional economic situation in Asia and also to avoid being shut out should APEC develop into a more powerful economic actor on the international level. China's omission from APEC would have greatly weakened the regime's effectiveness, given its economic power and extensive ties to the other economies of the region. Equally, China's determination to join the GATT after having been excluded for so many decades was reflected in its activities within APEC, as Beijing found the regime an ideal staging area for initiatives designed to promote its bid to rejoin the world's largest international trade organisation, namely the GATT/WTO.[25]

The early years of APEC development, were marked by serious disagreements as to how APEC should evolve. A sizeable split in the regime's ranks contrasted the 'American model', stressing rigid timetables for liberalisation with the 'Asian model' which stressed gradualism and voluntary compliance of agreements.[26] While both the United States and Australia continued their support for an eventual Asia-Pacific free trade community, other members advocated a much less ambitious agenda. Japan was especially worried that APEC would develop an exclusive trading bloc along European lines, resulting in the ongoing GATT talks being eclipsed in importance. Other, smaller, Asian states were concerned their specific needs would be ignored by the large economic powers within APEC, namely America, China and Japan. Those particular concerns were partially addressed with the decision that every second APEC summit would be held in a southeast Asian country, stressing the importance of that region as a key player in the regime's development.[27]

Opinions also differed between Western and Asian members of APEC over the degree of 'institutionalisation' which would be permissible within the organisation, with the latter group espousing the same 'network-based' flexible and informal patterns of cooperation found in Asian business practices, in contrast to the 'firm-based' approach prevalent in the West, with more stress on rules and binding documentation.[28] Upon entering APEC, China strongly supported the idea of APEC as an informal body based on consensus-building and inclusion. As President Jiang noted in a speech to the forum in 1993, Asia's economic success was not owed to the creation of closed regimes, and that 'APEC should be an open, flexible and pragmatic forum for economic cooperation and a consultation mechanism rather than a closed, institutionalised economic bloc.'[29] Clearly, China's APEC policy was very much in line with southeast Asia's.

The Clinton administration had begun floating the idea of a security role for APEC in the early 1990s, but opposition from other members, including China, kept that idea from further development.[30] Also, many Asian members, including China, resisted US calls for accelerated tariff cuts within the forum. In a scathing 1994 editorial, one Chinese journal accused Washington of attempting to cement a dominant role within APEC through trade liberalisation at a too-rapid pace for Asian members to handle.[31] During APEC's first decade of development, the Asian view that the forum should proceed slowly remained prevalent, and APEC took gradual steps towards formalisation, establishing a small secretariat in Singapore in 1993, and adding an APEC Leaders' Meeting following the Seattle APEC summit the same year.[32]

The successful completion of the Uruguay Round in 1993, and subsequent founding of the World Trade Organisation, marked the end of the initial, 'reactive' phase of APEC's development, with the regime no longer focused on responding to the events leading to the Round's completion. Instead, APEC attempted to create improved trade conditions for members on a regional scale. This change in direction within APEC was best exemplified by the Bogor Declaration struck after the 1994 APEC summit in Indonesia, which called upon all members to achieve free trade and investment amongst themselves by 2010 for the developed economies and 2020 for the lesser-developed.[33] Although the dates could not be made binding, the Bogor Declaration remained the most ambitious of APEC's mandates. In 1995 during the Osaka summit, a blueprint for achieving the '2020' goals was introduced. This included policy harmonisation in key sectors such as energy, telecommunications, small- and medium-sized enterprises, and science and technology. Member economies were to present their individual plans to illustrate how they would contribute to regional free trade.[34]

It was during this period of APEC's development that China assumed a more vigorous role within the organisation, with an eye to promoting itself as a potential GATT member. In a speech in November 1994, then-Foreign Trade Minister Wu Yi called upon APEC to support China's GATT membership before the WTO's creation, noting that Beijing would find it difficult from outside the GATT to abide by Uruguay Round agreements, which would also hinder attempts at regional trade liberalisation.[35] Matching words with deeds, Chinese representatives created no small stir at the Osaka summit by announcing Beijing's plans to develop a convertible currency, reform its taxation system making it more accessible to foreign investment, and cut tariffs on 4,000 different items.[36]

The timing of these announcements was certainly no accident, since these reforms served not only to demonstrate China was serious about enhancing economic liberalisation on a regional level, it was also taking solid steps to prepare itself for WTO membership. China used subsequent APEC meetings to announce tariff reductions on manufactured goods, textiles and forestry products, and in 1999 announced it would amend its laws on copyrights, patents and trademarks (long a sticking point between China and the West) to better align them with WTO specifications.[37] Clearly, China was very concerned with making positive contributions to APEC not only to assist in the development of the forum, but also to demonstrate to the international community at large its readiness to assume the role of great economic power.

Unlikely oasis: China and the Asian financial crisis

Prior to 1997, few doubted China's potential for economic greatness in the coming century. Beijing was about to welcome its lost territory, the economic powerhouse of Hong Kong, back into the fold, with former Portuguese territory Macau to follow in December 1999. The country's economy was growing at a steady rate, and more importantly, China was translating its economic success into serious political clout. After many years of following economic rules drawn up by outsiders, China was starting to feel more comfortable setting some of its own guidelines. A major example of this was the confidence Premier Li demonstrated when he stated in 1996 that if the United States would not cease its tedious criticism of Chinese internal policies, his country would seek its business partners elsewhere, such as in Europe and Japan.[38] By the mid-1990s, China appeared ready to assume its place alongside other Asian economic tigers as a strong emerging market. The arrival of the Asian meltdown, however, put a temporary stop to this thinking from the Chinese government. Although one official described the overall impact of the Asian economic slowdown as 'minimal',[39] Beijing reacted with great alarm as the 'Asian flu' began to strike its southern neighbours, one by one, in late 1997 and early 1998.

The origins of the Asian financial crisis could be traced to Thailand, which opted to float its currency, the baht, in July of 1997, with the end result a dramatic drop in the currency's value. The root cause of the crash was dissatisfaction with Bangkok's economic fundamentals, including infrastructure deficiencies and questionable financial and banking practices. These same concerns transferred to Thailand's neighbours and included the combined problems of excessive foreign investment in southeast Asia, financial institutions with insufficient levels of supervision, and regional governments taking a lethargic approach to key economic reforms.[40] Within months Indonesia, Malaysia, and the Philippines also saw their currencies being devalued, and Bangkok, Manila and Jakarta were forced to apply for assistance from the International Monetary Fund. The effects of the economic contagion were not limited to southeast Asia. In October 1997, currency speculators challenged the pegging of the Hong Kong dollar to the American dollar, resulting in sharp stock market drops. In December, South Korea was affected, and Seoul, too, contacted the IMF for a substantial loan.[41] In Japan, which had been sinking economically for most of the 1990s, upper-tier financial institutions Yamaichi Securities and Hokkaido Takushoku Bank became insolvent in 1997, leading to further losses of economic confidence.[42] Any hopes that Tokyo would use its financial power to stabilise crisis-affected economies in Asia were dashed as Japan was forced to address its own domestic economic troubles.

To further complicate matters for Beijing, the Russian Federation also descended into economic crisis, leading to a steep devaluation of the rouble and increasing the level of political chaos by August 1998. As short-term result of the rouble's fall, regions in Russia's far east began purchasing more Chinese goods in lieu of pricier products of Japan, the United States, and South Korea.[43] Encircled by stricken economies, and stuck between Russia's faltering economy and financial crises spreading across east and southeast Asia, China was placed in the uncomfortable position of being both the barometer for those trying to determine the severity and duration of the meltdown, and the unlikely beacon of stability in the region, since it was one of very few regional economies not adversely affected by the downturn.

Moreover, China opted for the very risky option of not devaluating its currency during the height of the crisis, a devaluation of the yuan which would have placed Chinese exports in a more favourable position versus other battered Asian economies. The entire region feared a Chinese devaluation would increase the level of financial panic in Asia and prolong the crisis. Thus, China's announcement not to devalue its currency gained the country much political capital.[44] China was loathe to permit a devaluation because its government feared such action would set off a wave of counter-devaluations elsewhere in Asia, thus creating a vicious circle and deepening the crisis. There was concern about how such a devaluation would affect its chances for WTO admittance. As well, Beijing wanted to avoid an economic meltdown in Hong Kong, which threatened to occur mere months after the former British colony reverted to Chinese administration.[45]

Conventional wisdom concerning China's conduct during this time suggested that Beijing was able to avoid a serious economic downturn because its economy was still partially closed, and its currency insufficiently convertible, and thus less vulnerable to outside 'shocks'.[46] However, closer examination reveals China was able to weather that storm due to a variety of factors. These included the fact that the country was in the middle of an economic 'soft landing' by 1997, the Gross Domestic Product was a healthy 8.8 per cent and inflation hovered at slightly under 3 per cent, creating a barrier against external economic pressures.[47] The soft landing was the result of corrective measures taken by Beijing to curb inflation rates which threatened major economic derailment. When the inflation rate in China reached an incredible 27.7 per cent in October 1994, the government responded via a reform package which included lowering the economic growth rate, raising agricultural production, hastening industry restructuring, and exercising closer monitoring and control of food items.[48] The yuan was devalued in 1994, a move which greatly improved the competitiveness of the currency and may have prevented the need for devaluation at the height of the crisis. Both during and after the regional financial downturn, the yuan remained strong.[49]

The beneficial effects of China's economic emergency measures remained in place at the time of the Asian financial crisis. Other analysts pointed to the beneficial timing of the crisis for China, since by late 1997 any questions about China's leadership transition after Deng Xiaoping had been answered, with the Jiang regime sufficiently strong and unified to address the regional economic crisis.[50] Finally, China was also helped by its large foreign exchange reserves and current and capital account surpluses, which assisted in keeping the country's exchange rates stable.[51]

With Beijing the unwitting island of stability during the crisis, the Chinese government discovered greater means to improve its economic and political standing in the region. For example, the mere threat of a devaluation of the yuan was sufficient to pressure the United States and the Group of Seven economies to help stop the slide of the Japanese yen, which if left unchecked, would have adversely affected Chinese exports. Faced with this threat, the American Federal Reserve and the Bank of Japan stepped in to increase the yen's value.[52] In addition to this formidable 'stick', China employed the use of 'carrots' to further improve its political standing in the region, the most visible example being Beijing's contribution of US$4 billion in financial assistance to the crisis-hit economies of Indonesia, South Korea, and Thailand, including an unprecedented US$1 billion pledge to the International Monetary Fund for the organisation's aid package to Bangkok.[53] Such actions allowed China to steal away much of the regional spotlight from Japan, which had frequently been accused of focusing too much on its own internal problems at the expense of assisting with regional efforts to pull Asia out of the worst of the crisis.

Although China was able to escape the worst effects of the crisis, the regional economic downturn did magnify serious deficiencies in the Chinese economy with which Beijing continues to struggle. The first of these involved the country's fragile economic structure itself. Even before the onset of the regional financial crisis, questions were raised as to how long Beijing could maintain its impressive economic growth while staving off pressure for long-overdue attempts at economic reform.[54] Though China was fortunate enough not to suffer from the same levels of economic uncertainty as elsewhere in east and southeast Asia during 1997–8, the country shared similar difficulties with other Asia-Pacific countries, notably the widespread inefficient allocation of capital resources. In the Chinese case, far too much funding continued to be directed from Beijing to state-owned enterprises which frequently lost money and constituted a serious drag on future economic growth. As a result, many state-operated banks, which lent money to keep these SOEs on virtual life-support, began themselves to slip into insolvency. These difficulties predated the Asian crisis, but the meltdown served to highlight Beijing's economic deficiencies. In addition, the Chinese economy could continue to prop up its state-owned enterprises as long as the private, non-state sector continued to receive large investments from the rest of Asia. When these sources dried up, as other parts of Asia shied away from foreign investment until their own houses were in order, China found it more difficult to postpone serious reforms of its SOEs.[55]

A second problem illuminated by the meltdown was the inefficiency of the country's banking system. Despite major economic differences between China and many east and southeast Asian tigers, all shared the common problem of a lack of monitoring and regulation of financial institutions. This resulted in unrestrained borrowing, political manipulation, and a lack of competition among banks all across the Asia-Pacific; China was not immune to these problems. Indeed, in 90 per cent of transactions involving investors, the Chinese banks acted as intermediaries, far more often than banks elsewhere in the Pacific Rim. China's commercial banks were also not required to undergo independent audits, and three of the four largest banks in China did not even report annual financial statistics. With such a dearth of information, it was difficult to tell how much capital was lost due to mismanagement and corruption.[56]

The conclusion that can be drawn from these examples is that despite China's remarkable economic progress over the last two decades, the country is not yet ready to become part of a regional economic bloc except in the most informal of circumstances and via a very guarded process of integration. The effects of the Asian meltdown served to underline considerable flaws in the Chinese economic system which hindered trade liberalisation in China. As for APEC itself, the development of the organisation continued, albeit in a much more cautious vein.

Post-crisis APEC relations

A second event which dampened regional support for APEC was the collapse of the ambitious Early Voluntary Sectoral Liberalisation (EVSL) initiative developed during the 1997 Vancouver meeting. This programme called for the creation of clusters of trade liberalisation deals for select sectors which would have supplemented existing policies. However, sharp disagreement between members on how to integrate fisheries and forestry sectors created an impasse in the negotiations, which limped along until being quietly discarded in 1999.[57] Despite the regional problems and loss of confidence created by the crisis, the Bogor process of gradual trade liberalisation in the Asia-Pacific remained nominally on track.

In a speech at the 1999 leaders' meeting, President Jiang noted APEC had a role to play in ensuring 'regional peace and stability' as well as promoting economic growth. He added that the WTO (which China was still two years away from joining) was an important actor in global trade, but that the body was still 'not as complete and broadly representative' as it should be. Therefore, APEC was a force for improving the international trade system as well as furthering the interests of its own membership. In light of the crisis, Jiang noted that each economy had a right to address their financial problems in their own way, and that no country should impose solutions on others.[58] This was a clear reminder that China remained strongly opposed to attempts by powerful economic actors, such as the West, to force less developed countries to adopt trade liberalisation packages which would be detrimental to their interests.

China used its first opportunity to host an APEC gathering to trumpet the host city of Shanghai as an emerging economic powerhouse. Despite the overshadowing of the 2001 APEC meeting by the events of 11 September in the United States, China was hopeful the Shanghai conference would produce new economic agreements, cementing China's contribution to the APEC process. Both the US and China also attempted to ignore previous incidents of earlier in the year, including the Hainan 'spy plane' incident.[59] The main achievement of the 2001 gathering was the Shanghai Accord, designed to reflect economic changes in the region because of globalisation and the development of the high-technology-dominated 'new economy'. The accord committed APEC members to 'clarify' the path leading to the implementation of the Bogor 2020 agreements, an expansion of the Osaka Action Agenda to reflect changes in the new economy, augmenting the 'peer review' of Individual Action Plans (IAPs), and furthering the harmonis-ation of regional economic and technical cooperation (Ecotech) initiatives. At the same time, APEC's policies of voluntarism and flexibility were reconfirmed, stressing that further formalisation and rules-based policymaking were not being considered. In addition to the Shanghai Accord, participants gave their support for a new round of international trade negotiations within the WTO, an important policy in light of the 1999 failure in Seattle to launch a 'Millennium Round'.[60]

APEC Shanghai was also used as a platform for regional condemnation of the September 2001 terrorist attacks in the United States, and for the introduction of an accord condemning terrorism. Although there were concerns from outside observers about the 'depth' of the condemnation for terrorist activities, negotiations were cordial and the United States refrained from pushing for the specific ident-ification of the perpetrators of 11 September, namely the Al-Qaeda organisation led by Osama bin Laden, likely out of deference to the muslim nations attending the gathering. China played a strong role in the drafting of the document, despite concerns that Beijing would consider the matter as out-of-scope for an economics meeting.[61] This anti-terrorism declaration was the most highly visible security-related statement issued by APEC, only the second time a security issue reached the upper echelons of an APEC Summit. The first was in 1999 when concerns about escalating violence between the Indonesian government and separatists in East Timor were raised at the New Zealand APEC meeting. [62]

Since 9/11, APEC has attempted to incorporate policies aimed at combating terrorism and economic disruptions, a considerable change in the organisation when compared with the 1990s, when American-led proposals to discuss strategic interests within APEC were frequently rebuffed by Asian participants, China not excluded.[63] Nevertheless, any optimism that the forum will develop a more permanent security dimension should be tempered with the argument that there are many security issues within the Asia-Pacific region which APEC members, including China, would find too delicate to discuss within the forum, including territorial demarcation issues. Any move to expand security dialogue within APEC would likely be a slow and controversial process as long as members retain the right to override issues before they are added to the forum's agenda.

Over time, the question of whether APEC should develop into a more formal, rules-based body began to fade as general acceptance of its informal nature prevailed. By the time of the Shanghai Summit in 2001, even the United States, the strongest supporter for both formalisation of APEC and the expansion of the body into non-economic areas such as security, was mostly quiet on the subject. The other major division within APEC, over whether economic liberalisation should be accelerated within the organisation, continued to play a role in various meetings. Those members favouring further liberalisation at a more expedient pace included Australia, Canada, Hong Kong, New Zealand, Singapore and United States. This assemblage, colloquially known in some APEC policymaking circles as the 'Buick Group' since their first informal meeting was said to have taken place in a room with a poster featuring a Buick automobile, favoured APEC as a tool to further regional market opening and access. Opposing them were the so-called 'capacity-builders', dominated by the southeast Asian members, who favoured initiatives which focused more on improving regional business and economic development, such as human capacity-building and information technology development.[64] Within APEC, China has tried to avoid favouring either side while demonstrating caution towards any initiatives seen as moving too fast towards regional economic liberalisation.

School's in: China's education within APEC

In seeking to explain the reasons behind Chinese support for APEC, Zhang outlined four factors which provided China strong incentives for joining the organisation:

1   the large percentage of Chinese trade which flows to the Asia-Pacific region;
2   the need to avoid being marginalised by the growing trend in the Pacific Rim towards economic regionalisation;
3   a forum to address concerns about competition from other regional economies; and
4   China's need as an evolving power to have a stronger voice in regional affairs and diverse economic issues.[65]

All of these issues are certainly strong motivators for China's ascension to APEC and for its continued support of the regime. However, there also exist other rationales more connected to Beijing's goals of enhancing its economic, and by association, its political power on a regional and international level, as well as to allow the ruling regime to better manage the country's transition to capitalism while still maintaining its guiding role.

First and foremost, China views APEC as necessary to address the changing economic conditions among its neighbours in east and southeast Asia, and to make sure that Beijing is not placed at a major disadvantage in the area of Asia-Pacific trade, especially when China's economy is becoming more and more dependent on foreign trade. Beijing desires a cautious, gradual integration with the global economy, with focus on equality and mutual benefit. By advocating these ideas through APEC, China wishes to discourage the development of more exclusive trade regimes which could place the country at a greater disadvantage during its precarious opening to international markets. This idea would correspond to the 'general realist' idea suggesting states join institutions to further their national interests rather than out of concerns over creating a balance of power.[66] Moreover, using the 'club goods' argument put forth by Gruber,[67] an argument could be made that after so many of China's main trading partners (and present or potential economic competitors) entered APEC in 1989 and after, including the United States, Japan, and the 'little tigers' in southeast Asia, China did not wish to be left out of a promising regime. This would also coincide with the argument put forth by Swaine and Tellis that China would be prompted to join an institution if it fears that institution would be detrimental to Beijing's interests if it stayed on the sidelines.[68]

However, the question of the impact on China, had it stayed out of APEC, should not be overstated, since such an outcome was highly unlikely either from China's viewpoint or that of other APEC founders. As was demonstrated by the comments and actions of officials both within China and representing other APEC members in the 1980s and early 1990s, there was a great deal of regional support for China's admission because of its dominant role in the Asia-Pacific economy. As China continued to open its doors to foreign investment, its impact on regional trade would only increase in the future, thus making China's exclusion from APEC a complete non-starter. At the same time, China's large economy and trade potential, as well as APEC's focus on decision-making by consensus, allowed Beijing to further promote its own policies of economic multilateralism, while exercising a veto on the delicate issues of greater formalisation, 'spillover' into non-economic areas, and the actions of Taiwan, all without fear of becoming marginalised.

There was also a contributing factor that unlike in security institutions, the consequences of a member of an economic regime 'cheating' (i.e. carrying out activities which are contrary to the regime's rules or norms) would have a lesser impact on the rest of the group. As Lipson noted, the danger of immediate 'defection' from an economic regime is very low, since economic activities are usually very transparent and slow to take effect.[69] Therefore it can be said that China need not have feared serious damage, had another member decided to 'cheat'. An argument could also be made that China's tardiness in entering the APEC allowed it a small amount of breathing space in order to observe the early evolution of APEC from the near distance, yet it had entered by the time the more specific mandate of the regime was decided after the Bogor conference. Using a variation on Gershenkron's theory of the advantages of 'developing late', an assertion can be made that joining APEC well after Canberra favoured Beijing since it was able to benefit from foreknowledge of its rights and responsibilities upon attaining membership.[70]

Another considerable advantage for China in maintaining its relations with APEC was that the organisation provided a 'middle step' in formulating Beijing's trade policies in preparation for WTO membership and also, in a much broader sense, for the completion of China's opening to the global economy. The APEC meetings during the 1990s provided an indispensable forum from which China could trumpet its determination to join the World Trade Organisation, as well as the advantages to both Beijing and the rest of the world should China gain admission. Examples of this were seen during the 1994 Bogor Summit and the Osaka Summit the following year. In Bogor, Chinese representatives attempted to convince naysayers that denying China WTO membership would result in a growing economic giant unaffected by the rules of the international trade system.[71]

APEC also provided China with the means to directly address its trade issues with its major competitor and trading partner, the United States. For example, Beijing had been at odds with Washington in the months before the Bogor summit over the possibility of the latter removing most favoured nation (MFN) trade status from Beijing. In response, Beijing attempted to demonstrate the value of what it termed the 'big cake', namely the Chinese economy, to the United States.[72] The 1993 APEC meeting in Seattle proved an excellent staging ground for advertising the 'cake'. During Chinese President Jiang Zemin's visit to Seattle for the first APEC leaders' summit in November of that year, he included a stop at the nearby Boeing aircraft manufacturing plant, and spoke of the importance of developing further economic ties between America and China. The visit, coupled with the simultaneous arrival in Beijing of Germany's Chancellor Helmut Kohl, accompanied by various heads of German multinationals, was a public relations success which underscored the importance of China to the international market. By May 1994, facing both internal and external pressures, the Clinton government opted not to link China's human rights record to its MFN status, representing one of that administration's most glaring foreign policy reversals.[73] Since that time, APEC has proven valuable for both sides to gauge each other's economic and trade policies within a less formal environment than that of bilateral summits.

The lack of a clear hierarchy within APEC meant no single member would be able to seek a leadership role within the organisation, at least not without a very dramatic restructuring of APEC's goals and ideals. China thus avoids the uncomfortable position of being forced to stave off a drive for leadership by a rival power, such as the United States or Japan, and would not require stronger leadership itself to prevent its interests from being subjugated. As Mahbubani noted, contrary to the European model of institutional cooperation, Asian institutions such as APEC are being shaped largely by middle or small powers rather than great ones.[74] The non-hierarchical nature of APEC has permitted China to participate and contribute to the organisation to better serve its foreign policy and trading needs without the same level of concern over what Grieco described as 'relative gains'. Relative gains theory suggests that states who cooperate are not only worried about what goods they accrue from cooperating, but whether other partners are gaining more, thus creating power asymmetries, often a large obstacle towards deepening cooperation.[75] While it cannot be said that each member of APEC has equal weight within the organisation, since differences in economic and political power among members are very great, the consensus-based structure of APEC minimises concerns that differences in power could be used to the detriment of less-powerful members.

In participating in an economic organisation which includes both Hong Kong and Taiwan as members, China was better able to facilitate its economic relations with its two most important non-state trading partners. The importance of this link was demonstrated by the so-called 'Greater China' effect, the increasing economic linkages over the past two decades between Taiwan, Hong Kong, and the coastal regions of the People's Republic. This *troika*, which evolved due to the converging economic goals of each economy, developed despite the formidable political constraints on all sides and the difficulties of setting up bilateral or trilateral meetings to address the problems of coordinating three different economies.[76] This advantage was lessened somewhat after Hong Kong reverted to Chinese rule after 1997, but APEC remains a valuable conduit for Beijing–Taipei economic discourse, even though the organisation has not been instrumental in addressing the larger political issues between the two sides.

Finally, similar to China's expanding relations with the World Trade Organisation, APEC serves as a means of solidifying the country's economic reforms and adding another layer of 'outside peer pressure'. Beijing has used this to demonstrate the need to complete its opening process to the international economy, despite reservations and protests on the domestic level. The Chinese government has used APEC meetings to tout the country's progress in adapting to the realities of globalisation and interdependence. For example, in 1994 President Jiang acknowledged the trend towards growing integration of global economics, and stated that issues ranging from trade to technical development to capital flows were all 'interdependent global issues' requiring international cooperation and a universal agreement on norms,[77] a far cry from Maoist doctrine. By the Brunei summit in 2000, the president went further in stating that engaging in economic globalisation was an 'objective requirement and inevitable outcome' for any nation's economic development.[78] Although APEC has neither the breadth nor the rules-based structure of the WTO, the Asia-Pacific forum has provided not only a platform for the Chinese leadership to demonstrate the benefits and necessity of greater economic liberalisation, but also a testing area for Chinese efforts to improve its economic relations with its Asian neighbours.

The future of APEC remains in flux, and questions remain as to whether this informal regime will achieve the level of policy cohesion necessary for its continued success. APEC's development has not precluded the establishment of other preferential trading arrangements designed to better address the specific economic problems of post-crisis Asia. By the late 1990s, this group had begun to gain higher visibility and influence in Asia, presenting new challenges and opportunities for China.

Pass the spaghetti: The ASEAN-Plus-Three and other PTAs

Since the Asian financial crisis, other forms of economic cooperation in Asia-Pacific began to take shape, and again China found itself at centre stage. Many economies in Asia began seeking alternatives to international and regional-level trade regimes in the form of bilateral and small-multilateral trade agreements, out of unhappiness with the response from larger regimes, including APEC, to the crisis. Several other reasons prompted this policy switch, including the extension of the NAFTA agreement southward to encompass Latin America, resulting in a Free Trade Area of the Americas, and the 1995 and 2004 expansions of the European Union, bringing its membership to 25 countries. As well, China, along with Japan and Korea, decided to abandon their traditional distrust of PTAs and joined southeast Asia in forging more exclusive trade links. Beijing's economic power was an attractive carrot for other Asian and non-Asian economies, and by mid-2004 China had completed a PTA with Hong Kong and had expressed interest in negotiating PTAs with Australia, Chile, New Zealand, South Africa, South Korea, and the Gulf Cooperation Council in the Middle East.[79]

A more ambitious free trade arrangement was first floated by then-Premier Zhu Rongji in 2000, namely an ASEAN-China Free Trade Agreement (ACFTA). Both sides showed great enthusiasm for this groundbreaking proposal, since Beijing would benefit from closer southeast Asian economic cooperation and ASEAN would overcome its relatively small economic base by linking itself closer with a rising China.[80] Should the ACFTA idea come to pass, and Chinese negotiators have recommended a deadline of 2010 for this agreement to be implemented, this PTA would involve 1.7 billion people and greatly increase the level of trade between the two sides.[81] This initiative acts as further proof that Beijing's confidence in areas of trade and economic negotiations has increased considerably since the 1990s, and with China in the WTO, this confidence may produce more proposals designed to further integrate the country into global markets.

As impressive as the ACFTA idea has been, this preferential trade agreement is one of many such accords created or under negotiation since the mid-1990s. Many of these agreements lie within the Pacific Rim, but some Asian economies have attempted to forge cross-regional free-trade ties, one example being Singapore's FTA negotiations with the United States, Canada, India and Jordan.[82] Although the proliferation of PTAs reflects a desire by East Asia to further its entrenchment into the international economy, some have expressed concerns that so many overlapping Pacific Rim trade agreements may produce a 'spaghetti-bowl effect', competing and conflicting trade deals which hinder rather than help the overall process of Asia-Pacific trade liberalisation.[83] One possible response to these concerns originated in the wake of the Asian financial crisis, namely the 'ASEAN-Plus-Three' regime.

In late 1997, ASEAN members invited delegations from China, Japan and South Korea to participate in the meetings in Kuala Lumpur.[84] More significantly, in November 1999, heads of ASEAN member states met with the leaders of the three northeast Asian states in Manila to discuss coordinating their economies better suggesting to some that a larger Asian economic bloc might slowly be taking shape. Although there had been much talk of expanding economic cooperation between ASEAN and northeast Asia's economic powers before the Manila meeting, this gathering produced support for a higher level of formalisation and established more concrete goals. Among the recommendations made during the summit was the creation of a *troika* to oversee urgent economic and security crises, movement towards the creation of a common market, and improved coordination of monetary and financial matters. Manila also marked a watershed in northeast Asian relations, as the gathering became the site of a tripartite meeting after Japanese Prime Minister Keizo Obuchi met with his counterparts from Korea and China to discuss joint economic issues. The end result was an agreement committing the three countries to the construction of a joint research body to explore various ways of institutionalising economic cooperation between them.[85]

The meetings between ASEAN and the three northeast Asian governments developed into regular events, leading to the development of a loose institution under the somewhat awkward title of 'ASEAN-Plus-Three'. Although the meetings themselves have been largely informal, they have nevertheless been the forum for many ambitious ideas to develop joint economic ties. The most far-reaching proposal thus far was the eventual creation of an Asian common market, similar in some ways to the European model, but less exclusive and less reliant on set rules and mandates.[86]

There is some irony to the development of the ASEAN-Plus-Three since in the early 1990s the government of Mahathir Mohammad of Malaysia had suggested a similar regional arrangement known as the East Asian Economic Group (EAEC). The main goal of this organisation would be to act as a 'balancer' for southeast Asia to use in countering the economic power of Japan, China, the United States, and emerging trade blocs in the west.[87] The term 'Group' was later changed to 'Caucus' to imply that this grouping would be informal and not imply a challenge to the mandate of APEC. The EAEC recommendation stemmed from concerns that the stalled Uruguay Round talks of the GATT would adversely effect economic conditions in Asia-Pacific, as well as the more general fear that the international trading system was too broad-based to properly address the specific economic concerns of the Asian region. The EAEC, therefore, would be comprised of Asian states exclusively.

The Clinton government came out strongly against the EAEC idea in the 1990s, largely out of concern such a group would eventually raise trade barriers to the United States and enact other protectionist policies.[88] The major stumbling block of the caucus idea was the reluctance of Japan, the largest economy in the proposed grouping, to accept the idea. Then-Prime Minister Toshiki Kaifu described the EAEC idea as being counterproductive to Asian interests and sought to distance Japan from the proposal when it became clear that 'non-Asian' countries would be excluded.[89] Until the end of the 1990s, the EAEC idea had fallen into near-total obscurity. However, with an APT regime comprised of the same membership as the proposed EAEC slowly taking root, reservations within Asia about the wisdom of setting up an exclusively Asian economic institution have not resurfaced. Since the end of the crisis, there was frustration in the region with the perceived mishandling of affected countries by the international financial regimes, especially the International Monetary Fund, widely blamed for exacerbating the severity of the economic 'contagion', notably in the most seriously affected states such as Indonesia, with prescribed remedies which did not adequately address Asia's specific financial problems.[90]

Another problem for the Asian economies was that since APEC's inception, the organisation has grown to incorporate great powers with interests outside of Asia, including the United States and Japan, as well as members outside of the Asian core, such as Mexico, Chile and Russia. Underlying concerns within Asia about whether APEC was growing too large and diverse to properly address the more specific economic issues within east and southeast Asia was likely another catalyst for the coming together of the APT. However, there is little sign that the APT is actively trying to supplant APEC as the primary trade regime within Asia, but rather the main goal of the APT appears to be the creation of a subsidiary institution more suitable to Asia's specific economic needs.

At the May and October 2000 APT meetings in Chiang Mai, Thailand, economic and financial ministers from ASEAN and the three northeast Asian economies agreed in principle to institutionalise the grouping. Citing the improving financial conditions in east Asia, the ministers announced a new initiative to fortify regional dialogue and cooperation among members. The Chiang Mai Initiative called for the simplified exchange of data on the flow of capital, improving financial surveillance in the region through a network of contact persons with an eye to establishing a foundation for a monitoring system, and creating a regional financing body to supplement international organisations. The underlying idea of the Chiang Mai Initiative was to create a currency swap mechanism, with agreement among members to provide loans in foreign currency funds from a reserve in case of a future crisis.[91] Bilateral currency swap arrangements between members were also encouraged.

Commentators have suggested that the Initiative may provide the blueprint towards a much-discussed Asian Monetary Fund (AMF), to assist member countries in case of an economic crisis. The origins of the AMF idea came from a Japanese proposal in September 2001 which recommended the development of a pool of capital which could be distributed to threatened Asian economies in the future. The idea was given support in Hong Kong, Taiwan, and Singapore, but was denigrated by the United States and Europe as both redundant and a challenge to the IMF integrity. China, not wishing to see Japan at the forefront of an Asian monetary organisation, also voiced its disapproval when the AMF idea was first floated but later softened its position.[92]

At the 2000 ASEAN-Plus-Three summit in Singapore, the 13 members agreed to study the possibility of a formalised East Asian Summit as well as a blueprint for a regional free trade and investment area. The major backer of a regional free trade deal was, surprisingly, China which viewed liberalised trade with its neighbours as a means to assist in its own policies of diversifying its trade.[93] At the conclusion of the meeting, the three leaders of northeast Asia pledged their support to ongoing cooperation with ASEAN, and issued their own statements concerning the directions in which each would like the new organisation to go. Within his own recommendations for the development of the organisation, Chinese Premier Zhu Rongji stressed that the developing regional bodies should try to complement each other rather than compete. In addition to the ACFTA idea, there were proposals for the joint development of the Mekong River basin region in southeast Asia, the expansion of internet capabilities and e-commerce in Asia, and the development of greater cooperation in the areas of human resources, tourism and agriculture. China joined its north Asian colleagues by encouraging the ongoing development of the Chiang Mai Initiative.[94] All three northeast Asian countries offered their support for an Initiative for Asian Integration (IAI), designed to encourage cooperation and assistance to less-developed Asian economies, and also agreed to participate in the development of an Asian 'IT belt', linking Asia's high technology centres.[95]

As the APT began to evolve, those members who would have been left out of a potential EAEC have expressed the same concerns about the APT, including Australia and New Zealand, two countries with important ties to Asian economies.[96] However, one scholar in Beijing dismissed any concerns that the APT would seek to supersede APEC as the paramount economic organisation in east and southeast Asia, noting that other members of APEC have also embarked upon creating smaller-scale financial regimes, and that Asia should be allowed to do so as well.[97] Thus far, the response from the United States towards the APT has been cautious, possibly a result of the organisation's newness and ambiguity. Equally, unlike the EAEC, adherents to the APT have taken concrete steps to remove any impression that they support regional exclusionist trade policies. The US did, however, speak out against the AMF idea when the concept was first floated during the dark days of the crisis in 1997. As Cai noted, this opposition may be a sign that America may still raise objections should the APT continue to develop into a more formalised institution.[98]

The development of the APT may be potentially problematic for another Asia-Pacific economy, namely Taiwan, which was omitted from the new organisation and is unlikely to be given an invitation in the near future, despite its extensive economic dealings with both northeast Asia and the ASEAN group. Inversely, this situation provides another incentive for Beijing to support the APT idea. Taipei's concerns about the new organisation stemmed not only from the possibility of being excluded from a developing Asian economic and trade zone, but also from worries that China may be encouraging regional free trade and the development of the APT as a roundabout method of economically isolating Taiwan. By the late 1990s, the growth of the Chinese economy, coupled with its stronger position in comparison to southeast Asia, also contributed to Taiwanese fears that Beijing may develop a form of economic hegemony over its southern neighbours, again leaving Taipei out in the cold.[99] Taiwan's tenuous economic situation at the beginning of the twenty-first century, largely due to the slowdown in the high-technology sectors, only added to Taiwanese sensitivities to any further development of the APT unless it could be afforded a role within the group.

The efforts of the APT, including the Chiang Mai Initiative, were lauded in an APEC Economic Leaders' Declaration after the Shanghai Summit of October 2001.[100] Despite the lofty goals of the ASEAN-Plus-Three during its first meetings, it was understood that many of its propositions, especially movement towards the creation of a common market, would have to overcome several obstacles. First, although the APT is a smaller and more exclusive body than APEC, there are still huge disparities not only in economic development between members, but also in terms of enthusiasm for, and capabilities to absorb, trade liberalisation and approaches to economic globalisation. The Asian financial crisis served to illustrate, and at times even intensify, these differences.[101] In addition, those economies most affected by the financial downturn have recovered at different rates, and each is expressing various degrees of confidence in their ability to participate effectively in a future Asian economic grouping.

There is also the question of how the creation of an east Asian economic organisation will affect the region's overall dependence on trade with the West, especially the United States and Europe. It is this factor which will likely prevent the development of an exclusive Asian trading region at the same level of formality, or exclusivity, as the EU or even NAFTA. The members of the ASEAN-Plus-Three, especially the advanced economies of Japan and South Korea, as well as states like Singapore which are heavily dependent on export-oriented economics, will need to remain vigilant to avoid the impression that greater economic institutionalism in Asia will affect economic relations with the West. In the case of the United States, most Asian economies have worked to maintain, or in the case of China and Vietnam improve, their economic relationships with Washington. No major economy in Asia, not even China, can afford to give the impression that they are seeking to distance themselves from the American giant.

As for Europe, ties between the APT countries and European Union have also become more institutionalised during the 1990s. The biannual Asia-Europe Meeting (ASEM) has become an increasingly important forum within which APT members may discuss common economic developments with the members of the EU. Begun in March 1996 in Bangkok after recommendations by the Singaporean government, the Asia-Europe Meetings bring together heads of state and government as well as foreign ministers from the original seven members of ASEAN, China, Japan, South Korea, and the member states of the European Union.[102] The primary goals of these gatherings are to encourage cross-regional dialogue, and to promote economic cooperation in other areas such as culture, education, and labour issues. China has engaged ASEM by co-proposing new initiatives on combating corruption and transnational crime, as well as promoting an environmental ministers' meeting and policies on forestry and sustainable development.[103] Beijing's enthusiasm for the ASEM meetings, and engagement with Europe as a whole, stems from both the desire to augment Sino-European economic relations and to add another component to its expanding multilateral engagement policies.[104]

There is also the matter of China itself, which possesses not only a rapidly growing economy but also a large labour pool yet to be tapped to a significant degree on a regional level. Material and human resource flows are necessary talking points for the ASEAN-Plus-Three, and yet widely differing opinions on these matters will make the reaching of a consensus very problematic. There are also ongoing questions about China's overall role in the organisation, since although Beijing has been very receptive to the idea of the APT, there are nevertheless concerns among other members that China would use its growing economic position to dominate the decision-making processes of a new grouping, as well as establish itself as a potential economic rival to both Japan and ASEAN. Beijing's proposal for a cross-Asia trading bloc came at a time when there was still much disagreement within ASEAN as to how to achieve trade liberalisation amongst their own membership.

In his comparison of Asian economies in the years following the crisis, Overholt expressed concerns that ASEAN was 'a spent force, both economically and politically', at least for the short term. He also reflected upon declining confidence in Japan, noting that in the late 1980s, Tokyo was viewed as a juggernaut economic power doing everything right while China was seen as an incorrigible basket case. But at the beginning of the new century those roles had been reversed. Beijing, he added, had implemented reform measures which were sufficient to allow China to ride out the worst of the crisis, and be rewarded by the same levels of regional prestige which Japan saw during its growth years in the mid-1970s.[105] Indisputably, there has been a shift in economic power levels throughout Asia as a result of China's dramatic development. Yet, rather than examining the issue playing a zero-sum game, Beijing may be positioning itself as the actor capable of spearheading a true Pacific Rim economic community.

The 'flying geese' model of Asian economic development is facing great troubles as both the lead goose, Japan, and many trailing ones, in southeast Asia, are in danger of falling behind the large waterfowl formerly at the back, China. Looking at the changes in economic power between China and Japan, a better metaphor for China may not be a goose at all, but rather a phoenix rising from the ashes of the desolation of the Maoist era. These changes will greatly affect both the course of regional economic cooperation and the role which China will play in it. If the gap in economic performance between China and its neighbours grows, regional enthusiasm for any liberalised trade placing China in an even more superior economic position would likely wane.

Such a problem was predicted by Segal as a potential issue for the EAEC should that organisation ever come to fruition. He noted that not only would an EAEC have more difficulty developing more open economies than a cross-Pacific grouping, but that an organisation restricted to east and southeast Asian members would be hard-pressed to 'resist' a rapidly growing Chinese economy.[106] The same problem exists for the APT, especially in the wake of the financial crisis and the slow recovery of some crisis-hit Asian economies. The underlying question is whether the APT is able to develop with such large economic disparities between members, disparities which are likely to become even wider should China's dynamo continue. Until this obstacle is openly addressed, the APT is likely to retain a very informal and non-binding structure. However, signs began to appear in 2004 which suggested that there was some regional support for a more formalised regional economic community using the APT framework. China, along with Japan and Malaysia, have advocated the development of an 'East Asian Community' (EAC) which would further integrate economic cooperation between ASEAN and the three northeast Asian states.[107]

For now, as one commentator noted, it may be too early to describe the APT as a distinct institution or even as a 'cooperation mechanism'. Rather, the group could be best described as 'a channel' to primarily assist ASEAN in developing its political role in Asia and to improve its dealing with other outside organisations.[108] However, should economic competition between ASEAN and China intensify, questions may arise as to which side is leading and which is following. It should be remembered that when the EAEC was first proposed, it was assumed Japan would act as the zenith of that organisation. With the APT, that role may well be filled by Beijing in the very near future.

Community or hegemony?

China's brief history of multilateral economic engagement can be best described as tempestuous, not only for Beijing for also for the rest of the Asia-Pacific region. However, in spite of China's tentative and often conflict-ridden openings to regional economic institutions, the country has developed a much more cooperative and engaging stance than what was observed during the early 1990s, and clearly Beijing is anxious both to share in the rewards of closer Asian economic cooperation, and also to increase its visibility in the global economic arena via its membership in exclusive economic regimes. During the past two decades, Beijing has found regional economic regimes to be an indispensable part of the country's opening up to the global economy. APEC and the fledgling APT group are proving beneficial to China's development as an Asian economic power centre, and a future global one as well.

APEC, the APT, and various smaller PTAs in which Beijing is engaged have been increasingly used by China to demonstrate the country's growing economic power and to strengthen its financial relations with Asia-Pacific. Within APEC, China has been able to demonstrate its increasing economic prowess in an organisation containing other great economic powers, including the United States and Japan. As a member of the APT, Beijing has been able to specifically demonstrate its economic growth not only alongside southeast Asia, but more crucially, Japan. Most of the Asian members of APEC, especially in southeast

Asia, have continued to face varying degrees of economic, social, and political fallout from the Asian financial crisis, and as a result, overall regional enthusiasm for free trade and economic liberalisation has yet to reach pre-crisis levels. As the global economy was threatened with recession during much of 2001, the response in Asia was to once again look warily at growing Chinese economic power, which appeared to be largely resistant to the most recent downturn.

APEC and the various preferential trade agreements have fostered growth in China's economic prestige as well as its trade. These results have helped the Chinese government to further strengthen its economic reform initiatives on both the domestic and international levels. As with the WTO, Beijing has used both APEC and other free trade agreements as demonstration tools to promote the reform processes to its people. Issues which therefore must be addressed when examining Beijing's economic institutional relations in Asia include whether Chinese economic power will continue to grow at the same pace as it has during the 1990s, both in the absolute sense and in comparison to other APEC economic powers. Will this assist or complicate China's integration with Asian economies? Signs at present may point to the latter, since if China's relative economic power leads to a more dominant position *vis-à-vis* its Asian neighbours, and a balancing force, such as Japan, is unable to take shape, further institutional economic cooperation via APEC or by other means may be in danger from two fronts.

China's neighbours may be wary of a system promoting economic liberalisation which would fortify Beijing's superior economic position, and China itself may be less willing to follow institutional rules which may adversely effect its economic growth. At present, it is premature to speak of a possible Chinese economic hegemony in Asia, since the country has not yet completed its transition to a market economy. Domestic-level strains may lead to future financial and political strains which may force China to turn inward rather than seek greater economic power on a regional scale.

Although these two economic organisations do not yet have an official security dimension to them, peripherally they do have a strategic function both for China and for other members. First, during the late 1990s, political and security issues including East Timor and the problem of terrorism have been tentatively discussed within APEC, but in an informal and non-binding fashion which Beijing has found acceptable. The stage may be set for future political issues to be added to APEC's docket, but the process is likely to be slow and measured. Even so, this evolution may serve Chinese interests by allowing Beijing to better gauge regional-level security concerns. As will be further explained, a fledgling security regime already exists for the region, namely the ASEAN Regional Forum (ARF). However, APEC has the advantage of being better established, more inclusive, and less potentially threatening to China's own security interests. Second, China's policy of supporting a stable Asian periphery has been assisted by its support for regional economic organisations, especially since Beijing has frequently equated peace and stability with regional development and fair economic relations between states. Although China was not as directly affected by the financial crisis as many of its neighbours,

Beijing still has an interest in preventing future regional contagion which would not only disrupt Asian trade flows but also result in further political and social upheaval around China's periphery. The crisis demonstrated not only the fragility of emerging economies in Asia, but also how rapidly the socio-economic problems of one country can spread into others.

A dramatic shift in economic power which produces a widening gap between China and ASEAN or northeast Asia would create greater strains on APEC's cohesion, and at the very least would result in China seeking an expanded role in the organisation's decision-making process. It is certain, however, that China will not consider itself bound to the decision made in Bogor to achieve cross-APEC free trade by 2020 if it feels its economic interests would be curtailed. As for APEC itself, the future of the organisation in the post-crisis era remains clouded. In many ways, the forum is suffering through the same lack of direction and loss of confidence as the European Community of the 1970s and early 1980s, when serious doubts were raised as to whether it could continue to develop into a true European economic regime. However, detractors who question whether APEC will ever develop into a more structured economic community also need to remember that the unity established in Europe was the product of many decades of development. At barely fifteen years old, it is far too early to speculate on the organisation's future longevity, or lack thereof.

The development of the ASEAN-Plus-Three and other bilateral and regional PTAs, and China's enthusiasm for them, may signal a serious change in priorities among ASEAN and the Asia-Pacific which could lead to a diminishing of APEC's role as the leading economic institution in Asia. The growth of the various preferential trade agreements reflects lingering concern in Asia both that another currency crisis could develop in the future, and that international-level organisations such as the IMF would be unable to provide region-specific solutions should another case of economic contagion occur. The APT continues to show signs of development into a 'soft regime', providing a more comfortable milieu in which to address regional-specific economic issues without the use of rules and deadlines. It remains to be seen, however, whether this regime can reach the same level as APEC in terms of being a recognisable multilateral actor both on a regional and an international scale.

Regardless of the direction of either APEC or the PTAs, both groups have provided a large number of benefits for China as it continues to develop its external economic relations. The main benefit for both organisations has been their ability to provide sorely-needed information on the benefits and problems of opening up the Chinese economy to the outside world, and making use of that information to address larger-scale liberalisation on the global stage, not only with the WTO but also with great economic powers outside of Asia, especially the United States. Moreover, the price for attaining this information has been lower than it might have been, had China opted to eschew regional cooperation and instead rely on the topmost level (the international trade system), and the bottom-most (bilateral agreements). These benefits have added considerably to China's goal of attaining greater power through its economic goods, and as long as Asian regional organisations continue to follow an informal and egalitarian philosophy, the development of Asian economic organisations will continue to provide information as well as political and economic benefits to China for some time to come.

3

CHIMERAS OR PEACEBUILDERS?

China's new approach to strategic regimes

On contentious terrain, do not attack.
Sun-tzu, *The Art of War*

Diplomacy revisited? China and changes in Asian security

Following the end of the cold war, there was much speculation as to how the new international order would affect security and cooperation in the Pacific Rim. Compared to North America and Europe, security organisations in the Asia-Pacific region are much less developed. In contrast to the development of the North Atlantic Treaty Organisation (NATO), which was created during the height of the cold war and continues to link North America and Europe in a guarantee of mutual security, and the Organisation for Security and Cooperation in Europe (OSCE), no comparable structure exists in Asia despite the end of the cold war and the disappearance of the associated ideological boundaries which divided much of east and southeast Asia into Western and Soviet spheres of influence. As a result, concerns were raised that early-twenty-first century Asia may ultimately mirror early-twentieth-century Europe, marked by open power rivalries, highly fluid alliances, and eventual warfare which could drag major regional powers, and perhaps the entire international community, into a melée.

Should this scenario become reality, China would almost inevitably be a participant, and some realists concerned about China's increase in military strength suggest the country might actually be an instigator of future conflict, possibly seeking to take advantage of the cold war's end to improve its own regional security situation.[1] Many of the more intractable security issues in the Asia-Pacific are also related to Chinese strategic policy either directly (Taiwan and the South China Sea) or indirectly (Korea, southeast Asia). While Beijing eschewed the use of force to address these problems during the last decades of the cold war, arguments were made in the 1990s that China could not be counted on to disavow the use of military action in the future should the status quo begin to interfere with the country's long-term strategic aims. As a result, the 'China threat' school of thought espoused by some policymakers and academics which described China as an emerging danger to international order, often pointed to Beijing's potential as a regional-level aggressor in Asia in justifying claims that the country is a 'revisionist' power in addition to a growing global one.[2] These views prevail despite many assertions that various recent improvements in Chinese military power notwithstanding, the country would encounter serious problems conducting even limited, localised warfare, let alone challenging a global power like the United States for hegemony in Asia.[3]

Part of the rationale behind this idea stemmed not only from the lack of security communities in the region, but also due to the fact that Beijing during the cold war was highly suspicious of such regimes, a legacy of its initial exclusion from the United Nations, and its targeting by the UN during the 1950–3 Korean War. Despite the Communists' war-weariness, they chose to side with North Korea to confront the technologically superior American-backed UN forces. Beijing began to send troops across the Yalu River in October 1950, both to defend its borders and (officially) offer support for North Korea in return for Korean assistance in defeating the Kuomintang years earlier.[4] Chinese mistrust of security regimes continued after the Sino–Soviet split and throughout much of the cold war, and it has only been since the late 1990s that this negative view began to change.

Security in the Pacific Rim today has changed considerably from previous decades. While traditional security threats remain a primary concern of the region, the present strategic problems facing the region are far beyond issues related to state-to-state warfare, namely the threats of terrorism and extremism. From the dawn of the twenty-first century, and especially after 11 September 2001, it has been understood in Asia that many modern security matters are too complicated to address unilaterally and must be dealt with via group action. Therefore it is in the interests of Beijing, its Asian neighbours, and outside parties such as the United States, that solutions to the myriad 'trouble spots' in the Pacific Rim be administered in a peaceful and productive manner, ensuring China is engaged as a partner in the process.

With the fall of the USSR and the development of the international war on terrorism, China's approach to international strategic institutions has evolved from complete withdrawal to reluctant participant to active shaper. Although many security issues in the region remain volatile, including nuclear tensions on the Korean Peninsula, the Taiwan question, and terrorism in southeast Asia, a security framework is gradually taking shape in the Asia-Pacific, with Beijing an increasingly valued partner.

Arguably the most visible example of China's gradual acceptance of multilateral security cooperation has been the nascent ASEAN Regional Forum (ARF), a body dedicated to encouraging dialogue on mutual security concerns with various prospects for peacebuilding between nations of the Pacific Rim. An original member of the ARF, China has shown much enthusiasm for the organisation despite lingering concerns that some strategic issues may be brought to agenda which would threaten China's foreign and domestic policies. Although the dividing line separating China's views of 'acceptable' and 'unacceptable' topics of discussion within the ARF has steadily blurred since the 1990s, it has not disappeared. Beijing has made it clear that the ARF and other fledgling security organisations in the region should not discuss matters which Beijing considers domestic issues. This has led to the question of whether the emerging security dialogues in the region can be of real assistance to China and its neighbours in reaching a consensus on overlapping security issues.

The answer to this appears to be a cautious 'yes'. China's military has begun to grow in relation to that of the rest of the region, leading to concerns that the delicate balance of power in Asia may tip in China's favour, making the country less inclined to cooperate with its neighbours. However, Beijing maintains its interest in developing multilateral solutions to security problems, in partnership with its neighbours. As China continues to shape its post-cold war defence policy, it has developed a 'new security concept', stressing the role of partnerships and community-building in addressing regional security.[5] The ARF does have the potential to act as a platform for Beijing's development of its strategic interests, and China has not only continued to support the ARF, it has begun to take a more active role in its development and has shown signs of taking the lead in developing the forum into a much stronger platform for regional security policymaking.

China's more conciliatory stance towards solving regional security issues within multilateral dialogues is no longer limited to the ARF, as over the past five years China has shown new confidence within multilateral security regimes and has assumed a more active and positive role in other forms of security cooperation, including informal Track II regimes and, more recently, northeast Asian security talks designed to defuse the complicated crisis involving North Korea's alleged nuclear weapons development.

The origins of the ARF

In 2001, the ASEAN Regional Forum was described by a Chinese scholar as an organisation with an 'irreplaceable role'[6] in the Asia-Pacific, while a Western official in Beijing called the organisation 'useless'.[7] These differences of opinion mirror differing opinions in regional security literature as to the nature and efficacy of the ARF, and indeed whether the organisation has the potential to develop more fully into a strong strategic actor and a force for peacebuilding in the Asia-Pacific region. While it is likely there are elements of truth in both opinions, it can be said that the ARF is beginning to develop into an example of the growing importance of multilateral security institutions to China's strategic thinking.

During the cold war, security cooperation on a formal level was limited to either bilateral ties or American-led regimes. Communist encroachment in east and southeast Asia, including North Korea, Vietnam, Laos and Cambodia prevented the creation of geographically-based security organisations, and Washington opted to utilise traditional bilateral linkages between itself and its Asian allies. In addition to the stalwart US–Japan security relationship, Washington established bilateral treaties with allies Australia, the Philippines, South Korea and Thailand, while maintaining ambiguous support for Taiwan. Multilateral cooperation during this time was rare, and the few examples included the enfeebled South East Asian Treaty Organisation (SEATO), created in 1954, and the 1951 Australia–New Zealand–United States (ANZUS) treaty between Washington and the governments of Australia and New Zealand.[8]

The situation changed dramatically when the Soviet Union began its disengagement process from the region in the late 1980s. During that time, the Asian regional schisms created by the cold war's effect in the Pacific Rim all but vanished. Korea, still divided between a Stalinist north and a capitalist south, remains one glaring exception. In east Asia, relations between China, Japan and South Korea have been strengthened and reinforced by increased economic ties. Further south, the Association of Southeast Asian Nations (ASEAN), created in 1967 to provide a united front against communist aggression, welcomed former Soviet client states (Cambodia, Laos and Vietnam) into the fold during the 1990s. Moreover, the states of East and Southeast Asia have no clear ideological or strategic adversaries. While the atmosphere in the region became far more conducive to the creation of multilateral strategic communities during the 1990s, the process has been slow and marked with criticism and controversy.

The ASEAN Regional Forum, which would become the vanguard for regional attempts at creating an Asia-Pacific multilateral security institution, came into being in Bangkok in 1994. The membership of the forum is extensive, bringing together 23 members from both sides of the Pacific Ocean as well as the European Union.[9] The ARF's genesis was largely prompted by efforts of the Association of Southeast Asian Nations to encourage the swift withdrawal of Vietnamese occupational forces from next-door Cambodia, an occupation which was considered a serious detriment to southeast Asia's overall security. A Vietnamese pullout was also a policy of which China, as a then-friend of Phnom Penh and main rival in that region to Vietnam, was also strongly in favour. The two major goals of the ARF, from its inception, were to 'foster constructive dialogue and consultation on political and security issues of common interest and concern; and to make significant contributions to efforts towards confidence-building and preventive diplomacy in the Asia-Pacific region.'[10] Another incentive for the development of the ARF, according to Johnston and Evans' description, was the perceived need in southeast Asia to 'engage' China and to address its future strategic role in the Pacific Rim.[11] As a result, the China–ASEAN relationship is one of the most important linkages found within the ARF, and can be used as a barometer in determining the organisation's future development.

There were high hopes for the ARF at its inception, both in the region and in the United States. For example, President Clinton referred to the Forum as one of many 'overlapping plates of armour' which would work to stabilise Asia's security situation.[12] However, the ARF's development has been very slow and measured, and it is still far from emerging as a security community on the same level of formality as its Atlantic counterparts, leading some analysts to criticise the group as primarily a body for dialogue but little concrete action.[13] Exactly why the ARF has been so lethargic in its development has been the subject of much argument, but several reasons are commonly cited by regional analysts.

First, the organisation lacks a clear mandate beyond serving as an outlet for security dialogue, and an argument could be made that there is insufficient political will among members for strong action to be taken to address the most serious security issues in the Asia-Pacific. There is no obligation to enforce decisions and recommendations made by the Forum and therefore the ARF would be ineffective in promoting collective security in the region. Buzan and Segal, in examining the prospects for institutional development in the Asia-Pacific, blamed state weakness and inexperience in the field of multilateral behaviour for the slow and uncertain development of strategic institutions.[14] While this pessimistic assessment implied such conditions are chronic in the region, strong differences of opinion between state actors about which aspects of regional security are appropriate for multilateral dialogue remain a roadblock to a strengthening of regional strategic ties.

The ARF operates by consensus, a textbook example of what Lake referred to as an 'anarchic institution', one where full sovereignty and veto power of the entire membership is guaranteed. Members of these informal institutions have greater latitude in observing their national interests while still participating in the group.[15] As one forum policy paper offered, 'The ARF should also progress at a pace comfortable to all participants. The ARF should not move "too fast for those who want to go slow and not too slow for those who want to go fast".'[16] The difficulty lies in coming to a clear agreement within such a large and diverse body as to exactly what the minimum and maximum acceptable 'speeds' are.

The region nominally under the ARF's jurisdiction has been critiqued as too large and complex a geographical (and geopolitical) area to cover effectively. In addition to the large number of ARF members is the diversity of its membership, its adherents representing a wide range of political, economic, and most importantly, military capabilities. These capability 'gaps' have made it more difficult to forge agreements on security matters, especially since the ARF lacks any means of enforcing its rules and norms, or of settling disputes between members. Its 'subregional' security issues include the Korea problem, East Timor's independence from Indonesia, individual border disputes, and cross-border crime and terrorism, making multilateral agreements more difficult.[17]

Other security problems have been considered 'domestic' in origin, however their effects have frequently reached across borders. Examples include terrorism and abductions by the Islamic fundamentalist Abu Sayyaf group in the Philippines and ethnic and religious violence in Indonesia since the mid-1990s, as well as a terrorist bombing in that country in October 2002.[18] The ARF has been slow to adapt to the challenges of these security threats, as the organisation has adopted the informal norms of its parent, ASEAN, discouraging infringements on the sovereignty of its members. In addition to the ARF's consensual nature, the group was founded upon a pledge to avoid interference in others' sovereign affairs, a mandate borrowed whole from ASEAN's foreign policy. As a result, key security issues can be, and have been, purposely left off the group's agenda in the forum's meetings. This has led to very visible 'holes' in the ARF's effectiveness, adding fuel to critics' views of the ARF's perceived weakness.

Despite the forum's perceived weaknesses, China has been an enthusiastic member of the ARF since 1994, while refraining both from introducing new initiatives to the body and from playing a strong role in shaping its policy directions. Rather, Beijing remained comfortable with ASEAN continuing to play a lead role in the ARF and has been willing to participate in the forum's ongoing security dialogue, within acceptable limitations. According to Shirk, Beijing was unwilling to assume a leading role in determining the course of security relations in the region both out of concern for arousing fears it was attempting to dominate the process, and also that any such leadership role would go against traditional Maoist foreign policy doctrine decrying 'hegemonic' behaviour.[19] Beijing's original role in the ARF was one of consultative partner, but after the forum began to formalise its objectives, China became a full dialogue partner in June 1996,[20] an indication of the country's growing flexibility towards multilateral strategic dialogues.

The Chinese view of the ARF was that the group was created primarily to safeguard the strategic interests of the original six members of ASEAN, plus the more recent members (Cambodia, Laos, Myanmar and Vietnam), and then to keep the entire region engaged in security dialogues in order to create an improved atmosphere of peace and stability. In light of the diverse nature of the region, China maintained the position that creating and encouraging a milieu of regional trust was far more important than establishing a rigid rule of conduct within the organisation. The country's views on the role of the ARF involve the promotion of regional peace and stability as well as the encouragement of security dialogue between Asia-Pacific actors.[21]

However, Beijing made it clear during its first years of membership that it did not view the ARF as a body to build regional collective security, to settle disputes, or even for joint decision-making on mutual strategic issues, but rather strictly as a forum for dialogue and information-sharing. As Smith noted, China, along with ASEAN, attempted to discourage any attempt to build the ARF along the lines of the OSCE (then known as the Council for Security and Cooperation in Europe, or CSCE). China's objections stemmed from its perceptions that the CSCE's inclusion of human rights issues into its security dialogues contributed to the erosion of the Soviet Union, and for that reason Beijing's delegation to the ARF avoided any reference to the CSCE in its reports.[22] Such an omission serves to highlight Chinese sensitivity towards any steps taken by other ARF members to have the organisation echo its more structured Western counterparts.

However, this did not mean that Beijing was not required to alter its security policies as a result of participation in the ARF, nor has China's role in the organisation been entirely passive. For example, in 1995 all ARF members were strongly encouraged to produce defence white papers as a means of promoting greater military transparency among members. China had previously been loath to do this, especially at a time when the PLA was undergoing reform and modernisation, changing from a military based primarily on manpower to one more suitable to the realities of post-bipolarity warfare. However, 'peer pressure', especially from the United States, was apparently the catalyst for Beijing's issuing of a white paper on arms control and disarmament in November 1995, followed by a more general paper on Chinese defence policy in July 1998.[23] Beijing produced subsequent defence white papers in 2000 and 2002 which further detailed its security priorities.

China and the 'Track II' connection

Due to the often sensitive security issues which the ARF has attempted to address, many of the more delicate discussions and ideas on regional peacebuilding have come from so-called 'Track II' organisations which are not official in nature but permit discussions free from the glare of official government policy. 'Track II' is a term used to describe policy meetings or organisations whose members are normally comprised of academics, non-governmental organisations (NGOs), occasionally economic or business interests, and often government members or officials.[24] This form of multilateral cooperation has become increasingly visible in the Asia-Pacific and another vehicle enabling China to engage the Asia-Pacific.

Governmental participants in Track II have traditionally been lower-level officials and frequently present their personal opinions on matters rather than describe the stance of their respective agencies. Track II has oftentimes been used as a means to discuss highly sensitive political or strategic issues considered too delicate to address, directly, by governments. The two regions where Track II initiatives have been most visible have been the Middle East, especially in discussions concerning Israel–Palestinian issues, and in east Asia, where the lack of formal security regimes, higher levels of distrust among the major regional powers and the presence of a politically ambiguous actor, Taiwan, make formal regional security dialogue through the ARF and others extremely difficult. Thus, Track II organisations have developed into some of the most important tools permitting Asian actors to construct a viable regional security framework.[25]

The ARF, in developing its security policies, makes extensive use of Track II initiatives which it either directly or indirectly supports, and the ideas and policy recommendations which these less formal groups produce can often set the agenda for the ARF itself.[26] In addition, due to the less structured setting of Track II, participants have the breathing room to 'filter', to use Evans' term, various ideas so that they are more palatable at governmental level and may contribute to official foreign policymaking.[27]

By far the most visible of the Track II groups which influence the ARF is the Council for Security Cooperation in the Asia-Pacific (CSCAP). CSCAP was created in June 1993 in Kuala Lumpur, and currently consists of 20 members and five working groups covering specific aspects of regional security.[28] CSCAP's membership is derived from regional academics, non-governmental organisations and lower-level government officials, and as a result the group has more latitude to discuss regional security matters judged too controversial to add to the ARF mandate. Its official mandate is to provide mechanisms for political and security issues to be discussed by governmental, nongovernmental, and academic interests, to make policy recommendations, and to facilitate information exchange with interested actors.[29]

However, Chinese representatives openly questioned the idea that CSCAP was 'unofficial', since so many regional government members participate in the process, albeit in 'personal capacities.'[30] This viewpoint created problems when the inevitable issue of Beijing's participation, with Taipei's, in CSCAP was raised. China did not join CSCAP at its inception, only being granted admission in 1995 because of concerns about the role of Taiwan which, while not welcomed into the ARF, was seeking some role on the Track II level. As Evans noted, Beijing opted to view CSCAP as 'semi-governmental' in nature, rather than non-governmental.[31] The distinction is important, since Beijing has continuously attempted to parry any attempt by Taiwan to codify its desire for independence via acceptance into formal international organisations by discouraging Taiwan's institutional participation unless under very controlled conditions, as demonstrated by compromises within economic regimes such as APEC and the WTO, previously discussed.

Thus, two years of negotiations were needed in order to reconcile the terms of Beijing and Taipei's membership, and ultimately the terms of admission and participation greatly favoured the former. Taiwanese representatives are able to attend working group meetings as individuals, but formal Taiwanese representation is not permitted in the CSCAP Steering Committee, the highest-level decision-making body within the Council, or annual meetings. As well, the subject of cross-Strait security, which Beijing considers an internal issue, has been omitted from the Council's agenda.[32] Other agenda items considered overly sensitive or a matter of Chinese internal security, such as the status of North Korean refugees crossing the Chinese border, are also blocked by Beijing.[33]

Despite China's initial wariness in joining CSCAP, the country developed a greater interest for the process, and Chinese delegations to both CSCAP and the ARF have been drawn from similar circles, notably retired ambassadors and embassy officials.[34] China has participated in annual meetings and, with Malaysia and New Zealand, currently heads the Working Group on Cooperative and Comprehensive Security. The activities of CSCAP China, based in Beijing and founded in 1997, have included forecasting, setting up working groups and coordinating various political issues related to the CSCAP mandate. A representative from CSCAP China is chosen to meet with the ARF and to advise the Chinese government on relevant security matters.

As with China's views towards the ARF, the China CSCAP group has been advocating the development of a peaceful regional milieu in order to promote economic development. Additionally, non-traditional security issues such as illegal drugs, maritime security and cross-border crime have been promoted by CSCAP China as necessary agenda topics, especially since these issues preclude addressing by China alone. CSCAP China has suggested that economic security matters, such as the negative impacts of economic globalisation, should also be brought to the table in the near future.[35] Considering Beijing's front-line experience with some of the more detrimental effects of globalisation in the wake of the Asian financial crisis, which at times resulted in social disorder and even violence around China's periphery, Beijing is understandably interested in placing these issues, as well, on a multilateral agenda.

As with many other Track II organisations, much of CSCAP's most sensitive dialogues take place during informal 'hallway chats' where more personal observations can be aired and greater informality permitted. Chinese representatives have used these opportunities to either soften official stances, or occasionally to reinforce them.[36] CSCAP membership produces a similar set of advantages for China as does the ARF, since it is also non-binding, informal, and non-interventionist. As Lipson explained, agreements struck in such a fashion can be beneficial since their informality allows for flexibility, adaptability to changed circumstances, and a higher level of privacy than more structured agreements.[37] However, because CSCAP is Track II in design, this body has a handicap of being obliged to construct policy recommendations which not only have the support of the whole of the group, but are also able to be 'pushed through the ceiling' and incorporated into Track I foreign policy, normally a very challenging endeavour.

In short, CSCAP in its present format is 'safe' for China to embrace because of its informality and its relative obscurity, and acts as a useful instructional and information-gathering tool for Beijing, educating China as to concerns about policy and academic communities in other nations. Equally, Chinese actions within CSCAP suggest it remains enthusiastic about this form of Track II process despite, or perhaps because of, its limitations. Therefore, it is likely the engagement process on the Track II level will continue for the near future with China's participation and support.

It has yet to be determined, however, whether Track II initiatives in the Pacific Rim can actually yield positive contributions to peace and security in the region. Despite fewer restrictions on dialogue and recommendations than those of the ARF, Track II engagement in Asia has been slow, lacking any breakthrough agreements. One scholar lamented that at the start of the new century, 'Track II diplomacy has run out of steam in the Asia-Pacific'. His reasons were that the inter-state 'trust' developed within both the ARF and CSCAP had not yet produced concrete preventive diplomacy, and the more traditional security problems have endured in the region, with neither regime able to adequately address them.[38] It is too early to tell if this degree of pessimism is justified, but until the agreements made within Track II begin showing more tangible contributions to security policy on the inter-governmental level, scepticism about the usefulness of these talks will persist. At a time when the power levels in Asia are shifting rapidly, there may be less tolerance in the region for conversations without results.

Limitations to the ARF: the cases of Taiwan and the South China Sea

Although there have been many positive developments in the field of regional military transparency, there are still some Asian security issues which Beijing has been resistant to discussing within a multilateral setting such as the ARF. Just after joining the ARF, Beijing was concerned that despite its informal structure and dialogue, the forum could still be used to marginalise and manipulate China. Therefore, during the ARF's early stages China rebuffed any attempts by the group to play a more active and formalised role in regional strategic issues.[39] As well, there are some security issues which, at least conventionally, would fall under the ARF's mandate that China has been opposed to pursuing within that body since Beijing has determined them to be domestic issues to be addressed by China only. These are the Taiwan issue and the question of ownership rights to some small but strategically important islets in the South China Sea.

Beijing's reluctance to allow Taipei to participate formally in the ARF or CSCAP, or to permit discussion in an open forum of the possible security ramifications of the Taiwan question, is a reflection of the longstanding stance of the government of China that any and all issues pertaining to the present and future disposition of Taiwan are strictly an internal matter and not subject to multilateral debate. Beijing was concerned that political or strategic issues relating to Taiwan might be introduced to the ARF agenda unless the breakaway province was excluded from the forum. At present, Taipei and Beijing have met in meetings sponsored by ASEAN on largely technical issues, including maritime safety, climate, marine biology and legal issues, but that remains the extent to which Beijing is willing to participate in the process with a Taiwanese element present. In short, there can be no joint Beijing-Taipei participation in any workshop where strategic affairs are on the table.[40]

CSCAP China also considers the Taiwan and South China Sea issues to be domestic matters which have no place being discussed within a regional organisation.[41] After China was permitted to enter CSCAP, as per Beijing's wishes Taiwanese representatives could only enter as individuals.[42] Nevertheless, there have continued to be differences of opinion within CSCAP as to what the proper level of Taiwanese participation should be, and in the past there were rumblings from Beijing delegations that representatives from Taipei were engaging in various dialogues to degrees beyond (to China) acceptable levels.[43] Beijing maintains that the issue of Taiwan should best be settled through a direct settlement with Taipei, and therefore a multilateral approach, even on the Track II level, to lessening tensions in the Taiwan Straits is not an option.

Another sensitive topic, namely the status of the South China Sea and the islands within, is an even thornier issue since a number of powerful regional actors are large stakeholders in the outcome of this dispute, including China. The region has great geo-strategic value, being located along valuable sea routes which connect east and southeast Asia to regions westward, including the Middle East. Adding to the problem is the existence of a 'Macguffin' in the form of possible but unsubstantiated energy supplies.

Despite the almost insignificant size of the islands (many of which are underwater at various times and tidal shifts), they remain the largest security headache in southeast Asia, and by far the largest obstacle to improved China–ASEAN relations. Before the creation of the ARF, the ASEAN's members were reluctant to directly challenge Chinese claims in the South China Sea. For example, in 1992 ASEAN released a very tepid declaration on its South China Sea policies, not mentioning Beijing by name and calling upon all disputants to use 'restraint', and explore means of joint cooperation in dealing with that area's security problems.[44] This viewpoint has evolved only marginally under the ARF, which has not been able to act as a mechanism to defuse the ongoing controversy over control of the islands.

The main island groups with which China is contesting ownership are the Spratly Islands (known in China as the Nansha, and claimed wholly by China, Vietnam, and Taiwan, and partly by Malaysia, the Philippines, Indonesia, and Brunei), and the Paracel Islands (or the Xisha, and claimed by Vietnam but presently occupied by China). A third group, located in the East China Sea, are the Diaoyu/Senkaku Islands, claimed by China, Taiwan, and Japan. Like the Spratlys, the Diaoyutai/Senkakus have both strategic value and possible oil reserves. While China has not supported referring the dispute to the ARF, Beijing has taken great pains, as has Tokyo, to avoid military confrontation over the islets and to promote a dialogue-based solution to their future administration. Both sides have taken steps to dampen any nationalistic pressures over the islands, and have discouraged any calls for annexation.[45]

However, the Diaoyu/Senkaku issue has yet to be satisfactorily resolved, and the potential for an escalation in tensions remains should either side adopt a less-conservative approach to determining future administration of these islets. This was illustrated by incidents in July and August 1996 when members of two Japanese rightist organisations erected an improvised lighthouse and, subsequently, a Japanese flag in the disputed zone. In 2004, a turnabout took place when a small group of Chinese activists occupied one of the disputed isles and was temporarily detained by Japanese authorities.[46] For many years these islands have been a magnet for nationalist elements in both countries, but there is no support as yet for turning the matter over to international arbitration.

The Paracels, located south-east of China's Hainan Island and due west of Vietnam, were forcibly brought into the Chinese sphere of influence in 1974 after then-South Vietnam attempted to annex them as part of a provincial village. Shots were fired by Vietnamese naval forces after Chinese fishermen planted a flag on one of the Paracel islets, after which China responded with a counterattack by the People's Liberation Army capturing the islands.[47] Since that time, Chinese administration of the Paracels has been considered, at least by Beijing, to be a *fait accompli* despite ongoing counter-claims by Hanoi. The PLA has greatly fortified the Paracels over the past decade, establishing a military base on the largest atoll, Woody Island, complete with tank units, missile and patrol boats, a sizeable runway, and a communications and information-gathering centre. In addition to relieving much of the burden of monitoring the South China Sea region from the next-closest base in Hainan, the Woody Island fortifications would, in theory, facilitate any future operations of People's Liberation Army Navy (PLAN) throughout the Sea itself.[48] Thus, Chinese moves to develop the Paracels militarily make it unlikely that Vietnam would risk renewed violence into order to assert its own claims of ownership.

The other main South China Sea island group, the Spratlys, presents a much thornier political issue. China claims them in their entirety, while physically occupying only part of the region, with Vietnam, the Philippines and Malaysia also having a physical presence on the islands.[49] China's claim to the whole of the Spratlys (and indeed the South China Sea) is based on historical ties and records dating back at least four thousand years when Chinese fishermen routinely made use of the isles as bases of operations. Modern Chinese maps clearly indicate the Spratlys and the surrounding waters as Chinese territory. Although the exact date of China's discovery of the islands is in dispute, some Chinese officials have claimed that they were discovered at least as far back as the Han dynasty (during the third century BCE). Moreover, Beijing claims that the islands were continuously inhabited by the Chinese people, and during the Ming and Qing dynasties (from 1368 to the end of Imperial China in 1911), the Spratlys were under the official jurisdiction of the then-Qiongzhou prefecture.[50] However, the status of the islands under modern international law has remained nebulous.

Chinese claims to the islands were codified, albeit ambiguously, during the waning years of the Qing dynasty by a convention between China and Tonkin (now part of Vietnam) after the Sino-French War of 1884–5.[51] After 1949 the Chinese Communist Party maintained the imperial stance that the Spratlys were sovereign Chinese territory, although it refrained from using military force to back up its claims until 1988, when approximately four months of naval posturing in the region between Vietnam and China erupted in a brief battle in March of that year.[52] Although neither side was completely driven from the islands, the conflict did demonstrate a renewed determination on the part of Beijing to maintain its claims on the archipelago. Thus, a large part of China's claims to the Spratlys is nationalistic in nature, but it has been argued that China has framed its claims to the islands in terms of economic gains as well as military goals. As Liefer argued, Beijing's claims to the Spratlys have been perceived as a major rationale for the development of Chinese naval forces which are better able to operate away from the mainland, an ability otherwise known as a 'blue water capability'.[53]

The possession of these islands is not just a matter of national pride for the disputants, since there have been contested reports that the region may contain sizeable petroleum reserves. Estimates have ranged from 1 to 17.7 billion tonnes of oil and natural gas in the Spratlys.[54] However, some opposing voices have stated that the overall geological makeup of the islands precludes the existence of any sizeable quantities of oil and that without independent verification, it is impossible to justify the expensive and politically complicated extraction efforts.[55] Nevertheless, the prospect of potential energy reserves in the region continues to ensure that the question over final ownership of the Spratlys remains a sensitive one, and a perpetual obstacle to furthering good relations between China and the ASEAN states. In addition to the islands' energy potential, there would be a military advantage to the stewards of the islands, since the islands would provide a jumping-off point for an expanded Chinese blue-water navy. [56] The islands' location next to economically important sea-lanes (such as the Malacca and Balabac Straits) also makes the Sea valuable from a strategic viewpoint.

Hostile encounters between Chinese and ASEAN claimants in the region continued through the 1990s. One of the most visible was the PLAN's occupation in 1995 of Mischief Reef, which had been claimed by the Philippines. In September 1994, Philippine soldiers on the Spratly island of Mischief Reef took 55 Chinese fishermen into custody. Beijing responded by conducting a bloodless but still ominous seizure of the island by the PLAN, which was discovered to have added military posts to the reef in February 1995. [57] This was the first time China and an ASEAN member had ever come into direct military conflict. As Acharya noted, ASEAN had been hopeful that China would be willing to use such pressure only against Vietnam, based on past enmity. The fact that a Philippine claim was targeted, and bearing in mind that Manila maintained one of ASEAN's weaker militaries, scotched that assumption. However, China attempted to achieve a settlement by advocating that the dispute be settled through negotiation and joint research in the Spratlys, [58] but enthusiasm for this initiative has been muted in southeast Asia amid lingering questions of Chinese motives. Ambiguity on the subject of addressing the Spratlys issue appears to be the preferred method of both the Chinese government and the military, and neither actor has tied the same level of nationalistic importance to the islands as they have to Taiwan. [59]

During the 1990s, China's stand on the Spratlys did soften somewhat. Before that time, the security situation in Asia would have been more favourable for China to press its claims to the region through force. Beijing's main rival in the region, Vietnam, was weakened and still diplomatically isolated, the ASEAN states still needed China to bring about a satisfactory end to the Cambodia problem, and China was still very much in American favour as a counterweight to the USSR. Indeed, it was suggested that these factors might have made Chinese actions to solidify its role on the islets very likely. [60] However, as the cold war ended, these windows of opportunity closed one by one, and both the United States and southeast Asia are far more wary of potential Chinese military activity in the South China Sea, making a direct annexation of the islands far more risky for Beijing.

Thus, rather than bring its policies into direct conflict with ASEAN, China has opted to continue pursuing the policy of *gezhi zhengyi gongtong kaifa*, or 'putting the disputes aside and working toward joint development' of the region. [61] China did warily agree to place Spratly-related issues on the ARF agenda, but it rebuffed any attempts at binding negotiations through the ARF, accepting only small concessions such as the right of passage though Chinese-claimed areas and agreeing to Indonesia's claim to Natuna Island, north-west of Borneo in the South China Sea, while maintaining that both the Paracels and the Spratlys are Chinese territory. [62] For China, the ARF is not a welcome locale in which to discuss 'joint development' of the region, because unlike the issue of the Paracels, Chinese administration of the Spratlys is hardly a closed issue. At present, Beijing lacks the political will, not to mention the military means, to press its claim on the archipelago, and the ASEAN disputants have not been compelled to scale down their own claims there.

By the mid-1990s, China began to use the ARF as a face-saving means by sufficiently altering its overall Spratly policies to appear more accommodating on the issue. In 1995 Beijing used the annual ARF gathering to announce that it would be willing to use the United Nations Convention on the Law of the Sea (UNCLOS) as a baseline for future negotiations on the final status of the South China Sea, rather than pressing its historical claims placing the Chinese in a better position to claim the islets.[63] The Chinese government also demonstrated its willingness to 'work around' South China Sea matters, as evidenced by Beijing's full support in a 1997 China-ASEAN joint communiqué of ASEAN's policy of promoting a 'zone of peace, freedom and neutrality' (ZOPFAN) and a 'nuclear weapons free zone' (NWFZ) in southeast Asia. In return, ASEAN confirmed its continued support of the 'one China' policy in the same document.[64]

China, today, is more willing to place South China Sea questions on the forum's agenda, reflecting its greater comfort level with the ARF and its version of multilateral problem-solving. In November 2002, China and ASEAN signed a declaration in Phnom Penh, which outlined a code of conduct for all parties in the South China Sea, stressing the need for adherence to international law, peaceful dispute settlement, and joint cooperation on research, combating transnational crime and maritime security. All parties agreed to restrain themselves from engaging in provocative activities, such as occupying any uninhabited islands, which could again inflame tensions.[65]

The Phnom Penh accord is a strong step towards reducing regional tension over the issue of South China Sea sovereignty. The issue is still not resolved however, since as one Chinese military expert noted, Chinese claims to the region long predate the current regime in Beijing, and no government in Beijing wishes to risk appearing weak in the face of externally based challenges to Chinese state sovereignty.[66] This is especially true in such a delicate period, as a new government in Beijing attempts to set foreign policy. Thus, both Taiwan and South China Sea issues have the potential to create a serious deadlock within future regional security dialogues unless all sides strive to find a common ground upon which to successfully address these strategic matters.

Perception shift

It must be acknowledged that China's decision to participate in the ARF was a notable departure both from traditional foreign policy preferences for bilateral linkages (especially in matters related to security) and from a longstanding aversion to committing the country to a formal strategic regime. As Wang correctly pointed out, Communist China was among the first countries to be the target of multilateral security initiatives via an alliance, namely during the Korean War, after the People's Republic was named as an aggressor state by the United Nations and became subject to global ostracism and a damaging embargo.[67] With this in mind, it is little wonder that Maoist China had a fear of such multilateral security initiatives, and frequently branded them imperialist in nature and tools of the dominant great powers.

Dislike and distrust of 'alliances', which to the Maoist Chinese government were indistinguishable from any multilateral security initiatives, was a common theme of Mao's foreign policy, most notably in his critiques of the SEATO process in the 1950s, which he once denigrated as 'running counter to the trend of history'.[68] Peaceful coexistence, rather than alliances based on military agreements, dominated the traditional Chinese view of multilateralism, and vestiges of this thinking marked Chinese policy long after the passing of Mao in 1976. Another problem China had with multilateral security was that such regimes were seen by Beijing as requiring a specific enemy against which to align.[69] After the Sino-Soviet split in the 1960s, China was anxious to pursue a more independent policy between the two super-powers, and after the fall of the Soviet Union, Beijing wished to preserve that independence by rebuffing closer cooperation with Western alliances such as NATO.

Nevertheless, the end of the cold war did result in a thaw of sorts in China's perceptions of strategic multilateralism in Asia. In the late 1980s and early 1990s, Beijing stood with the other four permanent members of the UN Security Council in their drive to produce a lasting peace in Cambodia, and China was also present at the pivotal 1989 Paris Conference which called for the removal of foreign troops from Cambodian soil and the holding of free elections.[70] Beijing also hosted a conference which confirmed Prince Sihanouk as the head of the Supreme National Council, the preliminary government which would assume power before the holding of a supervised vote.[71] Such actions demonstrated China's desire not only to sever its relationship with the Khmer Rouge, a major obstacle to improved China-southeast Asian ties, but also to play a positive, cooperative role in ending the long cycle of warfare in Cambodia. In addition, China was not only willing to support a UN peacekeeping force to create a milieu suitable for free Cambodian elections, but also provided financial support and military personnel in the form of observers and engineers for that mission.[72]

During the 1990s, China also agreed to provide military observers to other UN operations in the Middle East and Africa.[73] During 1999–2000, after violence in the breakaway Indonesian province of East Timor (now the independent state of Timor Leste) was halted by a cease-fire, Beijing took the extraordinary step of supporting and participating in a United Nations peacekeeping operation there, despite the fact that the longstanding Timorese drive for independence was a clear example of the same 'splittism' which China had in the past argued was a challenge to international order. Gill and Reilly noted that Beijing's change of heart may have stemmed from the proximity of the disputed zone to China, and the need to provide a response to anti-Chinese violence in Indonesia which took place sporadically during the 1990s. Unlike the NATO operations in Kosovo in 1999 to which Beijing strongly objected, the Timor operation was wholly overseen by the United Nations, offering China a prominent role and therefore greater visibility in the process.[74]

China has experienced an opening-up to the prospects of multilateral security over the past decade, provided Chinese core interests are not directly challenged. This policy change has been especially visible since 9/11, as China has given its support to the international war on terrorism and American operations in Afghanistan, and has tolerated the ongoing American military presence in central Asia. As questions persist as to whether terrorism would continue to pose an international security threat, Beijing has begun to acknowledge a clear difference between 'positive' and 'negative' strategic intervention depending on specific circumstances.

Such new thinking on China's part has been reflected in its relations with the ARF. Finnegan correctly noted that participation in the forum by China (and the United States) runs counter to realist thinking which suggests that institutions tend to reflect the policies of great powers, and that these powers will only participate if they are certain to receive relative gains in comparison to other actors.[75] Waltz, in explaining the development and perpetuation of institutions, also explained that such regimes survive 'as long as they serve the major interests of their creators, or are thought to do so', their creators invariably being great powers.[76] However, neither the United States nor China has argued for a leadership role for themselves within the ARF, instead preferring to let the middle powers in ASEAN take the lead. Why then has China, as a great power, maintained a high level of enthusiasm and support for this organisation despite not having the loudest voice? The answer can be found by examining the contributions the ARF makes to Chinese power in exchange for Beijing's support.

First, there was the post-cold war security situation in China's periphery which presented Beijing with the opportunity to take advantage of a 'peace dividend' in the form of a relaxed strategic situation with no clear state-based security threats. Therefore, the perceived costs and risks of institutional cooperation were lowered after the cold war. For example, Lampton explained China's opening to multilateral organisations like the ARF as a product of improving relations with the West, and a reduction in overall tensions on the international level, as well as growing encouragement from the developing world. On the domestic level, he added, Beijing greatly desired a reduction in defence expenditures to assist with economic restructuring.[77] Such reductions also reflected Beijing's drive to reform the Chinese armed forces focusing less on strength of numbers and more on modern weaponry and high technology. On a broader scale, a cornerstone of China's post-cold war foreign policy was the encouragement of a stable periphery by which to create an improved atmosphere for China's socio-economic modernisation.

Second, China has recognised that modern security problems have become very difficult to address unilaterally with any degree of success and for any duration. Nor can bilateral talks be sufficient to address these sorts of non-traditional strategic issues which have affected the Asia-Pacific as whole.[78] As Evans noted, 'repeated statements of benign intent by Chinese officials, invocations of the 'five principles of peaceful coexistence' and even concrete steps by Beijing to improve bilateral relations with most of its Asian neighbours are increasingly ineffective in meeting international concerns.'[79]

As China's 2000 Defence White Paper noted, Beijing perceives the ARF's main value as an incubator for regional confidence-building measures (CBMs), defined as policies dedicated to reducing tensions between actors through information exchange and mutual assurances, and as a means to examine new security concepts and the preventive security options. The white paper added that China has pushed for regional cooperation within the ARF framework in the areas of military medicine and law, and the conversion of military technologies for civilian use, and has attended meetings on areas such as peacekeeping, maritime security, emergency rescue, and CBMs.[80] China has also been supportive of more recent initiatives in the areas of preventive diplomacy (working to defuse a crisis before it leads to violence), as well as more non-traditional security issues which Beijing itself has had to address, namely illegal drugs, smuggling and the transportation of illegal immigrants.[81] All of these matters, Beijing has determined, can be addressed with the highest efficacy through regional multilateralism.

Third, Chinese participation in the ARF, according to Beijing, is based on a broader policy of adopting a 'phased approach' to Asian regional security, while cognisant of 'regional conditions', meaning the political, social and economic diversity of the Asia-Pacific region. The Chinese government insisted that a security regime be of equal value to all members, that the security of other actors not be diminished by a regime, and that no actor should attempt to build strategic superiority via the creation of a regime.[82] Therefore, the structure of the ARF, led primarily by ASEAN but with no dominating members, is, for China, an ideal institution in which to participate while maintaining these foreign policies. These tenets are compatible with Beijing's 'five principles of peaceful coexistence'. Although the principles have been a staple of Chinese foreign policy since Maoist times, Beijing has reinvigorated them in the post-cold war international order, one which was becoming increasingly dominated by instances of humanitarian intervention and challenges to the absoluteness of state sovereignty.[83] Thus, cooperation with ASEAN using these principles of non-interference as a baseline is mutually beneficial since it offers a stronger counterweight to the more interventionist Western forms of strategic cooperation.

Fourth, on a regional level, China has placed a great deal of emphasis over the past decade on repairing and strengthening its relationships with the strategically important ASEAN nations. During China's period of isolation, the country was widely regarded among ASEAN members as, at best, an adversary, and at worst, a serious security threat to southeast Asia. After ASEAN's founding, the original six members were divided on how best to approach an emerging China following its foreign policy opening in the 1970s. Three ASEAN members opted to swiftly recognise the People's Republic (Malaysia in 1974 and the Philippines and Thailand the following year),[84] but the other three (Brunei, Indonesia, and Singapore) declined. Relations with Jakarta were a considerable sticking point in the wake of the attempted communist coup in Indonesia in 1965 which led to the suspension of relations with Beijing two years later. Chinese support for the brutal Khmer Rouge regime between 1975 and its ouster by Vietnamese forces in 1978 was also looked upon as damaging regional interference by surrounding states. Despite the Khmer Rouge's claims to advocate national self-sufficiency, China was actually instrumental in supporting the regime in Phnom Penh through trade and economic assistance.[85]

In addition, Beijing was accused of supporting militant opposition forces in southeast Asia, most notably in Thailand and Malaysia, and sowing discord by claiming that overseas Chinese populations in the region were under Beijing's authority. Both of these policies were scrapped by the 1990s, when the Chinese government ceased advocating 'party-to-party' relations with southeast Asian communist groups, and dropped any authority claims over its expatriat populations.[86] By the beginning of that decade, China had begun redeveloping itself as a partner in the region rather than a destabilising force.

The diplomatic impasse between Beijing and ASEAN did not end until August 1990, when ties were re-established following months of lower-level negotiations after the Suharto government in Jakarta faced mounting pressure from its business communities to take advantage of China's modernising economy. This paved the way for Chinese relations to be formalised with Singapore (October 1990) and Brunei (September 1991).[87] However, expatriat Chinese populations in southeast Asia remained a source of friction, especially in Malaysia and Indonesia, largely due to the disproportionate wealth they possessed in relation to local ethnic groups, and the result being periodic anti-Chinese riots.[88] The most recent such incident took place during the ouster of Indonesian President Suharto in May 1998, when many Chinese business interests were attacked during anti-government riots, and both Beijing and Taipei issued formal complaints.[89] However, the fact that China restrained itself from taking any action beyond verbal protests signalled Beijing's intention to avoid direct interference in regional domestic affairs.

Toward the end of the 1990s, the whole of ASEAN was again examining Beijing with increased anxiety, based on the perceived growth of Chinese military and political power and the fact that the pullout of Vietnamese forces from Cambodia meant the loss of a major issue unifying ASEAN and Chinese interests.[90] This motivated ASEAN states to include China in an evolving regional security structure which became the ARF. While China has been largely successful in developing stronger ties with ASEAN, not only with the ARF but also via economic agreements such as APEC, these relations are still relatively new and therefore quite fragile. In addition to the South China Sea issue, other potential sticking points, such as lingering questions about Beijing's opaque defence policies and increased economic competition between China and southeast Asia, still have the potential of adversely affecting the relationship.[91] Therefore, the regional information exchange available to China via these institutions is certainly not trivial for Beijing.

Since the early 1990s, Beijing has been concerned with dispelling concerns in east and southeast Asia that China's political, economic, and military development would become a threat to the region. Such concerns, it was feared, would provide the impetus for closer strategic ties between Washington and Tokyo, and might also lead to a regional body designed to check Chinese growth. ARF participation, therefore, served to bolster China's insistence that it had no desire to become a military threat to its neighbours.[92] Although such assurances have not completely alleviated these regional concerns, the use of a multilateral forum to attempt to dispel such perceptions was seen to yield greater results than acting unilaterally.

Finally, the ARF also has great importance to Chinese strategic interests on a more international level, since the regime has the ability to promote forms of security cooperation favoured by Beijing, while contributing to the dampening of other forms of security cooperation which China does not want to see come about in its periphery, namely alliances. Since the end of the cold war, China, as the largest of the remaining 'communist' states, has become increasingly sensitive to any moves by the West, particularly the United States, to either isolate it diplomatically or to otherwise curtail its continued opening to the international system. Beijing, well aware of the 'containment' policies Washington attempted to use towards weakening the Soviet Union, is concerned that the same tactic of building walls of American-friendly states around an adversary might be used on China as well.

Of even greater concern to Beijing, however, is the possibility of a regional military alliance being set up around China, perhaps to counter Chinese military and political growth. Swaine and Tellis pointed to this factor as the main reason why China overcame its original scepticism of the ARF and agreed to participate and then deepen its involvement. However, they also frame China's decision to join the forum as a 'constrained choice', since Beijing was concerned that by opting out, the ARF would form joint policies which would be detrimental to Chinese foreign policy.[93] It is not clear, however, to what degree this form of 'loss avoidance' played a role in China's engagement with the ARF, nor is it clear that fear of isolation, or being the victim of countries balancing against it, was the determining factor, as they imply, in China reconsidering ARF participation. A counter-argument can be made that, rather than simply avoiding a negative, China saw a way of turning a potential negative into a positive.

China's concerns about eventually being faced with counter-alliances are not abstract. The two examples of possible adversarial alliances are the 'theatre missile defence' (TMD) initiative, and more recently the so-called 'Four-Party Group', both of which only began to coalesce in the late 1990s. The US-led TMD initiative was proposed during the waning years of the Clinton administration and moved much closer to reality via field tests ordered by Clinton's Republican successor, George W. Bush. The idea of 'missile defence' in the United States is based on the perception that it is possible to negate the threat of incoming enemy missiles by destroying them in mid-flight, either with an intercepting projectile or by the use of a laser-based system to eliminate incoming missiles at a safe distance. This system could be deployed to service a particular area to assist allied nations, acting as an offshoot of 'national missile defence' (NMD), used to protect the home country, namely US territory.

Beijing has made no secret of its unwavering opposition to any kind of TMD development, and Chinese Ambassador for Disarmament, Sha Zukang, in explaining why such an initiative would weaken regional security rather than strengthen it, likened the concept to 'drinking poison to quench one's thirst.'[94] China's objections to TMD are threefold. First and foremost, despite American assurances that TMD could only be workable against a handful of incoming missiles, China is concerned that its own small missile stockpile could be rendered ineffective by a regional theatre missile defence. At present, Beijing has approximately 30 *Dongfeng*-5 (DF) intercontinental ballistic missiles and about 110 intermediate-range missiles (DF-3, DF-4, and DF-21).[95] A workable TMD system could greatly reduce China's offensive missile capabilities, increasing Chinese insecurities and prompting Beijing to develop countermeasures.

Second, the development of such a system would spark serious international legal ramifications which are of great concern in China. The Anti-Ballistic Missile (ABM) Treaty, signed in 1972 between the United States and the Soviet Union, severely restricts the development of missile defence systems. However, the development of improved missile technology in the developing world produced calls in the United States to alter the ABM Treaty to pave the way for a workable NMD and TMD regime. China has insisted that the treaty remain intact, due to its role in limiting international proliferation and promoting global stability. In light of India and Pakistan's forced entrance into the nuclear club after both states tested nuclear weapons in 1998, China grew increasingly concerned that norms and practices preventing the proliferation of weapons of mass destruction were fraying, and the American development of missile defence platforms was seen by Beijing as further erosion of these norms.

Washington issued a statement in December 2001 announcing the withdrawal of the United States from the ABM Treaty, an announcement which was met with restrained, but still critical, reactions in Beijing.[96] Moreover, Beijing's hopes that Moscow would continue to take its side in opposing the American withdrawal, especially after China, Russia and their central Asian allies issued a joint declaration decrying TMD development in the Asia-Pacific region in 1999, were dashed. A wedge was driven between Beijing and Moscow on missile defence after Russia's President Putin received assurances from Washington that the US was unable and unwilling to neutralise the still-formidable Russian nuclear arsenal through a TMD system, and as a result the Putin government's reaction to the American ABM Treaty withdrawal was muted.[97] Although issues such as the war on terrorism and security in Korea have brought China and America closer together diplomatically, this issue remains a potential sore point between the two powers.

Third, the United States has advocated the inclusion of Japan, and perhaps South Korea, in any regional missile defence regime. If such a system were to be deployed in east Asia, there remains the possibility that Taiwan could also be a beneficiary, strengthening domestic pressure in Taipei for independence.[98] Not only would the creation of a TMD group greatly damage Chinese sovereignty in the eyes of Beijing, but these partners could comprise a 'stealth' alliance against China.[99]

A second possible alliance, the 'Four-Party' group, also colloquially referred to as the 'little NATO' or the 'Pacific NATO', is even less defined than a possible

TMD alliance, but nevertheless is seen by Beijing as a possible harbinger of an anti-China coalition in the Asia-Pacific. Although the idea of a US-led regional security alliance in east Asia has its origins at least as far back as the failed SEATO initiative, renewed concerns were raised in Beijing in July 2001, during a visit by American governmental and military officials to Canberra, when discussions began concerning the building of closer military linkages between four states with complementary regional strategic policies, namely the United States, Japan, South Korea and Australia. Despite initial assurances that such a grouping would be informal, a commentary in the *Beijing Review* in September 2001 accused Australia of supporting the initiative out of fear of Chinese growth and power, as well as 'catering to the appetite of the US hawk.' America was portrayed as attempting to sow regional discord by transforming its bilateral ties in the Pacific Rim into a multilateral body which would 'change the military pattern of the Asia-Pacific region and produce more crises there'.[100]

Beijing has been concerned with advocating non-alliance based strategic cooperation via the ARF and other informal regimes. Three points worked in China's favour. First, many ARF participants were anxious to include China in the organisation, recognising it as a strong and indispensable actor in improving regional security relations. Second, the ARF was slow to coalesce and lacked a clear mandate, and would therefore be more open to the introduction of policies more favourable to the Chinese viewpoint. Third, after Tiananmen in 1989, and in the wake of international praise following Beijing's non-interference in US-led preparations leading up the Gulf War, Beijing was anxious to revive its push for improved political relations with north and southeast Asia. In short, through the ARF, China had the opportunity not only to make it more difficult for an anti-China alliance to be formed, but also to fortify valuable ties with neighbours and to advocate such ties based on shared interests rather than alliances.

For the present, the ARF is also attractive to China largely due to the lack of available alternatives to multilateral dialogue. Despite the progress which China has made in improving relations with its neighbours, Beijing is still far from able to construct security institutions under its own aegis. As one analyst noted, although China does attempt to address its own power projection weaknesses by attempting to establish links with other states based on concern about American and Western dominance, one major obstacle is that, unlike the West, China has little to offer in terms of material rewards for closer security cooperation.[101]

Beijing views its immediate surroundings facing different sorts of security challenges than during the cold war era. There is no identifiable state enemy in China's view, and a majority of the post-cold war security issues deal with non-traditional threats, including terrorism. Therefore, 'alliances' in the cold war sense are perceived by Beijing as useless and detrimental to peacebuilding efforts in the Asia-Pacific, since they increase the security of some at the expense of the rest.[102] Chinese participation in the ARF therefore acts as a more visible extension of this policy and as a means by which to advertise the preferences of a strategic institution based on dialogue and consensus rather than creating new alignments to replace the old.

For example, the ARF was used as a springboard for the announcement of China's new alternative to the alliance structure when then-foreign minister Qian Qichen announced his country's 'New Security Concept' (NSC) at the Forum's March 1997 meeting.[103] The NSC, and its numerous updates, states that in addition to the Five Principles, China supports confidence-building measures, mutual trust and understanding, and flexible cooperation as methods of addressing modern security problems, including the war on terrorism. The NSC also extends into the area of economic security, encouraging all countries to further open their markets to each other and work to remove inequalities and discrimination in the spirit of enhanced cooperation.[104] The ARF has provided China with a valuable sounding board, as well as a model for the development and advertisement of this 'new thinking'.

Another, possibly more groundbreaking, initiative which China has launched via the forum is its proposal to create an ARF Security Policy Conference (ASPC) which would address challenges to regional security, future areas of security cooperation and joint actions against terrorism. More significantly, the paper also advocated discussions of the security and military strategies of ARF members, military modernisation, defence industry conversion and technology and civil-military relations.[105] These ideas were circulated at an ARF Inter-Sessional Support Group on Confidence-Building Measures in Beijing in November 2003, and were then incorporated into the main ARF meeting in Jakarta in July 2004. The first ASPC meeting took place in Beijing later that year, with annual meetings to follow.[106] Considering Beijing's traditional hostility towards multilateral talks on military transparency, this is a remarkable policy shift on China's part and represents one more example of that country's greater understanding of the importance of international regimes in solving security problems.

Beijing's newfound interest in taking a more active role in multilateral strategic negotiations has not been limited to regional-level issues. One sub-regional issue, albeit one with great international implications in which China has also increased its level of participation, has been the sporadic but ongoing, talks to remove a possible nuclear threat from the Democratic People's Republic of Korea (DPRK). Although not a new issue, as North Korea's nuclear development first gained international attention in the early 1990s, the country's attempts to restart its nuclear programme in late 2002, and the difficult diplomacy which followed, presented both difficulties and opportunities for China.

China and the Korean nuclear crisis

Beijing's increasing legerdemain within multilateral security initiatives has been further enhanced by its participation in the various negotiations designed to end the crisis created by North Korea in the wake of Pyongyang's October 2002 admission that it was once again developing nuclear weapons capabilities, in defiance of the 1994 Agreed Framework between the United States and the DPRK. Under that agreement, North Korea promised it would dismantle its nuclear weapons programme and allow for full international inspections of its nuclear facilities in exchange for two light-water reactors and a series of fuel oil shipments from the United States, Japan and South Korea.[107] The agreement had been supported by Beijing as a suitable compromise to end the crisis, and behaved in a fashion which one American official called the 'smiling dragon' approach.[108]

News of Pyongyang's defiance resurrected the prospect of a nuclear DPRK capable of destabilising the delicate security arrangement throughout east Asia. Since the 1990s, when advancements in North Korea's nuclear programme first came to light, there has been speculation that should Pyongyang develop nuclear weapons and the means to deliver them, nearby states such as Japan and South Korea would have little choice but to develop nuclear weapons capabilities of their own, setting off a 'fire-chain' scenario which northeast Asia, including China, would not want. At the same time, Pyongyang's actions undermined South Korea's 'sunshine policy' of diplomacy towards the North which had begun optimistically in 1997.[109]

Moreover, the North Korean admission that it was reneging on the 1994 accord came at a time when US foreign policy under George W. Bush appeared to be hardening against the DPRK's Kim Jong-Il regime. This was evidenced by the US president's controversial January 2002 State of the Union Address, where he identified North Korea, along with Iran and Iraq under Saddam Hussein, as parts of an 'axis of evil'. China was among other international actors who questioned the validity of those remarks, noting that the three countries were not allied with each other and that such a statement distracted from the more pressing problem of international terrorism.[110]

China's policy towards the DPRK shifted considerably during the 1990s as a result of Beijing's expanded Asian diplomacy and increased political and economic ties with Pyongyang's rivals, including Japan and South Korea. Although China remains North Korea's most important ally in the region, Beijing has attempted to take a more balanced approach to security on the peninsula. Moreover, while China has raced ahead with economic reforms, North Korea remains isolated and mired in a command economy which has become increasingly unworkable, resulting in shortages and famine crises since the early 1990s. The increasing disparities in politics, ideology, economics and foreign policy between the two countries have changed a once solid relationship, often referred to as 'lips and teeth' during the cold war, to one of increasing wariness.

By the beginning of 2003, North Korea had removed seals and monitoring equipment on its Yongbyon nuclear reactor and announced it was withdrawing from the Nuclear Non-Proliferation Treaty, thus giving the country a legal green light to develop nuclear weapons. Adding to the tensions were two missile tests which the DPRK conducted in February and March 2003 in the Sea of Japan and the intercepting of an American reconnaissance plane, also in March.[111] The United

States expressed escalating levels of displeasure of North Korea's provocative actions, and halted shipments of fuel oil to the DPRK. However, as the Bush administration was occupied with the looming invasion of Iraq and had little diplomatic leverage with which to coerce Pyongyang into halting its nuclear weapons capability, Beijing found itself pushed to the forefront of the crisis.

Since the end of the cold war, China became the only major power with the ability to directly influence North Korea, largely due to the fact that Pyongyang remains heavily dependent on Chinese aid and fuel transfers to prop up its stubbornly Stalinist economy.[112] The post-October 2002 events in North Korea created a serious conundrum for Beijing. China has no more desire to see North Korea develop nuclear weapons than it did in 1993 during the previous nuclear crisis. Beijing's position on North Korean nuclear weapons is that they would threaten not only Pyongyang's continued existence, but would also constitute a hindrance to Sino-American relations and potential future threat to China itself.[113] Moreover, should North Korea go nuclear, it would be very difficult for its neighbours, especially Japan, South Korea and possibly Taiwan, to resist the nuclear option as well.

However, China and North Korea have a shared ideological history, and Beijing does not want to see Pyongyang collapse, an outcome which may lead to civil war, a refugee crisis, and increased Western military involvement next to a sensitive Chinese border. In addition, China has repeatedly stated its strong opposition to any military solution to North Korean aggressiveness.[114] Indeed, any use of force against Pyongyang would carry with it a very high risk of dragging in most of the powers of northeast Asia. The United States, which was embroiled in military operations in Afghanistan and preparing for a strike against Iraq which commenced in March 2003, also opted for a diplomatic solution to Pyongyang's intransigence and as a result, American and Chinese preferences converged and Beijing was given a larger role in addressing the crisis. The start of the Iraq war contributed to an increased sense of urgency in both China and North Korea to address the nuclear issue, since both states were concerned that once Baghdad was dealt with by US-led forces the DPRK might be a future target of American military intervention.[115]

Since the beginning of the second North Korean nuclear crisis Beijing has advocated a diplomatic solution, and has tried to provide a forum for regional negotiation as well as a conduit between North Korea and other concerned parties, namely the United States, South Korea, Japan and Russia. The first China-hosted meetings between American and DPRK officials in April 2003 not only ended poorly, but were marred by a North Korean admission that the country had already begun the reprocessing of more than 8,000 spent nuclear fuel rods. However, this statement was later proven incorrect due to a translation error, and in fact Pyongyang had only announced that it was close to the stage where it could begin the reprocessing.[116] North Korea made it clear that its nuclear weapons development programme would only be shelved in exchange for full diplomatic relations with the United States and considerable economic assistance, a compromise which Washington remained unwilling to make.

After much negotiation, North Korea accepted an invitation to what would become the first round of Six-Party Talks (SPT) hosted by Beijing and with representatives from both the Koreas, China, the United States, Japan and Russia. However, various pressures from China were instrumental in Pyongyang's return to the table, including a three-day shutdown of an oil pipeline between the two countries in February 2003. Beijing claimed that the halting was the result of an accident but the incident was viewed by many observers as a warning shot aimed at Pyongyang, designed to convince the Kim Jong-Il government to enter into negotiations.[117] In another arm-twisting move, Beijing announced in September of that year that People's Armed Police forces near the DPRK border would be replaced by as many as 150,000 PLA military personnel. Although the move was seen by many as a way for Beijing to address the increasingly troublesome problem of North Korean refugees slipping over the border into China, the military deployment also signalled an overall stronger tone with Pyongyang.[118]

In addition to pressuring North Korea to accept multilateral talks, Beijing also engaged in intense shuttle diplomacy, as demonstrated in July 2003 with Deputy Foreign Minister Dai Bingguo's frequent trips between Pyongyang and Washington in order to keep the negotiation process alive.[119] The United States was unwilling to accede to Pyongyang's demands for bilateral talks, so the best solution for China was to recommend a multilateral process. All of these events underscored the fact that Beijing was no longer going to remain aloof from North Korea's nuclear brinksmanship, and instead was determined to play an active, positive role in solving the issue via negotiations.

The first SPT in August 2003 produced few results save for an agreement to continue the talks and an affirmation that a nuclear-free Korean peninsula should be achieved while ensuring its security.[120] In the wake of a North Korean concession to allow a group of American experts to visit the Yongbyon site in January 2004, a second SPT meeting in Beijing was held the following month, but again produced no breakthroughs. A third Beijing SPT event took place in June 2004 with more tangible results. An offer was unveiled by the United States in the name of breaking the diplomatic impasse to allow North Korea to again receive fuel oil shipments in exchange for Pyongyang's dismantling of its nuclear programme and a resumption of inspections under a specific timetable. Washington also agreed to provide a 'provisional' assurance that the United States would not invade North Korea nor seek regime change by toppling its government.[121]

Although the Six-Party Talks have thus far not resulted in a satisfactory resolution to the North Korean nuclear crisis, China's willingness to play a strong role in the negotiations coupled with its ability to coerce Pyongyang into making concessions and remaining at the bargaining table, has made it an indispensable actor in the diplomatic process. The development of the SPT further demonstrates the increasing importance to China of the multilateral approach to international-level problem solving, while simultaneously demonstrating China's commitment to security cooperation based on consensus and confidence-building rather than formal regime-building.

Conclusions: the sociable dragon?

By continuing to support the ARF, which is and will likely remain, informal, non-binding and inclusive in the near-term, China hopes to further develop its regional strategic relations, and to deflect and deter the rise of other security institutions which may prove detrimental to Chinese strategic interests. However, the greatest challenges for the ARF, especially in the areas of border disputes and terrorism issues are still to come, and China will continue to be a determining factor in many of them. Shifts in military, political and economic power will continue in east and southeast Asia, likely resulting in China gaining more relative power than its surrounding neighbours. As a result, many multilateral relationships will be tested as China continues to weigh the benefits of cooperation versus the risks of surrendering too much of its sovereignty to international institutions. Much will depend not only on China's evolving foreign policy under the Hu Jintao government, but also on the actions taken by other ARF members (the United States, Japan and ASEAN), in pursuing their own interests in the Asia-Pacific.

Another test of the China-ARF relationship will take place as the ARF continues to deepen its mandate as a response to modern security challenges. Deepening the ARF would involve many changes, including the inclusion of more sensitive issues, such as the South China Sea, in some form onto the ARF agenda. There is also the question of whether the forum will develop a more structured framework, perhaps even developing into a formal security community. This prospect is no longer as daunting to Beijing as it was in the 1990s, as demonstrated by China's ASPC recommendation. With Chinese relations with its neighbours at very cordial levels, Beijing now has a great deal of self-assurance which it has used to pursue its security interests in the Asia-Pacific region through institutional cooperation and multilateral dialogues, while at the same time discouraging the development of alliances which would place China in a more defensive position. Also, after a decade of engagement with the ARF and other regional security institutions, Beijing is now more confident both in proposing new security initiatives and participating more fully in existing ones. In short, China's engagement of security institutions is increasingly echoing the behaviour of a conservative great power, rather than as a revisionist spoiler.

Potential Asian security pitfalls still remain, including the war on terrorism, the Taiwan Straits, Korea, and outstanding border disputes. Fortunately, a growing number of governmental and sub-governmental mechanisms are developing in the region to address them. At present, China shows no outward signs of displeasure with the increasing Asia-Pacific multilateral security dialogues such as the ARF and Six-Party Talks. Rather, Beijing's view of these regimes is that they serve as necessary tools not only for addressing post-cold war security challenges, but also for furthering Chinese aims of building a stable and peaceful periphery. The fact that China is willing to continue its cooperation with the ARF despite that body's weaknesses, and even to take the lead in other strategic talks such as the SPT and a nascent ASPC, illustrates the importance of China's evolving institutional relations, linkages which are necessary for Beijing to grow wiser to the ways of how such institutions can increase Chinese power and prestige within the international system.

4

LABYRINTH'S EDGE

China and the Shanghai Cooperation Organisation

> Do not drive the tiger from the front door, while letting the wolf
> get in the back.
>
> Hu Zhidang, Han Dynasty

China regards Eurasia

China's brief history of engagement with security regimes began with a highly conservative approach to multilateral cooperation as Beijing endeavoured to craft a new strategic policy to reflect the end of the cold war and its own changing security needs. However, since the mid-1990s this approach has subtly changed to reflect growing maturity and confidence allowing Beijing to more actively and effectively pursue its own goals within international security institutions. Moreover, as China continues to make adjustments to its New Security Concept (NSC), the country is finding new methods of developing its policy experiment on regional security approaches while addressing a growing security concern on its western frontier. While relations between China and Russia have warmed considerably since the early 1990s, other parts of the former Soviet Union, namely the central Asian republics, have presented new and unique challenges for Chinese security. Beijing's response has been to be the driving force behind the development of the Shanghai Cooperation Organisation (SCO) in June 2001.

The SCO, formerly known as the 'Shanghai Five', was a group uniting China with its old adversary, Russia, and the former Soviet republics of Kazakhstan, Kyrgyzstan, and Tajikistan. This organisation was created out of bilateral agreements in the late 1990s between China and the former Soviet republics in an effort to define their borders and strengthen security along their long and remote mutual frontier. As a result of Uzbekistan's membership in 2001 and the group's increased formalisation, the renamed SCO has grown well beyond its original mandate, and currently examines other security issues, including the problems of terrorism and separatism, while investigating other outlets to greater regional cooperation.

The demise of the Soviet Union has produced a new and distinct security dynamic for central Asia; a region, today, still attempting to define itself after the shock of sudden independence. The Russian Federation had to make similar adjustments, adapting to a transition from superpower to tenuous great power. Central Asia has become an increasingly important part of the world not only for China, but also for numerous other international actors. This, as a result of the region's proven and potential energy supplies, its prominent role in the war on terrorism after the 9/11 terrorist bombings and American-led military operations in nearby Afghanistan. The presence of American forces in central Asia since 2001 has the potential to alter the balance of power throughout a region which has historically been subject to great power competition.

What makes the SCO distinct from the organisations previously discussed is that, in addition to the fact that China has played a prominent role – arguably a paramount role – in the organisation's development, and has made use of the group to advocate its own specific foreign policies in addition to those shared by the organisation as a whole, the SCO represents one of the first cases of China taking the lead to develop a regional regime. Moreover, the SCO has allowed China to refine and develop its NSC, multilateral security cooperation based on community building rather than formal alliances. Notwithstanding Beijing's comparative lack of experience in participating so fully in the shaping of a multilateral institution, China has succeeded in helping to develop the Shanghai group into a body which addresses strategic issues which Beijing could not reconcile unilaterally. The study of the SCO is therefore an essential test case for measuring current Chinese approaches to international-level security institutions.

Good fences make good neighbours: the origins of the 'Five'

Since the break-up of the USSR in 1992, the former Soviet republics in central Asia have become increasingly important in foreign policy calculations of the People's Republic of China. Since the early 1990s, China has attempted to increase its visibility in Asia by improving relations with its neighbours and seeking to mend fences with old adversaries such as Russia and Central Asia. However, Chinese engagement with the former Soviet central Asian republics has been marred by the rising number of strategic concerns in the region, including weak governments, secessionist forces, political and religious extremism and mounting concerns that an international rivalry may be developing over central Asia's abundant energy resources. Many of these issues directly affect both the domestic and foreign policies of China, and rather than remaining aloof from the challenges which central Asia presents, Beijing is opting for a policy of engagement, making use of its powerful position in the region to offer political and economic support in the hopes of creating an atmosphere of greater peace and stability.

The fall of the Soviet Union produced a handful of new states in central Asia, distinguished by small, often heterogeneous, populations and central governments largely left over from the Soviet era, which for the most part were ill-equipped for the rapid transition to independence. The original borders of the socialist republics in central Asia were delineated in Stalinist times, often purposefully ignoring the ethnic makeup of the region, resulting in nationalities split amongst different states. As such, a mix of ethnicities dominates the region, its cultures and its languages, often with little in common save for their mutual subaltern status within the USSR.[1] After the break-up, the central Asian governments had to build their new states largely from the top down. As with other regions emerging from forms of colonialism, the business of state building contained many elements of risk and the potential for great instability as these governments were forced to develop economies, infrastructure, and state identities within a very short timeframe.

However, central Asia has faced the additional problems of being very late developers, restructuring command economies which had previously been tied exclusively to Moscow. Even before the break-up, many of the central Asian republics suffered economically under the Soviet regime, and as a result a series of informal and sometimes illegal networks was created, leading to corruption and black markets. Many of these networks were based along ethnic or regional ties, and continued to be maintained even after the republics gained independence.[2] Despite the region's extensive energy resources, in the form of petroleum and natural gas reserves, as well as considerable mineral deposits, the region as a whole remains largely poor, with weak governments ill-prepared for free markets and globalisation. All of the central Asian republics suffered economic decline after 1992, save for Kazakhstan, due to its oil revenues, and attempts at socio-economic reform in the region have been either lethargic or, in the case of Turkmenistan and Uzbekistan, ossified.[3] Before the SCO was created there was also little regional cooperation, a factor which allowed China a freer hand in advocating the development of the Shanghai group, since it was one of the few areas in China's periphery lacking regimes which could compete for influence with China.

The underdeveloped nature of the central Asian republics has prompted their governments to retain varying degrees of authoritarianism in the hopes of 'catching up' to the mainstream world economy at a faster pace, echoing in some ways the 'developmental' policies which appeared decades ago in Taiwan and South Korea.[4] What separates the current political and economic reform policies of today's central Asia and yesterday's east Asia, however, is that in the former there are fewer avenues for financial development, a more isolated geographic locale, and instead of the American umbrella which benefited the east Asian 'dragons', central Asia must instead contend with different external actors vying for primarily economic gains. Although the American military presence in the region since 9/11 has provided a stabilising factor of sorts, US efforts in central Asia have been focused on anti-terrorism operations with little emphasis on internal problems of development.

Moreover, a majority of the leaders in the region are former communists with little experience in the intricacies of free market economics, and are therefore more vulnerable to the ravages of economic globalisation which has defined the post-cold war international system. Since the region is also heavily dependent on fossil fuels as its primary resource, there exists the considerable risk of 'rentierism' (becoming dependent on income, or 'rents', from external sources at the expense of capital for domestic taxation) which greatly hinders democratic development since governments are less dependent on taxes for sustainability. As has also been noted, governments heavily dependent on energy exports have the potential to use these funds to fortify their positions against dissent and to discourage the development of domestic actors which may favour further democracy.[5] Such conditions have already begun to develop in central Asia.

Contributing to the complex strategic situation in central Asia is Russia, which despite its decline in power remains a very formidable player, further complicating the still-evolving security milieu of the region since the administrations of Boris Yeltsin and Vladimir Putin in Moscow have periodically shown willingness to influence the affairs of other post-Soviet states in Russia's 'near abroad'. The question of Moscow's role is of special concern in central Asia, since that part of the former Soviet Union has been less successful in developing independent identities than, for example, the Baltic or Caucasus regions. Following independence, all the new states in Central Asia also retained strong economic and political linkages to Moscow.

Since the early 1990s although steps were taken to rebuild military hierarchies in the Central Asian republics and agreements were struck to coordinate regional strategic issues, insecurities still abound.[6] The successor organisation to the Soviet Union, the Commonwealth of Independent States (CIS) was originally conceived as the primary strategic institution in central Asia and the other Soviet successor states, save the Baltic nations. However, in the decade since its creation, that organisation accomplished little in coordinating regional security in central Asia, other than ensuring a continued Russian presence.[7] As a result, the 1990s was best defined as an institutional vacuum in Central Asia in strategic issues, economic and political areas.

The most important foreign policy task for the central Asian republics following independence was to cultivate new friends and allies to assist with their transition and economic and political development. In addition to Russia, other states with political or cultural ties to the region, such as Iran, Turkey and Pakistan, wanted to extend their influence over the politically uncertain region. The renewed competition for influence in central Asia gave rise to the now conventional thinking that a renewed 'Great Game', similar to the diplomatic scramble in the region at the beginning of the twentieth century, only with different players, had begun. For China, it was essential to avoid being left behind in the scramble during the 1990s to secure good relations in central Asia, especially in light of the region's borders on China's fragile and isolated western frontier. In addition to Russia, China's western border lies opposite Kazakhstan, Kyrgyzstan, and Tajikistan, as well as Afghanistan, India, and Pakistan (via the disputed territory of Kashmir).

China's far west, most notably the region of Xinjiang, with a population of about 19.3 million, counts Muslim peoples among its population who share similar ethnic backgrounds with populations in Central Asia. According to China's 2000 population census, the country's Muslim community makes up a very small percentage of the total population (about two per cent) but in absolute terms that translates to approximately 20.3 million persons. Islamic ethnicities within China include about 9.8 million Hui (an amorphous term relating to Muslims of largely Han Chinese extraction), 8.4 million ethnic Uyghurs, and 1.25 million Kazakhs, with smaller percentages of Dongxing, Kyrgyz, Salar, Tajik and Uzbek peoples.[8] The independence of the former central Asian republics has increased Beijing's sensitivity to separatist leanings within China's Muslim minority, and hastened the requirement for Beijing to recognise the new states and acknowledge their borders.

Two other reasons can be cited for the suddenness of Beijing's overtures to central Asia. First, China wished to continue the process of rebuilding its international linkages after the repercussions of Tiananmen Square in 1989. The former Soviet states provided rich diplomatic opportunities to demonstrate Beijing's commitment to regional peace and stability. Also, Beijing was determined not to allow Taiwan to gain a diplomatic beachhead in central Asia by cajoling the republics into recognising Taipei rather than the People's Republic.[9] The Chinese government was successful in that endeavour, as all of the central Asian states recognised one China with Beijing as the capital.

After taking this first step of recognition, China then approached the region with intentions of resolving the numerous border disputes inherited from the former USSR. Since the Sino-Soviet split in the early 1960s, protecting China's western border against Soviet encroachment was extremely taxing to the People's Liberation Army. As one Chinese scholar described it, the large amount of capital, personnel and material which needed to be diverted to the country's northwest in the 1970s and 1980s represented 'a heavy burden on our shoulders'.[10] It was estimated that by the mid-1980s about 500,000 Soviet Red Army forces were deployed near the Chinese border, while PLA forces in China's northern and western borders were numbered at between 800,000 and 1.5 million.[11] It was hoped that once the borders with Russia and other successor states could be legally demarcated, China could take advantage of warmer relations with Moscow and the new republics to begin a phased reduction of PLA forces.

The process began with proposals to reduce military forces on their mutual borders and ease trade restrictions through new travel linkages. The changes were especially profound for Kazakhstan, as China soon became the republic's second most important market for exports.[12] The economic opening between China and central Asia had begun even before the Soviet break-up, in the wake of the thaw between Moscow and Beijing during the late 1980s. Despite traditional mistrust between China and the peoples across its western border, a factor dating at least as far back as the building of the Great Wall, Beijing was committed to allaying any regional concerns that China would be a security threat to Central Asia.[13]

The promise of enhanced trade became China's most important carrot in the competition for influence in central Asia, as was shown by then-Premier Li Peng's successful tour of the region in 1994. During his visit to Uzbekistan, Li spoke candidly about recreating the old 'silk road' trade route through the region,[14] a message that was well-received throughout his travels. However, at the time of his visit, the sundering of the USSR was still very recent, and great care was taken during initial diplomatic contacts to avoid alienating Russia or to imply China was seeking a power base in the region to counter Moscow.[15]

Beijing was also largely successful in its bid to swiftly resolve outstanding border issues between it and three central Asian states. The Chinese government signed agreements with Kazakhstan which ratified their common borders in 1994, 1997 and 1998, and a final agreement with Bishkek, Kyrgyzstan which finalised the Sino–Kyrgyz frontier was signed in August 1999.[16] Talks on demarcating the Chinese boundary with Tajikistan in the Pamir region, a process complicated by the area's mountainous terrain, were finally completed in May 2002 after Dushanbe, Tajikistan, agreed to cede a thousand square kilometres of land in the Murgab District to China, a small percentage of the 28,000 km² which was originally under dispute.[17]

Another difficult security issue for China which required resolving ahead of closer Sino-central Asian linkages was the question of the leftover Soviet nuclear weapons stockpiles in Kazakhstan, which along with Russia, Belarus, and Ukraine had inherited segments of the USSR's nuclear arsenal. Beijing was greatly concerned about the possibility of Kazakhstan retaining some level of nuclear capability, thus placing another nuclear power (in addition to Russia, India, and Pakistan) on Chinese borders. Beijing, like others in the international community, was also distressed at the possibility of nuclear material from Kazakhstan being transferred to potentially hostile non-nuclear states. However, shortly after the USSR's dissolution, Kazakhstan, Belarus and Ukraine all agreed to transfer the whole of their respective nuclear weapons stockpiles to Russia. The remaining nuclear arms on Kazakh soil were removed in May 1995, four months after China officially agreed, in accordance with its policy of not using nuclear arms against non-nuclear states, not to use or threaten the use of nuclear weapons against Kazakhstan.[18]

In the wake of this agreement which settled so many long-standing border disputes between China and the former Soviet Union, Beijing and its other dialogue partners found themselves with a useful platform for talks on other security matters. This convergence of interests permitted an expansion of the security agenda between the five states and the series of bilateral agreements to be folded into a multilateral organisation with much growth potential.

Demonstrating confidence: foundations of the SCO

In May 1989, the warming of Sino-Soviet relations was codified in a joint communiqué in Beijing when Gorbachev visited the Chinese capital. The agreement promised issues between the two sides would be settled peacefully and that both countries would work to reduce troops on their shared border and to increase economic, cultural, and scientific ties. The Soviet delegation promised to work towards greater nuclear disarmament and stated its support for the 'one China' policy.[19] These issues would carry over to the dialogue between Beijing and the four ex-Soviet Republics with which it shared borders – Russia, Kazakhstan, Kyrgyzstan and Tajikistan – in November 1992. All five actors were eager to reach an accord which would provide the confidence-building measures necessary to reduce border tensions along the long Sino-CIS border, allowing for a reduction of the armed forces stationed there.

In April 1996, talks culminated in the Five-Power Agreement, signed in Shanghai, which would regulate military activity in the border regions and forbid exercises which could be perceived as threatening by other signatories.[20] The agreement also encouraged strategic information-sharing, conducting of joint exercises and increasing contact between the armed forces personnel of signatory countries. After the signing, there was an increase in bilateral meetings between Chinese and Russian military officials, inspections and Chinese arms purchases.[21] In April 1997, a second agreement placed limits on the number of soldiers and weapons which could be deployed by all five sides inside a 100 km buffer zone, with each participant restricted to a maximum of 130,400 soldiers, 3,900 tanks and 4,500 armoured vehicles within the zone. Specific details on the geographic reach of the agreement, reduction procedures, information sharing and verification, and inspections were also added.[22]

These agreements proved beneficial for all actors, as the pact gave Russia renewed outlets to East Asia, and filled an institutional vacuum in central Asia. A regional strategic apparatus had been slow to develop since the beginning of the 1990s due to the weakness of central Asian state governments and the relatively underdeveloped military forces in the region, save for Uzbekistan's.[23] For China, the 1996 and 1997 accords served the dual purposes of reducing tensions on what had been a very tense frontier in the past, and increasing the level of Beijing's persuasive power within central Asia.

More importantly for China, its negotiators were able to add the same clause to its agreements with the central Asian states which it had introduced in its Treaty of Friendship and Cooperation with Mongolia in 1994, namely that all sides would be dissuaded from entering into unfriendly alliances. This clause, at least tacitly, discouraged the development of military pacts between Moscow and its central Asian neighbours.[24] Since the 1997 accord, the five signatories agreed to further meetings to coordinate shared security concerns. Although the group had yet to be codified into a formal institution, the 'Shanghai Five' became the most important means by which China could address its evolving foreign policies with Russia and central Asia.

In helping to create the Shanghai Five, China brought together a collective, which evolved from the Five-Power Agreement and the subsequent treaty, by helping to build a regime based on addressing mutual perceived insecurities in the region. All of the actors involved were concerned with the stability of the governments and states in central Asia, since any further destabilisation would likely spill across borders, including those of China and Russia. At the Five's summit in Dushanbe in July 2000, the focus of the security discussions shifted from border demarcation and demilitarisation to the mutual problems of regional terrorism and separatism. Due in large part to Beijing's diplomacy, the Dushanbe talks ended with an agreement to establish an anti-terrorism centre, originally planned for the Kyrgyz capital of Bishkek, and a joint declaration calling for enhanced security cooperation amongst the five states.[25]

The Shanghai Five took an important step towards greater formalisation and international visibility in June 2001 when, while welcoming the group's newest member, Uzbekistan, into the fold, a declaration which formed the genesis of the Shanghai Cooperation Organisation was signed. The founding of the SCO signalled both a desire to deepen the structure of regional cooperation and also to expand its mandate beyond purely security matters. According to the declaration, the SCO's mandate was to encourage regional cooperation with the strategic, economic and cultural spheres and to call for peace and a just international order.[26]

The organisation's official charter was unveiled at its second conference in St. Petersburg in June 2002. Key points addressed by the document included the confirmation that a Regional Anti-Terrorism Structure (RATS) would be created to address area security issues, support for central Asia as a nuclear-weapons-free zone, and that the government in Beijing is the sole government of China, with Taiwan as a part of China. The charter also gave support to other peace-building initiatives in the Asia-Pacific region, including the ASEAN Regional Forum (ARF) and to peace talks concerning the Korean Peninsula and south Asia. The charter affirmed the SCO was 'neither a bloc nor a closed alliance', was not directed against any third party and would be based on respect for mutual interests and common approaches to dealing with regional and international problems.[27] In June 2003 a permanent secretariat was established in Beijing and Chinese ambassador Zhang Deguang was named the organisation's first secretary-general.[28]

The security wing of the SCO also began to match words with deeds. In October 2002, PLA personnel and the Kyrgyz armed forces held a joint military anti-terrorism exercise on the border between the two countries, the first such manoeuvre and the first to be held under SCO auspices. A larger-scale operation which included mock assaults on terrorist positions and involved all SCO members (save Uzbekistan) was completed in August 2003. The two-part exercises were notable not only due to their scope but also for the fact that they took place at both the frontier city of Ucharal, Kazakhstan and in Xinjiang, the first time that Beijing ever sponsored multilateral military exercises within Chinese borders.[29] After considerable delay, and a location change from Bishkek to Tashkent, the RATS centre was formally launched during the SCO's summit in June 2004. This anti-terrorism organisation was given the mandate of cooperating with both the SCO's membership and other international organisations in combating terrorism, separatism and extremism as well as creating an information nexus and think-tank dedicated to the study of terrorism.[30]

With the growth of the Shanghai grouping since 2001, the question of new members has been growing increasingly significant for China and the SCO as a whole and has been influenced by the fact that the admission of Uzbekistan has not been without its problems for the group. Although Uzbekistan suffered from the same set of security concerns as its neighbours in the region (terrorism and religious extremism), Tashkent was still looked upon with some wariness by some Shanghai Five members. Uzbekistan's population (27 million) is far greater than that of all of the other central Asian states, and its armed forces are relatively more developed. Moreover, Uzbekistan had been seen by those both inside and outside the region, as a potential 'pivot state' in the region due to its conservative foreign policies, independence from Russia's sphere of influence, and seemingly stable regime.[31] During the 1990s, China maintained an interest in increasing trade with Tashkent, since Uzbek territory rests along the historical 'silk road' trade route which Beijing wishes to revive. The addition of Uzbekistan to the SCO appeared, initially, to favour China's expanding central Asian diplomacy.

Uzbekistan, however, has demonstrated that it is unwilling, despite its SCO membership, to sever relations with other great powers. In October 2001, Tashkent brokered a security agreement with the United States, pledging mutual support to combat terrorism and allowing American forces to use Uzbek installations.[32] That same month, the American media revealed that Tashkent had actually conducted secret military operations with American military forces for at least a year before the September 2001 terrorist bombings.[33] In spite of Uzbekistan's shifting orientations, however, there has been little damage to SCO-Uzbek relations since 2001. Nevertheless, the SCO's decision to move the anti-terrorism centre from Bishkek to Tashkent could be seen as another means, in addition to strategic and economic incentives, of keeping Uzbekistan linked to the organisation.

With the initial success of the SCO's founding, questions were raised as to whether and how the group would expand its membership. The only former Soviet central Asian republic outside of the SCO, Turkmenistan, has opted for a largely neutral role in regional affairs and has no immediate ambitions to join the group. Since 2000, there has been sporadic talk of India and Pakistan joining the organisation. In January 2001, Islamabad made a formal request for admission to the Shanghai Five and, tellingly, the head of Pakistan's Inter-Services Intelligence, Lt-General Mahmud Ahmed, contacted China directly to gauge Beijing's support for Pakistan's request.[34] The actions of Pakistan strongly suggested that despite the organisation professing to be egalitarian, China retains the position of 'first among equals', at least in the perception of potential new members.

The possible inclusion of Pakistan and/or India into the SCO would create problems for the organisation, and China has thus far remained non-committal on either proposal. First, including both countries would present an entirely new set of security issues, centring on the conflict in Kashmir, which the forum would initially be ill-prepared to address. Second, including these two sizeable regional powers would potentially dilute China's now-extensive influence within the SCO, especially since both India and Pakistan have been anxious to improve ties with the central Asian republics. Third, admitting Pakistan and not India would heighten the international perception the SCO was developing into a partisan strategic organisation, an impression which Beijing has consistently attempted to dispel. One of the main tenets of China's post-cold war foreign policy has been to decry the persistence of military alliances, which are seen as detrimental to international peace and stability. As such, it is unlikely the SCO is prepared to widen the scope of its security interests into the thorny issues of south Asia, especially Kashmir, and therefore full membership by Delhi or Islamabad in the immediate future may not be viable. However, the granting of observer status (a position Uzbekistan had previously enjoyed) to these two governments is a possibility and may be a compromise welcomed by SCO members.

The question of SCO increasing its membership was partially addressed following the SCO's Tashkent Summit in June 2004 when Mongolia was granted observer status. At the suggestion of Russian President Putin, the idea of a SCO-Afghanistan liaison group was also explored;[35] a remarkable policy shift considering that when the organisation was formed Kabul – under the Taliban – was a focus of the SCO's security concerns. Should the organisation continue to develop further integration in its security policies and in other areas such as economic development, other states in the region may continue to knock on the SCO's door, especially those seeking alternatives to Western-dominated regimes. It remains to be seen how receptive the SCO will be to these new requests for membership.

By advocating specific mandates for the organisation and having a strong voice in determining its development, the Shanghai Cooperation Organisation is becoming one of China's most valuable assets in dealing with the new political and strategic realities of its western frontier. This does not mean, however, that the organisation is not facing serious obstacles to maintaining its integrity and its future goals. Among the issues to be addressed by Beijing and the organisation's membership before it can continue to develop effectively is the question of how China and the SCO can combat the increasingly dangerous spread of cross-border religious extremism and terrorism which affects the entire SCO membership. Also, probably the most important in the short term for the SCO, is the question of whether the American military presence in central Asia as a result of its operations in Afghanistan will marginalise the effectiveness of the organisation. In addressing these issues, China's response may be crucial both to the success of the SCO and to the country's own ambitious foreign policies in the central Asian region.

Fundamentalism and 'splittism' in China's backyard

Despite China's successes in gaining security assurances from Russia and central Asia after 1992, and the rapid establishment of cordial relations and trade ties between Beijing and its western neighbours, the past decade has seen the emergence of a new set of security issues which have threatened to destabilise the Sino-central Asian region. The bilateral border agreements which Beijing had struck with governments in central Asia would prove insufficient to deal with these new threats and therefore China has had to look more seriously at a multilateral alternative. These developing menaces were what Chinese specialists termed 'the three evils': extremism, separatism, and terrorism.[36] The advent of these 'evils' would be a defining point in the development of the SCO, and of China's strategic policies in the region.

The first few years following the break-up of the Soviet Union marked an uneasy transition not only for the regimes of central Asia, but also its citizens. Many of the peoples of central Asia turned towards rediscovering traditional Islamicist religious and political thought which had been suppressed during the Soviet era. In the beginning of the post-USSR transitional period, political thought in the region was dominated by traditional Jadidist thinking, a path that stressed education, the modernisation of religion, and self-determination. Jadidism was adapted by the central Asian states as a means of bridging their pre-Soviet Muslim histories and Soviet-era secularism.[37] However, it was not long into Central Asia's political transition when less tolerant ideological strains from other parts of the Islamic world began to be imported into the region from Afghanistan, Pakistan and Saudi Arabia.[38] These developments would have serious ramifications for central Asia and its immediate neighbours, including China.

Beijing's concern with the rise of secessionist and Islamic fundamentalist movements in central Asia is a product of concerns about how these developments will influence the Muslim population in Xinjiang. The prospect of 'splittism', the traditional term used by China to describe a forcible breaking away of Chinese territory, has been of paramount concern for Beijing since the founding of the People's Republic. The far western region of China is sparsely populated and largely underdeveloped, a factor which led to Beijing's 'open up the west' campaign, begun in 2000 as a series of government modernisation initiatives designed to promote socio-economic growth in western China.[39]

It is partially because of this disparity in development, that China's far west remains the most volatile part of Chinese territory. Despite its remoteness, Xinjiang is a major strategic asset to China for its proximity to central Asian trade routes and for its petroleum and mineral reserves.[40] Therefore, Beijing is sensitive to the problem of separatism in that territory. In seeking to restrain extremist factions within its Muslim populations, China has linked itself through a common cause not only to the central Asian regimes, but also to Russia, which struggled against armed Islamic-based insurrections throughout the 1990s in northern Caucasus provinces of Chechnya and Dagestan.[41]

Since the beginning of the 1990s, there have been frequent incidents of unrest among Muslim separatists in Xinjiang, and Beijing has responded to these challenges in several ways. Internally, the Chinese government has encouraged migration of Han Chinese into Xinjiang and increased economic development in the province as a method of dampening popular support for secessionism. Externally, China has endeavoured to maintain good relations with much of the Islamic world as a means of avoiding state-based support for Muslim separatists in Xinjiang. Once the states of central Asia achieved independence, China was quick to establish relations with the governments in that region, in part, for these same reasons.[42] For example, Kazakhstan, Kyrgyzstan and Uzbekistan all have considerable Uyghur populations, and China has been anxious to avoid ethnic conflict occurring under the guise of reuniting Muslim peoples on either side of the Sino-central Asian borders.

Most of the successor states in central Asia retained their secular, ex-communist governments which ruled without strong opposition forces. The exception was Tajikistan, which in 1992 descended into a five-year civil war as a result of cleavages between ethnicities and even between different communist factions.[43] Despite the relatively peaceful transfer of power in most of central Asia during the early 1990s, a political and social void of sorts was created in this region after the abrupt transition to independence, leaving many states in central Asia open to influences from other strains of Islamic-based thinking, including religious extremism. During the 1990s, Islamic fundamentalism became the most visible form of opposition to the political status quo in the region, and the most crucial security concern across central Asia. Although many of the central Asian fundamentalist movements were domestic in origin, launched in opposition to regional state governments, there were also concerns about terrorism spilling over from Taliban-held Afghanistan.

A watershed event in the recent political history of central Asia was the pullout of Soviet military forces in Afghanistan in 1988–9, and the subsequent fall of the Moscow-backed Najibullah regime in 1992. The USSR tried, and failed, between 1978 and 1989 to bring Afghanistan into its orbit via military force, leaving the country in a shambles physically and economically.[44] The resulting power vacuum led to civil war as the various *mujahideen* rebel groups, formerly united in their opposition to a decade of Soviet occupation, were unable to construct a successor government acceptable to all factions and ethnicities within the country. Emerging from the conflict was the previously unknown fundamentalist Islamic group known as the Taliban, whose members are primarily Pashtun by ethnic origin and Sunni in faith. Two years after emerging from obscurity in Pakistan, Taliban forces in 1996 captured the Afghan capital of Kabul from its primary rival, the Northern Alliance, a loose conglomerate of separate multiethnic groupings, including Tajiks, Uzbeks and Shi'ite Hazaras.[45]

By the end of the 1990s, the Taliban government had become an international concern, especially in the wake of its harbouring of terrorists led by political extremist and former Saudi entrepreneur Osama bin Laden. Bin Laden, and the Al-Qaeda ('The Base') terrorist network he led, had been accused of masterminding the bombings of American embassies in Kenya and Tanzania in August 1998, and the bombing of the American naval vessel USS *Cole* in October of 2000.[46] Ultimately, al-Qaeda was held responsible for the hijacking of four American commercial airliners and the subsequent destruction of 11 September 2001.

When the Taliban came to power, threats of international isolation and deteriorating economic conditions in Afghanistan did little to loosen the regime's grip on power. Before 9/11, Taliban leaders had refused to extradite bin Laden, even after a December 2000 vote by the United Nations Security Council to place sanctions on the regime, while strengthening an existing flight embargo and a ban on weapons shipments to Afghanistan.[47] As a result of American military intervention after the 9/11 terrorist attacks, the Taliban were driven from power, and in December 2001 an interim coalition government led by President Hamid Karzai and composed of former Northern Alliance adherents and Pashtun moderates took power with American backing.[48] However, despite the continued presence of international peacekeepers the country remains weakened and fragile, with many regions beyond central governmental control. China has been one of many countries to offer aid and development assistance to Kabul as a means of staying involved in that country's recovery. However, such activity has not been without its dangers, as demonstrated by the murder in June 2004 of eleven Chinese construction workers in northern Afghanistan by suspected Taliban militias.[49]

Although the Taliban is the most visible of the Islamic extremist organisations which have operated in central Asia, it is by no means the only group. The Islamic Movement of Uzbekistan (IMU), created in the late 1990s, was derived from a group of local religious leaders who formed a coalition called Adolat ('Justice') earlier in the decade. In 1991 Adolat attempted to establish Islamic law in the city of Namangan, located within the Uzbek section of the Ferghana Valley region, and adopted violent methods in the wake of a government crackdown. After the movement was banned by the Karimov regime in March 1992, those members who escaped arrest fled to Afghanistan and Tajikistan, and the IMU was founded by these elements in the city of Kabul.[50] After mobilising, IMU forces sought greater influence within the Ferghana Valley, an isolated region of central Asia which straddles the borders between Uzbekistan, Tajikistan and Kyrgyzstan. With a population of 10 million, the valley is the most densely-populated region in central Asia, and home to a heterogeneous citizenry of 65 per cent Uzbeks, 20 per cent Kyrgyzs and approximately 10 per cent Tajiks. This valley is also an important source of energy supplies, cotton and land supporting the agricultural and industrial sectors of all three countries.[51]

After its founding, the IMU declared a *jihad* (holy war) against the Uzbek government, and has attempted to disrupt Uzbekistan and the surrounding region both politically and economically. In 1999, the IMU staged an unsuccessful assassination attempt against President Karimov and engaged in bombings and hostage-taking, including the kidnapping of foreign nationals.[52] Although its activities were restricted to central Asia, the international profile of the IMU increased considerably after the Clinton government in the United States recognised the group as a terrorist organisation in September 2000 and promised support for Tashkent in combating the group.[53] However, eradicating the threat from the IMU proved extremely difficult for local governments, as the group had found sanctuary in northern Afghanistan and had used training facilities there, operated by both the Taliban and Osama bin Laden.[54] The military leader of the IMU, Juma Namangani, was, before his reported death in November 2001, said to be a close ally of bin Laden, and had hoped to recruit Afghan militants to assist in his campaign to destabilise Uzbekistan.[55]

China's concern with the growth of the IMU stemmed directly from its reported linkages with Uyghur extremist separatists, who, according to one analyst, had been active in Islamic resistance movements since the 1980s when they joined with the Afghan *mujahideen* to combat the Soviet occupation. After the Soviet pullout, he added, soldiers of Uyghur origin remained active within Afghanistan, fighting and training in Afghanistan with IMU and Taliban forces.[56] These events have heightened Chinese concerns that Uyghur separatist forces could be strengthened with outside aid to the point where they may present a threat to Chinese border and internal security.

The Ferghana region is home to non-militant groups which also advocate revolutionary change in central Asia, and by extension western China. The most visible of these has been the Hizb ut-Tahrir al-Islami, or the Party of Liberation, which has greatly expanded its influence in the region since the break-up of the Soviet Union. The primary goal of the Hizb is the unification of all Muslim peoples throughout central Asia and, later, the entire Islamic community, under a single political entity, a *khilafat* or 'Caliphate'. The rapid spread of the Hizb has been attributed to the group's extensive use of communications resources both modern (including email correspondence) and traditional (paper leaflets).[57] The result has been the creation of an entrenched network by which the Hizb has spread its teachings.

The rise of Islamic revolutionary groups such as the Taliban, the IMU and the Hizb further complicate the situation for China, since there remains the potential for the importation of extremist philosophies into Xinjiang, possibly leading to increased ethnically based tensions and organised rebellion against Chinese rule.[58] In addition to harbouring militants from other parts of central Asia, Afghanistan has been accused of offering sanctuary to Uyghur militants hoping to smuggle weapons and aid to separatists in China. In November 2001, Chinese Vice-Premier Qian Qichen estimated that a thousand Muslims of Chinese origin had trained with Al-Qaeda forces in Afghan camps,[59] demonstrating the importance to Beijing of combating Islamic extremism in Central Asia.

After 9/11, the American promise to eliminate terrorist threats from Afghanistan permitted China to relinquish its policy of taking a conservative approach to the Taliban regime in the hopes of preventing their support for Uyghur separatists.[60] Soon after the bombings, China's 76 km border with Afghanistan, accessible via the narrow Wakhan Corridor, was sealed. Once the Al-Qaeda terrorist organisation in Afghanistan was identified by the United States as the source of the attacks, Beijing agreed to support Western efforts against international terrorism, including military action in Afghanistan, while refraining from attempts to link the matter with other issues such as Taiwan.[61] However, this support was not without reservations. Beijing advised restraint and caution in dealing with the Afghanistan threat, and called for the United Nations Security Council, where China has veto power, to be advised on American military actions.[62]

By the end of the 1990s, the political and security situation in central Asia had further deteriorated, with many of the former Soviet regimes there becoming increasingly authoritarian as a result of threats from Islamic militants operating out of central Asia, outside the rule of law. The development of the Shanghai Five-turned-SCO as a multilateral security community represented an ideal avenue for China to address these issues with five like-minded governments.

The June 2001 meeting in Shanghai of the Shanghai Five was notable not only for the expansion and formalisation of the organisation into the SCO, but also because the group agreed to an increased focus on regional security issues beyond strictly border matters. The membership of the newly-created SCO agreed to formally support Russian and Chinese efforts to fight ethnic-based separatism within their borders, while the central Asian republics would receive assistance with their own problems of Muslim fundamentalism. Soon after 9/11, the SCO attempted to better define its own role within the US-led international war on terrorism.

In January 2002, China's Information Office of the State Council released a report in the weekly *Beijing Review* accusing so-called 'East Turkestan' extremist groups of instigating over two hundred separate terrorist incidents in Xinjiang between 1990 and 2001. These included bombings, murders, poisonings, arson, and establishing networks to purchase arms and organise civil discord. The report concluded that these East Turkestan terrorists were 'closely connected' with international terrorist forces, had the 'unstinting support' of Osama bin Laden, and were integral parts of his organisation.[63] During the same month, leaders of the SCO met again in Beijing to discuss mutual concerns of regional terrorism in the wake of 9/11. They released a statement calling for the battle against terrorism to be fought on both international and domestic levels, and that 'this struggle should not engender bias or adopt double standards'. Chinese Foreign Minister Tang Jiaxuan added that all SCO members had pledged their support to Beijing's struggle with East Turkestan terrorists.[64]

Despite the political and economic benefits to China of closer cooperation with central Asia, the most visible mandate of the SCO has been to strengthen strategic cooperation amongst members and to combat non-state-based security threats from terrorist and extremist organisations. These ties have proven invaluable to China as a method of augmenting its border security on its sensitive western frontier, while at the same time addressing the problems of terrorism which since the turn of the century have assumed international importance. In late September 2001, when a spokesperson for the Chinese Foreign Ministry was asked about a possible role for the SCO in the American-led international coalition against terrorism, the response was a somewhat ambiguous pledge that the SCO had a 'unique role' to play in the global fight against terrorism, and that China was 'pushing forward and actively participating in the anti-terrorist cooperation within the Organisation's framework'.[65]

The American focus on central Asia as a result of its Afghanistan operations has complicated the SCO's development. In the face of competition from the United States, the SCO will need to develop a clearer mandate to avoid becoming marginalised by other international actors. Despite the domination of the war on terrorism on central Asian policies, however, another strategic issue, energy, continues to assert itself. In addition to Beijing's concerns about the security of its western frontier, China is swiftly finding itself in competition for central Asia's substantial, but still underdeveloped, fossil fuel reserves.

The 'black gold' variable

In addition to central Asia's strategic locale, the region's attractiveness to the international community stems largely from its current and potential energy resources in the form of oil (in Kazakhstan, Uzbekistan, and in and around the Caspian Sea) and natural gas (Kazakhstan, Uzbekistan and Turkmenistan). The countries with these resource endowments have restructured their economies so that these resources are their dominant export and the foundation of their economic development. However, the remote geography of central Asia, in addition to its poor infrastructure, has made it extremely difficult to tap and transport energy from these reserves to interested markets without the development of new pipelines and refineries. Therefore the governments of central Asia have opted to strike deals with foreign governments and corporations to assist with the extraction and transportation costs.

The energy situation in Central Asia is of great importance not only to China's foreign policy but also to its long-term domestic development planning. As a result of the country's rapid economic growth, China's need for imported raw materials, including aluminium, copper, zinc and iron ore, has increased sharply since the early 1990s.[66] This requirement for commodity imports is also apparent in China's energy sector. As of 2000, approximately 69 per cent of domestic energy needs were derived from inefficient and environmentally unfriendly coal, with oil comprising another 25 per cent and other sources, including natural gas, nuclear and hydro-electrical power, far behind. In 1993, China, as the second-largest energy consumer in the world, was forced to become a net importer of petroleum, a development with serious ramifications for both its future development and its security concerns.[67] Automobiles are one major contributing factor. Although the number of privately owned vehicles is still very low compared to the West, demand is increasing as more of the population is able to afford cars. However, China also needs new energy supplies for industrial fuels and electricity requirements.[68]

The modernisation push in China has taken a huge toll on the country's energy supplies. A walk through Beijing on a warm day will demonstrate some of the current and potential problems. Traffic jams in the capital have become endemic as the city rushes to complete a sixth ring road, and more apartment buildings have been fitted with air-conditioning units as citizens try to stay cool. Strains on the electrical grid during the summer of 2004 forced conservation measures in large cities, including Beijing, Shanghai and Guangzhou, and concerns have been raised that energy shortages will increase as the country continues to develop. China is the second-largest energy consumer in the world, but *per capita* uses only about 10 per cent of the energy consumed in the United States.[69] The situation today is far different from the pre-reform era, wherein a large majority of the country's energy needs were met via domestic sources.

While Beijing has attempted to develop its domestic energy resources, the results have been mixed at best. Hopes that fossil fuels in the Xinjiang's Tarim Basin would alleviate China's energy shortfall are far from certain,[70] and ambitious hydroelectric projects have also been problematic for Beijing. These include the controversial Sanxia (Three Gorges) hydroelectric project, expected to come online no sooner than 2009 at a cost of about US$25 billion and, by project's end, more than a million displaced persons as a result of the associated flooding of inhabited lands. Since its inception the project has been inundated by protests, accusations of local corruption and incidents of substandard construction.[71] Other ambitious dam projects along the Nu, Upper Mekong, and Jinsha Rivers have also drawn criticism from local environmental groups for their potential impact on the surrounding land.[72]

With this in mind, Beijing has become increasingly interested in acquiring access to oil reserves from foreign sources. Beijing has sought oil-trade ties with states in the Middle East and north Africa, including those which were placed under American sanctions, such as Iran, Iraq, Libya and Sudan, as well as Oman, Saudi Arabia and Yemen. Beijing has also pursued joint ventures in sub-Saharan Africa, Peru and Venezuela.[73] In July 2004 it was announced that Beijing was close to commencing free trade talks with the Gulf Cooperation Council (GCC), an organisation which includes oil-rich states of Saudi Arabia, Kuwait and the United Arab Emirates.[74] Beijing's increasing need for foreign oil and gas is also starting to affect not only Chinese foreign policy but other international issues as well, as was demonstrated by Beijing's September 2004 opposition to United Nations sanctions against Sudan in response to atrocities in that state's Darfur region and its reluctance in November of that year to support UN Security Council action against Iran as a response to its alleged nuclear weapons development. China has extensive oil partnerships with both states despite their 'rogue' status.[75]

There are also two other potentially oil-rich regions closer to China which are of special interest, namely the South China Sea, which as noted, may contain underwater oil reserves and, unsurprisingly, central Asia and the Caspian region. Although estimates of the quantity of petroleum in the central Asian region have been hotly disputed, ranging from an optimistic 200 billion barrels to a more conservative 90 billion,[76] China remains very interested in securing greater access to these supplies and much of Beijing's central Asian diplomacy has focused on energy development.

In seeking central Asian energy deals, the first country Beijing approached was Kazakhstan, which possesses an estimated two billion tonnes of oil and another 1,100 billion cubic metres of natural gas, but had only rudimentary oil production facilities, and lacked pipelines suitable for exporting its fossil fuels.[77] By 1997 Beijing was able to acquire 60 per cent of the central Asian republic's Aktyubinsk oilfield. That same year, the China National Petroleum Corporation (CNPC) outbid Russian and Western oil companies to land an exclusive contract to develop Kazakhstan's Uzen oilfield, one of the largest fields in the country and located near the Caspian Sea. These deals, worth a total of more than US$9 billion, involve the construction of extensive pipelines between Kazakh and Chinese territory.[78] In May 2004, another investment agreement was signed between the CNPC and KazMunaiGaz of Kazakhstan calling for construction, set to begin in August of that year, of a 1,240 km pipeline from Atasu, Kazakhstan to Xinjiang. This project is one of three segments of a 3,000 km link which, when completed, will transport up to 20 million tonnes of oil annually from the Caspian Sea to China.[79] In 2000 President Jiang and officials from the CNPC also visited Turkmenistan and signed an agreement to assist Ashgabat in developing its oil and gas fields, and to construct a 5,000 km oil pipeline from eastern Turkmenistan to China.[80] With these agreements in place, China is better positioned to assist in the economic and political development of key central Asian states as well as securing invaluable new energy resources.

However, China is far from alone in seeking to develop central Asian energy supplies; rather it has faced considerable competition from Russia, the West, and Iran in a bid for influence. Much of the current competition is focused on the best method of transporting petroleum via pipelines from the Kazakh/Caspian Sea region to markets and, predictably, much of the debate has centred not only on financial and technical considerations, but also on political costs and benefits. The United States, with its comparatively large financial resources, advocated the establishment of a pipeline which would carry Caspian oil from Kazakhstan to Baku, Azerbaijan, through Georgia and then to the Mediterranean port of Ceyhan in Turkey. Despite the complications of this route, including its length (1760 km) and the high costs involved in building the link, an estimated US$3 billion,[81] the 'Baku-Tbilisi-Ceyhan' (BTC) link does have significant political advantages for the West, since Azerbaijan, Georgia and Turkey are all US allies.

Russia and Iran countered the BTC proposal with alternative routes which would make use of their territories, including links to the Persian Gulf, supported by Teheran, and a path north-westward from Baku to the Russian port of Novorossiysk, supported by Moscow despite the routing which would take the pipeline through disputed areas in the Caucasus, including Chechnya.[82] The United States made little secret of its view that under optimal conditions central Asia could serve as a possible supplementary fuel source, potentially countering dependence on the Arabian Peninsula and Persian Gulf should the latter regions become too unstable. This would place China in a less advantageous position *vis-à-vis* its own regional energy policies. Although American military operations in Iraq since 2003 have shifted its external energy priorities somewhat, Washington remains interested in central Asia as a source of energy supplies for Western markets.[83] However, all existing and proposed central Asian pipeline projects, including those supported by Beijing, may have costs not only in construction but also maintenance and security, as the unstable political situation in much of the Trans-Caspian region may make pipelines tempting targets for terrorist attack.

It is still too early to determine the role of central Asia's energy on Chinese political initiatives in that region. It remains in China's interest to be engaged in the region in order to avoid being thwarted by competing powers, and the SCO, while not directly involved with energy security, is still an important outlet permitting China to address its energy interests in central Asia. If the members of the group grow closer, Beijing will have the means to develop into an even more powerful economic influence in the region, allowing for more economic initiatives which may lead to further joint energy development. However, if there is intensified competition within central Asia by various great powers for the rights to exploit the region's energy supplies, the SCO cannot remain aloof from this rivalry. In the short term, however, the SCO serves Chinese interests in the energy area by ensuring an institutional link to the energy-producing states in which Beijing has shown increasing interest.

The United States and the SCO in a post-9/11 world

At the time of the SCO's founding, American influence in central Asia was negligible compared to that of Russia and China. This was largely due both to geographical constraints, and to an ongoing US policy advocating greater democracy in the region in order to improve the economic and security situation there, calls which did little to stop the trend towards further authoritarianism in central Asia.[84] However, well before the events of 9/11, the United States had been demonstrably less chary of projecting its military power into central Eurasia. This was evidenced in a November 1994 American military operation, codenamed 'Operation Sapphire', which retrieved 600 kg of uranium from Ust-Kamenogorsk in eastern Kazakhstan for safekeeping in the United States. Concerns had been raised that the poorly guarded nuclear facility was at high risk of being plundered.[85] In August 1998, US armed forces fired cruise missiles at camps in Afghanistan which were reportedly overseen by Osama bin Laden. The attacks were in response to his alleged role in the bombings of American embassies in Kenya and Tanzania earlier in the month. American actions in Afghanistan at that time provided proof to Beijing that the United States no longer considered central Asia to be outside its sphere of influence, and served to augment Chinese concerns about Western encroachment in its backyard.[86]

In addition to direct influence in central Asia, the United States and its allies were able to establish significant institutions in the region which may serve to challenge Chinese security interests there. The most visible example is the extension of the Organisation for Security and Cooperation in Europe (OSCE) into central Asia. Since the OSCE first opened a liaison office in Tashkent in 1995, the organisation has established centres in Ashgabat, Almaty and Bishkek in order to coordinate regional activities. The OSCE, comprising 55 members in Europe and North America, was created to promote regional security dialogue, information exchange, human rights and fair elections among members. Although still limited in its direct operations in central Asia, there remains the possibility that the OSCE could become a serious rival for Beijing in the competition for regional influence there.

The North Atlantic Treaty Organisation (NATO) has also increased its visibility in the region over the past decade. Since the break-up of the Warsaw Pact more than a decade ago, NATO has sought to engage former Pact nations and former Soviet Republics in the hopes of creating a milieu designed to prevent the re-emergence of an anti-Western bloc and to promote democratisation. The primary tool that NATO uses to promote these goals is the Partnership for Peace (PfP), created in 1994. All six former Soviet central Asian republics are members of the PfP, and their activities have included military exchanges and joint exercises.[87] Beijing had been wary of the development of the PfP, viewing it as a thinly veiled tool for American containment policy of China, and was concerned about Western military activity so close to Chinese borders.[88]

The events of 9/11 and after have, to phrase it mildly, completely changed the strategic picture for both China and the SCO. In preparation for military operations in Afghanistan in the fall of 2001, the United States was able to establish bases within three SCO member states, Kyrgyzstan, Tajikistan and Uzbekistan, as well as in nearby Pakistan, in an effort to forcibly oust the Taliban regime from Kabul and hunt al-Qaeda forces.[89] Although much of Afghanistan has been pacified and presidential elections were successfully completed in October 2004, American forces remain on the ground in many parts of the country while other international peacekeepers patrol Kabul and areas north of the capital. At the start of 2005, there was no firm exit strategy for American forces in central Asia.

These developments have placed China in a serious dilemma. On one side, China has benefited from the improvement of central Asian security after the end of the Taliban regime. The Chinese government has successfully been able to link the activities of Uyghur separatists in Xinjiang, which Beijing claims are organised within an 'East Turkestan Islamic Movement' (ETIM) to former Al-Qaeda camps in Afghanistan. In August 2002, after much lobbying on China's part, the United States designated the ETIM as a terrorist organisation, a move praised by Beijing and seen as a way for Washington to continue to enlist China's help in the war on terrorism.[90] Since 9/11, Washington and Beijing have greatly synchronised their policies in regards to combating international terrorist organisations, and the US military presence in central Asia has mitigated Beijing's security concerns to a degree.

From a different viewpoint, however, the American military presence in central Asia can be viewed as a bane to China's central Asian and SCO policies. Beijing now faces the possibility of its SCO compatriots developing closer strategic ties to the United States, in addition to a long-term Western military presence at its back door. Adding to this is the fact that Pakistan, a longstanding Chinese ally, was successfully courted by Washington as an ally in the war on terrorism. As previously noted, Beijing is very sensitive to the prospect of American containment of Chinese power. After the US began courting central Asian support for military intervention in Afghanistan soon after 9/11, some Chinese academics warned that the government in Beijing, and especially the PLA, would be alarmed at an extended American military presence in the region.[91] Since the central Asian military operations began, there has been little attempt by Washington to directly engage either China or Russia in consultations concerning the American military presence, leading to concerns that should the United States maintain military forces in Afghanistan and surrounding states for the long term, the SCO and China's own regional policies run the risk of being pushed aside. Moreover, Beijing, along with Moscow, would increasingly attempt to balance American power in the region.[92]

Thus, it is important to question whether the SCO will become a partner or a rival to Western strategic interests in central Asia, and more importantly, will the SCO have the power to play either part? It would be very premature to state that the US presence in central Asia has already sidelined the SCO, since the American role in the region has been very issue-specific, namely waging war on terrorists. China, by contrast, has the geographic advantage of being able to engage in a more multifaceted foreign policy approach to central Asia which may prove more durable in the longer term.

SCO cooperation and benefits for China

The SCO can be considered a distinct institution in the sense that it counts among its members very young states with underdeveloped rates of participation in either regional or international institutions, along with two established regional great powers. It can also be argued that in the history of institution building, it has been rare to witness the creation of a security-based regime with members possessing very disparate levels of political and military power. This asymmetry has allowed China to play a prominent role in the development of this institution, as well as allowing Beijing to mould the grouping to better address specific Chinese strategic issues. However, beyond these assertions, it is also possible to draw parallels with other security regimes in explaining why the SCO came about and what China's strategic interests are in developing this institution further.

As explained in the previous chapter, China's history in its dealings with multilateral security organisations has been very short and oftentimes reluctant, since through most of its history China has remained outside such structures. More-over, many of the concepts inherent in such organisations, including collective security, have traditionally been an anathema to Chinese concepts of the sanctity of borders, the importance of state sovereignty and an opposition to 'hegemonism', the domination of weaker powers by greater ones. Nevertheless, changes in security perceptions both on the international level and in China's periphery have prompted a re-evaluation of Chinese thinking on matters relating to multilateral security.

The Shanghai group, therefore, is an important case study of this new thinking, not only because of its recent origins since the cold war but also because it combines the traditional Chinese preference for bilateral security agreements using consensus-based decision-making with evolving multilateralism, a model which China has stated might be useful in other parts of the Asia-Pacific region.[93] Unlike other security organisations such as the ARF, in which China has been largely content to play the role of observer rather than shaper, Beijing has consistently been at the forefront on the SCO, and its earlier iterations, from the beginning and has worked to change the focus of the organisation from border-related issues to anti-terrorism and greater political and economic ties.

In addition, the organisation has developed in keeping with Chinese preferences for security relations based on confidence-building, achieving consensus based on common interests and mutual benefit, rather than cold-war-era alliances which stressed the acquisition of armaments.[94] Beijing, along with its SCO partners, has stressed that the organisation is not exclusive and is not directed against an outside party. Rather, the group has focused on improving regional conditions through increased political and economic contacts, in addition to joint action against illegal activities, including terrorism, smuggling and unlawful migration.[95] In addition, the Shanghai group represents one of the few security organisations which China had a direct hand in creating, thus allowing Beijing to determine its direction at the onset, as opposed to other security-based organisations which China joined after their inceptions, such as the UN Security Council or the Nuclear Non-proliferation Regime.

In seeking to explain the impetus which led to the development of the SCO, the most obvious response would be that it was a reaction to external pressures. For example, Adler and Barnett have argued that the first stage in the maturation process of a security community is the appearance of a) changes in technology, demography, economics, or the environment; b) new interpretations of social reality; and c) external threats.[96] Certainly the first two factors are present in central Asia, since the end of the Soviet Union significantly changed the political, demographic and strategic landscape of the region, leading to both new opportunities and new concerns for China and the post-Soviet republics. The third prerequisite is less distinct however. Although there are certainly serious security threats in central Asia, they are not necessarily external in nature. Instead of an outside threat which forces other states to come together for mutual protection, the threats in central Asia are largely internal in the form of Islamic fundamentalism and secessionism. In this way, the mandate of the SCO is very similar to that of the ASEAN in the first few years following its creation in 1967. Although ASEAN members had concerns about the growing threat of external actors (such as communist Vietnam), the primary sources of insecurity for the majority were internally-based groups, mainly communist insurgents wishing to topple member governments in the region.[97]

The same vulnerabilities are present in the SCO, since although one could argue that Afghanistan was an 'external' threat due to its support for groups seeking to violently alter the political status quo in central Asia, most of the threats to the region are still 'home-grown', developing within central Asia itself. For the four central Asian republics, the stakes are no less than state integrity and regime survival, since the governments in Astana, Dushanbe, Bishkek and Tashkent are highly susceptible to crippling shocks from the opposition forces in the region. The situation is less dire for Russia and China, but with both states undergoing complex transitions both politically and economically, large-scale disruptions on their most vulnerable frontiers are not desirable, especially since they would distract both countries from more pressing issues both domestically and regionally.

In the case of Russia, the Putin government is still combating economic stagnation, corruption and the ongoing problems of maintaining security in its Caucasus region, especially Chechnya. China's security interests are still largely concentrated eastward, and focus on Taiwan, southeast Asia and the United States. Therefore, Beijing is arguably in the best position of the six to confront the internalised threats from central Asia, but cooperation with its SCO colleagues provides tools to address its insecurities in this region where China's traditional forms of military power (i.e. nuclear, missile-based) are not efficacious. Moreover, the development of the SCO may serve to bolster security conditions on China's western border and, in theory, allow Beijing to focus on its more exigent strategic concerns to the east.

There is also the 'alone together' syndrome as another external reason for the SCO's development.[98] This theory, coined by Ispahani to describe the development of the Gulf Cooperation Council on the Arabian Peninsula and the Organisation of Front Line States in Southern Africa in the 1980s, can also be somewhat applicable to the case of the SCO. In explaining the development of these types of security organisations in the developing world, Ispahani noted four factors. These are the dissolution of larger pacts, often those with superpower involvement, the growing gap between the developed and developing world as to the nature of economic, political, and social issues, the security vacuums created by the departure of colonial powers, and the effects of a nuclear stalemate between the United States and Soviet Union, their rivalry spilled over into the developing world, leading to the need to create a 'united front' against being drawn into superpower proxy conflicts. Of these, the first three issues have a strong relation to the case of the SCO, since the fall of the USSR did involve the removal of a larger security pact as well as creating a security vacuum in central Asia on the borders of Russia and China.

In addition, the current security threats which the region is facing, including direct threats to SCO members' state integrity from extremist groups, has largely differed from those addressed by Western security organisations. As to the fourth factor, although the age of superpower rivalry ended along with the USSR, the central Asian region has become a nexus for various other rivalries, including regional powers vying for political influence, economic actors competing for energy riches, and different branches of religious ideologies seeking to establish beachheads. Such strains would be difficult for any region to endure, but for one as fragile as central Asia, it is understandable that the need to create stabilising institutions would be so strong.

Beijing has been largely successful in the crafting of the Shanghai Cooperation Organisation, and has clearly taken up the position as first among equals in the group. Since the regime's inception, China has been able to use its political and persuasive powers to shape the SCO's agenda to align with its very distinctive security interests and concerns. Specifically, Beijing was first able to use the forum's structure to strike agreements on military deployments on the Sino-central Asian frontier, thus allowing China the freedom to greatly reduce its military commitments there in keeping with the PLA's desire to modernise and place more of an emphasis on technology rather than strength of numbers. Later, China was able to use the Shanghai Five mechanism to convince its central Asian partners to refrain from offering support to Muslim minorities in China, thus assisting in the removal of a serious potential threat to Chinese sovereignty on its western frontier. However, in addition to the primary function of addressing border and frontier security issues, Beijing's membership in the SCO has brought about other peripheral security and power benefits, 'private goods' which China would not have been able to obtain without the organisation.

First, the development of the SCO served to facilitate China's policy of ensuring the stability of the country's vulnerable western frontier; more specifically, Xinjiang. As Harris noted, despite the remoteness of the province and the considerable amount of resources required by Beijing to maintain it, the area is vital to Chinese security interests since it provides a buffer zone between China's core provinces and other countries, it contains natural resources important to Chinese economic growth, and it provides a needed window into central Asia which began to grow in importance after the demise of the USSR.[99] China is wary of any foreign-based influences, both state and non-state in nature, which may erode Chinese sovereignty over Xinjiang. At the same time, Beijing wishes to retain control of the territory while avoiding the same levels of military build-up which were necessary in the years after the Sino-Soviet split in the early 1960s. Maintaining good relations with Russia and central Asia is therefore crucial to ensuring the safety of China's far west and the SCO acts as another means to achieve that goal.

Second, the creation of the SCO is a natural extension of China's policy of developing more amicable relations in the international system, and it acts as an increasingly visible example of these initiatives. The trend began in the 1980s when Beijing began developing a 'stable periphery' policy, encouraging more cordial relations with its neighbours in order to facilitate its ongoing economic and security policy reforms, to gain insight from the newly industrialising economies in east Asia, and to discourage the evolution of security threats on Chinese borders.[100] The SCO has further validated China's new regional friendship policies, adding weight to Beijing's policy of presenting a more businesslike and congenial face both to its periphery and to the world as a whole.

Central among these has been Beijing's desire to re-establish friendly relations with the Russian Federation, relations which had been placed in a deep freeze in the decades following the Sino-Soviet split. Due to the lengthy border between the two states, any Chinese initiative to create a stable periphery along its western frontier would not succeed without more cordial relations with Moscow. Fortunately for Beijing, at the end of the cold war, Russian and Chinese foreign policy concerns came increasingly closer to alignment, influenced by both countries' concern about American power in Eurasia and joint preference for the development of a multipolar international system rather than US hegemony.

Moscow in the 1990s wanted to increase economic ties with the Asia-Pacific region based on the Russian far east's energy supplies, its strategic location as a transport corridor, as well as it being a destination for foreign labourers and a source of scientific expertise.[101] China has played an important part in that engagement process. However, Beijing's relationship with Russia is not without its differences as issues such as trade imbalances which have favoured Beijing, illegal and unregulated cross-border trade, Moscow's concerns over high levels of Chinese immigration into the Russian far east, and lingering historical distrust, have persisted.[102] Nevertheless, both countries have been anxious to advertise the growing levels of amity between the two, which culminated in the Treaty on Good Neighbourliness, Friendship and Cooperation which was signed in July 2001, largely due to Chinese efforts.[103] Although it is unlikely at this time that the two countries will enter into an alliance comparable to that which existed before the Sino-Soviet split, Beijing is nevertheless interested in keeping Moscow engaged as an important regional actor despite its loss of political power and prestige as a result of the fall of the USSR.

Since the inception of the SCO, the organisation has provided a multilateral institutional framework which has served to augment the warming Sino-Russian relationship, which Beijing has found invaluable in increasing its international visibility. As Knudsen suggested, the original 1996 agreement between Russia, China, and the central Asian border states had the added purpose of allowing Beijing to 'bring Russia back in' in order to provide a greater balance among other great powers in the Asia-Pacific region and to prevent one regional actor from developing too great a monopoly.[104] However, it is too early to judge whether the current Sino-Russian friendship will endure as a sign of increasingly converging political and strategic interests, or act as a marriage of convenience based on mutual suspicion of American foreign policy motives. At present, the SCO has served to fortify Beijing's relations with Moscow, an important component of China's post-cold-war regional foreign policy.

Third, the development of the SCO offered China the opportunity to establish a diplomatic foothold in an increasingly important region. With the overlap between NATO partners and the SCO membership, it was suggested the Shanghai group might act as a bridge between Chinese and Atlantic security interests.[105] The need for this linkage has grown since 9/11, and at the same time the strategic engagement of central Asia has offered China a larger window not only into Eurasia, but well beyond. For example, since 2003 Sino-European Union relations have warmed considerably due to increased economic ties and shared policies on issues relating to Iraq's security and the role of the United Nations in settling international disputes.[106] Thus, the SCO has the potential to act as a physical and political bridge between these two entities. As well, China's engagement with both Russia and central Asia can be seen as a way for Beijing to dilute further Western influence in the region.

Fourth, China's powerful position within the SCO has allowed the group to act as a stronger sounding board for international-level security policies in which Beijing has a strong stake. The SCO has provided the most visible model of Beijing's New Security Concept via the use of informal cooperation and community-building rather than through hierarchical alliances. Since the end of the cold war, China's security thinking has expanded to include a far more hetero-geneous approach to defence and strategy, including diplomacy, economic factors, developing mutual interests, as well as separating short-term fundamental issues from longer-term strategic goals. These philosophies have been successfully injected into the SCO, and although opinion is still very much divided as to how strong a role the organisation can play in Eurasian security, the SCO has disting-uished itself in its approach to addressing the region's highly complex security dynamic.

Finally, the creation of the SCO has allowed China, and other members, to create a more comprehensive set of tools with which to address non-security issues, most notably increased economic cooperation. As Ross noted, Beijing has the added advantage over Moscow in extending its influence over central Asia due to China's strong economic presence.[107] Any development of an economic or trade mechanism within the SCO would therefore be beneficial to Chinese financial, as well as political, interests.

When the SCO met in Almaty, Kazakhstan, in September 2001, a memorandum of understanding on economic cooperation was unanimously approved. The main agreements in the memorandum included the development of joint ventures, improving transportation and communications infrastructure, and cooperation on power generation, tourism, agriculture, credit and banking, water and the environment.[108] These initiatives may allow China to further strengthen the Silk Road policy of developing a conduit for Chinese trade through central Asia, as well as to further develop the economy of its own far western provinces. Should SCO plans to develop its economic and cultural sectors prove viable, this would be an example of the 'spillover' process, described by Nye as a situation whereby 'imbalances created by the functional interdependence or inherent linkages of tasks can press political actors to redefine their common tasks'.[109]

Although a formal SCO security community may be a long way off, the deepening of the SCO mandate, greatly supported by China, demonstrates a significant development in Beijing's new thinking on the utility of international institutions. Beijing has the potential to gain several goods from the SCO process beyond border security, including economic gains, regional prestige and a strength-ened hand in dealing with other great powers, especially the United States, as the international community faces possible competition over influence in Central Asia.

The SCO's next role: cooperation model or chess piece?

At the beginning of the twenty-first century, the central Asian region could be categorised into three distinct sets of actors. First, there are the former Soviet republics in the region which, along with Afghanistan, are faced with weak governments, poor infrastructure and a variety of challenges to state authority. Although one country, Uzbekistan, has been better able to develop an independent identity over the past decade, these states are still especially vulnerable to both inside and outside political pressures. Second, there are the regional powers, namely India, Iran, Pakistan, and Turkey, who have, to varying degrees, viewed central Asia as an arena in which to strengthen their respective regional positions.

Finally, there are the great powers, China, Russia, and the United States, who have recognised their need to engage the region both because of central Asia's considerable economic potential, mostly in the form of energy, and its capability of serving as an incubator for terrorism and extremist organisations, as the events of September 2001 tragically demonstrated. All of these states are circling the region, seeking greater influence while ensuring rivals do not do the same. As a result, central Asia risks becoming a whirlwind, and the potential for an expanded conflict there remains a clear possibility as a result of these overlapping rivalries.

The security dynamic in central Asia is changing very rapidly, and it is still unclear which direction the region will take in the coming years. Keeping this uncertainty in mind, China is very concerned that this frontier not be transformed into a threat either to Chinese security or to its foreign policy interests. Chinese engagement in central Asia has been and remains a very risky endeavour due to the weak political structure of the region, and the highly problematic security challenges throughout. If these relations are mishandled by Beijing, there would be serious impact within China's own borders in Xinjiang. The Chinese government is determined to prevent the growth of non-state security challenges in the form of the 'three evils' in central Asia. In addition, China is aware that it is now in direct competition with other great powers for regional influence, a situation greatly complicated by the presence of American forces in central Asia after 9/11. The United States, far more capable to provide both security and economic 'carrots' to the region than Russia or China, has provided an extra layer of difficulty for Beijing.

Nevertheless, China's role in the creation and evolution of the SCO is one of the most significant foreign policy initiatives to emanate from that country in the last decade. More importantly, the forum represents a successful endeavour by China to help in the creation of an international security institution which observes the parameters of Chinese foreign policy as it relates to cooperation with such organisations, namely that the SCO, despite its increased formalisation after 2001, remains consensus-based, not directed towards a specific adversary, and is flexible enough to allow for new issues to be raised. China's position of being the strongest player in the Shanghai group, economically and politically, has also allowed Beijing to take the lead in directing the SCO to examine issues important not only to the whole, but also to China specifically.

The question which remains is whether the rapidly shifting power distribution in central Asia as a result of increased rivalries by local and regional states, and capped by the sudden increase in American influence, will create untenable strains on the organisation which China may be unable to reconcile. Moreover, future conflicts in the region could have their genesis in a variety of sources: state collapse, a resurgence of extremist activities, regional frictions, and rivalries over energy development in the Caspian region. The true test of the SCO's effectiveness will be based on how it addresses these future challenges, and whether it remains a tool for peace rather than a participant in a new Great Game.

The Shanghai Cooperation Organisation is still very young, and it is still unclear whether the forum will develop into a more formalised security community or retain its informal status. Its future will also depend on the maintenance of relative good will between its two most formidable members, China and Russia, and whether the group can succeed in addressing its current issues, namely the reductions in regional tension caused by terrorism, cross-border smuggling and secessionist forces which still bedevil the governments of all six members. Despite the growing number of challenges facing the SCO, Beijing will be very reluctant to see its most ambitious experiment in developing a regional security regime end in failure. Regardless of which direction the forum takes, however, the SCO will remain an important case study for the overall examination of Chinese engagement with international institutions.

5

SEEKING MODERNITY

China's institutional openings and shifts in international power

> Opportunity must not be lost when the gods smile.
> Li Jing, Tang Dynasty

China steps out

'Look around', a Western diplomat said as we walked along the Embassy Row district in Chaoyang, Beijing on a typically humid September day. 'This is one of the few places in the world where the population goes to bed at night safe in the knowledge that when they get up, things will be just a little bit better. There are few other places in the world where that can be said'. While this statement may oversimplify China's social and political situation, it also contains many elements of truth. Since the Dengist reforms, China's domestic-level economic development and its international stature have grown at rates faster than those of rising powers of the past. From the start of the twenty-first century, China has demonstrated growing confidence in its interactions with the global community. This has resulted in the increased use of international institutions as a means of developing and enhancing Chinese power in the international system. Therefore, to understand the dynamics of China as a great power, and as a future global power in the areas of politics, economics, and military capability one must begin with the variable of China's cooperation with international institutions.

China's interactions with others, small and large powers alike, increasingly reflect greater maturity and self-assurance in foreign policymaking, a preference for conservative thinking, and a respect for state sovereignty. Of course, the power capabilities of states do not remain constant and the end of the cold war was merely the latest in a series of power shifts in the international system producing new winners and new challengers. If, as appears likely, China continues to grow in relation to other great powers to the point where it has the ability to redefine international order, what might be the outcome?

One argument cautions that China's increased interactions with the global community, especially in terms of economic ties, should not be interpreted as a sign the region around China is bound to become more pacified. This view dominated much strategic study in the 1990s. As Nye lamented, 'it has become fashionable to say that the world after the cold war has moved beyond the age of power politics to the age of geoeconomics. Such clichés reflect narrow analysis. Politics and economics are connected. International economic systems rest upon international political order'.[1] Mearsheimer pointed to China as being 'the key to understanding the future distribution of power in Northeast Asia', and warns that Chinese economic growth may translate into considerable future regional instability.[2] Finally, Huntington's oft-discussed 'Clash of Civilisations' theory includes a description of China as a rising power within a highly unstable Asian region, while Sino-American relations are described as very tenuous.[3] Until 9/11, China loomed large in the strategic thinking of other great powers, including the United States. Is the warming of Sino-American relations, as a result of their mutual anti-terrorism policies, a long-term diplomatic shift or a temporary marriage of convenience?

Another argument stresses Beijing's ambition to assume the privileges of great-powerdom in the international system, preferring cooperation over conflict. One study points to Chinese caution and conservatism in its dealings with the international system, stressing China's rationality and eagerness to continue its cooperation with other states within the boundaries of international rules and norms of behaviour.[4] Nathan and Ross argued that despite China's considerable development both economically and militarily, it remains vulnerable to outside pressures from other greater powers.[5] Beijing may be unwilling to engage in belligerent behaviour which would risk its newfound international status, its fragile domestic reforms, the safety of its markets and its strengthened international ties. In other words, Beijing is reaping many benefits from increased international cooperation, including that from international institutions. Much of China's power has developed through cooperation, a situation that the country is unwilling to change at the present time.

In order to reconcile these arguments, one should define the China of today. Schweller described four types of states in relation to two variables, their level of satisfaction with international order and the lengths to which they will go to change it in order to serve their needs. 'Lion' states are willing to pay high costs to protect what they have but will accept only small costs to improve upon what they have. They are normally large powers which prefer the status quo. 'Lamb' states are unwilling to assume high costs either to protect what they have or to gain more, thus making them weakened states. 'Jackals' are very concerned about protecting what they have, but will pay even higher costs to gain more. They are commonly categorised as potential great powers dissatisfied with the status quo. Finally, 'Wolves' are states which place more emphasis on what they covet than what they already have, often entering into reckless military adventures in the name of further gains.[6]

Using these criteria, categorising China is not difficult. Adherents to the 'China threat' school of thought might define Beijing as a jackal, pointing to its rising power and apparent dissatisfaction with the international system, as well as its military modernisation and its opposition to many Western policies and ideologies. However, in terms of its current behaviour both within international institutions and in more general terms of its security interests, *China is a lion*, and has already begun to adopt the foreign policy perceptions of great power and potential global power.

China's foreign policy behaviour would suggest an unwillingness to engage in revisionist behaviour and its need to take its place as a peer among other great powers. Although Beijing has moved toward a more extroverted foreign policy and improved its military to better address its power projection deficiencies, Beijing has shown a marked unwillingness to use force over the past half century unless perceived core interests, primarily state sovereignty, were threatened.[7] Where past, and likely future, problems lie is when China's core interests, including Taiwan, greater access to the Pacific, and a larger share of international resources and markets, overlap the interests of others, including the United States.

China's activity strongly suggests a greater emphasis on either status quo preservation or measured evolution of various facets of international order. In keeping with 'lion-like' behaviour, Beijing has shown little sign that it is willing to pay high costs or take great risks in employing force to improve its standing in the international hierarchy. Whether this situation will continue depends greatly on how its rising power affects its foreign policy activities, especially *vis-à-vis* other great powers, and how and whether the United States and other powers will accept the rise of China.

In examining China's motives for cooperation with international institutions, one can identify three stages in the development of Beijing's policy towards such regimes. First was a period of general avoidance and suspicion, which dominated the time between the founding of the People's Republic and the opening to the United Nations and later to the West in the 1970s. The lack of recognition by many countries of the regime in Beijing, coupled with the Mao Zedong government's suspicions of international security and economic institutions being utilised by the West to dominate the international system and erode the communist revolution, prevented China from effectively engaging the global community through the growing number of international regimes created after the cold war.

The second stage was the cautious, conservative opening to institutions, particularly economic-based regimes such as the International Monetary Fund and the GATT, as a means of promoting China's foreign policy independence of the 1980s. The breaking with the Soviet Union and gradual opening to the United States and its allies came about while greater confidence was developed by Beijing, reducing its fears of becoming marginalised in the international system. Furthermore, the end of the Maoist era with its erratic domestic and foreign policy developments during the Cultural Revolution was succeeded by the reformist policies of Deng Xiaoping after 1979, who advocated economic liberalisation and a greater opening to international dialogue and trade to reverse the damage created by previous attempts at modernisation via command economics and political isolation. With Deng's shift in policy priorities and his assertion that the 'colour of the cat' was not important, China began a period of economic growth and international opening which increasingly included international and regional organisations.

The third stage was the post-Tiananmen, post-cold war expansion of China's institutional engagements to include more regionally-based economic regimes such as APEC and the APT as well as strategic institutions such as the ARF and SCO. Following Tiananmen, Beijing was anxious to improve relations both with its immediate neighbours and with other parts of the world. These initiatives were also inspired by the demise of the Soviet Union, since this removed Moscow as one of Beijing's largest security concerns, paving the way for warmer Sino-Russian relations. As well, the end of the cold war created more stability around other parts of China's periphery, such as in southeast Asia, as enhanced initiatives to foster regional cooperation replaced former rivalries. China's newfound skill and confidence enabled it to not only react to existing international regimes, but to influence their development and even call for and develop new institutions.

China feared, during the 1990s, that the international system was drifting towards unipolarity, with the United States at the apex. Beijing repeatedly professed its preference for a multilateral system with a number of great powers preventing a concentration of power. Thus, China increased its participation with interstate institutions in order to ensure a continued role in shaping the evolving post-cold war international order. Furthermore, greater institutional engagement served as an outlet for China's more nationalistic foreign policies which flourished under the Jiang regime and have continued under Hu Jintao. The dawn of globalisation and the events of 9/11 further underscored the fact that China needed to engage in greater cooperation regionally and internationally, and on a Track I and Track II basis.

A fourth stage in China's institutional engagement has quietly begun over the past few years, defined by the sophisticated and confident utilisation of institutions to advance Chinese power in the international system. As was previously described, China's developing relations with international institutions revolved around six 'goods' of great importance to the development of Chinese power. These goods have been obtained from increased interactions with inter-state regimes.

The advantages of institutions I: economic regimes

It is easy to forget in the midst of the growing number of reports detailing China's economic growth, development and trade, as well as glowing predictions of the impact of the country's vast market potential, that China is still a developing country in many ways and has had a very short time, compared to other great powers, to adjust to the complexities of the global economic system. Both on an international and on a regional level, China can be considered a late developer. Examining China's international economic impact, Segal's 1999 polemic warned against overestimating Chinese power. He reminded readers that China's ranking in terms of percentage of global gross national product and human development was still very low.[8]

China's market reforms after 1978, and the acceleration of the economic liberalisation process during the early 1990s, took place well after its neighbours, Japan, South Korea and southeast Asia, all participated in the 'Asian Miracle' which led to wide-ranging regional economic growth from the 1980s until a reality check arrived in the form of the financial crisis. Great enthusiasm for China developed in the early 1990s, when the country was identified as a soon-to-be economic powerhouse. At that time, a 'Beijing scramble' mentality, one in which companies 'scrambled' for Chinese market access, appeared in the West, but this enthusiasm did not match reality.[9] Much of China's economy remains under central control or influence, the domestic reform process remains far from completion, and the gap between rich and poor represents a considerable social and economic obstacle to further growth. In short, China had, and still has, a great deal of economic catching up to do before it ascends to the upper tier of the world's most powerful economies.

However, despite these formidable obstacles, indicators of economic growth, including annual gross domestic product, foreign investment, a rapidly-developing middle class and increased trade, all point to remarkable gains over the past twenty-five years. China's economy has proven itself to be both attractive and resilient. Beijing has been able to adjust to shocks of the financial crisis and the SARS outbreak while continuing to record impressive growth in gross domestic product. Also, in examining Chinese behaviour towards economics and trade-based institutions since the Dengist reforms, a conclusion can be made that Beijing was swift in developing a level of poise and understanding necessary to abide by the rules and norms of these regimes.

The case studies examined in this book support the assertion by Wang that China is, at least for now, currently more content with participation in economic institutions than in strategic ones.[10] However, this factor is not unique to the Chinese case, as part of the reason why Wang's assertion is apodictic can be drawn from previous studies of regime behaviour. Milner noted that one of the most crucial functions of regimes is preventing cheating or defection by one party. Regimes have the ability to reduce concerns about defection, because regimes involve information exchange between members, and about members, and facilitate transactions. Moreover, the mere fact that a given regime exists means that its members are comfortable enough with each other and with the rules or norms of that regime.[11]

Since Beijing began its process of institutional engagement, it has been more receptive to institutions which focus on trade and economic cooperation issues rather than on security matters, perhaps because cooperation in economic and security areas involves different 'stakes'. As Lipson explained, states within economic regimes rarely must concern themselves with the potential of another member breaking rules since most such actions would be slow to develop and difficult to conceal.[12] Jervis noted that security issues usually spark more competitiveness between states and that the stakes are much higher in the strategic realm than the economic. A state is also commonly able to defend itself against external economic problems without adversely affecting other states' interests and can take such defensive measures at a more leisurely pace than during a security emergency.[13] A feature of many current economic regimes are measures which permit members to suspend obligations without withdrawing from the regime altogether. Even though the use of such 'escape clauses' may carry some degree of penalty, their existence has assuaged concerns that members would be completely locked into international economic agreements.[14] All of these features of modern economic regimes may explain why states often view economic regimes as more congenial to their interests.

In the case of China, its current economic strength and its current and potential market power has served to increase its role in global trade and financial issues. Impressive Chinese economic fundamentals, including government stability, a highly trained and educated workforce, rapid growth in the industrial and services sectors, and support from overseas diaspora have enabled China to increase its economic growth an average of approximately 9.5 per cent per year since the Dengist reforms.[15] Not only has China developed into a powerful exporter, but it has become a strong importer, purchasing approximately US$187 billion worth of foreign goods for domestic consumption in 2003, and is an enthusiastic supporter of foreign joint ventures, all measures which have increased enthusiasm for economic openness from both Chinese firms and citizens.[16]

Much economic development lies ahead for China, since large numbers of the population still have not benefited from the economic reforms. The wealth gap between the prosperous coast and underdeveloped interior remains a serious domestic problem. In 2003, the country's gross national income per capita stood at approximately US$1,100 according to the World Bank, and the 2004 Human Development Report released by the UN Development Programme (UNDP) placed China in 94th place of 177 states in its development index.[17] Despite these obstacles, the country's latent and kinetic economic power has grown to where it cannot be ignored or marginalised.

China's growing economic power has allowed the country to negotiate with trading and financial regimes from a far stronger position than when it first opened up to the global market. Admittedly, the country's advantage of being a *presence gigantesque* did not prevent its negotiation process of joining the GATT/WTO from lasting well over a decade. However, China's important role in international affairs defined the question of when and how, not if, China could join. Yet to be revealed is how China's economic power will affect its actions and those of other members within the organisation, and what kind of role China will play in the current international trading round of negotiations launched after the Doha meeting.

China has been presented with many incentives to develop positive relationships with multilateral economic regimes. From a domestic-level viewpoint, the opening to international economic institutions, especially the WTO, has assisted the government in implementing reform initiatives throughout many sectors within China, including the state bureaucracy, state-owned enterprises, private business, trade of goods and services, the military, and banking and financial services. The country's economic success has been linked to its ability to adapt to international markets, including its institutions, just as it has linked the legitimacy of its communist regime to its ability to provide for the Chinese people and move the country further towards economic development and modernity.

Whether the Communist Party can continue to tie the country's economic successes to participation in economic regimes will greatly depend on the amount of financial trauma created as reforms continue and whether the government can absorb these socio-economic shocks. Since the end of the cold war the Chinese government has largely been accepting of the WTO and the Asian initiatives designed to improve regional trade flows and to avoid a repeat of the political and economic circumstances which created the Asian financial crisis. China had remained sufficiently insulated from the regional economic system to endure the Asian flu with just a slight bout of sniffles. However, should the domestic impact of greater international competition create a political backlash against Beijing, China's institutional commitments may be scaled back.

As well, should Asia itself suffer an economic relapse, the effects on China may be considerably more severe as Beijing continues to open up more of its economy to regional and international participation. At the beginning of the new century there appeared little evidence China would scale down its economic opening policies, since its comfort level with liberalised trade has extended beyond international and regional trade regimes into smaller-scale preferential trade agreements in Asia and increasingly elsewhere in the world. The true test of the resiliency of China's opening to the global economy, and its associated regimes, will be in how it conducts itself within an increasingly dense network of trade obligations.

The 'information question' is another factor in examining China's relations with international regimes. As Keohane noted, asymmetrical information, when one party knows more than another, can lead to serious problems in state interaction. However, regimes by their nature provide information, reducing the risks involved in making international agreements. Thus, he argues, economic regimes are beneficial in reducing the perceived risks of economic transactions and in reducing the costs of various interactions since regimes reduce gaps in information flow which may lead to conflicts between partners.[18] The Chinese case is no exception. As a late developer, China has not only been required to quickly learn the rules of procedure in the global economy but also has been placed at risk of adverse treatment by more advanced economies, a situation that a Chinese Communist Party with its legitimacy largely based on continued economic growth can ill-afford.

Every institution which China decides to engage has the potential to provide information on international rules and norms, whether area-specific or of a more general nature, as well as the policy orientations of other participants in a given regime. Beijing appears to have made much use of economic institutions in assisting with its rapid transition from command to liberal economics. In the cases of the

WTO, the Asia Pacific Economic Cooperation (APEC) forum and the Asean-Plus-Three (APT), China has utilised these regimes not only for the shared benefit of increasing trade flows between it and the international community, but also to increase its knowledge of multilateralism, international norms and the preferences of other political actors. Within the WTO, Beijing has the ability to better understand international trade discourse, while its membership and size ensures Beijing of a role in the shaping of future trade developments. APEC and the APT provide China with the ability to gain further insights into the economic recovery since the financial crisis of East Asia and to further examine how the development processes of the economically advanced states in the region could act as models for future Chinese growth.

On the international level, the advantages of these regimes are also clear. Since China is becoming increasingly tied to the global economy through trade, joint ventures, international investment and foreign assistance, it is in China's interests to ensure this global economy evolves in ways which are compatible with Beijing's goals. In joining both regional and international economic institutions, Beijing has spoken out against protectionism or favouritism in global trade while seeking to distinguish itself as a large developing power. At the same time it has used these bodies to promote its growing economic and market power and to solidify economic relations both with neighbours and with international markets, ensuring continued economic growth.

From a liberalist viewpoint, China's institutional relations may provide further insight into whether economic interdependence is a contributor to peaceful state behaviour, an issue which has divided many international relations specialists.[19] A caveat needs to be offered, however, since China has not yet fully opened its economy either to institutional rules or to the global market as a whole. Moreover, China's positive views of APEC and the ASEAN-Plus-Three stem from the fact that they do not actively promote formalised regional economic integration, but rather more efficient coordination of regional trade and development. Therefore, it would be premature to examine these two organisations as forces for regional peacebuilding.

From a *realpolitik* viewpoint, China's approach to regional economic regimes may be seen as a method of building Beijing's regional-level economic strength. Both APEC and the APT have served to demonstrate China's increasingly important role in Asia, both economic and to a larger degree, political. The current economic hierarchy within the Asia-Pacific has the potential to shift in Beijing's favour, and the coming decade may see China supplant Japan as the economic 'core' of the region. Beijing has also made use of both groups to gain further advantage in its ongoing diplomatic rivalry with Taiwan. In the case of the APEC forum, although Taipei is a member, Beijing has exercised control over the degree to which the island can represent itself at forum meetings, while simultaneously taking advantage of one of the few windows available into Taiwan's economic policies. Taiwan is currently shut out of the APT and should this organisation develop into a more formal Asian economic community, the island will be placed at an even more serious disadvantage. For Beijing, its stature within the organisation as well as its economic health compared to many other members of the group, including Japan and much of southeast Asia, guarantees it a strong voice in the development of the APT and may provide China with a united front to better address issues important to it on an international level.

Beijing's muted support and reserved approach to APEC is becoming starkly contrasted to a more assertive approach within the APT and its mandate of increasing regional trade. Within the Asean-Plus-Three milieu, China has begun to emerge as a driving force, particularly in light of its proposals to increase the pace of developing east and southeast Asian free trade and because Beijing's economy is one of the strongest in post-crisis Asia. In short, Beijing has been able to take advantage of still partially recovering ASEAN economies, Japan's sporadic financial doldrums and rising regional and international interest in Chinese markets and economic growth, which will further intensify as a result of China's WTO admission. Although there is no guarantee this regional economic hierarchy will remain static, the APT and the rising number of preferential trade agreements which Beijing is negotiating serve to reflect China's growing financial power and strength both on a regional scale and an international scale.

The advantages of institutions II: strategic regimes

Over the past decade, China's relations with its immediate neighbours, as well as with other parts of the world, have steadily improved as the country pursued a programme of developing stronger ties leading to further political and economic cooperation. Beijing's relations with security institutions have also gone from cold to cordial, and the level of Chinese interest and participation in such regimes has grown since the beginning of the 1990s. This increasing interest can be explained in various ways. First, China is developing confidence that it can cooperate with these regimes while maintaining a necessary level of sovereignty and state security. Second, many of the strategic institutions which have developed around China since the end of the cold war contain both frameworks and mandates more suited to specific Chinese interests both at an international and domestic level.

Third, China's ongoing concern about being marginalised by other states, and especially by other great powers, the nightmare 'containment' scenario, has prompted its use of institutions to help thwart such potential international initiatives. Fourth, the security issues which China is attempting to address today are less within the realm of 'state vs. state' and more in relation to non-traditional threats such as terrorism, separatism and international crime. These new security dangers have proven too difficult for China to address alone, necessitating the cultivation of friends and allies to solve these complex problems.

Thus, the cost–benefit ratio of Beijing's engagement with international strategic institutions has been altered to the degree that China believes these organisations provide enough goods to be worth the risks and loss of sovereignty of institutional cooperation. The clearest symbol of this level of comfort is the creation of the Shanghai Cooperation Organisation, the first major strategic institution constructed primarily under Chinese influence. Beijing's proposals to expand the mandate of the ARF and its stronger, more positive participation in the Korean Six-Party Talks provide additional proof of this rising comfort level.

China originally approached post-cold war security institutions with wariness due, in part, to unfavourable historical encounters with them. Chinese interests in Korea were targeted by the UN in the early 1950s, and that body's recognition of the Republic of China instead of the mainland in 1971 contributed to Beijing's isolation during the first decades of the cold war. Even after China gained further international visibility and recognition, the country was still influenced by fears these regimes would force Beijing to make its defence policies less opaque, providing greater confidence to China's adversaries and reducing the Chinese deterrence abilities.[20] This anxiety still tends to permeate the Chinese approach to participation in strategic regimes, regardless of the level of formality or rules of the regime in question, but is no longer as high a concern as it was in the 1990s and before.

China's participation in security institutions has helped the country to pursue a primary foreign policy goal of maintaining a stable periphery to ensure that it can continue its social and economic development unimpeded by regional crises. China's periphery is currently at a level of peace unprecedented since the end of the Second World War. Beijing is unwilling to take this stability for granted and instead operates on the assumption that the international system remains in a transitional period from a bipolar world dominated by superpower rivalry to either a multipolar one, which Beijing would favour for its ability to bring about checks and balances on state power, or a unipolar one dominated by the United States, which Beijing has argued would be detrimental to global peace and stability. In addition to concerns about great-power alignment, China faces a host of non-traditional security threats which may adversely affect its desire for sustained regional stability. These include the 'three evils' of separatism, terrorism and extremism, all of which may be imported into China from abroad, as well as the smuggling of arms, drugs and persons, piracy, and maritime security.

With the beginning of the new century, the international war on terrorism has affected many parts of the world, and the question of nuclear proliferation has affected Asia with concerns that North Korea may barge into the nuclear club. Economic security has risen in importance as trade linkages have proven themselves vulnerable to terrorism and health crises, including SARS and avian flu. China lacks the power and abilities to address all of these problems unilaterally and although Beijing has built up many strong bilateral relationships based on security interests, such ties have been deemed insufficient to address these new security threats. Therefore, China's approach to multilateral security has softened appropriately towards organisations which discuss these matters on a regional scale, including the United Nations, ARF and even APEC.

At the same time, China is concerned with the development of regional security organisations which may exclude or align against China. This has been demonstrated by China's sceptical view of the inroads the Organisation of Security and Cooperation in Europe (OSCE) and the North Atlantic Treaty Organisation (NATO) have made into the former Soviet Union and closer to China's western border. Neither the proposed 'Four Party Group' composed of the United States and select Pacific Rim allies, based on shared defensive interests, nor the 'theatre missile defence' regime based on American anti-missile technology transfers to select allies, have gelled into actual alliances or even communities. Nevertheless China's harsh criticism of both groups demonstrated the high level of sensitivity to possibly being ringed by unfriendly alliances.

Such concerns have helped shape Chinese approaches to regional security institutions, since, as Swaine and Tellis correctly noted, China tends to join institutions if it fears they may turn against Chinese interests if Beijing allows itself to be left out,[21] an idea which was also explored in Gruber's study noting states may be prompted to join institutions, even when they are concerned about the short-term costs and might prefer to remain outside, out of 'fear of being left behind'.[22] However, as Rosecrance pointed out in his critique of Gruber's hypotheses, in real world situations it is possible for a state to remain outside an organisation yet still benefit from it, since on many occasions the 'goods' which an institution produces (such as more regional security) cannot be limited to members. As well, he stated, if a state sees an organisation being built up which runs counter to that state's interests, rather than joining despite the hardships, a state may decide to work against that organisation. Finally, a state may enter into an organisation not feeling forced to but rather with the idea that its position within the group may improve over time.[23]

Applying this question to China, one recognises the fear of being left out is certainly a factor in that country's engagement with strategic institutions. One of China's largest security concerns is to become the object of a Western-led policy of 'containment' or 'strategic encirclement', taking measures to restrain Chinese power by maintaining military alliances intended to balance against Chinese military power. By enlisting the assistance of West-friendly states such as Japan, a containment policy would prevent China from projecting its power in the region.[24] China's development of multilateral as well as bilateral ties to its Asian neighbours may serve to frustrate future attempts at containment by making the process too difficult and costly.

For example, had China been left out of the ARF, security agreements might possibly have been struck which could have adversely affected Beijing's policy on sensitive security matters, specifically Taiwan and the dispensation of the South China Sea territories, making Beijing's policies towards these areas more difficult to maintain. In the case of the Shanghai Five/SCO, the stakes were even higher for China, since its western frontier faced a myriad of security problems due to central Asia's weak states and extremist movements, coupled with very weak institutional development save, perhaps, for the Commonwealth of Independent States. Thus, for China to avoid institution-building would have meant the risk of increased lawlessness and extremism spilling over Chinese borders, forcing China to divert a much larger amount of capital and military resources westward in order to protect its border from these threats. Another unfavourable outcome might have been an expanded Western or Russian presence in the region increasing China's vulnerability and possibly cutting off Chinese influence in a politically and economically important region. China's enthusiasm for the SCO, therefore, serves as a means to ward off both sets of dangers.

However, the loss-avoidance idea provides only a partial rationale for Chinese association with regional security regimes, and to help complete the picture it is also helpful to examine the attractiveness of the regimes themselves. In short, the development of what Lake termed 'anarchic institutions',[25] those which are based on the maintenance of full sovereignty among members and therefore lack a hierarchy, has been crucial to China enjoying more comfortable relationships with strategic regimes. These types of institutions often provide each member with an equal voice and veto of mandates and rules and, in theory, prevent the development of blocs which would force resolutions on unwilling members. This form of cooperation formed the basis of China's New Security Concept which, as demonstrated by the SCO and the Six-Party Talks, has evolved from theory to reality in select cases.

According to neo-realist theory, a major hurdle in encouraging institutional cooperation is the idea that not only are states concerned about what they themselves gain from interstate cooperation, but they are also highly sensitive to what other partners may gain, especially if there is the perception that others gain more.[26] This problem is mitigated should an institution be anarchic, since others' gains can be verified by other members. While persuasive and 'soft' power are always factors in any institution so long as different members possess different levels of power, including military, economic, and so forth, an anarchic institution prevents a dissenting state from having to agree with the majority or defect from the organisation. This added security reduces the risk of cheating and strengthens the integrity of the regime itself. Thus, the development of anarchic regimes such as the ARF and CSCAP has been the lynchpin of China's acceptance of deeper engagement with strategic institutions.

For example, had the ARF developed as a more formal organisation with set rules and a hierarchical structure, it is unlikely China would have had the same level of interest in joining since doing so would have increased its perceived vulnerability. Rather, China may have worked to discourage the creation of such a regime, and its important role in maintaining Asia-Pacific security may have enabled it, more than other states, to press its policies more effectively. From another viewpoint, China may have benefited from strategic arrangements created by the ARF (including confidence-building measures, maritime security agreements, and so forth), even without membership. However, the fact that the ARF is informal, lacks rules of conduct and has a consensus-based system, allowing any member a veto makes the organisation a more comfortable one for China.

Using its veto power, Beijing has prevented sensitive issues such as those involving Taiwan and the ultimate status of the South China Sea archipelagos from being discussed at ARF meetings. As for the SCO, China might have been able to obtain the security it needed by relying on the individual bilateral agreements it signed with Russia and various central Asia states. However, since the SCO is also based on consensus, and at present China retains a first among equals status within the organisation because of its comparatively strong political and economic power, China is even more content with a multilateral approach to maintaining Eurasian security.

A related rationale for China's engagement with security institutions is based on China's desire to improve its overall prestige in the international order and to develop a security role in keeping with its status as a great power (*daguo*) and developing global power. Previous great powers relied heavily on material and military power to achieve their lofty status. However, the presence of the United States at the apex of the current post-cold war international hierarchy, coupled with the existence of nuclear weapons which many great power states possess, further discourages an attempt by China to improve its standing in the international order by means of force. Beijing has instead relied on participation in security institutions as one method of demonstrating its increasing importance to global security. Although China was granted a seat at the UN Security Council in 1971, and demonstrated its own nuclear capability seven years before that, the country still seeks to develop its status as a modern great power.

Key to this goal has been the restoration of linkages between China and its neighbours. Many of these links were severed during the cold war period due to either ideological differences or territorial issues. China's ambitious doctrine of 'leaning to one side' and becoming a valued member of the communist collective soured along with the Sino-Russian relationship,[27] leaving China isolated and vulnerable, forcing a détente with the United States. At the same time, China was facing challenges from many areas of its long border: the USSR to the north, Vietnam to the south and the US allies Japan and South Korea to the east. In the 1990s, China adopted a multidirectional diplomatic initiative to improve regional ties, a move meant to ensure such levels of vulnerability of its borders would not be seen again.

Much of this work was achieved through bilateral negotiations which resulted in security and economic agreements and occasionally a formalised 'partnership', such as those of the 1990s with Russia, France, ASEAN and Pakistan.[28] However, pursuing improved ties through strategic organisations provided additional benefits supplementing existing bilateral linkages. For example, the southeast Asian states which comprised ASEAN were anxious to bring China into a security nexus and thus supported China joining the ARF as a means of engaging Beijing. Conversely, Beijing was anxious to repair damaged relations with southeast Asia following years of rancour during the cold war, which in the case of Vietnam had erupted into full-fledged warfare. Thus, membership in the ARF, as well as the APT economic grouping, proved to be an ideal method for Beijing to augment the bilateral ties which it was forging with the region in the 1990s.

In the case of the SCO, the break-up of the Soviet Union presented China with a host of new states with whom Beijing was anxious to solidify ties, not only since there was concern Taiwan would make diplomatic inroads in central Asia, but also because swiftly establishing diplomatic ties with central Asia would give China a larger window into a region bordering the country's highly sensitive far western regions. At the same time, the independence of the central Asian states opened up the possibility of a renewed 'Great Game', a competition between great powers for regional influence and resources. As Rashid noted, what separates the present 'game' from the one played between Russia and Great Britain in the nineteenth century has been the present-day development of extremist organisations such as the Taliban and Al-Qaeda which have become global security threats and have forced the United States, Russia and China to coordinate their efforts to combat these threats.[29] However, it is unclear whether this great power cooperation in central Asia will prevail as the region's energy resources continue to be tapped. Should increased great power competition recur, Beijing requirement to ensure a continued visibility in central Asia is fulfilled by the SCO.

The ARF and the SCO have also acted as useful platforms for China to accentuate its doctrine of the New Security Concept. The development of this new thinking on security and cooperation stemmed from Chinese displeasure at the methods employed by other great powers, especially those in the West, to assure their security since the end of the cold war. A 1997 editorial in the *Beijing Review* noted that standard security practices among states were the creation of alliances designed to counter a mutual enemy, large powers protecting smaller ones, and weaker states deferring to stronger ones. Moreover, state security and state cooperation were traditionally seen by realists as being 'incompatible' with each other, since measures taken by one country to better protect itself invariably created insecurities in others, a nod to the Western international relations concept of the 'security dilemma'. However, the piece argued that at the close of the twentieth century, states' security interests had become so intertwined that it was necessary to approach the ideas of security and cooperation from a different, more conciliatory standpoint.[30] The NSC draws heavily on the 'five principles of peaceful coexistence', and stresses equality and non-discrimination, mutual trust and benefits and the non-interference in states' sovereign affairs.[31] Additionally, China has advocated including political, economical and technological cooperation as a further means of strengthening ties between states, rather than using only military power as a basis for linkages.[32]

During the course of the 1990s, the Chinese government developed this concept as a strategic paradigm to counter the alliance-based forms of cooperation favoured by Western powers during the cold war, but which, in China's view, were being inappropriately carried over into the post-cold war international system. A prime example of this is the ongoing strategic relationship between the United States and Japan.[33] These ideas were also elaborated upon within China's 2000 National Defence White Paper, which stressed that 'multilateral security dialogue and cooperation in the Asia-Pacific region should be oriented towards and characterised by mutual respect instead of the strong bullying the weak, cooperation instead of confrontation, and seeking consensus instead of imposing one's will on others'.[34] This form of security thinking was judged by China to be more compatible with its strategic interests during the transitional period away from cold war bipolarity.

A major area of contention between China and Western powers at the turn of the new century is the issue of when it is appropriate for security concerns to override norms of national sovereignty in the name of humanitarian intervention. Despite a softening on this question over the past decade, and especially since 9/11, the concept of 'humanitarian intervention' will continue to be seen by China as a game played by the rich and powerful, a game which brings differences in state power and abilities into stark relief. As such, it is highly improbable that Beijing will attain a level of comfort with the idea of state intervention in a unilateral fashion on humanitarian grounds, and will prefer that such actions be taken under the aegis of the UN. Beijing's acceptance of American actions in Afghanistan after 9/11 may indicate a change in Beijing's stance on the question of state sovereignty and military intervention.

However, this may be a temporary position. As long as China remains concerned that the United States may circumvent international norms and institutions as occurred with the Kosovo and Iraq operations, and as long as China fears it may be the victim of such practices in the future, distrust will continue. Institutions such as the ARF or its Track II subsidiaries would provide useful sounding boards to address the problems of intervention. Indeed, both the ARF and the SCO have been cited as examples of the effectiveness of this new security thinking both for China and across Asia.[35] In Beijing's view, they both represent security developments based on confidence- and consensus-building, while maintaining respect for the boundaries of state sovereignty.

The blueprint for China's proposed new security thinking has not been completely formulated, and is at present distinguished as much by what it is against, namely alliances and zero-sum strategic concepts, as what it is for, consensus-based, equal, and non-interventionist state cooperation. Nevertheless, China may continue to make use of both strategic institutions to further develop and promote this new thinking as a means of attempting to counter the development of alliances and hierarchical security institutions around China's periphery. What remains to be seen is whether Beijing's New Security Concept can accomplish this, especially since, as Duffield noted, China's rapid growth in military and economic power may strengthen the very American-based alliances Beijing argues against and possibly even create new ones.[36] Thus, Beijing is anxious to make use of existing 'anarchic' institutions in the Asian region to promote the development of security, based on non-alliance principles and hopefully to convince other actors in the region tthat the development of an anti-China bloc would be detrimental to regional peace.

Finally, China has approached strategic institutions hoping to obtain spillover benefits which go beyond strictly military matters. In the case of the ARF, China has cooperated with the organisation as a means to assure neighbours it is not a threat to the stability of the Asia-Pacific and one of the benefits of this goodwill may be increased political and economic ties between the region and Beijing. More specifically, China has supported initiatives within the ARF which promote cooperation in areas beyond strategic matters. These include technology development, medicine and legal issues which would be beneficial to Chinese foreign policy and increase necessary ties with the region.

As for the SCO, Beijing has shown a great deal of enthusiasm for formalising that regime, not in the direction of creating a Eurasian NATO, but rather with an eye to creating a regional community which goes beyond security issues and also addresses issues of trade, joint development and culture. Such a development would hopefully serve to maintain peaceful relations on China's long western border and provide trade routes, long sought after by Beijing, between the Chinese coast and the Eurasian heartland. Chief among those trade concerns will inevitably be energy flows as the central Asia/Caucasus region gradually develops the wherewithal to extract and transport its oil and supplies to international markets. A twenty-first century China growing increasingly dependent on outside energy supplies to fuel its burgeoning economy cannot afford to overlook the importance of its central Asian relations.

However, it is likely that due to both the ongoing threat of extremism and terrorism in the region, coupled with a likely longer-term American interest in the area as part of its international operations against terror, security matters will remain at the apex of the SCO's activities in the foreseeable future. In light of the fact the SCO is currently styling itself as a means for policy coordination on strategic and political matters in central Asia, the organisation may prove a useful partner in international efforts to promote peace in what is developing into a highly unstable region. Although the SCO is still very young and its mandate is still evolving, it does have the advantage of being the 'person on the scene', an important asset should international security concerns, especially the war on terrorism, deepen in central Asia.

It is too early to determine whether China's warming approach to international strategic institutions is the beginning of a long trend or a matter of political expediency. If one assumes the former, these institutions may act as a means for a maturing China to both solidify its great power status by addressing problems which the country cannot effectively handle alone and to take a more active role in the development of international security. Or these institutions may present a means to gain information about the security practices of possible rivals on a regional level, as well as *vis-à-vis* other great powers, especially the United States. Once China develops its military, political, economic and persuasive powers more effectively, a pessimistic view would suggest that Beijing would disengage from the commitments of security institutions in favour of more direct unilateral actions. Whichever future scenario is correct, and there is the possibility that elements of both futures may become reality, Chinese power has been greatly assisted by its engagement of security regimes.

Gains, losses, and Chinese power

Regimes, as Krasner noted, are created when the distribution of power among a given set of countries is relatively equal, but problems in coordination are present.[37] It should be added, that for a regime to appear, not only must power levels of potential members be compatible, but there must be at least a minimum of policy coordination and amicable relations between the partners. After the end of the cold war, these conditions were present in the case of China, since while the country was more powerful than many of its partners, in terms of its exposure to international discourse, China was very much the student. Examining Beijing's current relationship with international institutions, the cost–benefit measurement greatly favours continuing to create and strengthen international linkages. How long will this particular situation last and what will be the next stage of China's cooperation with international regimes? To answer these questions, it is necessary to examine the ability of such regimes to provide China with the goods it desires and the costs the country will be willing to assume in the future to reap maximum benefits from multilateral diplomacy via these institutions.

In both economic and political regimes, China at the start of the twenty-first century appears to be slowly but perceptibly moving away from Kim's 'maxi-mini' principle of engaging institutions to gain the maximum number of rights while minimising the associated responsibilities. The term was used to describe Chinese participation in the UN and to account for its policy of oscillating between 'tacit cooperation and aloofness' within that organisation. In other words, he noted that Chinese conservatism in its participation in the UN can be traced to its desire to accrue the most benefits while assuming the least costs.[38] Economy noted that the principle could be applied to China's associations with international regimes as a whole, suggesting Beijing employs international institutions to enhance its state economic capabilities rather than to transfer state sovereignty to an international decision-making body.[39]

The 'maxi-mini' idea can arguably imply that China's approach to international regimes is distinct to the Chinese case. In reality, a strong case can be made that any given state approaches an international institution first with the question of how the regime can benefit the state, and only secondly vice versa, if at all. Differences in state approaches to international institutions can be found in the degree to which each state maximises the benefits of cooperation while minimising the costs. China, being a great power and developing global one, is in a better position to do so than many other nations.

When examining Beijing's interactions with international institutions since the end of the cold war, one may question whether China has become increasingly more willing to accept higher costs in cooperating with international institutions in order to accrue future gains. This would provide evidence that although the 'maxi-mini' principle can be used to describe some facets of Chinese behaviour towards international institutions, it does not reveal the entire picture. Furthermore, as China grows in both political and economic power, the country can less afford to take a 'maxi-mini' approach to institutional cooperation which 'maxi-mini' implies.

To examine the economic case studies, Beijing's participation within APEC, the ASEAN-Plus-Three and various emerging preferential trade agreements in Asia has resulted in many gains for China, including heightened regional prestige, windows into other important regional economies, and tutelage in the art of foreign economic interactions, giving China more weight in interacting with the global economic system. Since the rules of these two organisations are consensus-based, China need not fear being 'ganged up on' by other members and having its own policies dictated by outsiders. Within these regimes China has the luxury of pursuing the largest possible number of gains at a very low cost. Yet, China's slow but steady evolution towards lead goose status in the 'flying geese' economic configuration within Asia, as well as the growing number of economic ties China is forging with the rest of Asia, have placed additional pressures on Beijing. Thus, an argument can be made that as long as China continues to tie its economic growth to external trade and economic liberalisation, Beijing cannot afford to view economic institutional cooperation in a 'zero-sum' fashion. It was painfully proven to Asia in 1997 that an economic downturn in one country can drag in unwitting neighbours as well.

In the case of the WTO, China has had to pay a large admission price and did not have the luxury of entering into this group on its own terms. Instead, the process of joining was lengthened by China's many incremental attempts to improve its economic liberalisation practices and laws to a point where other WTO members would accept China's accession. The economic impact of China's WTO membership is bound to be severe in the short term, especially in the sensitive areas of financial services and agriculture. Having entered the organisation, the rules-based structure of the WTO system requires that if China attempts to act in an overly 'selfish' manner, it would be the subject of punitive actions from other members and/or the WTO's dispute settlement body. Thus, China must play by the rules to a sufficient degree to maintain membership benefits.

It can be argued China's huge market and growing economic power may provide a temptation for the country to act less cooperatively within the WTO, since other members might not wish to aggravate their lucrative linkages with Beijing. However, the WTO will act as a strong incentive for the government of Hu Jintao to push forward with the economic reform programmes needed to maintain its levels of economic growth and the Party must maintain the goodwill of the Chinese populace. In the case of the WTO, China needs to take the costs with the benefits for maximum gain from its association with the organisation.

On the strategic side, the cases of the ASEAN Regional Forum (ARF) and the Shanghai Cooperation Organisation (SCO) provide differing views of the 'maxi-mini' principle. The ARF, like APEC, is consensus-based, which has allowed China the opportunity to block any multilateral initiatives which would challenge its security interests, namely Taiwan and the security situation in the South China Sea. The lack of binding rules within the ARF has permitted China to press its policies of insisting the above two issues are domestic in nature and best handled by Beijing, alone. Thus, China's participation in the ARF could best be described as pursuing private goods (keeping other members away from matters tied to Chinese sovereignty as well as gaining insights into other members' strategic interests) at little cost. Should the strategic picture in the region change as a result of the creation of more formal security arrangements, China may need to further engage the ARF to ensure its security interests are not marginalised. However, the idea of leaving China out of multilateral security dialogues is one which is becoming less and less viable as Beijing takes a more active approach to international security problems.

The cost–benefit equation is considerably murkier in the case of the SCO, for although this organisation also operates by consensus, the nature of the membership and the mandate of the Shanghai group have forced China to assume more costs in order to reap the rewards. First and foremost, China acted 'against type' by not only supporting and cooperating with a security institution, but was, in fact, the major impetus for the SCO's creation in the first place and continues to play the strongest role in determining the policies of the group. Second, the SCO has within its membership one strong state (China), one faltering state (Russia), and four weaker ones (Kazakhstan, Kyrgyzstan, Tajikistan and Uzbekistan). Therefore, China has had to assume a leadership role in shaping the SCO to keep the organ-isation from losing forward momentum, since an erosion of the SCO could result in China being less able to address its security concerns in the region, as well as facing a diminishing of its own stature within Central Asia, which is developing into one of the most contested strategic arenas in Asia due to its geographic location and oil and gas supplies.

Another factor was the rapid arrival of American interests and military in central Asia as a result of 9/11 and the subsequent military campaign in Afghanistan. China may consider the SCO as the best institution available to counter an entrench-ment of Western interests in the region, but such a task would be extremely difficult until the United States disengages from the region. Since the United States entered central Asia and began to enlist regional actors, including some SCO members, to assist American forces with the Afghanistan campaign in exchange for aid and assistance, neither China nor Russia has had the ability to match these rewards. Thus, the SCO was unable to provide a counter-offer and was almost totally eclipsed during the campaign to unseat the Taliban government. However, the SCO is participating in the war on terrorism and is a valuable source of intelligence and expertise in a region which had often been overlooked before 9/11.

In short, the 'maxi-mini' principle offers a limited explanation for determining why China chose to cooperate with international institutions. Moreover, as these relationships develop, this principle may become less important as China further matures as a great power and develops the confidence required for a deepening of its institutional commitments. As well, it has been argued that in seeking to replicate the successes of rivals, a given country may tend to adopt their policies. In the case of great powers, it was asserted that the risks of operating within an anarchic global system compelled upper-tier states to copy the successful policies of other actors, especially in terms of security matters.[40] Keeping this in mind, it might explain why China seeks the use of international institutions to gain assurances of both economic and strategic security. This idea may also help explain why China took the extraordinary step of creating a security regime, the SCO, largely under its own aegis.

What those commitments will look like once China evolves further as a global power is unclear. For the present, China is in the process of shedding its 'fight or flight' reflex as applied to international regimes, as a result of increased confidence but also because of the regimes' ability to enhance Chinese power. Will China remain conservative or will it use its growing power to address what it sees as deficiencies in the status quo? To answer this question one should consider the role of the world's lone superpower and how its relations with China will shape the foreign policies of both states.

The eagle meets the dragon

The United States and China must make better use of multilateral security institutions to better address their mutual strategic concerns. A string of unpleasant incidents between the United States and China, many of which have involved the militaries or intelligence agencies of one or both sides, has taken place since the early 1990s. These have included the *Yinhe* incident, the embassy bombing in Belgrade and the release of the Cox Report in 1999 which detailed accusations of Chinese espionage. Chinese military actions during the 1996 Taiwanese elections also brought about a restrained but nevertheless formidable American naval response.[41] Finally, the April 2001 Hainan incident demonstrated the potential for danger when Chinese and American military forces come into direct contact.

The late 1990s saw a polarisation of opinions within US policy and academic circles over whether China should be 'engaged' or contained. This period also saw the rise of a vocal group of China detractors, known in some American policy circles as the 'blue team', which favoured a harsher military and political stance against a rising China and who accused those favouring an engagement policy as being the 'red team', supporters of conciliation.[42] As Roy summarised, the 'China threat' school of thinking points to China's burgeoning military budget and foreign weaponry acquisitions, the incompatibility of Western and Chinese thinking on issues such as liberalisation, democracy and human rights, and the fact that rising powers tend to practice hegemonic foreign policies as their external interests grow in number.[43]

More conservative strains of this idea suggest that China's rapid economic growth and overall power development will produce instability on the domestic and international levels, which may create friction with Beijing's foreign relations. Wilkinson argued that 'it would be hard for China to sustain long-term economic growth and military modernisation without provoking its neighbours and the United States to coalition, containment, and encirclement'.[44] Kristof cited historical examples of rapid growth precipitating destabilisation and occasionally the use of force in certain nations, including Germany under Wilhelm II, Imperial Japan and the United States of the nineteenth century, which had exercised its growing power in Latin America. He added that Chinese insecurities and differing political perceptions between Beijing and Washington would likely cause the latter to view the former as 'prickly, mulish, and fiercely independent'.[45]

There are several arguments against a rising Chinese threat. Those offered by Roy include the restraints on Chinese behaviour caused by Beijing's linkages with international markets and the need for the CCP to encourage a stable periphery, thereby permitting it to continue internal reforms; a history of conservative foreign policy and strategic behaviour; and the PLA's outdated weaponry and the need to modernise to keep pace with its neighbours.[46] In the 1990s, the containment versus engagement conundrum touched off what Kim referred to as a 'spectrum of opinions' over how a rising China should be addressed,[47] but in actuality this debate spins around a central problem: is China dissatisfied with the current international system and, if so, to what degree is China willing to improve the international order in its favour?

On the Chinese side, remarks have been made by members of the People's Liberation Army which suggest that at least one segment of the Chinese armed forces is unhappy with American foreign and military policy. These include a comment made by a PLA official during Sino-American tensions over Taiwan in the mid-1990s, namely that the US would defer using nuclear weapons against China since Washington cares 'a lot more about Los Angeles than you do about Taipei. If you hit us, we will hit you too'.[48] Equally, the popularity within China of such nationalist tomes as 1996's *China Can Say No*, which espoused nationalist and anti-American doctrines, was not overlooked by those suspicious of Chinese sentiment against the West, even though they were not universally accepted by intellectuals.[49] Criticisms of excessive Chinese jingoism, such as the 1998 book *China Should Not be 'Mr. No'* were even reviewed in China's *People's Daily* newspaper, highlighting the book's assertion that 'narrow nationalism' and hawkish world-views were partially responsible for the demise of the USSR.[50] Still, these developments do suggest the intellectual mainstream in China struggles with questions of nationalism and how it should be translated into foreign policy, especially in a period of regime transition.

In addition, American military superiority and technology aptly demonstrated in the first Gulf War, Kosovo, Afghanistan, and second Gulf War campaigns, over the past decade, have acted as formidable reality checks on Chinese military thinking. One study noted that in the wake of America's successful campaign against Serbian forces in 1999, one that was fought almost exclusively by air power, opinion within the PLA was split over how best to address a future American threat. Old-school adherents stressed 'people's war' theories of consistently moving and hiding troops from enemy attack; modernists favoured attempting to match American military technology; conservatives, fearing that an arms race would help bankrupt China as it did with the USSR, instead favoured the 'asymmetrical warfare' approach using the PLA's available weapons. As well, a text circulated in

1999 by two PLA colonels brought the 'asymmetrical warfare' argument a step further by arguing that '*chaoxian zhan*' (unlimited warfare), the use of any and all different techniques designed to wear down Western forces may be justified to preserve Chinese interests.[51]

Although these quotes and works suggest a strain of Chinese hawkish thinking within the country's armed forces and policy circles, the larger picture suggests that any problems with the United States have been more than balanced by strategic realties and conservatism within the Chinese defence infrastructure. According to Ross, mainstream PLA analysts do study the practice of 'asymmetrical warfare', going to battle against a superior foe, but for the most part they are critical of inflammatory language used to demonstrate the supposed ease with which China would defeat the United States, and the prevailing opinion within mainstream PLA thinking is that American superiority in modern warfare should be taken as a given.[52] Thus, a rush to conflict with the West is not perceived as something sought by a majority of the PLA leadership.

However, these differences of opinion within the Chinese military do not mean that the PLA and their government supporters in China have discounted the United States as a present and future adversary. As Shambaugh explained, frustration within military and civilian circles with American hegemonic behaviour, including its practice of encouraging democratic development, its domination of global trade, the maintenance and sometimes strengthening of American military alliances, US interventionism in domestic conflicts, and its willingness to use military force to pursue political and economic policies drove Chinese suspicion of American strategic motives. A prevailing view in Beijing was that the encouragement of a multipolar (*duojihua*) international order would prevent the United States from developing into an even greater hegemonic power.[53]

During the first few months of the George W. Bush administration in the United States, it appeared the American position *vis-à-vis* China was hardening. The Hainan incident took place on the heels of a report by American Defense Secretary Donald Rumsfeld calling for a reorientation of US military priorities away from the European theatre and more towards Asia, indicating that Russia was becoming less of a strategic threat and China and North Korea should be the United States' most serious security concerns.[54] Soon after the detained American military personnel on Hainan Island were released, Bush stated his country would do 'whatever it takes' to defend Taiwan,[55] an apparent departure from previous American policy of maintaining opaqueness on the 'One China' issue. Talk of a new kind of cold war continued.

The events of 9/11 rapidly changed that view. The international war on terrorism, led by the United States, represents a new facet of the Sino-American relationship. Although China has shown unwavering support for the eradication of terrorist activity, based on its indigenous problems with ethnic separatism and extremism near the country's western frontier, the current American campaign may still pose problems for future Chinese foreign policy. The impressive steps which China has taken to improve relations with other states both inside and outside its periphery have not completely allayed Chinese fears of containment by the United States and its allies, and the spectre of a future China being ringed by American forces and allies, even under the aegis of the fight against international terrorism, will remain of concern in Beijing's foreign policymaking.

American military efforts to capture Al-Qaeda leaders and oust the Taliban regime required assistance from front-line states near Chinese borders, including Pakistan, Russia, Tajikistan and Uzbekistan, all countries with which China either has strong relations, or was actively seeking closer ties. The rationale for China's reluctance to pose a more serious challenge to American military efforts to combat terrorism, even though those efforts have included direct interference in the sovereign affairs of various countries, can only partially be explained by China's own antipathy towards terrorism and concerns the extremist forces which the United States targeted were also potential dangers to Chinese security.

Another factor in China's muted response to America's newly activist foreign policy is most certainly the need for Beijing to avoid costly international entanglements at a very delicate phase in China's domestic politics. For only the third time in the short history of the People's Republic, the country underwent a leadership transition in 2002–3 with the top leadership positions of President and Communist Party Head being passed from Jiang Zemin to Hu Jintao. However, after 2003, Jiang's interest in becoming an *éminence grise*, a power behind the throne, was evidenced by his decision to stay on as head of the powerful Central Military Commission (CMC), which oversees the armed forces, until officially agreeing to step down in September 2004 with Hu succeeding him. From that position, Jiang was briefly able to wield a great deal of influence, echoing the late 1980s and early 90s when Deng Xiaoping continued to shape domestic and foreign policy despite having technically withdrawn from the leadership role.[56] With Jiang in retirement, the Hu administration will now have the opportunity to further clarify and deepen the nascent policy ideas behind the 'peaceful rise' concept.

The new government in China has focused much of its attention towards addressing domestic affairs, including economic reform, poverty alleviation, healthcare and social issues. However, once the new leadership has solidified its position, it is very likely China will further concentrate on pursuing its policies on the international level and this may involve future diplomatic brushes with the United States. It would be premature to suggest that the current atmosphere of improved cordiality between the two powers will endure beyond the short term, as there are many outstanding issues in Sino-American relations which may sour the current entente. Beijing has been critical of many aspects of America's security policy under President George W. Bush, including missile defence development, the US withdrawal from the Anti-Ballistic Missile Treaty, and the National Security Strategy document released by Washington in September 2002 which suggested that pre-emptive and, if necessary, unilateral force may be used in order to preserve American and international security.[57] Such talk is an anathema to China's developing views of global security through cooperation and the aegis of international law.

There are also signs that the United States maintains serious concerns about China. The subject of human rights in China remains a contentious issue between the two countries despite a perceived sidelining of the subject after 9/11.[58] From an economic viewpoint, China's rapid rise has raised US concerns about an undervalued Chinese currency and the country's swiftly expanding share of international exports, leading to concerns about China becoming a mercantilist power in Asia.[59] However, with China in the WTO and growing increasingly bound by various international trade rules on the regional and international level, it is difficult to predict whether US–China trade relations will ever descend into serious acrimony.

Washington also remains troubled about China's military modernisation. In the 2004 annual report to Congress by the US Department of Defense, concerns were raised about Beijing's increases in defence spending, the modernisation of Chinese air, ground and sea-power, advances in missile and heavy-lift capabilities, information and space technology, as well as changes in strategic thinking which take into account the American success in toppling the Hussein regime in Iraq. The report also outlined various scenarios for Chinese military force against Taiwan, and Beijing's possible responses to foreign intervention during an attack on the island.[60] China's successful launch of a person into space in October 2003 also has strategic implications for the United States, despite Chinese assertions that space exploration should be peaceful. The success of the *Shenzhou V* spacecraft has raised concerns that China will soon be able to improve its missile capabilities and eventually produce anti-satellite weapons, resurrecting a cold war spectre of an arms race in space between the two powers.[61]

Taiwan also remains a possible source of future Sino-American disputes. The very close victory by President Chen Shui-bian of the traditionally pro-independence Democratic Progressive Party (DPP) in the March 2004 elections, coupled with a simultaneous referendum asking whether Chinese missile emplacements should be aimed towards Taiwan, angered Beijing. The possibility that Chen may try to replace the Taiwanese constitution and make it the subject of a referendum in 2006 is a strong concern for Beijing, which views such an action part of a gradual move towards independence. After Chen was belatedly sworn into office in May 2004 following a review of the balloting, Beijing issued a warning that Taipei would face severe punishment if it moved 'recklessly' towards independence, but at the same offered to soften its stance towards the island should it decide to abide by the 'One China' principle, a provision Chen has reputedly rejected.[62] The Bush administration attempted to walk a fine line between the two sides, attempting to dissuade the Chen government from holding the referendum during a visit by Premier Wen in December 2003,[63] and continuing to express hope that both sides can come to a diplomatic solution to the regional tensions.

Further evidence of the delicacy of the situation took place in July 2004 when China held a series of military manoeuvres on the South China Sea island of Dongshan in order to simulate an assault on Taiwan, while at almost the same time Taiwanese and American armed forces were holding their own separate manoeuvres.[64] Should cross-Strait relations deteriorate, several variables would come into play. Would Taipei risk further moves towards independence and what actions might Beijing take to press its sovereignty on the island? Moreover, what would be an American response to increased tensions, especially since much foreign policy attention and resources from Washington remain directed towards the war on terrorism?

Great power conflict between China and the United States is far from inevitable, and comparisons between the current Sino–American relationship and the superpower rivalry of the previous century can only be made to a point. The differences between the two countries are not as ideological, but rather stem from political and economic differences. At the same time, China neither has nor wants the ability to construct a ring of allied periphery states along the same vein as the Warsaw Pact which augmented the international power of the Soviet Union. Rather, China has opted to conduct its foreign policy within the current Western-dominated international order, which includes increasing participation in international institutions.

Thus, the United States and other nations should continue to encourage the process of China's integration within multilateral regimes as a means of keeping a growing China engaged in the international system. For both sides there is an increasing need to understand the other's politics and policy goals for the new century. America must find a means of channelling Chinese power by encouraging Beijing to further participate in international institutions designed to bring collective goods to all members.

Increased Sino-American engagement within various regimes will also provide the information necessary for Washington to better construct what one American analyst termed a 'purple' policy for China, namely a mixture of 'red team' thinking (treating China as a potential partner), and 'blue team' thinking (considering China a potential competitor).[65] Such a violet-hued approach would demonstrate the rewards of Chinese cooperative behaviour and the serious consequences of the unilateral use of force to address Chinese grievances. For China, further engagement with the United States within regimes will provide the country with the window into American policy necessary to avoid future crises, as well as to gain further insight into the responsibilities of developing into greater power.

Reconsidering modern-day great powers

The case of China has offered a valuable means to measure the development of the first rising global power since the end of the cold war and the proliferation of international regimes. The most important conclusion which can be drawn from this study is that international institutions have developed into an essential tool for measuring the foreign policy goals of rising powers. This is not to say that traditional measurements, including material capabilities, military and economic power, persuasive and 'soft' power and policy coordination with other states, are not as relevant to the case of China or to future rising powers. Rather, it has been argued that institutions have been playing an increasingly important role in the shaping of foreign policies and perceptions of a rising China, and therefore this variable must be more closely studied when gauging present and future Chinese power. As demonstrated, China's increasing enthusiasm for engaging various international regimes of many different stripes has become a key facet of the country's post-cold war international relations and this process has not only affected China's international perceptions, but has also changed the character of many institutions in which Beijing has chosen to participate.

Moreover, this book has endeavoured to examine the question of whether institutions can be used as tools to accommodate rising global powers. In the past institutions were far fewer and played a negligible role in guiding the activities of rising powers or allowing other powers to better address the power shift created by countries seeking to advance their status in the global hierarchy. Examining China, some conclusions concerning this question can be made. First, there is little indication that institutions have directly curtailed Chinese foreign policy behaviour, especially relating to strategic matters. Instead, China has routinely asserted its power to ensure that various institutions either do not infringe on areas which Beijing believes to be its exclusive domain, especially matters related to the status of Taiwan and indeed any areas which are perceived as possibly compromising Chinese security interests, but also economic and political sovereignty, including trade, tariffs and energy.

Second, although the use of institutions as 'sticks' to discourage perceived improper behaviour by China is lacking, regimes are proving their worth as 'carrots', offering incentives for Beijing to alter its foreign policy activities with the promise of goods which China would be unable or unwilling to obtain unilaterally. Many examples have appeared as the number of institutions has grown. From an economic viewpoint, the WTO offered such a number of goods (prestige, participation in global trade regulation, a catalyst for ongoing domestic-level political and economic reform) that Beijing was willing to pay a high price in the form of risky and delicate governmental and economic restructuring to obtain an elusive admission ticket to the organisation. In the case of APEC and the APT, the rewards are less distinct, but a clear advantage was given to China by being perceived within Asia as the developing lynchpin economy in the region, all with relatively little cost to China itself.

Examining the strategic realm, the ARF gave China a needed window into the security activities of its Asian neighbours, including Taipei, while at the same time granting the power to curtail any development of an 'anti-China' security bloc and preventing unwanted regional incursions into the South China Sea region. The SCO provided China with an even greater array of carrots, including protecting its sensitive western border, increasing its influence in a geo-politically important region (central Asia) and providing a possible counterweight to Western and Russian influences there. In short, institutions have allowed China to pursue foreign policy goals which would not have been viable had it acted unilaterally.

The SCO is also the centre of a third point about institutions accommodating rising powers. China, itself, appears to be shedding some of its concerns about regimes and has instead actively sought to develop some of its own, in this case, the Shanghai group. Admittedly, the SCO is still very new and largely untested and it is too soon to tell if this regime will be considered in the future as a deviant case or as the forerunner of other China-led regimes. However, an important element in measuring the development of rising global powers in the future is not only how they cooperate and react to existing institutions, but also whether and how they take the initiative to create regimes of their own. The two most recent global powers, the United States and the Soviet Union, were very adept at regime creation, although their methods differed. The US relied on shared interests and rewards, while the USSR-led regimes heavily depended on force, as well as proxy leaders in satellite countries, to maintain cohesion.[66] In the post-cold war world the United States, as the world's largest power, is frequently the guiding influence within many international organisations.

Will a growing China also seek to develop further institutions on its own as part of its development as a rising power? Beijing lacks the wherewithal to create 'counter-regimes' to balance the United States and is instead content to make use of Western-created and dominated institutions. This may not mean, however, that as China grows in power and confidence it will not attempt to forge its own regimes. The question is whether they would be used to further integrate China into the international system, or rather to mount a challenge to the status quo. All these points should be examined not only in the Chinese case, but also in debating whether such studies can be transferred to other rising powers in the future.

Another aspect of China's institutional relations and how they may affect this area of international relations theory is the question of how domestic and international level policies influence each other within a rising power. Within international relations theory, there has been much study of how domestic policy can affect foreign policy perceptions, and vice versa, but in the case of China's institutional relations, distinct variables come into play. One is that the great emphasis which the Chinese regime has placed on perpetuating itself has spilled over into China's foreign policy behaviour as the government's ideology has shifted from Maoism to nationalism. The second is that, since the beginning of the Dengist reforms, domestic and foreign policies within China have become increasingly intertwined, and thus success or failure on one level can readily affect the other.

A third point is that since leaders are directly answerable to the party apparatus, the international level can be a place where individual lawmakers potentially enhance their position within the government. Conversely, foreign policy failures can adversely affect government officials, as illustrated by Zhu Rongji's tenuous hold on the premiership during the rancorous WTO negotiations of the 1990s. Adding to this dynamic is the fact that during much of the history of the People's Republic, there has been a clear separation between public and 'informal' internal politics, also known as the *yang feng/yin wei* dichotomy ('outwardly obedient/ inwardly defiant'), the latter being a set of policies and directives kept private within the CCP's inner circle.[67] Even within the post-Dengist period of Chinese reform, the informal level of Chinese politics has been very difficult to examine due to the secretiveness of the decision-makers at the centre of the Chinese party system. However, the survey of China's engagement processes with international institutions, as with other investigations into Chinese foreign policy, has provided information on domestic-level decision-making as well. In short, examining China's institutional relations provides another window into Beijing's often complex domestic policy processes and political development, and is therefore worthy of further study.

Implications for international relations

From a more theoretical viewpoint, it can be said that there exists a considerable amount of common ground rich for future study between realism, especially structural realism which focuses on the distribution of state capabilities within an anarchic international milieu,[68] and institutionalism, which stresses their role in state behaviour. What has been generally agreed upon among international relations theorists in the post-cold war period, is that the current international order is marked by anarchy (although there are differences between schools as to the degree), and that states still rise and fall in power absolutely and in relation to each other. Despite the uncertainty created by these anarchic conditions, and the lack of an overreaching extra-state legal system, international regimes and institutions have been growing steadily in number over the past century. As well, a growing number of new institutions are being based on voluntary participation, rather than as a result of the strong dominating the weak,[69] for example those countries in Eastern Europe which were annexed into the Soviet sphere of influence, as its institutions, during the middle of the twentieth century.

Where the literature is presently underdeveloped, however, is in gauging the effect of institutions of various types on the process of power acquisition by great powers and potential global ones. According to traditional realism, institutions do not have a significant impact on state behaviour. Rather, as Evans and Wilson explained, according to traditional realism 'international regimes are merely arenas for acting out power relationships. Conceptualised in this way, the idea of regimes has little to offer over and above that which can be discovered through traditional, state-centric and interest-based, means of analysis. They are neither autonomous nor intervening variables: they do not have a life of their own, nor do they in any significant sense affect international outcomes'.[70] However, the traditional realist viewpoint on regimes has been joined, according to Krasner, by both a 'modified' realist stance, which suggests that institutions act as guideposts for state behaviour, and the 'Grotian' model which further stipulates that regimes have become well-integrated into domestic and international-level political interactions, and have developed into a source of influence on state behaviour.[71]

Clearly, international institutions are not irrelevant for rising global powers. This study has endeavoured to demonstrate that institutions can act as a means to better obtain and channel the power necessary for a great power to develop into a global one without resorting to the use of force, a method of power-acquisition made unacceptably risky by the presence of nuclear weapons. Great power war, which was often used to address or solidify power shifts, is no longer an attractive option in the post-nuclear, post-cold war system, since its effects can be damaging on a global scale. China's conservative foreign policy has adapted engagement with international institutions as a more effective way, one which is based on maintaining external stability, of developing its power in the global arena.

The study of institutions can be beneficial to the areas of neo-realism which address the question of international outcomes, more specifically international events such as inter-state cooperation or conflict.[72] Although it remains arguable to what degree institutions act as a constraint on state behaviour, it can be stated that the growing number of international institutions provides tools (greater outlets for cooperation, information exchange, education, paths to increased trade or strategic coordination) which can affect international outcomes, often in a positive fashion, by discouraging conflict. These effects are even more important when great powers are brought into the equation, since institutions have not only the potential to provide the goods mentioned above, but also the means of acquiring the power necessary for select states to advance to global power status.

While material capabilities certainly cannot be ignored in the study of how a state makes the transition to becoming a global power, this work has argued that another sphere, the ability to effectively make use of the goods available though cooperation via international institutions, also needs to be addressed. This area could potentially represent a bridge between the evolving neo-realist school and institutionalist theory. At the same time, more study must be focused on the role of 'anarchic' institutions, which are becoming increasingly visible in Asia as an alternative to the structured, hierarchical ones found in North America and Europe, and what role they have played in easing not only China but other Asian states into further institutional cooperation. Despite Mearsheimer's assertion that 'there is no institution with any real power in Asia',[73] China and its neighbours have been increasingly willing to join anarchic institutions even though many, like APEC and the ARF, are without independent rules and norms of enforcement. The question is whether these anarchic institutions will remain a preferred method of inter-state cooperation in the coming years or whether more traditional regimes take hold in Asia once states become more comfortable with more formal means of cooperation. If it is the latter, what role will China play: a spoiler seeking to inhibit more structured institutions, or the centre of a new twenty-first century Asian community?

The post-cold war international system is being presented with the first potential global power, China, to rise during a period of global institutional development. In the case of China, what needs to be examined are the areas of great and global power development and state-to-state relations within a global system which is primarily anarchic, but has also been the beneficiary of a large and growing amount of international institutions. As Ruggie and Caporaso argued, while engaging in multilateral activity is not without costs, it does entail a significant commitment to shape policies which move beyond strictly national interests.[74] Therefore, the decision to enter into such activity is not one made lightly. Yet in the post-cold war system, many states, including a rising global power such as China, are rushing towards multilateral activity and joining institutions. The solution to addressing these differences is to examine how institutions have developed into an important tool for China to increase its power in the international system.

Scenes from a Chinese crossroads

The growth of Chinese power over the past three decades is one of the most important events in the modern international system and will inevitably be used as a measurement for future studies of great power development. What makes China's rise distinct from its predecessors, however, is the fact that the country is growing within a global milieu which is becoming increasingly saturated with international institutions. Rather than ignore them and concentrate on power acquisition *vis-à-vis* other great powers, China has chosen to directly engage regimes of many stripes in order to obtain further resources, knowledge and abilities to continue evolving as a great power and a potential global power. Unlike other great powers of the past which opted to enhance their power via the use of force and the development of far-reaching military and economic power, China has instead made use of the current international order, including its regimes, to attain greater power in the international system. The result of this engagement is that China is increasingly pursuing a conservative foreign policy increasingly dedicated to cooperation and joint problem-solving.

The question now is whether the pace of China's foreign policy opening will increase, decrease or stay at the levels mandated by the Jiang and Hu regimes as the country continues to grow. The answer to this will be found both in Beijing's ongoing domestic reform policies and the expansion of its foreign policy interests on the international level. One certainty, however, is that the emerging international system can no longer afford to ignore the rise of China, and international regimes will be one important arena for the examination and understanding of the rise and development of Chinese power. It will be necessary to the study of China's evolving role in the world to look beyond material capabilities and power politics to gain further knowledge of how China cooperates with the international system. International institutions have provided China both with pathways to its development as a great power and reflections of many possible futures for the Chinese state.

NOTES

INTRODUCTION

1 The *zhoubian* concept is elaborated in Mel Gurtov and Byong-Moo Hwang, *China's Security: The New Roles of the Military* (Boulder, CO and London: Lynne Rienner, 1998), 67–70.

2 Jane Perlez, 'Asian Leaders Find China a More Cordial Neighbour', *The New York Times*, 18 October 2003, A1.

3 Andrew J. Nathan and Bruce Gilley, *China's New Rulers: The Secret Files* (2nd edn) (New York: New York Review of Books, 2003), 234–5.

4 Evan S. Medeiros, 'China Debates Its "Peaceful Rise" Strategy', *YaleGlobal*, 22 June 2004, yaleglobal.yale.edu/article.print?id=4118.

5 'Backgrounder: China's Road of Peaceful Rise', *XinhuaNet*, 23 April 2004. news.xinhuanet.com/english/2004-04/23/content_1436850.htm.

6 'Hu Jintao Addresses the Brazilian Parliament (full text)' Foreign Ministry of the People's Republic of China, 13 November 2004. www.fmprc.gov.cn/eng/wjdt/zyjh/t170363.htm.

7 Samuel S. Kim, 'China's International Organizational Behaviour', in *Chinese Foreign Policy: Theory and Practice,* ed. Thomas W. Robinson and David Shambaugh (Oxford: Clarendon Press, 1994), 405.

8 Robert O. Keohane, 'Lilliputians' Dilemmas: Small States in International Politics', *International Organization* 23(2) (Spring 1969): 295.

9 Susan Strange, 'The Persistent Myth of Lost Hegemony', *International Organization* 41(4) (Autumn 1987): 565–71.

10 Joseph S. Nye Jr., *The Paradox of American Power: Why the World's Superpower Cannot Go It Alone* (Oxford and New York: Oxford University Press, 2002), 8–12. See also Joseph S. Nye Jr., *Soft Power: The Means to Success in World Politics* (New York: Public Affairs Books, 2004).

11 Walter Russell Mead, 'America's Sticky Power', *Foreign Policy* 141 (March/April 2004): 46–53.

12 Keohane, 'Lilliputians' Dilemmas', 296.

13 Kenneth N. Waltz, *Theory of International Politics* (New York: Random House, 1979), 129–31.

14 Colin S. Gray, 'The Continued Primacy of Geography', *Orbis* 40(2) (Spring 1996): 258.

15 Andrew J. Nathan, *China's Transition* (New York: Columbia University Press), 218.

16 Hang-Sheng Cheng, 'A Midcourse Assessment of China's Economic Reform', in *The China Reader: The Reform Era*, eds. Orville Schell and David Shambaugh (New York: Vintage Books, 1999), 311–21.

17 *Constitution of the People's Republic of China*, Amendment Fourth (6), 14 March 2004.

18 Ted C. Fishman, 'The Chinese Century', *The New York Times Magazine*, 4 July 2004, 6.24.

19 Ligang Song, 'China', in *East Asia in Crisis: From Being a Miracle to Needing One?* ed. Ross H. McLeod and Ross Garnaut (London and New York: Routledge, 1998), 105–7.

173

20 Elizabeth M. Prescott, 'SARS: A Warning', *Survival* 45(3) (Autumn 2003): 207–13.

21 'SARS, A Valuable Lesson for Chinese Government to Learn', *People's Daily*, 8 June 2003; Joseph Fewsmith, 'China and the Politics of SARS', *Current History* 102(665) (September 2003): 250–5; Jacques deLisle, 'SARS, Greater China, and the Pathologies of Globalisation and Transition', *Orbis* 47(4) (Fall 2003): 587–604.

22 See Nicholas R. Lardy, 'China and the Asian Contagion', *Foreign Affairs* 77(4) (July/August 1998): 78–88; Edward S. Steinfeld, 'The Asian Financial Crisis: Beijing's Year of Reckoning', *Washington Quarterly* 21(3) (Summer 1998): 37–51; Elizabeth C. Economy, 'Reforming China', *Survival* 41(3) (Autumn 1999): 21–42.

23 Randall Peerenboom, *China's Long March Toward Rule of Law* (Cambridge: Cambridge University Press, 2002), 450–1.

24 Erica S. Downs, 'The Chinese Energy Security Debate', *The China Quarterly* 177 (March 2004): 21–4.

25 Paul Roberts, *The End of Oil: On the Edge of a Perilous New World* (Boston and New York: Houghton Mifflin, 2004), 143–6.

26 *FY04 Report to Congress on PRC Military Power Pursuant to the FY2000 National Defense Authorization Act: Annual Report on the Military Power of the People's Republic of China*, (Washington, DC: United States Department of Defense, 2004), 16.

27 '70 Chinese Navy Sailors Killed in Submarine Disaster', *Xinhua*, 2 May 2003, news.xinhuanet. com/english/2003-05/02/content_856531.htm.

28 See John Wilson Lewis and Xue Litai, *China Builds the Bomb* (Stanford, CA: Stanford University Press, 1988).

29 See David Shambaugh, *Modernizing China's Military: Progress, Problems and Prospects* (Berkeley, CA and London: University of California Press, 2002), 70–72; You Ji, *The Armed Forces of China* (London and New York: I.B. Taurus, 1999), 132–8; James A. Boutilier, 'Standing into Heavy Seas: The New Maritime Environment in Northeast Asia', *Cancaps Papier*, 29, (March 2002) 3.

30 Bates Gill, 'China's Newest Warships', *Far Eastern Economic Review*, 27 January 2000, 30.

31 For information on the J-10 fighter, see Craig Hoyle and Yihong Chang, 'China to Lift Veil on its J-10', *Jane's Defence Weekly* (20 March 2002): 16–7.

32 You, *The Armed Forces of China,* 90, 112–7.

33 Chen Wen, 'The New Mandate of Heaven', *Beijing Review*, 23 October 2003, 5.

34 See Jack Goldstone, 'The Coming Chinese Collapse', *Foreign Policy* 99 (Summer 1995): 35–52; and Arthur Waldron, 'After Deng the Deluge: China's Next Leap Forward', *Foreign Affairs* 74(5) (September/October 1995): 148–53.

35 Lowell Dittmer, 'Leadership Change and Chinese Political Development', in *The New Chinese Leadership: Challenges and Opportunities after the 16th Party Congress*, ed. Yun-han Chu, Chih-cheng Lo and Ramon H. Myers (Cambridge: Cambridge University Press, 2004), 10–32; Joseph Kahn, 'Hu Takes Full Power in China As He Gains Control of Military', *The New York Times*, 20 September 2004, A1.

36 John J. Mearsheimer, *The Tragedy of Great Power Politics* (New York and London: W.W. Norton, 2001), 30–36; Jack S. Levy, *War in the Modern Great Power System, 1495–1975* (Lexington, KY: The University Press of Kentucky, 1983), 10–19.

37 Robert Gilpin, *War and Change in International Politics* (Cambridge: Cambridge University Press, 1981), 13.

38 Gilpin, *War and Change in International Politics*, 95. See also Christopher Layne. 'The Unipolar Illusion: Why New Great Powers Will Rise', *International Security* 17(4) (Spring 1993): 10–11.

39 Layne, 'The Unipolar Illusion', 11–16.

40 Robert O. Keohane, 'International Institutions: Two Approaches', *International Studies Quarterly* 32 (1988): 379–96.

41 John J. Mearsheimer, 'The False Promise of International Institutions', *International Security* 19 (Winter 1994–5): 5–49.

42 See Stephen D. Krasner, 'Structural Causes and Regime Consequences', in *International Regimes*, ed. Stephen D. Krasner (Ithaca, NY: Cornell University Press, 1983), 2.

43 Lisa L. Martin, 'An Institutionalist View: International Institutions and State Strategies', in *International Order and the Future of World Politics*, ed. T.V. Paul and John A. Hall (Cambridge and New York: Cambridge University Press, 1999), 78–98.

44 Jeffrey W. Legro and Andrew Moravcsik, 'Is Anybody Still a Realist?' *International Security* 24(2) (Fall 1999): 5–55. See also Hans J. Morgenthau, *Politics Among Nations: The Struggle for Power and Peace* (4th edn), (New York: Alfred A. Knopf, 1967), 4–14; and John A. Vasquez, 'The Realist Paradigm and Degenerative versus Progressive Research Programs: An Appraisal of Neotraditional Research on Waltz's Balancing Proposition', *American Political Science Review* 91(4) (December 1997): 899–912.

45 Joseph M. Grieco, 'Anarchy and the Limits of Cooperation: A Realist Critique of the Newest Liberal institutionalism', *International Organization* 42(3) (Summer 1998): 485–507.

46 John Gerard Ruggie, 'Multilateralism: The Anatomy of an Institution', *International Organization* 46(3) (Summer 1992): 561–98.

47 Kishore Mahbubani, 'The Pacific Way', *Foreign Affairs* 74(1) (January/February 1995): 100–11.

48 The term refers to the perceived nexus of these bilateral agreements, the 1951 US-Japan Mutual Security Treaty. See Kent E. Calder, *Pacific Defense: Arms, Energy and America's Future in Asia* (New York: William Morrow, 1996), 151.

49 For example, see Brian L. Job, 'Track 2 Diplomacy: Ideational Contribution to the Evolving Asian Security Order', in *Asian Security Order: Instrumental and Normative Features*, ed. Muthiah Alagappa (Stanford, CA: Stanford University Press, 2003), 241–79, and Peter J. Katzenstein, 'Regionalism in Comparative Perspective', *Cooperation and Conflict* 31(2) (1996): 123–59.

50 Martin, 'An institutionalist view', 78.

51 Thomas J. Christensen, 'Chinese Realpolitik', *Foreign Affairs* 75(5) (September/October 1996): 37–52.

52 Elizabeth Economy, 'The Impact of International Regimes on Chinese Foreign Policy-Making: Broadening Perspectives and Policies … But Only to a Point', in *The Making of Chinese Foreign and Security Policy in the Era of Reform*, ed. David M. Lampton (Stanford, CA: Stanford University Press, 2001), 251.

53 Michael Oksenberg and Elizabeth Economy, 'Introduction: China Joins the World', in *China Joins the World: Progress and Prospects*, ed. Michel Oksenberg and Elizabeth Economy (New York: Council on Foreign Relations Press, 1999), 22–3.

54 Joseph Y.S. Cheng and Zhang Wankun, 'Patterns and Dynamics of China's International Strategic Behaviour', in *Chinese Foreign Policy: Pragmatism and Strategic Behavior*, ed. Suisheng Zhao (Armonk, NY and London: M.E. Sharpe, 2004), 180–83.

55 Chia Siow Yue, 'Economic Cooperation and Integration in East Asia', *Asia-Pacific Review* 11(1) (2004): 4–8.

56 Evan Medeiros and M. Taylor Fravel, 'China's New Diplomacy', *Foreign Affairs* 82(6) (November/December 2003): 24.

57 The author wishes to thank Flora Wan for her contributions to this argument.

58 For theories of late developers, see Alexander Gerschenkron, *Economic Backwardness in Historical Perspective: a Book of Essays* (Cambridge, MA: Harvard University Press, 1962).

59 Kenneth N. Waltz, 'Structural Realism after the Cold War', *International Security* 25(1) (Summer 2000): 18–26.

60 Ruggie, 'Multilateralism', 586.

61 Grieco, 'Anarchy and the Limits of Cooperation', 487. See also Robert Powell. 'Anarchy in International Relations Theory: The Neorealist-Neoliberalist Debate', *International Organization* 48(2) (Spring 1994): 326–9.

62 Hongying Wang, 'Multilateralism in Chinese Foreign Policy: The Limits of Socialization?' In *China's International Relations in the 21st Century*, ed. Weixing Hu, Gerald Chan and Daojiong Zha (Lanham, MD and Oxford: University Press of America, Inc., 2000), 71.

63 Gerald Segal, 'Does China Matter?' *Foreign Affairs* 78(5) (September/October 1999): 33.

64 For historical analyses into China's domestic and foreign policies, see Ross Terrill, *The New Chinese Empire and What it Means for the United States* (New York: Basic Books, 2003) and Alastair Iain Johnston, *Cultural Realism: Strategic Culture and Grand Strategy in Chinese History* (Princeton, NJ: Princeton University Press, 1995).

65 Alastair Iain Johnston, 'China's Militarized Interstate Dispute Behaviour 1949–1992: The First Cut at the Data', *The China Quarterly* 153 (March 1998): 1–30.

66 The nature of Chinese strategic culture has been the subject of considerable controversy. Conventional scholarly wisdom regarding a purported traditional Chinese aversion to warfare and a preference for defensive operations has been challenged by scholars such as Alastair I. Johnston and Andrew Scobell. Both argue that China possesses multiple strands of strategic culture and China's record of military behaviour in the dynastic and post-1949 eras is not consistent with that depicted by conventional scholarly wisdom. See Johnston, *Cultural Realism* and Andrew Scobell, *China's Use of Military Force: Beyond the Great Wall and the Long March* (Cambridge: Cambridge University Press, 2003).

67 Kalevi J. Holsti, *The State, War, and the State of War* (Cambridge: Cambridge University Press, 1996), 36–40.

68 Shambaugh, *Modernizing China's Military*, 90.

69 T.V. Paul, 'Nuclear Taboo and War Initiation in Regional Conflicts', *Journal of Conflict Resolution* 38(4) (December 1995): 696–717.

70 John Wilson Lewis and Xue Litai, *China's Strategic Seapower: The Politics of Force Modernization in the Nuclear Age* (Stanford, CA: Stanford University Press, 1994), 211–4.

71 See Mark W. Zacher, 'The Territorial Integrity Norm: International Boundaries and the Use of Force', *International Organization* 55(2) (Spring 2001): 215–50.

72 Elizabeth Wishnick, *Mending Fences: The Evolution of Moscow's China Policy from Brezhnev to Yeltsin* (Seattle, WA and London: University of Washington Press, 2001), 24–43.

73 Harlan W. Jencks, 'China's "Punitive" War on Vietnam: A Military Assessment', *Asian Survey* 19(8) (August 1979): 801–15.

74 See Johnston, 'China's Militarized Interstate Dispute Behaviour 1949–1992'.

75 Richard McGregor, 'China to Join Nuclear Non-proliferation Group in Big Shift over Foreign Policy', *Financial Times*, 13 April 2004, 1.

76 Bates Gill, 'Two Steps Forward, Two Steps Back: The Dynamics of Chinese Nonproliferation and Arms Control Policy-Making in an Era of Reform', in *The Making of Chinese Foreign and Security Policy in the Era of Reform*, ed. David M. Lampton (Stanford, CA: Stanford University Press, 2001), 257–88. See also David M. Lampton, *Same Bed, Different Dreams: Managing US-China Relations, 1989–2000* (Berkeley,CA and London: University of California Press, 2001), 169–70.

77 'Some Thoughts on Establishing A New Regional Security Order', Statement by Ambassador Sha Zukang at the East-West Center's Senior Policy Seminar, 7 August 2000, (Honolulu: Ministry of Foreign Affairs of the People's Republic of China, 2000). www.fmprc.gov.cn/eng/5180.html.

78 Yi Ding, 'Upholding the Five Principles of Peaceful Coexistence', *Beijing Review* (February 26–March 4, 1990): 13–6.

79 Li Cheng, *China's Leaders: The New Generation* (Lanham, MD and Oxford: Rowman and Littlefield, 2001), 69–80.

80 David Shambaugh, 'China's Military Views the World: Ambivalent Security.' *International Security* 24(1) (Winter 1999/2000): 52–79.

81 Erik Eckholm. 'A Quiet Roar: China's Leadership Feels Threatened by a Sect Seeking Peace', *The New York Times,* 4 November 1999, A10.

82 Yong Deng, 'Research Note: The Chinese Conception of National Interests in International Relations', *The China Quarterly* 154 (June 1998): 308.

83 Ann Kent, 'China, International Organisations, and Regimes: The ILO as a Case Study in Organisational Learning', *Pacific Affairs* 70(4) (Winter 1997–8): 521.

84 Boutros Boutros-Ghali, *An Agenda for Peace 1995*. (2nd edn) (New York: United Nations, 1995), 44.

85 George A. Lopez and David Cortright, 'Containing Iraq: Sanctions Worked', *Foreign Affairs* 83(4) (July/August 2004): 90–1.

86 Robert O. Keohane, *After Hegemony: Cooperation and Discord in the World Political Economy* (Princeton, NJ: Princeton University Press, 1985), 85–109.

87 Stephen D. Krasner, 'Global Communications and National Power: Life on the Pareto Frontier', *World Politics* 43(3) (April 1991): 336–66.

88 Lisa L. Martin, 'Interests, Power, and Multilateralism', *International Organization* 46(4) (Autumn 1992): 770.

89 *China's National Defence in 2002* (December 2002) news.xinhuanet.com/english/2002-12/10/content_654634.htm.

90 Charles Krauthammer, 'The Unipolar Moment', *Foreign Affairs* 70(1) (Winter 1990/91): 23–33; Michael Mastanduno, 'Preserving the Unipolar Moment: Realist Theories and US Grand Strategy after the Cold War', *International Security* 21(4) (Spring 1997): 49–88.

91 Lampton, *Same Bed, Different Dreams*, 77–8.

92 John Wong and Zheng Yongnian, 'Nationalism and Its Dilemma: Chinese Responses to the Embassy Bombing', *Reform, Legitimacy, and Dilemmas: China's Politics and Society* ed. Wang Gongwu and Zeng Yongnian (Singapore: Singapore University Press and World Scientific Publishing, 2000), 321–43.

93 Sheng Lijun, 'Bush's New China Policy: Air Collision, Arms Sales, and China-US Relations', *Pacific Focus: Inha Journal of International Studies* 14(2) (Fall 2001): 57–86.

94 X [George F. Kennan], 'The Sources of Soviet Conduct', *Foreign Affairs* 25(4) (July 1947): 566–82.

95 Gurtov and Hwang, *China's Security: The New Roles of the Military*, 71.

96 Denny Roy, 'China's Reaction to American Predominance', *Survival* 45(3) (Autumn 2003): 68.

97 Marc Lanteigne, 'Tipping the Balance: Theatre Missile Defense and the Evolving Security Relations in Northeast Asia', Working Paper 34. Institute of International Relations, University of British Columbia, Vancouver, Canada, January 2001.

98 Paul Kennedy, *The Rise and Fall of Great Powers: Economic Change and Military Conflict From 1500 to 2000* (London: Unwin Hyman, 1988), xxiii, 439.

99 Ronald L. Tammen, Douglas Lemke, Carole Alsharabati, Brian Efird, Jacek Kugler, Allan C. Stam III, Mark Andrew Abdollahian and A.F.K. Organski, *Power Transitions: Strategies for the 21st Century* (New York and London: Chatham House, Seven Bridges Press, 2000), 156–7.

100 Mearsheimer, *The Tragedy of Great Power Politics*, 396–402.

101 Nicholas R. Lardy, 'China's Economic Growth in an International Context', *The Pacific Review* 12(2) (1999): 163–71.

102 David Zweig, 'China's Stalled "Fifth Wave": Zhu Rongji's Reform Package of 1998–2000' *Asian Survey* 41(2) (March/April 2001): 231–47; Economy, 'Reforming China', 21–42.

103 Minxin Pei, 'Rotten from Within: Decentralized Predation and Incapacitated State', in *The Nation State in Question*, ed. T.V. Paul, G. John Ikenberry and John A. Hall (Princeton, NJ: Princeton University Press, 2003), 321–49.

104 Jonathan Watts, 'China Admits First Rise in Poverty since 1978', *The Guardian*, 20 July 2004. www.guardian.co.uk/print/0,3858,4974418-103681,00.html.

105 Thomas G. Moore, 'China and Globalization', *Asian Perspective* 23(4) (1999): 65–95; see also Yongnian Zheng, *Globalization and State Transformation in China* (Cambridge and New York: Cambridge University Press, 2004).

106 Stuart Harris, 'China and the Pursuit of State Interests in a Globalizing World', *Pacifica Review* 13(1) (February 2001): 26–9.

107 Bates Gill, 'Limited Engagement', *Foreign Affairs* 78(4) (July–August 1999): 65–76.

108 Stephen Haggard, *The Political Economy of the Asian Financial Crisis* (Washington, DC: Institute for International Economics, 2000), 3.

109 For example, see Amy Myers Jaffe and Steven W. Lewis, 'Beijing's Oil Diplomacy', *Survival* 44(1) (Spring 2002): 115–34.

110 Wenguo Cai, 'China's Membership in the GATT/WTO: Historical and Legal Issues', *China and the World Trade Organisation: Requirements, Realities, and Resolution*, ed. Wenguo Cai, Murray G. Smith, and Xu Xianquan (Ottawa: Centre for Trade Policy and Law, 1996), 10–25.

111 Alexander Wendt, 'Anarchy is What States Make of It: The Social Construction of Power Politics', *International Organization* 46(2) (Spring 1992): 391–425.

112 See Suisheng Zhao, *A Nation-State by Construction: Dynamics of Modern Chinese Nationalism* (Stanford, CA: Stanford University Press, 2004) for a learned overview of the history of Chinese nationalism.

113 Michel Oksenberg, 'China's Confident Nationalism', *Foreign Affairs* 65(1) (Winter 1986): 501–23.

114 Fei-Ling Wang, 'Self-Image and Strategic Intentions: National Confidence and Political Insecurity', in *In the Eyes of the Dragon: China Views the World*, ed. Yong Deng and Fei-Ling Wang (New York and Oxford: Rowman and Littlefield, 1999), 22–4.

115 Jiang Zemin, 'How Our Party is to Attain the "Three Represents" under the New Historical Conditions' (25 February 2000), in *Jiang Zemin on the 'Three Represents'* (Beijing: Foreign Languages Press, 2003), 7–13.

116 Guangqui Xu, 'The Chinese Anti-American Nationalism in the 1990s', *Asian Perspective* 22(2) (1998): 193–218.

117 For a more comprehensive description of Chinese nationalism directed against the United States after the Belgrade and Hainan incidents, see Peter Hays Gries, *China's New Nationalism: Pride, Politics and Diplomacy* (Berkeley, CA: University of California Press, 2004).

118 Xiao Gongqin, 'Zhongguo Minzu Zhuyi de Lishi yu Qianjing' ('The History and Prospect of Chinese Nationalism'), *Zhanli yu Guanli* 2, (1996); cited in Suisheng Zhao, 'Chinese Nationalism and Authoritarianism', in *China and Democracy: Reconsidering the Prospects for a Democratic China*, ed. Shuisheng Zhao (New York and London: Routledge, 2000), 255.

119 See Robert Art, 'To What Ends Military Power?', *International Security* 4(4) (Spring 1980): 4–35.

120 Albert O. Hirschman, *Exit, Voice, and Loyalty: Responses to Decline in Firms, Organisations, and States* (Cambridge, MA: Harvard University Press, 1972).

121 Gerald Chan, *Chinese Perspectives on International Relations: A Framework for Analysis* (Basingstoke: Macmillan Press; New York: St Martin's Press, 1999), 115–23.

1 RED LIGHT, GREEN LIGHT

1 'China Becomes WTO Member', News Release, Ministry of Foreign Trade and Economic Cooperation, People's Republic of China, 11 December 2001. 202.96.57.185:7777/Detail.wct? RecID=14&SelectID=4&ChannelID=1951&Page=1.

2 See Robert Gilpin, *The Political Economy of International Relations* (Princeton, NJ: Princeton University Press, 1987), 190–91.

3 Wenguo Cai, 'China's Membership in the GATT/WTO: Historical and Legal Issues', in *China and the World Trade Organisation: Requirements, Realities, and Resolution*, ed. Wenguo Cai, Murray G. Smith and Xu Xianquan (Ottawa: The Centre for Trade Policy and Law, 1996), 11–2.

4 Nancy Bernkopf Tucker, 'The Taiwan Factor in the Vote on PNTR for China and its WTO Accession', *National Bureau of Asian Research NBR Analysis* 11(2) (2000). www.nbr.org/publications/analysis/vol11no2/essay1.html.

5 Mao Zedong, 'Systematically and Completely Destroy Imperialist Domination in China' (5 March 1949), in *On Diplomacy* (Beijing: Foreign Languages Press, 1998), 62–3.

6   Chen Jian, *Mao's China and the Cold War* (Chapel Hill, NC and London: University of North Carolina Press, 2001), 51.

7   Justin Yifu Lin, 'Economic Reform and Development Strategy in China', in *China's Entry to the WTO: Strategic Issues and Quantitative Assessments*, ed. Peter Drysdale and Ligang Song (London and New York: Routledge, 2000), 30.

8   William Feeney, 'Chinese Policy in Multilateral Financial Institutions', in *China and the World: Chinese Foreign Policy in the Post-Mao Era*, ed. Samuel S. Kim (Boulder, CO and London: Westview Press, 1984), 269.

9   Chu-yuan Cheng, 'Mainland China's Modernization and Economic Reform: Process, Consequences, and Prospects', in *Forces for Change in Contemporary China*, ed. Bih-jaw Lin and James T. Myers (Columbia, SC: University of South Carolina Press, 1993), 265–73.

10 Justin Yifu Lin, Fang Cai and Zhou Li, *The China Miracle: Development Strategy and Economic Reform* (Hong Kong: The Chinese University Press, 1998), 128–9.

11 Lu Aiguo, *China and the Global Economy since 1840* (Basingstoke: Macmillan Press, 2000), 126.

12 The World Bank, *China 2020: Development Challenges in the New Century* (Washington, DC: The World Bank, 1997), 2–4.

13 See W.W. Rostow. 'The Take-Off Into Self-Sustained Growth', in *The Economics of Underdevelopment*, ed. A. Agawala and S. Singh (New York: Oxford University Press, 1963), 171–2.

14 Kenneth Lieberthal, *Governing China: From Revolution Through Reform* (New York and London: W.W. Norton, 1995), 149–53.

15 Harold K. Jacobson and Michael Oksenberg, *China's Participation in the IMF, the World Bank, and GATT* (Ann Arbor, MI: University of Michigan Press, 1990), 41–2.

16 'The United Nations and the World Economy', and the 'The Declaration on the Establishment of a New International Order', in *The United Nations and Just World Order*, ed. Richard A. Falk, Samuel S. Kim, and Saul H. Mendlovitz (Boulder, CO and Oxford: Westview Press, 1991), 281–91.

17 Yongjin Zhang, *China in International Society Since 1949: Alienation and Beyond* (Oxford and New York: St Martin's Press, 1998), 226.

18 Margaret M. Pearson, 'The Case of China's Accession to the WTO', in *The Making of Chinese Foreign and Security Policy in the Age of Reform*, ed. David M. Lampton (Stanford, CA: Stanford University Press, 2001), 340.

19 Susan Shirk, *How China Opened its Door: The Political Success of the PRC's Foreign Trade and Investment Reforms* (Washington, DC: The Brookings Institution, 1994), 34–40.

20 Willem van Kemenade, *China, Hong Kong, Taiwan, Inc.: The Dynamics of a New Empire* (New York: Vintage Books, 1997), 160–2.

21 Lu Jianren, 'China's Experience in Utilizing ODA and APEC Development Cooperation', in *APEC and Development Cooperation*, ed. Mohamed Ariff (Singapore: Institute of Southeast Asian Studies, 1998), 103–7.

22 Feeney, 'Chinese Policy in Multilateral Financial Institutions', 271.

23 Nicholas R. Lardy, *China's Unfinished Economic Revolution* (Washington, DC: Brookings Institution Press, 1998), 63.

24 Jacobson and Oksenberg, *China's Participation in the IMF, the World Bank, and GATT*, 92–4.

25 Nicholas R. Lardy, *China in the World Economy* (Washington, DC: Institute for International Economics, 1994), 44–7.

26 Yoichi Funabashi, Michel Oksenberg and Heinrich Weiss, *An Emerging China in a World of Interdependence: A Report to the Trilateral Commission* (New York, Paris and Tokyo: The Trilateral Commission, 1994), 43.

27 Zhang, *China in International Society since 1949*, 234–5.

28 Pearson, 'The Case of China's Accession to the WTO', 341.

29 James Mann, *About Face: A History of America's Curious Relationship with China: From Nixon to Clinton* (New York: Vintage Books, 2000), 262–3.

30 Russia, meanwhile, had applied to but had not gained admission to the WTO as of mid-2004. See Nicholas R. Lardy, *Integrating China into the Global Economy* (Washington, DC: Brookings Institution Press, 2002), 63, 198 note 2.

31 Jacobson and Oksenberg, *China's Participation in the IMF, the World Bank, and GATT*, 102.

32 William R. Feeney, 'China and the Multilateral Economic Institutions', in *China and the World: Chinese Foreign Policy Faces the New Millennium*, ed. Samuel S. Kim (Boulder, CO and Oxford: Westview Press, 1998), 257.

33 Stephen Green, *China's Stockmarket: A Guide to its Progress, Players and Prospects* (London: The Economist, 2003), 11–12.

34 Michael Yahuda, 'Deng Xiaoping: The Statesman', *The China Quarterly* 135 (September 1993), 558.

35 Richard Baum. *Burying Mao: Chinese Politics in the Age of Deng Xiaoping* (Princeton, NJ: Princeton University Press, 1994), 342–4.

36 Nicholas D. Kristof and Sheryl Wudunn, *China Wakes: The Struggle for the Soul of a Rising Power* (New York: Vintage Books, 1994), 344.

37 Doug Guthrie, *Dragon in a Three-Piece Suit: The Emergence of Capitalism in China* (Princeton, NJ: Princeton University Press, 1999), 150–3.

38 See Jeremy Brooks Rosen, 'China, Emerging Economies, and the World Trade Order', *Duke Law Journal* 46(6) (April 1997): 1521 and 1521 note 19.

39 John H. Jackson, 'Managing the Trading System: The World Trade Organisation and the Post-Uruguay Round GATT Agenda', in *Managing the World Economy: Fifty Years After Bretton Woods*, ed. Peter B. Kenen (Washington, DC: Institute of International Economics, 1994), 131–6.

40 Asif H. Qureshi, *The World Trade Organisation: Implementing International Trade Norms* (Manchester and New York: Manchester University Press, 1996), 5.

41 David M. Lampton, *Same Bed, Different Dreams: Managing US-China Relations, 1989–2000* (Berkeley, CA and London: University of California Press, 2001), 117.

42 Richard Nixon, *Beyond Peace* (New York: Random House, 1994), 125–6.

43 Margaret M. Pearson, 'The Case of China's Accession to the GATT/WTO', in *The Making of Chinese Foreign and Security Policy in the Era of Reform*, ed. David M. Lampton (Stanford, CA: Stanford University Press, 2001), 342.

44 James Mann, *About Face: A History of America's Curious Relationship with China: From Nixon to Clinton* (New York: Vintage Books, 2000), 345–6.

45 Yasheng Huang, 'Sino-US Relations: The Economic Dimensions', in *In the Eyes of the Dragon: China Views the World*, ed. Yong Deng and Fei-ling Wang (Lanham, MD and Oxford: Rowman and Littlefield, 1999), 170–3.

46 Stuart Harris, 'China's role in the WTO and APEC', in *China Rising: Nationalism and Interdependence*, ed. David S.G. Goodman and Gerald Segal (New York and London: Routledge, 1997), 140–1.

47 Margaret M. Pearson, 'China's Integration into the International Trade and Investment Regime', in *China Joins the World: Problems and Prospects*, ed. Elizabeth Economy and Michel Oksenberg (New York: Council on Foreign Relations Press, 1999), 180–1.

48 Alastair Newton and Robert Subbaraman, *China: Gigantic Possibilities, Present Realities* (New York: Lehman Brothers, 2002), 78.

49 Margaret M. Pearson, 'China and Major Economic Institutions', in *Engaging China: the Management of an Emerging Power*, ed. Alastair Iain Johnston and Robert S. Ross (London and New York: Routledge, 1999), 218.

50 Qureshi, *The World Trade Organisation: Implementing International Trade Norms*, 129.

51 Shi Guangsheng, 'China's Foreign Economic Trade in the 21st Century', in *China's Century: The Awakening of the Next Economic Powerhouse*, ed. Laurence J. Brahm (Singapore and New York: John Wiley and Sons, 2001), 119–25.

52 Pearson, 'China and Major Economic Institutions', 225–6.

53 Pearson, 'The Case of China's Accession to the GATT/WTO', 350.

54 Ian Johnson and Eduardo Lachica, 'China Hinders Its Own Bid for WTO, Adding New Trade Barriers as Old Ones Fall', *The Wall Street Journal*, 20 May 1997, A15.

55 Lampton, *Same Bed, Different Dreams*, 178–9.

56 Joseph Fewsmith, 'The Political and Social Implications of China's Accession to the WTO', *The China Quarterly* 167 (September 2001): 579–80.

57 Feng Chen, 'Order and Stability in Social Transition: Neoconservative Political Thought in Post-1989 China', *The China Quarterly* 151 (September 1997): 593–613.

58 Joseph Fewsmith, *China since Tiananmen: The Politics of Transition* (Cambridge: Cambridge University Press, 2001), 214–17.

59 Fewsmith, 'The Political and Social Implications of China's Accession to the WTO', 574.

60 In 2003 the SETC was merged with the Ministry of Foreign Trade and Economic Cooperation (MOFTEC) to form the Ministry of Commerce, responsible for overseeing domestic and international trade. On the subject of the MITI, see Chalmers Johnson, *MITI and the Japanese Miracle: The Growth of Industrial Policy, 1925–1975* (Stanford, CA: Stanford University Press, 1982).

61 Dali L. Yang, 'Rationalizing the Chinese State: The Political Economy of Government Reform', in *Remaking the Chinese State: Strategies, Society, and Security*, ed. Chien-min Chao and Bruce J. Dickson (London and New York: Routledge, 2001), 36–8.

62 Edward S. Steinfeld, 'The Asian Financial Crisis: Beijing's Year of Reckoning', *Washington Quarterly* 21(3) (Summer 1998): 49.

63 Information concerning the MII (in Chinese) can be viewed at www.mii.gov.cn/.

64 Kathleen Hartford, 'Cyberspace with Chinese Characteristics', *Current History* (September 2000): 256.

65 Blaise Zerega. 'What Would Mao Think?', *Red Herring* 83 (October 2000): 120–32.

66 Pearson, 'The Case of China's Ascension to the GATT/WTO', 362.

67 Elizabeth C. Economy, 'Reforming China', *Survival* 41(3) (Autumn 1999): 33–5. See also David Scheff, *China Dawn: The Story of a Technology and Business Revolution* (New York: HarperCollins, 2002).

68 'The Battle for Cyberspace', *The China Reader: The Reform Era*, ed. Orville Schell and David Shambaugh (New York: Vintage Books, 1999), 256–9. See also Geremie R. Barmé and Sang Ye, 'The Great Firewall of China', *Wired* 5.06 (June 1997): 138–51, 174–8.

69 Joseph Kahn, 'China Is Filtering Phone Text Messages to Regulate Criticism', *The New York Times,* 3 July 2004, A3.

70 '15th Statistical Survey on the Internet Development in China', *China Internet Network Information Center*, July 2004. www.cnnic.net.cn/download/2005/012701.pdf.

71 Lester J. Gesteland. 'Internet Not Fully Open to Foreigners under China WTO – Experts', *ChinaOnline*, 17 November 1999. www.chinaonline.com/topstories/991117/c9111751.asp.

72 Mel Gurtov and Byong-Moo Hwang, *China's Security: The New Roles of the Military* (Boulder, CO and London: Lynne Rienner, 1998), 192.

73 See James Mulvenon, 'Soldiers of Fortune, Soldiers of Misfortune: Commercialization and divestiture of the Chinese Military-Business Complex, 1978–99', in *Remaking the Chinese State: Strategies, Society, and Security*, ed. Chien-min Chao and Bruce J. Dickson (London and New York: Routledge, 2001), 204–27.

74 You Ji, *The Armed Forces of China* (London and New York: I.B. Tauris, 1999), 65–7.

75 Susan V. Lawrence and Bruce Gilley, 'Bitter Harvest', *Far Eastern Economic Review*, 29 April 1999, 22–5.

76 James Mulvenon, 'Your Guess Is As Good As Mine: PLA Budgets, Proposals and Discussions at the Second Session of the 10th National People's Congress', *China Leadership Monitor* 11 (Summer 2004), www.chinaleadershipmonitor.org/20043/jm.pdf.

77 Helene Cooper and Bob Davis, 'Overruling Some Staff, Clinton Denies Zhu What He Came For', *The Wall Street Journal*, 9 April 1999. A1, A6; Helene Cooper and Bob Davis, 'Barshefsky Drove Hard Bargain, but Lost to Politics', *The Wall Street Journal*, 9 April 1999, A24.

78 A declassified copy of the Cox Report of May 1999 can be read via *CNN.com* at www.cnn.com/ ALLPOLITICS/resources/1999/cox.report/.

79 Robert L. Suettinger, *Beyond Tiananmen: The Politics of US-China Relations, 1989–2000* (Washington, DC: Brookings Institution, 2003), 287–304.

80 Lampton, *Same Bed, Different Dreams*, 184–5.

81 Fewsmith, *China since Tiananmen*, 210.

82 Di Yinqing and Zheng Gang, 'Why is the United States Anxious to Resume Talks with China on China's Entrance to the WTO?' *Gaige naican* (*Internal Reference Material on Reform*), 8, 20 April 1999: 39–42. Reprinted in *The Chinese Economy* 33(2) (March/April 2000): 6–12.

83 David Zweig, 'China's Stalled "Fifth Wave": Zhu Rongji's Reform Package of 1998–2000', *Asian Survey* 41(2) (March/April 2001): 236.

84 Susan V. Lawrence and Shawn W. Crispin, 'Double-Edged Fury', *Far Eastern Economic Review* (20 May 1999): 10–13.

85 See James Miles, 'Chinese Nationalism, US Policy and Asian Security', *Survival* 42(4) (Winter 2000–1): 51–71.

86 Joseph Fewsmith, 'China and the WTO: The Politics Behind the Agreement', *National Bureau of Asian Research NBR Report* (November 1999), 5–6. www.nbr.org/publications/report.html.

87 'In Historic Pact, US Opens Way for China to Finally Join WTO', *The Wall Street Journal*, 16 November 1999, A1, A19.

88 'Big Business Seeks Benefits amid Details of China Deal', *The Wall Street Journal*, 16 November 1999, A19.

89 'China Raises Five Proposals for Next Round Trade Talks', Embassy of the People's Republic of China in the United States of America, 2 December 1999. www.china-embassy.org/eng/7036.html.

90 Lampton, *Same Bed, Different Dreams*, 188; Pitman Potter, 'The Legal Implications of China's Accession to the WTO', *The China Quarterly* 167 (September 2001): 597.

91 Fang Yan, 'China Throws Itself into International Competition: Agriculture Faces a New Challenge', *Economy and News*, 2 (1993). Reprinted in *China's Economic Reform: A Study with Documents*, ed. Christopher Howe, Y.Y. Kueh and Robert Ash (London and New York: RoutledgeCurzon, 2003), 278–90.

92 'USTR Releases Details on US-China Consensus on China's WTO Accession', Office of the United States Trade Representative Press Release 1–38, 14 June 2001. www.ustr.gov/releases/2001/06/01-38.htm; 'China and US Clinch WTO Deal', BBC News, 9 June 2001, news.bbc.co.uk/hi/english/business/newsid_1379000/1379461.stm.

93 'Jiang Zemin's Speech on Party's 800th Anniversary (part V)', *China Daily*, 1 July 2001. www1.chinadaily.com.cn/highlights/docs/2001-07-01/17467.html.

94 Susan V. Lawrence, 'The Life of the Party', *Far Eastern Economic Review* 18 October 2001, 37–40. See also Li Minsheng. 'Entrepreneurs from Non-Public Sector Hail Jiang Speech', *Beijing Review* 9 August 2001, 11–14.

95 Interview, Canadian scholar, February 2002.

96 *Constitution of the People's Republic of China* (4th edn) (Beijing: Foreign Languages Press, 1999).

97 'Accession of the People's Republic of China', World Trade Organisation WT/L/432, 23 November 2001. www.mac.doc.gov/China/ProtocolandDecision.pdf.

98 Joseph Kahn, 'World Trade Organisation Admits China, Amid Doubts', *The New York Times*, 11 November 2001, A16.

99 'China's Permanent Mission to the WTO Inaugurated', *Xinhua*, 28 January 2002. news.xinhuanet.com/english/2002-01/28/content_257650.htm.

100 'WTO Ministerial Conference approves accession of Chinese Taipei', WTO News, 2001 Press Releases. www.wto.org/english/news_e/pres01_e/pr253_e.htm.

101 'WTO membership protocol signed', *Beijing Review*, 22 November 2001, 4.

102 Todd Crowell and David Hsieh, 'Setting China's Direction', *Asiaweek* 1 September 2000, 28.

103 Cheng Li, *China's Leaders: The New Generation* (Lanham, MD and Oxford: Rowman and Littlefield, 2001), 157 9.

104 Andrew J. Nathan and Bruce Gilley, *China's New Rulers: The Secret Files* (2nd edn) (New York: New York Review Books, 2003), 101–2.

105 Peter Gourevitch, 'The Second Image Reversed: The International Sources of Domestic Politics', *International Organisation* 32(4) (Autumn 1998): 883.

106 Robert D. Putnam, 'Diplomacy and Domestic Politics: The Logic of Two-level Games', *International Organisation* 42(3) (Summer 1998): 427–60.

107 Lampton, *Same Bed, Different Dreams*, 184.

108 Zhang Guochu, 'Employment after WTO Accession', *Beijing Review*, 21 March 2002, 16–7.

109 Fewsmith, 'The Political and Social Implications of China's Accession to the WTO', 582.

110 Jagdish Bhagwati, 'Don't Cry for Cancun', *Foreign Affairs* 83(1) (January/February 2004): 57–60.

111 Gustavo Capdevila, 'G-22 Warmup for Post-Cancun Talks', *Asia Times*, 4 October 2003. www.atimes.com/atimes/Global_Economy/EJ04Dj01.html; 'WTO narrows trade focus to seek July agreement', *Business Times* (Singapore) 7 May 2004. business-times.asia1.com.sg/story/ 0,4567,116024,00.html.

112 Lardy, *Integrating China into the World Economy*, 110–11.

113 Kellie S. Tsai, *Back-Alley Banking: Private Entrepreneurs in China* (Ithaca, NY and London: Cornell University Press, 2002), 47–59.

114 Peter Wonacott, 'China Begins Career as a WTO Member', *The Wall Street Journal*, 11 December 2001, A14.

115 Gordon G. Chang, *The Coming Collapse of China* (New York: Random House, 2001), 194–209.

116 Gilpin, *The Political Economy of International Relations*, 31–4.

117 Madelyn C. Ross, 'China's International Economic Behaviour', in *Chinese Foreign Policy: Theory and Practice*, ed. Thomas W. Robinson and David Shambaugh (Oxford and New York: Clarendon Press, 1994), 437.

118 Lanxin Xiang, 'The China Debate and the Civilization Debate', *Issues and Studies* 34(10) (October 1998), 85.

119 For example, see Paul Dibb, David D. Hale and Peter Prince, 'The Strategic Implications of Asia's Economic Crisis', *Survival* 40(2) (Summer 1998), 5–26.

120 Cui Zhiyuan, 'Jiaru shijie maoyi zuzhi bushi Zhongguo dangwu zhiji' ('Entering the WTO is Not an Urgent Task for China'), *Zhongguo yu shijie* (*China and the World*), internet journal, cited in Fewsmith, 'The Political and Social Implications of China's Accession to the WTO', 586.

121 Lardy, *Integrating China into the Global Economy*, 16–18.

122 'Something Rotten in the State of China', *The Economist*, 16 February 2002, 37–8.

123 See Huang Weiding, 'Fighting Corruption Amidst Economic Reform', in *China's Century: The Awakening of the Next Economic Powerhouse*, ed. Laurence J. Brahm (Singapore and New York: John Wiley and Sons, 2001), 39–55.

124 Erik Eckholm, 'Chinese Hear from Premier on Threats to Economy', *The New York Times*, 6 March 2002, A5.

125 'To Get Rich is Glorious', *The Economist*, 19 January 2002, 33–4.

126 Geremie R. Barmé, 'The Revolution of Resistance', in *Chinese Society: Change, Conflict and Resistance*, ed. Elizabeth J. Perry and Mark Selden (New York and London: Routledge, 2000), 201.

127 Thomas G. Moore, 'China and Globalization', *Asian Perspective* 23(4) (1999), 65–6.

128 Fewsmith, 'The Political and Social Implications of China's Accession to the WTO', 588–9.

129 Janice Gross Stein, 'International Cooperation and Loss Avoidance: Framing the Problem', in *Choosing to Cooperate: How States Avoid Loss*, ed. Janice Gross Stein and Louis W. Pauly (Baltimore, MD: Johns Hopkins University Press, 1993), 22.

130 'China Files First WTO Compliant, Demands Talks with US', *China Daily* 15 March 2002. www1.chinadaily.com.cn/news/2002-03-15/60982.html.

131 Paul Blustein, 'China Agrees to Resolve Dispute Over Tax Breaks', *Washington Post*, 9 July 2004, E01.

2 FLYING GEESE AND RISING PHOENIX

1 Chia Siow Yue, 'Economic Integration and Cooperation in East Asia', *Asia-Pacific Review* 11(1) (2004): 3.

2 The twenty-one member economies of APEC are Australia, Brunei, Canada, Chile, China (People's Republic), Hong Kong (China), Indonesia, Japan, Korea (South), Malaysia, Mexico, New Zealand, Papua New Guinea, Peru, Philippines, Russia, Singapore, Chinese Taipei (Taiwan), Thailand, the United States, and Vietnam. Three multilateral bodies, the Association of Southeast Asian Nations (ASEAN), the Pacific Economic Cooperation Council (PECC), and the Pacific Islands Forum, act as observers.

3 Ippei Yamazawa, 'On Pacific Economic Integration', *The Economic Journal* 102 (November 1992): 1523.

4 Steven Radelet and Jeffrey Sachs, 'Asia's Reemergence', *Foreign Affairs* 76(6) (November/December 1997): 52.

5 Miles Kahler, 'Legalization as Strategy: The Asia-Pacific Case', *International Organization* 54(3) (Summer 2000): 559–63.

6 Kent E. Calder, *Pacific Defense: Arms, Energy and America's Future in Asia* (New York: William Morrow, 1996), 151.

7 Peter C.Y.Chow, 'Asia-Pacific Economic Integration in Global Perspective', in James Hsiung (ed.) *Asia Pacific in the New World Politics*, 1993 (Boulder, CO: Lynne Rienner Press), 204.

8 Manoranjan Dutta, *Economic Regionalization in the Asia Pacific: Challenges to Economic Cooperation* (Northampton, MA: Edward Elgar, 1999), 21.

9 Yong Deng, *Promoting Asia-Pacific Economic Cooperation* (New York: St. Martin's Press; Basingstoke: Macmillan Press, 1997), 55–8.

10 Robert Gilpin, *The Political Economy of International Relations* (Princeton, NJ: Princeton University Press, 1987), 199.

11 See Andrew Moravcsik, 'Negotiating the Single European Act', in *The New European Community: Decisionmaking and Institutional Change*, ed. Robert O. Keohane and Stanley Hoffman (Boulder, CO and London: Westview Press, 1991), 41–84.

12 Chow, 'Asia-Pacific Economic Integration in Global Perspective', 195.

13 Kym Anderson, 'Europe 1992 and the Western Pacific Economies', *The Economic Journal* 101 (November 1991): 1547–9.

14 Andrew Elek, 'Asia-Pacific Economic Cooperation (APEC)', in *Southeast Asian Affairs 1991* (Singapore: Institute of Southeast Asian Studies, 1991) 37.

15 Donald Crone, 'Does Hegemony Matter? The Reorganization of the Pacific Political Economy', *World Politics* 45 (July 1993): 518–20.

16 Yamazawa, 'On Pacific Economic Integration', 1528–9.

17 'Australia's Hawke Views China's APEC Inclusion', *Xinhua*, 15 April 1991 *Foreign Broadcast Information Service – China* [FBIS-CHI-91-073], 16 April 1991, 17–18; Yongjin Zhang, *China in International Society since 1949: Alienation and Beyond* (New York: St. Martin's Press, 1998), 239.

18 Crone, 'Does Hegemony Matter?', 524.

19 Gary Klintworth, 'China's Evolving Relationship with APEC', *International Journal* 50(3) (Summer 1995): 489–90.

20 'Qian Qichen on the World Situation', *Beijing Review* 15 January 1990, 15–16.

21 'Li Peng on Domestic and World Issues'. *Beijing Review* 1 July 1991, 27.

22 Don Oberdorfer, *The Two Koreas: A Contemporary History* (Reading, MA: Addison-Wesley, 1997), 243–4.

23 Victor D. Cha, 'Engaging China: The View from Korea', in *Engaging China: The Management of an Emerging Power*, ed. Alistair Iain Johnston and Robert S. Ross (New York and London: Routledge, 1999), 44.

24 Crone, 'Does Hegemony Matter?', 78–9.

25 Zhang, *China in International Society since 1949*, 240.

26 Margaret M. Pearson, 'China and Major Economic Institutions', in *Engaging China: The Management of an Emerging Power*, ed. Alastair Iain Johnston and Robert S. Ross (New York and London: Routledge, 1999), 217.

27 'Aimless in Seattle', *The Economist,* 13 November 1993, 36.

28 Nicole Gallant and Richard Stubbs, 'APEC's Dilemmas: Institution-Building around the Pacific Rim', *Pacific Affairs* 70(2) (Summer 1997): 206.

29 'Jiang Zemin's 20 November Speech to APEC Leaders', *Beijing Review*, 29 November 1993, *Foreign Broadcast Information Service – China* [FBIS-CHI-93-290] 2 December 1993, 3–4.

30 Richard K. Betts, 'Wealth, Power and Instability: East Asia and the United States after the Cold War', *International Security* 18(3) (Winter 1993/94): 72.

31 Jiang Xiaoyan, 'Dispute Over APEC Development Orientation', *Shijie Zhishi*, 1 November 1994, *Foreign Broadcast Information Service – China* [FBIS-CHI-94–220] 15 November 1994, 11–13.

32 Gallant and Stubbs, 'APEC's Dilemmas', 212–14.

33 Hiromoto Seki, 'APEC: New Paradigm for Asia-Pacific Relations', *Asia-Pacific Review* 3(1) (Spring/Summer 1996): 131–6.

34 *Osaka Action Agenda: Implementation of the Bogor Declaration*. Ministry of Foreign Affairs, Japan. November 1995. www.mofa.go.jp/policy/economy/apec/1995/agenda.html.

35 'Wu Yi Urges APEC to Support Entry into GATT', *Xinhua*, 11 November 1994, *Foreign Broadcast Information Service – China* [FBIS-CHI-94-220], 15 November 1994, 11.

36 'China's Sackful of Surprises', *The Economist*, 25 November 1995, 33.

37 Johnny Chi-Chen Chiang, 'Conceptualizing the APEC Way: International Cooperation in a Non-institutionalized Regime', *Issues and Studies* 36(6) (November/December 2000), 190–1.

38 Yoichi Funabashi, 'Bridging Asia's Economics-Security Gap', *Survival* 38(4) (Winter 1996–7): 103–4.

39 Interview, Hong Kong legal expert, Hong Kong SAR, September 2001.

40 Paul Dibb, David D. Hale, and Peter Prince, 'The Strategic Implications of Asia's Economic Crisis', *Survival* 40(2) (Summer 1998): 6–11.

41 Stephen Haggard, *The Political Economy of the Asian Financial Crisis* (Washington, DC: Institute for International Economics, 2000), 3–4.

42 Edward J. Lincoln, 'Japan's Financial Mess', *Foreign Affairs* 77(3) (May/June 1998): 62.

43 Elizabeth Wishnick, *Mending Fences: The Evolution of Moscow's China Policy from Brezhnev to Yeltsin* (Seattle, WA and London: University of Washington Press, 2001), 175–6.

44 Xiao-Ming Li, 'China's Macroeconomic Stabilization Policies Following the Asian Financial Crisis', *Asian Survey* 40(6) (November/December 2000): 938. See also A. S. Bhalla and D. M. Nachane, 'The Economic Impact of the Asian Financial Crisis on India and China', in *Financial Liberalization and the Asian Crisis*, ed. Ha-Joon Chang, Gabriel Palma, and D. Hugh Whittaker (Basingstoke and New York: Palgrave, 2001), 242.

45 Pang Zhongying, 'Globalization and China: China's Response to the Asian Economic Crisis', *Asian Perspective* 23(1) (1999): 125–6.

46 Edward S. Steinfeld, 'The Asian Financial Crisis: Beijing's Year of Reckoning', *The Washington Quarterly* 21(3) (Summer 1998), 37.

47 Ligang Song, 'China', in *East Asia in Crisis: From Being a Miracle to Needing One?* ed. Ross H. McLeod and Ross Garnaut (New York and London: Routledge, 1998): 105.

48 See Gene Hsin Chang and Jack Hou, 'Structural Inflation and the 1994 "Monetary" Crisis in China', *Contemporary Economic Policy* 15 (July 1997): 73–81.

49 Bhalla and Nachane, 'The Economic Impact of the Asian Financial Crisis on India and China', 238.

50 Alvin Y. So, 'China under the Shadow of the Asian Financial Crisis: Retreat from Economic and Political Liberalization?' *Asian Perspective* 23(2) (1999): 90–1.

51 Li, 'China's Macroeconomic Stabilization Policies Following the Asian Financial Crisis', 939–42.

52 David M. Lampton, *Same Bed, Different Dreams, Managing China-US Relations, 1989–2000* (Berkeley, CA, Los Angeles, CA and London: University of California Press, 2001), 242–3.

53 Thomas G. Moore and Dixia Yang, 'Empowered and Restrained: Chinese Foreign Policy in the Age of Interdependence', in *The Making of Chinese Foreign Policy in the Era of Reform*, ed. David M. Lampton (Stanford, CA: Stanford University Press, 2001), 220–2.

54 Kiichi Saeki, 'The Rise of China: Threats, Uncertainties, and Opportunities', *Asia-Pacific Review* 2(1) (1995): 204.

55 Steinfeld, 'The Asian Financial Crisis: Beijing's Year of Reckoning', 37–8.

56 Nicholas R. Lardy, 'China and the Asian Contagion', *Foreign Affairs* 77(4) (July/August 1998): 78–9.

57 Peter A. Petri, 'APEC and the Millennium Round', in *Asia Pacific Economic Cooperation (APEC): Challenges and Tasks for the Twenty-First Century*, ed. Ippei Yamazawa (New York and London: Routledge, 2000), 105.

58 'Further Cooperation Needed for APEC's Development', *Beijing Review*, 27 September 1999, 9–10.

59 Michael Vatikiotis, Ben Dolven, and David Murphy, 'Terror Throws Us Together, For Now', *Far Eastern Economic Review*, 1 November 2001, 36–40.

60 In 2003 the SETC was merged with the Ministry of Foreign Trade and Economic Cooperation (MOFTEC) to form the Ministry of Commerce, responsible for overseeing domestic and international trade. On the subject of the MITI, see Chalmers Johnson, *MITI and the Japanese Miracle: The Growth of Industrial Policy, 1925–1975* (Stanford, CA: Stanford University Press, 1982).

61 Interview, Canadian government official, November 2001.

62 'Getting a Bit More Serious about Security', *The Economist*, 27 October 2001, 42–3.

63 For example, see Michael Richardson, 'China and US Clashing Anew in Pacific Forum: Differences on Security and Trade begin to Disrupt Asian Meeting', *International Herald Tribune*, 16 November 1995, 1, 8.

64 Interview, Canadian government official, November 2001.

65 Zhang Yunling, 'China and APEC: Interests, Opportunities, and Challenges', in *From APEC to Xanadu*, ed. Donald C. Hellmann and Kenneth B. Pyle (Armonk, NY: M.E. Sharpe, 1997), 196.

66 Richard Rosecrance, 'Has Realism Become Cost-Benefit Analysis?' *International Security* 26(2) (Fall 2001): 135.

67 Lloyd Gruber, *Ruling the World: Power Politics and the Rise of Supranational Institutions* (Princeton, NJ: Princeton University Press, 2000).

68 Michael D. Swaine and Ashley J. Tellis, *Interpreting China's Grand Strategy: Past, Present, and Future* (Santa Monica, CA: Rand, 2000), 135–6.

69 Charles Lipson, 'International Cooperation in Economic and Security Affairs', *World Politics* 37 (October 1984): 1–23.

70 See Alexander Gerschenkron, *Economic Backwardness in Historical Perspective: A Book of Essays* (Cambridge, MA: Harvard University Press, 1962).

71 Patrick E. Tyler, 'China Pressing to Join Trade Club', *The New York Times* (14 November 1994): D1, D5.

72 Lampton, *Same Bed, Different Dreams*, 43–5.

73 James Mann, *About Face: A History of America's Curious Relationship with China, From Nixon to Clinton* (New York and Toronto: Vintage Books, 2000), 292–4.

74 Kishore Mahbubani, 'The Pacific Way', *Foreign Affairs* 74(1) (January/February 1995): 110.

75 Joseph M. Grieco, 'Anarchy and the Limits of Cooperation: A Realist Critique of the Newest Liberal Institutionalism', *International Organization* 42(3) (Summer 1998): 485–507.

76 Amos A. Jordan and Jane Khanna, 'Economic Interdependence and Challenges to the Nation-State: The Emergence of Natural Economic Territories in the Asia-Pacific', *Journal of International Affairs* 48(2) (Winter 1995): 436.

77 'President Jiang Zemin's Keynote Speech at the Informal APEC Leadership Meeting, 15 November 1994', Foreign Ministry of the People's Republic of China, 15 November 1994, us-mirror.fmprc.gov.cn/eng/5122.html.

78 'Speech by President Jiang at the Eighth APEC Informal Leadership Meeting, 16 November 2000', Foreign Ministry of the People's Republic of China, 16 November 2000, www.fmprc.gov.cn/eng/topics/3755/3791/3793/3797/t19403.htm.

79 Chia Siow Yue, 'Economic Cooperation and Integration in East Asia', *Asia-Pacific Review* 11(1) (2004): 2–4; Zhang Jin, 'Progress Made in Free Trade Talks with GCC', *China Daily*, 5 July 2004: 9. www.chinadaily.com.cn/english/doc/2004-07/05/content_345486.htm.

80 John Wong and Sarah Chan, 'China-ASEAN Free Trade Agreement: Shaping Future Economic Relations', *Asian Survey* 43(3) (May/June 2003): 507–9.

81 Barry Desker, 'In Defence of FTAs: From Purity to Pragmatism in East Asia', *The Pacific Review* 17(1) (March 2004): 13–14.

82 Yue, 'Economic Integration and Cooperation in East Asia', 5.

83 Jagdish Bhagwati and Arvind Panagariya, 'Preferential Trading Areas and Multilateralism: Strangers, Friends, or Foes?' in *The Economics of Preferential Trade Agreements* (Washington DC: The AEI Press, 1996), 53–4.

84 Jürgen Haacke, 'The ASEANization of Regional Order in East Asia: A Failed Endeavour?' *Asian Perspective* 22(3) (1998): 7–47.

85 Kevin G. Cai, 'Is a Free Trade Zone Emerging in Northeast Asia in the Wake of the Asian Financial Crisis?' *Pacific Affairs* 74(1) (Spring 2001): 13.

86 Lester J. Gesteland, 'China, ASEAN Ponder Asian Common Market', *ChinaOnline* 29 November 1999, www.chinaonline.com/topstories/991129/c9112952.asp.

87 Peter J. Katzenstein, 'Regionalism in Comparative Perspective', *Cooperation and Conflict* 31(2) (1996): 139–40.

88 Joseph M. Grieco, 'Realism and Regionalism: American Power and German and Japanese Institutional Strategies During and After the Cold War', in *Unipolar Politics: Realism and State Strategies After the Cold War*, ed. Ethan B. Kapstein and Michael Mastanduno (New York: Columbia University Press, 1999), 329–30.

89 Grieco, 'Realism and Regionalism', 322–3; Nishiguchi Kiyokatsu. 'Toward an East Asian Free Trade Area', *Japan Quarterly* (January–March 1993): 14.

90 See Paul Dibb, David D. Hale and Peter Prince, 'The Strategic Implications of Asia's Economic Crisis'. *Survival* 40(2) (Summer 1998): 5–26.

91 'The Chiang Mai Initiative', Discussion Paper, Special ASEAN Finance Deputies Meeting (AFDM) +3, 6 May 2000, Chiang Mai, Thailand. www.mfa.go.th/dea/chiangmai_initiative.htm.

92 David P. Rapkin, 'The United States, Japan and the Power to Block: the APEC and AMF Cases', *The Pacific Review* 14(3) (2001): 394–8, 405n36; Marc Lanteigne. 'ASEAN Plus Three and the Changing Roles of Economic Institutions in the Post-Crisis Asia Pacific Region', *Trading Arrangements in the Pacific Rim* Release 2001-1 (January 2001): 4.

93 'The Best Things in Life', *The Economist*, 2 December 2000, 42.

94 'Premier Zhu Rongji Attending the Summit between ASEAN and China, Japan and South Korea (10 + 3) Issuing An Important Speech (25 November 2000)', Ministry of Foreign Affairs of the People's Republic of China. us-mirror.fmprc.gov.cn/eng/6063.html.

95 'Press Statement by Chairman, 4th ASEAN Informal Summit, Singapore, 25 November 2000', Media Secretariat, ASEAN Informal Summit, Singapore. www.aseansummit2001.org.bn/org/as2001/4aispr.htm.

96 Peter Montagnon, 'Disillusion Leads to Growing Spirit of Co-operation among Asian Nations', *Financial Times*, 21 July 2000, 12.

97 Interview with Chinese scholar, Beijing, September 2001.
98 Cai, 'Is a Free Trade Zone Emerging in Northeast Asia in the Wake of the Asian Financial Crisis?', 16.
99 Hsu Tung-ming, 'Pay heed to ASEAN's tilt toward the mainland', *Taipei Times* 3 December 2001. www.taipeitimes.com/news/2001/12/03/story/0000114192.
100 'APEC Economic Leaders' Declaration: Meeting New Challenges in the New Century (21 October 2001)', Ministry of Foreign Affairs of the People's Republic of China, 21 October 2001. us-mirror.fmprc.gov/eng/19019.html.
101 Richard Stubbs, 'ASEAN Plus Three: Emerging East Asian Regionalism', *Asian Survey* 42(3) (May/June 2002): 451.
102 Christopher M. Dent, 'The Asia-Europe Meeting and Inter-Regionalism: Towards a Theory of Maximum Utility', *Asian Survey* 44(2) (March/April 2004): 215–16.
103 Christopher Bo Bramsen, 'ASEM: A New Dimension in Asian-European Relations', in *China's Century: The Awakening of the Next Economic Powerhouse*, ed. Lawrence J. Brahm (Singapore: John Wiley and Sons, 2001), 89–97.
104 Interview with European Union Embassy official, Beijing, April 2004.
105 See William H. Overholt, 'Asia's Continuing Crisis', *Survival* 44(1) (Spring 2002): 97–114.
106 Gerald Segal, 'East Asia and the "Constrainment" of China', *International Security* 20(4) (Spring 1996): 114.
107 Richard McGregor, David Ibison and Shawn Donnan, 'China, Japan and Malaysia Back Fresh Move to Create "East Asian Community"', *Financial Times*, 5 August 2004, 6.
108 Xiao Zhou, 'What is "Ten plus Three"?' *Beijing Review,* 11 December 2000, 8–9.

3 CHIMERAS OR PEACEBUILDERS?

1 Barry Buzan and Gerald Segal, 'Rethinking East Asian Security', *Survival* 36(2) (Summer 1994): 3–21.
2 Denny Roy, 'Hegemon on the Horizon: China's Threat to East Asian Security', *International Security* 19(1) (Summer 1994): 149–68.
3 See Michael G. Gallagher, 'China's Illusory Threat in the South China Sea', *International Security* 19(1) (Summer 1994): 169–94; Michael O'Hanlon, 'Why China Cannot Conquer Taiwan', *International Security* 25(2) (Fall 2000): 51–86; Brian Job, André Laliberté and Michael D. Wallace, 'Assessing the Risks of Conflict in the PRC-ROC Enduring Rivalry', *Pacific Affairs* 72(4) (Winter 1999–2000): 513–35.
4 T.V. Paul, *Asymmetric Conflicts: War Initiation by Weaker Powers* (Cambridge and New York: Cambridge University Press, 1994), 86–91.
5 David M. Finkelstein, 'China's "New Concept of Security"', in *The People's Liberation Army and China in Transition*, ed. Stephen J. Flanagan and Michael E. Marti (Washington, DC: National Defence University Press, 2003), 197–209.
6 Interview, Chinese scholar, Beijing, September 2001.
7 Interview, Western official, Beijing, September 2001.
8 John S. Duffield, 'Why is There No APTO? Why is There No OSCAP? Asia-Pacific Security Institutions in Comparative Perspective', *Contemporary Security Policy* 22(2) (August 2001): 72–3.
9 The ARF's membership includes all ten ASEAN states (Brunei, Cambodia, Indonesia, Laos, Malaysia, Myanmar/ Burma, Philippines, Singapore, Thailand and Vietnam), as well as Australia, Canada, China (People's Republic), the European Union, India, Japan, Mongolia, New Zealand, the Russian Federation, North and South Korea and the United States.
10 'The Objectives of ARF', Association of Southeast Asian Nations, 1994. www.aseansec.org/print.asp?file=/amm/objarf1.htm.
11 Alastair Iain Johnston and Paul Evans, 'China and Multilateral Security Institutions', in *Engaging China: The Management of an Emerging Power*, ed. Alastair Iain Johnston and Robert S. Ross (New York and London: Routledge, 1999), 256–7.

12   Robert A. Manning and Paula Stern, 'The Myth of the Pacific Community', *Foreign Affairs* 73(6) (November/December 1994): 88.

13   Robert Karniol, 'Why Asia must Search for a Security Structure Formula', *Jane's International Defence Review* 2/2000 (February 2000): 42.

14   Barry Buzan and Gerald Segal, 'Rethinking East Asian Security', *Survival* 36(2) (Summer 1994): 15–17.

15   David A. Lake, 'Beyond Anarchy: The Importance of Security Institutions', *International Security* 26(1) (Summer 2001): 130.

16   'The ASEAN Regional Forum: A Concept Paper', The Association of Southeast Asian Nations, 1995. www.aseansec.org/print.asp?file=/politics/arf_ch2c.htm.

17   Various interviews, Beijing, September 2001.

18   Steven Rogers, 'Beyond the Abu Sayyaf: The Lessons of Failure in the Philippines', *Foreign Affairs* 83(1) (January / February 2004): 15–20; see Seng Tan and Kumar Ramakrishna, 'Interstate and Intrastate Dynamics in Southeast Asia's War on Terror', *SAIS Review* 24(1) (Winter-Spring 2004): 91–105.

19   Susan L. Shirk, 'Chinese Views on Asia-Pacific Multilateral Security Cooperation', *NBR Analysis* 5(5) (Seattle: National Bureau of Asian Research, 1994), 12.

20   Thammy Evans, 'The PRC's Relationship with the ASEAN Regional Forum: Realpolitik, Regime Theory or a Continuation of the Sinic Zone of Influence System?' *Modern Asian Studies* 37(3) (2003): 746–51.

21   Interview, Chinese scholar, Beijing, September 2001.

22   Smith, 'Multilateralism and Regional Security in Asia', 13.

23   Bates Gill, 'Two Steps Forward, One Step Back: The Dynamics of Chinese Nonproliferation and Arms Control Policy-Making in an Era of Reform', in *The Making of Chinese Foreign and Security Policy in the Era of Reform*, ed. David M. Lampton (Stanford, CA: Stanford University Press, 2001), 277–9.

24   Brian L. Job, 'Track 2 Diplomacy: Ideational Contribution to the Evolving Asia Security Order', in *Asian Security Order: Instrumental and Normative Features*, ed. Muthiah Alagappa (Stanford, CA: Stanford University Press, 2003), 241–79.

25   Xavier Furtado, 'Bridge Over Troubled Waters: Strengthening the Role of Track II Security Mechanisms in the South China Seas', *Cancaps Papier* 19 (February 1999), 11.

26   Alastair Ian Johnston, 'The Myth of the Asian Way? Explaining the Evolution of the ASEAN Regional Forum', in *Imperfect Unions: Security Institutions over Time and Space*, ed. Helga Haftendorn, Robert O. Keohane, and Celeste A. Wallander (Oxford and New York: Oxford University Press, 1999), 300–02.

27   The idea of 'filtering' was coined by Paul Evans, quoted in Johnston, 'The Myth of the Asian Way?', 303.

28   CSCAP's current members are Australia, Cambodia, Canada, European CSCAP, India, Indonesia, Japan, Malaysia, Mongolia, New Zealand, North Korea, New Guinea, People's Republic of China, Philippines, Russian Federation, Singapore, South Korea, Thailand, United States, and Vietnam. Its working groups oversee Comprehensive and Cooperative Security, Confidence and Security-Building Measures, Maritime Cooperation, North Pacific Dialogue, and Transnational Crime.

29   A copy of the CSCAP Charter, (drafted in December 1993 and amended in August 1995) can be viewed at www.cscap.org/revised.

30   Johnston, 'The Myth of the Asian Way?', 303.

31   Paul Evans, 'The New Multilateralism and the Conditional Engagement of China', in *Weaving the Net: Conditional Engagement with China*, ed. James Shinn (New York: Council on Foreign Relations, 1996), 261.

32   Johnston and Evans, 'China and Multilateral Security Institutions', 257, 271 (note 72).

33   Interview with Canadian scholar, December 2001.

34   Interview with Canadian scholar, December 2001.

35   Interview, Chinese security policy official, Beijing, September 2001.

36 Interview with Canadian scholar, December 2001.

37 Charles Lipson, 'Why are Some International Agreements Informal?' *International Organization* 45(4) (Autumn 1991): 495–538.

38 Tsuyoshi Kawasaki, 'Formulating Canada's Grand Strategy in Asia', *International Journal* 56(1) (Winter 2000–2001): 136.

39 Andrew J. Nathan and Robert S. Ross, *The Great Wall and the Empty Fortress: China's Search for Security* (New York: W.W. Norton, 1997), 115.

40 Jusuf Wanandi, 'ASEAN's China Strategy: Towards Deeper Engagement', *Survival* 38(3) (Autumn 1996): 122.

41 Interview, Chinese security policy official, Beijing, September 2001.

42 Jianwei Wang, 'Managing Conflict: Chinese Perspectives on Multilateral Diplomacy and Collective Security', in *In the Eyes of the Dragon: China Views the World*, ed. Yong Deng and Fei-ling Wang (New York: Rowman and Littlefield, 1999), 86.

43 Interview with Canadian scholar, December 2001.

44 'ASEAN Declaration on the South China Sea', ASEAN Secretariat, 1992, www.aseansec.org/print.asp?file=/politics/pol_agr5.htm.

45 Erica Strecker Downs and Phillip C. Saunders, 'Legitimacy and the Limits of Nationalism: China and the Diaoyu Islands', *International Security* 23(3) (Winter 1998/99): 114–46.

46 Downs and Saunders, 133–4; Joseph Kahn, 'China Tells Japan to Release 7 Arrested on Disputed Island', *The New York Times*, 26 March 2004, A9.

47 Mel Gurtov and Byong-Moo Hwang, *China's Security: The New Roles of the Military* (Boulder, CO and London: Lynne Rienner, 1998), 260–1.

48 You Ji, *The Armed Forces of China* (New York and London: I.B. Tauris, 1999), 217.

49 Mark J. Valencia, *China and the South China Sea Disputes*, Adelphi Paper 298, (Oxford: Oxford University Press, 1995), 8–11.

50 Michael Bennett, 'The People's Republic of China and the Use of International Law in the Spratly Islands Dispute', *Stanford Journal of International Law* 28(425) (Spring 1992): 434–5.

51 Xavier Furtado, 'International Law and the Dispute Over the Spratly Islands: Whither UNCLOS?' *Contemporary Southeast Asia* 21(3) (December 1999): 388–90.

52 Gurtov and Hwang, *China's Security*, 263.

53 Michael Leifer, 'Chinese Economic Reform and Security Policy: The South China Sea Connection', *Survival* 37(2) (Summer 1995): 49–50.

54 Valencia, *China and the South China Sea Disputes*, 10.

55 Furtado, 'Bridge Over Troubled Waters', 10. See also Robert A. Manning, *The Asian Energy Factor: Myths and Dilemmas of Energy, Security, and the Pacific Future* (New York and Basingstoke: Palgrave, 2000), 190.

56 Robert S. Ross, 'China and Southeast Asia: The Challenge of Economic Competition', in *Southeast Asia in the New World Order*, ed. David Wurfel and Bruce Burton (London: Macmillan Press, 1996), 159.

57 Gurtov and Hwang, *China's Security*, 265. See also Frédéric Lasserre, *Le Dragon et la Mer: Stratégies géopolitiques chinoises en mer de Chine du Sud* [The Dragon and the Sea: China's Geopolitical Strategies in the South China Sea] (Montreal: Harmattan, 1996), 137–41.

58 Amitav Acharya, 'ASEAN and Conditional Engagement', in *Weaving the Net: Conditional Engagement with China*, ed. James Shinn (New York: Council on Foreign Relations, 1996), 223–4; Benito Lim, 'Political Changes in China and Their Implications on the Philippines', in *Crisis and Transformation in Northeast Asia: Implications for the Philippines*, ed. Xavier A. Furtado (Manila: De La Salle University Press, 1999), 66.

59 You, *The Armed Forces of China*, 226.

60 John W. Garver, 'China's Push Through the South China Sea: The Interaction of Bureaucratic and National Interests', *China Quarterly* 132 (December 1992): 1028.

61 Suisheng Zhao, 'China's Periphery Policy and Its Asian Neighbours', *Security Dialogue* 30(3) (September 1999): 341.

NOTES

62 Gurtov and Hwang, *China's Security: The New Roles of the Military*, 266.

63 You, *The Armed Forces of China*, 222.

64 Lee Lai To, 'China's Relations with ASEAN: Partners in the 21st Century?' *Pacifica Review* 13(1) (February 2001): 65.

65 'Declaration on the Conduct of Parties in the South China Sea', The Association of Southeast Asian Nations, 2002, www.aseansec.org/13165.htm.

66 You, *The Armed Forces of China*, 221.

67 Jianwei Wang, 'Chinese Perspectives on Multilateral Security Cooperation', *Asian Perspective* 22(3) (1998): 105.

68 Mao Zedong, 'On the Intermediate Zone, Peaceful Coexistence, Sino-British and Sino-U.S. Relations (24 August 1954)' in *On Diplomacy* (Beijing: Foreign Languages Press, 1998), 122–5.

69 Wang, 'Chinese Perspectives on Multilateral Diplomacy and Collective Security', 84.

70 'Letter dated 30 August 1990 from China, France, the USSR, the United Kingdom and the United States transmitting statement and framework document adopted by their representatives at meeting in New York, 27–28 August 1990'. A/45/472-S/21689, 31 August 1990. Reprinted in *The United Nations and Cambodia, 1991–1995* (New York: United Nations, Department of Public Information, 1995), 88–92.

71 Steven R. Ratner, 'The Cambodia Settlement Agreements', *American Journal of International Law* 87(1) (1993): 1–41.

72 Wang, 'Chinese Perspectives on Multilateral Diplomacy and Collective Security', 76–8.

73 Samuel S. Kim, 'China and the United Nations', in *China Joins the World: Progress and Prospects*, ed. Elizabeth Economy and Michel Oksenberg (New York: Council on Foreign Relations Press, 1999), 54.

74 Bates Gill and James Reilly, 'Sovereignty, Intervention, and Peacekeeping: The View from Beijing', *Survival* 42(3) (Autumn 2000): 48–50. See also Allen Carlson, 'Helping to Keep the Peace (Albeit Reluctantly): China's Recent Stance on Sovereignty and Multilateral Intervention', *Pacific Affairs* 77(1) (Spring 2004): 9–27.

75 Michael J. Finnegan, 'Constructing Cooperation: Toward Multilateral Security Cooperation in Northeast Asia', *Asian Perspective* 23(1) (1999): 84.

76 Kenneth N. Waltz, 'Structural Realism after the Cold War', *International Security* 25(1) (Summer 2000): 26.

77 David M. Lampton, *Same Bed, Different Dreams: Managing US-China Relations, 1989–2000* (Berkeley, CA and London: University of California Press, 2001), 164.

78 Interview, Chinese scholar, Beijing, September 2001.

79 Paul Evans, 'The New Multilateralism and the Conditional Engagement of China', 252.

80 Information Office of the State Council of the People's Republic of China, *China's National Defence in 2000*, (Beijing: New Star Publishers, 2000), 48–50.

81 Interview, Chinese scholar, Beijing, September 2001.

82 'Some Thoughts on Establishing a New Regional Security Order. Statement by Ambassador Sha Zukang at the East-West Center's Senior Policy Seminar', Ministry of Foreign Affairs of the People's Republic of China, 7 August 2000. www.fmprc.gov.cn/eng/5180.html.

83 For example, see Yi Ding, 'Upholding the Five Principles of Peaceful Coexistence', *Beijing Review* 26 February–4 March 1990, 13–16.

84 Wang Gungwu, *China and the World since 1949: The Impact of Independence, Modernity, and Revolution* (London and Basingstoke: Macmillan Press, 1977), 159.

85 Elizabeth Becker, *When the War Was Over: Cambodia and the Khmer Rouge Revolution* (New York: PublicAffairs Book Group, 1998), 294–5.

86 Wanandi, 'ASEAN's China Strategy: Towards Deeper Engagement', 118–19.

87 Lee, 'China's Relations with ASEAN', 62–4.

88 Acharya, 'ASEAN and Conditional Engagement', 225.

89 Graham Hutchings, *Modern China: A Companion to a Rising Power* (London and New York: Penguin Books, 2001), 324.

90   Michael Leifer, *The ASEAN Regional Forum*, Adelphi Paper 302 (Oxford: Oxford University Press, 1996), 17.
91   Wanandi, 'ASEAN's China Strategy', 119.
92   Shirk, 'Chinese Views on Asia-Pacific Multilateral Security Cooperation', 7–8.
93   Michael D. Swaine and Ashley J. Tellis, *Interpreting China's Grand Strategy: Past Present and Future* (Santa Monica, CA and Washington, DC: Rand, 2000), 136.
94   Speech by Chinese Ambassador Sha Zukang, Canadian Department of Foreign Affairs and International Trade, Ottawa, February 2001.
95   *The Military Balance: 2003–2004* (London: The International Institute for Strategic Studies, 2003), 170.
96   Jasper Becker, 'Shock of the New for PLA Strategists', *South China Morning Post*, 20 December 2001. china.scmp.com/lifestyle/ZZZA2DSYAVC.html.
97   Kori Urayama, 'China Debates Missile Defence', *Survival* 46(2) (Summer 2004): 128–9.
98   Charles L. Glaser and Steve Fetter, 'National Missile Defense and the Future of US Nuclear Weapons Policy', *International Security* 26(1) (Summer 2001): 82.
99   Marc Lanteigne, 'Tipping the Balance: Theatre Missile Defence and Evolving Security Relations in Northeast Asia', IIR-UBC Working Paper No. 34 (January 2001): 17–28.
100   Xiao Zan, '"Mini NATO" in Asia-Pacific Region Plan by the US and Australia', *Beijing Review*, 13 September 2001, 10.
101   Bob Catley, 'The Bush Administration and Changing Geopolitics in the Asia-Pacific Region', *Contemporary Southeast Asia* 23(1) (April 2001): 159.
102   Jianwei Wang, 'Chinese Perspectives on Multilateral Security Cooperation', *Asian Perspective* 22(3) 1998: 123–5.
103   Finkelstein, 'China's "New Concept of Security"', 197.
104   'China's Position Paper on the New Security Concept 06/08/2002', Permanent Mission of the People's Republic of China to the United Nations Office at Geneva and other International Organizations in Switzerland, 31 July 2002. genevamission.fmprc.gov.cn/eng/33227.html.
105   'Draft as of November 6, 2003, ARF Security Policy Conference – A Concept Paper for Discussion', ARF Inter-Sessional Support Group, Beijing, November 2003.
106   'Chairman's Statement of the 11th ASEAN Regional Forum, Jakarta, 2 July 2004', ASEAN Regional Forum. www.aseansec.org/16246.htm.
107   David E. Sanger, 'North Korea Says It Has a Program on Nuclear Arms', *The New York Times*, 17 October 2002, A1; James Dao, 'The Pact That the Koreans Flouted', *The New York Times*, 17 October 2002, A12.
108   Joel S. Wit, Daniel B. Poneman and Robert L. Gallucci, *Going Critical: The First North Korean Nuclear Crisis* (Washington, DC: Brookings Institution Press, 2004), 343.
109   Yong Shik Choo, 'Handling North Korea: Strategy and Issues', *SAIS Review* 23(1) (Winter–Spring 2003): 44–5.
110   Wang Hongwei, 'Pondering on Bush's "Axis of Evil" Remarks', *Beijing Review*, 14 March 2002, 6–7.
111   Ming Liu, 'China and the North Korean Crisis: Facing Test and Transition', *Pacific Affairs* 76(3) (Fall 2003): 358.
112   Morton Abramowitz and Stephen Bosworth, 'Adjusting to the New Asia', *Foreign Affairs* 82(4) (July/August 2003): 121–2.
113   Liu, 'China and the North Korean Crisis', 357.
114   Tae-hyo Kim, 'The Six-Way Multilateral Approach: Dilemma for Every Party', *Korea and World Affairs* 27(3) (Fall 2003): 348–9.
115   Andrew Scobell, 'China and North Korea: The Limits of Influence,' *Current History* 102(665) (September 2003): 275.
116   Daniel A. Pinkston and Phillip C. Saunders, 'Seeing North Korea Clearly', *Survival* 45(3) (Autumn 2003): 83–4.
117   Karen deYoung and Doug Strack, 'Beijing's Help Led to Talks: US Cuts Demands on North Korea', *The Washington Post*, 17 April 2003, A1.

118 Joseph Kahn, 'China Moves Troops to Area Bordering North Korea', *The New York Times*, 16 September 2003, A3.
119 Kyung-Ae Park, 'North Korea in 2003: Pendulum Swing between Crisis and Diplomacy', *Asian Survey* 44(1) (January/February 2004): 142.
120 'Vice FM Wang Yi, Head of Chinese Delegation to the Six-Party Talks Gives a Press Conference', Ministry of Foreign Affairs of the People's Republic of China, 30 August 2003. fmprc.gov.cn/eng/wjb/zzjg/yzs/gjlb/2701/2705/t2552.htm.
121 David E. Sanger, 'U.S. to Offer North Korea Incentives in Nuclear Talks', *The New York Times*, 23 June 2004, A3.

4 LABYRINTH'S EDGE

1 Ronald Grigor Suny, 'Provisional Stabilities: The Politics of Identities in Post-Soviet Eurasia', *International Security* 24(3) (Winter 1999/2000): 164–8.
2 Rajan Menon and Hendrik Spruyt, 'The Limits of Neorealism: Understanding Security in Central Asia', *Review of International Studies* 25 (1999): 88–9.
3 Charles William Maynes, 'America Discovers Central Asia', *Foreign Affairs* 82(2) (March/April 2003): 122–3.
4 See Chalmers Johnson, 'Political Institutions and Economic Performance: The Government-Business Relationship in Japan, South Korea, and Taiwan', *The Political Economy of the New Asian Industrialism*, ed. Frederic C. Deyo (Ithaca, NY and London: Cornell University Press, 1987), 136–64.
5 Michael L. Ross, 'Does Oil Hinder Democracy?' *World Politics* 53 (April 2001): 325–61. See also Giacomo Luciani, 'Resources, Revenues, and Authoritarianism in the Arab World: Beyond the Rentier State?' in *Political Liberalization and Democratization in the Arab World. Volume 1: Theoretical Perspectives*, ed. Rex Brynen, Bahgat Korany, and Paul Noble (Boulder, CO and London: Lynne Rienner, 1995), 211–27.
6 Oumirserik Kasenov, 'Central Asia: National, Regional, and Global Aspects of Security', in *Security Dilemmas in Russia and Eurasia*, ed. Roy Allison and Christoph Bluth (London: Royal Institute of International Affairs, 1998), 188–91.
7 Lena Jonson and Roy Allison, 'Central Asian Security: International and External Dynamics', in *Central Asian Security: The New International Context*, ed. Roy Allison and Lena Jonson (London: Royal Institute of International Affairs, and Washington, DC: Brookings Institution, 2001), 2.
8 The author wishes to thank Dru C. Gladney for information on China's 2000 population census.
9 Yasmin Melet, 'China's Political and Economic Relations with Kazakhstan and Kyrgyzstan', *Central Asian Survey* 17(2) (1998): 236–7.
10 Interview, Chinese scholar, Beijing, September 2001.
11 Robert A. Scalapino, 'Asia in a Global Context: Strategic Issues for the Soviet Union', in *The Soviet Far East Military Buildup: Nuclear Dilemmas and Asian Security*, ed. Richard H. Solomon and Masataka Kosaka (Dover, MA: Auburn House, 1986), 27–8.
12 Andrew J. Nathan and Robert S. Ross, *The Great Wall and the Empty Fortress: China's Search for Security* (New York and London: W.W. Norton, 1997), 51.
13 Shireen T. Hunter, *Central Asia since Independence* (Westport, CT: Praeger Publishers, 1996), 125–7.
14 John Anderson, *The International Politics of Central Asia* (Manchester and New York: Manchester University Press, 1997), 196–7.
15 Shiping Tang, 'Economic Integration in Central Asia: The Russian and Chinese Relationship', *Asian Survey* 40(2) (March/April 2000): 367.
16 Sun Zhuangzhi, 'China and Central Asia in the New International Climate', *The Times of Central Asia* (25 January 2001). www.times.kg/2001/N4/new-01.shtml.

17 Sergei Okhotnikov, 'China and Central Asia after the Beginning of the Antiterrorist Operation in Afghanistan', *Central Asia and the Caucasus* 5(17) (2002): 20; Evan Medeiros and M. Taylor Fravel, 'China's New Diplomacy', *Foreign Affairs* 82(6) (November / December 2003): 26.

18 Guangcheng Xing, 'Security Issues in China's Relations with Central Asian States', in *Ethnic Challenges Beyond Borders: Chinese and Russian Perspectives of the Central Asian Conundrum*, ed. Yongjin Zhang and Rouben Azizian (New York: St. Martin's Press, 1998), 204–7.

19 'Sino-Soviet Joint Communiqué, Beijing, 18 May 1989', *Beijing Review*, 29 May 1989, 15–17.

20 John W. Garver, 'Sino-Russian Relations', in *China and the World: Chinese Foreign Policy Faces the New Millennium*, ed. Samuel S. Kim (Boulder, CO and Oxford: Westview Press, 1998), 122–3.

21 Kenneth W. Allen, 'Confidence-Building Measures and the People's Liberation Army', *Remaking the Chinese State: Strategies, Society and Security*, ed. Chien-min Chao and Bruce J. Dickson (New York and London: Routledge, 2001), 235–6.

22 David Shambaugh, *Modernizing China's Military: Progress, Problems and Prospects* (Berkeley, CA and London; University of California Press, 2002), 288; Genrikh Kireev, 'The Serpentine Path to the Shanghai G-5', *International Affairs* (Moscow) 49(3) (2003): 90–1.

23 Barry Buzan and Ole Wæver, *Regions and Powers: The Structure of International Security* (Cambridge and New York: Cambridge University Press, 2003), 426.

24 Mel Gurtov and Byong-Moo Hwang, *China's Security: The New Roles of the Military* (Boulder, CO and London: Lynne Rienner, 1998), 76.

25 Bruce Pannier, 'Tajikistan: Shanghai Five Discuss Separatist Threats, Trade', Radio Free Europe/Radio Liberty, 5 July 2000. www.rferl.org/nca/features/2000/07/f.ru.000707151138.html; David Stern, 'Central Asia Plan to Fight Terrorism', *Financial Times*, 6 July 2000, 12.

26 'Declaration on the Establishment of the Shanghai Cooperation Organisation', 15 June 2001, Permanent Mission of the Republic of Kazakhstan, missions.itu.int/~kazaks/eng/sco/sco02.htm.

27 'Declaration by the Heads of the Member States of the Shanghai Cooperation Organisation', Ministry of Foreign Affairs of the Russian Federation, Information and Press Department, 10 June 2002, www.ln.mid.ru/Bl.nsf/arh/CBC1EA4D4C4C826A43256BD400330C09?OpenDocument.

28 Matthew Oresman, 'The Moscow Summit: Tempered Hope for the SCO', *Central Asia-Caucasus Analyst*, 4 June 2003, www.cacianalyst.org/view_article.php?articleid=1462.

29 'China, Kyrgyzstan Hold Joint Anti-terror Military Exercise', *Xinhuanet,* 11 October 2002, news.xinhuanet.com/english/2002-10/11/content_593548.htm; 'Five State Army Drill Targets Terrorism', *China Daily,* 7 August 2003, www1.chinadaily.com.cn/en/doc/2003-08/07/content_252628.htm. See also 'Joint Anti-Terrorism Exercise', *PLA Daily*, 2003, english.pladaily.com.cn/special/5army/index.htm.

30 'Anti-Terror Body Launched at SCO Summit', *Xinhua*, 17 June 2004, www.chinadaily.com.cn/english/doc/2004-06/17/content_340281.htm.

31 See S. Frederick Starr, 'Making Eurasia Stable', *Foreign Affairs* 75(1) (January/February 1996): 80–92; and Henry L. Clarke, 'An American View of Uzbekistan', *Central Asian Survey* 18(3) (1999): 373–83.

32 'Joint Statement between the Government of the United States of America and the Government of the Republic of Uzbekistan', Press Statement, Richard Boucher, Spokesman, Washington DC, Bureau of Public Affairs, US Department of State, 12 October 2001, www.state.gov/r/pa/prs/ps/2001/5354.

33 Thomas E. Ricks and Susan B. Glasser, 'US Operated Secret Alliance with Uzbekistan', *Washington Post*, 14 October 2001, A01.

34 'Pakistan Bid to Join Shanghai Five Group', *Dawn,* 4 January 2001. www.dawn.com/2001/01/04/top10.htm.

35 'Central Asia Gets New Image in Tashkent, Astana', *Pravda*, 17 June 2004, newsfromrussia.com/world/2004/06/17/54426_.html.

36 Interview, Chinese scholar, Beijing, September 2001.

37 Abdujabbar A. Abduvakhitov, 'The Jadid Movement and its Impact on Contemporary Central Asia', in *Central Asia: Its Strategic Importance and Future Prospects*, ed. Hafiz Malik (New York: St. Martin's Press. 1994), 65–75.

38 Ahmed Rashid, 'The Fires of Faith in Central Asia', *World Policy Journal* 18(1) (Spring 2001): 45.

39 David S.G. Goodman, 'The Campaign to "Open up the West": National, Provincial-level and Local Perspectives', *The China Quarterly* 178 (June 2004): 317–34.

40 Ahmad Lutfi, 'Blowback: China and the Afghan Arabs', *Issues and Studies* 37(1) (January/ February 2001): 161–2.

41 See Anatol Lievan, *Chechnya: Tombstone of Russian Power* (New Haven, CT and London: Yale University Press, 1999).

42 Witt Raczka. 'Xinjiang and its Central Asian Borderlands', *Central Asian Survey* 17(3) (1998): 396–403; Magid, 'Handle With Care', 17.

43 Stuart Horseman, 'Uzbekistan's Involvement in the Tajik Civil War 1992–1997: Domestic Considerations', *Central Asian Survey* 18(1) (1999): 37–8.

44 Ralph H. Magnus and Eden Naby, *Afghanistan: Mullah, Marx and Mujahid* (Boulder, CO and Oxford: Westview Press, 2002), 158–61.

45 Citha D. Maass, 'The Afghanistan Conflict: External Involvement', *Central Asian Survey* 18(1) (1999): 65–6; Ahmed Rashid, *Taliban: Militant Islam, Oil and Fundamentalism in Central Asia* (New Haven, CT and London: Yale Nota Bene, 2001), 55–66.

46 Steve Coll, *Ghost Wars: The Secret History of the CIA, Afghanistan, and bin Laden, from the Soviet Invasion to September 10th, 2001* (New York: Penguin Press, 2004), 403–4; 532–3.

47 Barbara Crossette, 'Tough Sanctions Imposed on Taliban Government Split UN', *The New York Times*, 20 December 2000, A20.

48 Angelo Rasanayagam, *Afghanistan: A Modern History* (London and New York: I.B. Tauris, 2003), 254–7.

49 Victoria Burnett, 'China's Lofty Ambitions in a Shattered Kabul', *Financial Times*, 23 October 2003, 15; Carlotta Gall, 'Taliban Suspected in Killing of 11 Chinese Workers', *The New York Times*, 11 June 2004, A13.

50 Pauline Jones Luong and Erika Weinthal, 'New Friends, New Fears in Central Asia', *Foreign Affairs* 81(2) (March/April 2002): 63–4. See also Rashid, 'The Fires of Faith in Central Asia', 51–3.

51 Kenneth Weisbrode, *Central Eurasia: Prize or Quicksand? Contending Views of Instability in Karabakh, Ferghana and Afghanistan*, Adelphi Paper 338, (New York: Oxford University Press, 2001), 45–7.

52 Ahmed Rashid, *Jihad: The Rise of Militant Islam in Central Asia* (New Haven, CT and London: Yale University Press, 2002), 159–67.

53 'Intent to Designate as Foreign Terrorist Organisation the Islamic Movement of Uzbekistan/ Fact Sheet: Islamic Movement of Uzbekistan', U.S. Department of State Office of the Spokesman Press Statement, 15 September 2000. secretary.state.gov/www/briefings/statements/2000/ ps000915b.html.

54 Rashid, 'The Fires of Faith in Central Asia', 53.

55 See Agam Shah, 'IMU Likely to Survive Juma Blow', Institute for War and Peace Reporting *Reporting Central Asia* No. 94, 14 December 2001. www.iwpr.net/index.pl?archive/rca/ rca_200112_94_1_eng.txt.

56 Rashid, *Jihad*, 204.

57 Rashid, *Jihad*, 115–36; Rajan Menon, 'The New Great Game in Central Asia', *Survival* 45(2) (Summer 2003): 190.

58 M. Ehsan Ahrari, 'China, Pakistan, and the "Taliban Syndrome"', *Asian Survey* 40(4) (July/ August 2000): 668–9.

59 Philip P. Pan and John Pomfret, 'Bin Laden's Chinese Connection', *Washington Post*, 10 November 2001, A20.

60 David Murphy and Susan V. Lawrence, 'Beijing Hopes to Gain from U.S. Raids in Afghanistan', *Far Eastern Economic Review,* 4 October, 2001, 18, 20.

61 Stephen M. Walt, 'Beyond Bin Laden: Reshaping US Foreign Policy', *International Security* 26(3) (Winter 2001/02): 67.

62 Charles Hutzler, 'Is Central Asia Big Enough for U.S., China?' *The Wall Street Journal,* 24 September 2001, A19.

63 Information Office of the State Council, '"East Turkestan" Terrorist Forces Cannot Get Away with Impunity'. *Beijing Review,* 31 January 2002, 14–20.

64 Elisabeth Rosenthal, 'China, Russia, and Four Neighbors Seek Common Front on Terror', *The New York Times,* 8 January 2002, A12; Tamora Vidaillet. 'China and Russia Seek to Reassert Anti-terror Role', *Reuters Asia,* 8 January 2002, asia.reuters.com/printerfriendly.jhtml?StoryID =496895.

65 'Foreign Ministry Spokesman's Press Conference, 28 September2001', Foreign Ministry of the People's Republic of China, 2001. us-mirror.fmprc.gov.cn/eng/18532.html.

66 David Hale, 'China's Growing Appetites', *The National Interest* (Summer 2004): 138–9; 'The Hungry Dragon', *The Economist,* 21 February 2004: 58–60.

67 Erica S. Downs, 'The Chinese Energy Security Debate', *The China Quarterly* 177 (March 2004): 21–4.

68 Paul Roberts, *The End of Oil: On the Edge of a Perilous New World* (New York: Houghton Mifflin, 2004), 143–5.

69 Howard W. French, 'China's Boom Brings Fear of an Electricity Breakdown', *The New York Times,* 5 July 2004, A4; Geoffrey York, 'Darkness Descends over the Forbidden City', *The Globe and Mail,* 9 July 2004, A3.

70 Tang, 'Economic Integration in Central Asia', 366–7.

71 Elizabeth Economy, *The River Runs Black: The Environmental Challenge of China's Future* (Ithaca, NY and London: Cornell University Press, 2004), 207.

72 Jim Yardley, 'Dam Building Threatens China's "Grand Canyon"', *The New York Times,* 10 March 2004, A1, A12.

73 See Amy Myers Jaffe and Steven W. Lewis, 'Beijing's Oil Diplomacy', *Survival* 44(1) (Spring 2002): 115–34.

74 Zhang Jin, 'Progress Made in Free Trade Talks with GCC', *China Daily,* 5 July 2004, www.chinadaily.com.cn/english/doc/2004-07/05/content_345486.htm.

75 See Richard Spencer, 'Tension Rises as China Scours the Globe for Energy', *The Telegraph,* 19 November 2004. news.telegraph.co.uk/news/main.jhtml?xml=/news/2004/11/19/wchina19.xml.

76 Sergei Troush, *China's Changing Oil Strategy and its Foreign Policy Implications,* Brookings Center for Northeast Asian Policy Studies Working Paper, (Fall 1999). www.brook.edu/fp/cnaps/papers/1999_troush.htm.

77 Yelena Kalyuzhnova, *The Kazakhstani Economy: Independence and Transition* (New York: St Martin's Press, 1998), 123–6.

78 Nozar Alaolmolki, *Life after the Soviet Union: The Newly Independent Republics of the Transcaucasus and Central Asia* (Albany, NY: State University of New York Press, 2001), 8. See also Stuart Parrott, 'China's Great Game', *Asia Inc.* 7(3) (October 1998): 40–43.

79 'New Pact to Pipe Kazakh Oil to China', *China Daily,* 18 May 2004, english.peopledaily.com.cn/200405/18/eng20040518_143613.html.

80 Bruce Pannier, 'Central Asia: US Interests Suffer Setbacks', Radio Free Europe/Radio Liberty, 18 July 2000, www.rferl.org/nca/features/2000/07/F.RU.000718150038.html.

81 'Baku-Tbilisi-Ceyhan (BTC) Pipeline', *Caspian Development and Export,* 24 July 2004. www.caspiandevelopmentandexport.com/ASP/BTC.asp.

82 Abraham S. Becker, 'Russia and Caspian Oil: Moscow Loses Control', *Post-Soviet Affairs* 16(2) (2000): 104–22.

83 Roberts, *The End of Oil,* 56.

84 Pannier, 'Central Asia: US Interests Suffer Setbacks'.

85 Michael R. Gordon, 'US, in a Secret Deal, Removes Bomb Fuel in Ex-Soviet Republic', *The New York Times*, 23 November 1994, A1, A10.

86 Guangcheng Xing, 'China and Central Asia', in *Central Asian Security: The New International Context*, ed. Roy Allison and Lena Jonson (London: Royal Institute of International Affairs; New York: Brookings, 2001), 167.

87 Kasenov, 'Central Asia: National, Regional, and Global Aspects of Security', 203–4.

88 David Shambaugh, 'Sino-American Strategic Relations: From Partners to Competitors', *Survival* 42(1) (Spring 2000): 104.

89 Menon, 'The New Great Game in Central Asia', 189.

90 'Decision to Put ETIM on Terror List Hailed', *China Daily*, 28 August 2002, 1; Philip P. Pan, 'Separatist Group in China Added to Terrorist List', *Washington Post*, 26 August 2002, A9.

91 Mark O'Neill, 'PLA Sees Afghan Conflict as Threat to Border Stability', *South China Morning Post*, 20 September 2001. Reprinted via *NAPSNet Daily Report* at www.nautilus.org/napsnet/dr/0109/SEP21.html#item3.

92 S. Neil MacFarlane, 'The United States and Regionalism in Central Asia', *International Affairs* (London) 80(3) (2004): 459. See also Andrew Higgins and Charles Hutzler, 'China Fails to Win Antiterror Spotlight', *The Wall Street Journal*, 19 October 2001, A11, A13.

93 Jianwei Wang, 'Chinese Perspectives on Multilateral Security Cooperation', *Asian Perspective* 22(3) (1998): 103–132.

94 'Some Thoughts on Establishing a New Regional Security Order', Statement by Ambassador Sha Zukang at the East-West Center's Senior Policy Seminar, August 2000, Honolulu. Reprinted at www.fmprc.gov.cn/eng/5180.html.

95 *China's National Defense in 2000*, The Information Office of the State Council, Beijing, PRC, October 2000, 51–5.

96 Emanuel Adler and Michael Barnett, 'A Framework for the Study of Security Communities', in *Security Communities*, ed. Emanuel Adler and Michael Barnett (New York and Cambridge: Cambridge University Press, 1998), 29–65.

97 Amitav Acharya, 'Regionalism and Regime Security in the Third World: Comparing the Origins of the ASEAN and the GCC', in *The (In)security Dilemma: National Security of Third World States*, ed. Brian L. Job (Boulder, CO: Lynne Rienner, 1991), 143–64.

98 Mahnaz Zehra Ispahani, 'Alone Together: Regional Security Arrangements in Southern Africa and the Arabian Gulf', *International Security* 8(4) (Spring 1984): 152–75.

99 Lillian Craig Harris, 'Xinjiang, Central Asia and the Implications for China's Policy in the Islamic World', *The China Quarterly* 133 (March 1993): 115–17.

100 Suisheng Zhao, 'China's Periphery Policy and its Asian Neighbours', *Security Dialogue* 30(3) (September 1999): 335–46.

101 Mikhail Titarenko and Vassilii Mikheev, 'The Asia-Pacific Region and Russia', *International Affairs* (Moscow) 47(3) (2001): 63–5.

102 Elizabeth Wishnick, *Mending Fences: The Evolution of Moscow's China Policy from Brezhnev to Yeltsin* (Seattle, WA and London: University of Washington Press, 2001), 163–76; Evgenii Afanasiev and Kirill Barskii, 'China: Our Relations Do Not Fear Frost', *International Affairs* (Moscow) 49(5) (2003): 78–9.

103 Lowell Dittmer, 'The Sino-Russian Strategic Partnership: Ghost of the "Strategic Triangle"?' in *Chinese Foreign Policy in Transition*, ed. Guoli Li (New York: Walter de Guyter, 2004), 225.

104 Olav Knudsen, 'What Promise for Regional Collective Security? A Comparison of the Baltic Sea Region and Northeast Asia', *Pacific Focus: Inha Journal of International Studies* 14(2) (Fall 1999): 33.

105 Strobe Talbott, 'From Prague to Baghdad: NATO at Risk', *Foreign Affairs* 81(6) (November/December 2002): 51–2.

106 Lanxin Xiang, 'China's Eurasian Experiment', *Survival* 46(2) (Summer 2004): 112–13.

107 Robert S. Ross, 'The Geography of the Peace: East Asia in the Twenty-First Century', *International Security* 23(4) (Spring 1999): 84.

108 'Shanghai Cooperation Organisation States Come to Terms on Economic Cooperation', *Russian Observer*, 14 September 2001. www.russianobserver.com/stories/2001/09/13/1000391594/1000469222.html.

109 Joseph S. Nye, 'Comparing Common Markets: A Revised Neofunctional Model', in *Regional Integration: Theory and Research*, ed. Leon N. Lindberg and Stuart A. Scheingold (Cambridge: Harvard University Press, 1971), 200.

5 SEEKING MODERNITY

1 Joseph S. Nye, 'East Asian Security: The Case for Deep Engagement', *Foreign Affairs* 74(4) (July/August 1995): 90.

2 John J. Mearsheimer, *The Tragedy of Great Power Politics* (New York and London: W.W. Norton, 2001), 396–400.

3 Samuel P. Huntington, *The Clash of Civilizations and the Remaking of World Order* (New York: Simon and Schuster, 1996), 221–9.

4 Mark Daniell, 'China in a World of Risk', in *China's Century: The Awakening of the Next Economic Powerhouse*, ed. Laurence J. Brahm (Singapore and New York: John Wiley and Sons, 2001), 99–107.

5 Andrew J. Nathan and Robert S. Ross, *The Great Wall and the Empty Fortress: China's Search for Security* (New York and London: W.W. Norton, 1997), 226–37.

6 Randall L. Schweller, 'Bandwagoning for Profit: Bringing the Revisionist State Back In', *International Security* 19(1) (Summer 1994): 72–107.

7 Alastair Iain Johnston, 'China's Militarized Interstate Dispute Behaviour 1949–1992: A First Cut at the Data', *The China Quarterly* 153 (March 1998): 1–30.

8 Gerald Segal, 'Does China Matter?' *Foreign Affairs* 78(5) (September/October 1999): 25–29.

9 Joe Studwell, *The China Dream: The Quest for the Last Untapped Market on Earth* (New York: Atlantic Monthly Press, 2002), 98–107.

10 Jianwei Wang, 'Managing Conflict: Chinese Perspectives on Multilateral Diplomacy and Collective Security', in *In the Eyes of the Dragon: China Views the World*, ed. Yong Deng and Fei-ling Wang (Lanham, MD and Oxford: Rowman and Littlefield, 1999), 83.

11 Helen Milner, 'International Theories of Cooperation among Nations', *World Politics* 44 (April 1992): 475–8.

12 Charles Lipson, 'International Cooperation in Economic and Security Affairs', *World Politics* 37 (October 1984): 17.

13 Robert Jervis, 'Security Regimes', *International Organisation* 36(2) (Spring 1982): 358–60.

14 See B. Peter Rosendorff and Helen V. Milner, 'The Optimal Design of International Trade Institutions: Uncertainty and Escape', *International Organization* 55(4) (Autumn 2001): 829–57.

15 Alastair Newton and Robert Subbaraman, *China: Gigantic Possibilities, Present Realities* (New York: Lehman Brothers, 2002), 16–18.

16 George J. Gilboy, 'The Myth Behind China's Miracle', *Foreign Affairs* 83(4) (July/August 2004): 35–8.

17 'GNP Per Capita 2003, Atlas Method and PPP', The World Bank. www.worldbank.org/data/databytopic/GNIPC.pdf; 'Human Development Report 2004: Human Development Index', United Nations Development Programme. hdr.undp.org/presskit/hr2004/pdf/presskit/HDR2004_PKE_HDI.pdf.

18 Robert O. Keohane, *After Hegemony: Cooperation and Discord in the World Political Economy* (Princeton, NJ: Princeton University Press, 1984), 93–5.

19 For example, see Erik Gartzke, Quan Li, and Charles Boehmer, 'Investing in the Peace: Economic Interdependence and International Conflict', *International Organisation* 55(2) (Spring 2001): 391–438.

20 Thomas J. Christensen, 'China, the US-Japan Alliance, and the Security Dilemma in East Asia', *International Security* 23(4) (Spring 1999): 71.

21 Michael D. Swaine and Ashley J. Tellis, *Interpreting China's Grand Strategy: Past, Present and Future* (Santa Monica, CA: Rand, 2000), 135–6.

22 Lloyd Gruber, *Ruling the World: Power Politics and the Rise of Supranational Institutions* (Princeton, NJ: Princeton University Press, 2000), 47.

23 Richard Rosecrance, 'Has Realism Become Cost–Benefit Analysis?' *International Security* 26(2) (Fall 2001): 147–8.

24 See Gerald Segal, 'East Asia and "Constrainment" of China', *International Security* 20(4) (Spring 1996): 107–35; and Gideon Rachman, 'Containing China', *The Washington Quarterly* 19(1) (1995): 129–39.

25 David A. Lake, 'Beyond Anarchy: The Importance of Security Institutions', *International Security* 26(1) (Summer 2001): 130.

26 Joseph M. Grieco, 'Anarchy and the Limits of Cooperation: A Realist Critique of the Newest Liberal Institutionalism', *International Organization* 42(3) (Summer 1988): 485–507.

27 Chen Jian, *Mao's China and the Cold War* (Chapel Hill, NC and London: University of North Carolina Press, 2001), 44–6.

28 Joseph Y.S. Cheng and Zhang Wankun, 'Patterns and Dynamics of China's International Strategic Behaviour', in *Chinese Foreign Policy: Pragmatism and Strategic Behavior*, ed. Suisheng Zhao (Armonk, NY and London: M.E. Sharpe, 2004), 180–83.

29 Ahmed Rashid, *Jihad: The Rise of Militant Islam in Central Asia* (New Haven, CT and London: Yale University Press, 2002), 205–7.

30 A. Ying, 'New Security Mechanism Needed for Asian-Pacific Region', *Beijing Review*, 18 August 1997, 6–7.

31 'Some Thoughts on Establishing a New Regional Security Order', Statement by Ambassador Sha Zukang at the East–West Center's Senior Policy Seminar, 7 August 2000, Honolulu. Ministry of Foreign Affairs for the People's Republic of China, 2000. www.swedenembassy.fmprc.gov.cn/eng/5180.html.

32 H. Lyman Miller and Liu Xiaohong, 'The Foreign Policy Outlook of China's "Third Generation" Elite', *The Making of Chinese Foreign and Security Policy in the Era of Reform*, ed. David M. Lampton (Stanford, CA: Stanford University Press, 2001), 144.

33 Alastair Iain Johnston and Paul Evans, 'China's Engagement with Multilateral Security Institutions', *Engaging China: the Management of an Emerging Power*, ed. Alastair Iain Johnston and Robert S. Ross (London and New York: Routledge, 1999), 260–1.

34 *China's National Defence in 2000*, (Beijing: Information Office of the People's Republic of China, October 2000), 48.

35 'Some Thoughts on Establishing a New Regional Security Order', Statement by Ambassador Sha Zukang at the East–West Center's Senior Policy Seminar, 7 August 2000. www.swedenembassy.fmprc.gov.cn/eng/5180.html.

36 John S. Duffield. 'Why is There No APTO? Why is There No OSCAP? Asia-Pacific Security Institutions in Comparative Perspective', *Contemporary Security Policy* 22(2) (August 2001): 87.

37 Stephen D. Krasner, 'Global Communications and National Power: Life on the Pareto Frontier', *World Politics* 43(3) (April 1991): 336.

38 Samuel S. Kim, 'China and the United Nations', *China Joins the World: Progress and Prospects*, ed. Elizabeth Economy and Michael Oksenberg (New York: Council on Foreign Relations Press, 1999), 60–71.

39 Elizabeth Economy, 'The Impact of International Regimes on Chinese Foreign Policy-Making: Broadening Perspectives and Policies... But Only to a Point', *The Making of Chinese Foreign and Security Policy in the Era of Reform*, ed. David M. Lampton (Stanford, CA: Stanford University Press, 2001), 232–3.

40 Christopher Layne, 'The Unipolar Illusion: Why New Great Powers Will Rise', *International Security* 17(4) (Spring 1993): 15–16. See also Kenneth N. Waltz, *Theory of International Politics* (Reading, MA: Addison-Wesley, 1979), 127–8.

41 David M. Lampton, *Same Bed, Different Dreams: Managing US–China Relations 1989–2000* (Berkeley, CA and London: University of California Press, 2001), 39–63.

42 Eric A. McVadon, 'A Purple China Policy for the US', *Far Eastern Economic Review*, 21 December 2000, 29.

43 Denny Roy, 'The "China Threat" Issue: Major Arguments', *Asian Survey* 36(8) (August 1996): 759–62.

44 David Wilkinson, 'Unipolarity without Hegemony', *International Studies Review* 1(2) (Summer 1999): 162.

45 Nicholas D. Kristof, 'The Rise of China', *Foreign Affairs* 72(5) (November/December 1993): 71–3.

46 Roy, 'The "China Threat" Issue', 762–5.

47 Kim Taeho, 'A Reality Check: The "Rise of China" and its Military Capability toward 2010', *The Journal of East Asian Affairs* 12(2) (Summer/Fall 1998): 324.

48 Allen S. Whiting, 'China's Use of Force, 1950–96, and Taiwan', *International Security* 26(2) (Fall 2001): 129–30.

49 Joseph Fewsmith, *China since Tiananmen: The Politics of Transition* (Cambridge and New York: Cambridge University Press, 2001), 154–6.

50 James Miles, 'Chinese Nationalism, US Policy and Asian Security', *Survival* 42(4) (Winter 2000–1): 53–4.

51 June Trufel Dreyer, 'The PLA and the Kosovo Conflict', *Strategic Studies Institute Monograph* (May 2000), 7–17.

52 Robert S. Ross, 'The Stability of Deterrence in the Taiwan Strait', *The National Interest* 65 (Fall 2001): 71–2.

53 David Shambaugh, 'China Views the World: Ambivalent Security', *International Security* 24(3) (Winter 1999/2000): 61–7.

54 Aleksandr Shumilin, 'Pentagon Re-Targeting', *Izvestia*, 27 March 2001. Reprinted in *NAPSNet Daily Report*, 28 March, 2001, www.nautilus.org/napsnet/dr/0103/MAR28.html#item19.

55 Peter Hays Gries and Thomas J. Christensen, 'Correspondence: Power and Resolve in US China Policy', *International Security* 26(2) (Fall 2001): 159.

56 Gang Lin, 'Leadership Transition, Intra-Party Democracy, and Institution Building in China', *Asian Survey* 44(2) (March/April 2004): 255; 'Hu Takes over Jiang as China's Military Chief', *Xinhua*, 19 September 2004. news.xinhuanet.com/english/2004-09/19/content_1995255.htm.

57 Adam Ward, 'China and America: Trouble Ahead?' *Survival* 45(3) (Autumn 2003): 40–3.

58 Rosemary Foot, 'Bush, China and Human Rights', *Survival* 45(2) (Summer 2003): 167–86.

59 Gilboy, 'The Myth Behind China's Miracle', 38; 'China's PM Defends Currency Peg', BBC News, 7 October 2003. news.bbc.co.uk/go/fr/fr/-/2/hi/business/3170088.stm.

60 'FY04 report to Congress on PRC Military Power: Pursuant to the FY2000 National Defense Authorization Act: Annual Report on the Military Power of the People's Republic of China', United States Department of Defense, 29 May 2004. www.defenselink.mil/pubs/d20040528 PRC.pdf.

61 William S. Murray III and Robert Antonellis, 'China's Space Program: The Dragon Eyes the Moon (and Us)', *Orbis* 47(4) (Fall 2003): 645–52.

62 Chang Yun-Ping, 'Chen Drafts Timetable on Constitution', *Taipei Times*, 12 November 2003, 1; Philip P. Pan, 'China Offers Double-Edged Notice to Taiwan', *Washington Post*, 17 May 2004, A14.

63 David E. Sanger, 'US Asks Taiwan to Avoid a Vote Provoking China', *The New York Times*, 9 December 2003, A1.

64 Edward Cody, 'China, Taiwan and US Display Military Might', *Washington Post*, 27 July 2004, A18.

65 McVadon, 'A Purple China Policy for the US', 29.

66 Lake, 'Beyond Anarchy: The Importance of Security Institutions', 139–41.

67 See Chalmers Johnson, 'What's Wrong with Chinese Political Studies?', *Asian Survey* 22(10) (October 1982): 921.

68 Kenneth N. Waltz, 'Structural Realism after the Cold War', *International Security* 25(1) (Summer 2000), 5–41.
69 Donald J. Puchala and Raymond F. Hopkins, 'International Regimes: Lessons from Inductive Analysis', *International Regimes*, ed. Stephen D. Krasner (Ithaca, NY and London: Cornell University Press, 1983), 70–9.
70 Tony Evans and Peter Wilson, 'Regime Theory and the English School of International Relations: A Comparison', *Millennium: Journal of International Studies* 21(3) (Winter 1992): 330.
71 Stephen D. Krasner, 'Structural Causes and Regime Consequences: Regimes as Intervening Variables', *International Regimes*, ed. Stephen D. Krasner (Ithaca, NY and London: Cornell University Press, 1983), 5–10.
72 See Jeffrey W. Taliaferro, 'Security Seeking Under Anarchy: Defensive Realism Revisited'. *International Security* 25(3) (Winter 2000/01): 128–61.
73 Mearsheimer, *The Tragedy of Great Power Politics*, 364.
74 John Gerard Ruggie, 'Multilateralism: the Anatomy of an Institution', *International Organisation* 46(3) (Summer 1992): 561–598; James A. Caporaso, 'International Relations Theory and Multilateralism: the Search for Foundations', *International Organisation* 46(3) (Summer 1992): 599–632.

REFERENCES

Abduvakhitov, Abdujabbar A. 'The Jadid Movement and its Impact on Contemporary Central Asia', in *Central Asia: Its Strategic Importance and Future Prospects*, edited by Hafiz Malik, 65–76 (New York: St Martin's Press, 1994).

Acharya, Amitav. 'Regionalism and Regime Security in the Third World: Comparing the Origins of the ASEAN and the GCC', in *The (In)security Dilemma: National Security of Third World States*, edited by Brian L. Job, 143–64 (Boulder, CO: Lynne Rienner, 1991).

—— 'ASEAN and Conditional Engagement', in *Weaving the Net: Conditional Engagement with China*, edited by James Shinn, 220–48 (New York: Council on Foreign Relations, 1996).

—— 'Collective Identity and Conflict Management in Southeast Asia', in *Security Communities*, edited by Emmanuel Adler and Michael Barnett, 198–227 (Cambridge, New York and Melbourne: Cambridge University Press, 1998).

Adler, Emanuel and Michael Barnett. 'A Framework for the Study of Security Communities', in *Security Communities*, edited by Emanuel Adler and Michael Barnett, 29–65 (New York and Cambridge: Cambridge University Press, 1998).

Afanasiev, Evgenii and Kirill Barskii, 'China: Our Relations do not Rear Frost,' *International Affairs* (Moscow) 49(5) (2003): 71–80.

Ahrari, M. Ehsan. 'China, Pakistan, and the "Taliban Syndrome"', *Asian Survey* 40(4) (July/August 2000):658–71.

Alaolmolki, Nozar. *Life after the Soviet Union: The Newly Independent Republics of the Transcaucasus and Central Asia* (Albany, NY: State University of New York Press, 2001).

Allen, Kenneth W. 'Confidence-Building Measures and the People's Liberation Army', in *Remaking the Chinese State: Strategies, Society and Security*, edited by Chien-min Chao and Bruce J. Dickson, 228–56 (New York and London: Routledge, 2001).

Anderson, John. *The International Politics of Central Asia* (Manchester and New York: Manchester University Press, 1997).

Anderson, Kym. 'Europe 1992 and the Western Pacific Economies', *The Economic Journal* 101 (November 1991): 1538–51.

Ball, Desmond. 'Arms and Affluence: Military Acquisitions in the Asia-Pacific Region', *International Security* 8(3) (Winter 1993/4): 78–112.

Barmé, Geremie R. 'The Revolution of Resistance', in *Chinese Society: Change, Conflict and Resistance*, edited by Elizabeth J. Perry and Mark Selden, 198–220 (New York and London: Routledge, 2000).

Barmé, Geremie R. and Sang Ye. 'The Great Firewall of China', *Wired* 5.06 (June 1997): 138–51, 174–8.

202

Baum, Richard. *Burying Mao: Chinese Politics in the Age of Deng Xiaoping* (Princeton, NJ: Princeton University Press, 1994).

Becker, Abraham S. 'Russia and Caspian Oil: Moscow Loses Control', *Post-Soviet Affairs* 16(2) (2000): 91–132.

Becker, Elizabeth. *When the War Was Over: Cambodia and the Khmer Rouge Revolution* (New York: PublicAffairs Book Group, 1998).

Becker, Jasper. 'Shock of the New for PLA strategists', *South China Morning Post* (20 December 2001). www.china.scmp.com/lifestyle/ZZZA2DSYAVC.html.

Beijing Review. 'Sino-Soviet Joint Communiqué, Beijing, 18 May 1989' (29 May 1989): 15–17.

—— 'Qian Qichen on the World Situation' (15 January 1990): 14–17.

—— 'Li Peng on Domestic and World Issues' (1 July 1991): 24–27.

—— 'Foreign Ministry News Briefing' 20 September 1999): 11.

—— 'Further Cooperation Needed for APEC's Development' (27 September 1999): 9–10.

—— 'WTO membership protocol signed' (22 November 2001): 4.

Bennett, Michael. 'The People's Republic of China and the Use of International Law in the Spratly Islands Dispute', *Stanford Journal of International Law* 28(425) (Spring 1992): 425–50.

Bernkopf Tucker, Nancy. 'The Taiwan Factor in the Vote on PNTR for China and its WTO Accession', National Bureau of Asian Research *NBR Analysis* 11(2) 2000 Essay 1. www.nbr.org/publications/analysis/vol11no2/essay1.html.

—— (ed.) *China Confidential: American Diplomats and Sino-American Relations, 1945–1996* (New York: Columbia University Press, 2001).

Betts, Richard K. 'Wealth, Power and Instability: East Asia and the United States after the Cold War', *International Security* 18(3) (Winter 1993/4): 34–77.

Bhalla, A. S. and D. M. Nachane. 'The Economic Impact of the Asian Financial Crisis on India and China', in *Financial Liberalization and the Asian Crisis*, edited by Ha-Joon Chang, Gabriel Palma and D. Hugh Whittaker, 237–53 (Basingstoke and New York: Palgrave, 2001).

Blank, Stephen. 'Every Shark East of Suez: Greater Power Interests, Policies and Tactics in the Transcaspian Energy Wars', *Central Asian Survey* 18(2) (1999): 149–84.

Boutros-Ghali, Boutros. *An Agenda for Peace 1995*, 2nd edn (New York: United Nations, 1995).

Brahm, Laurence J. 'Conclusion', in *China's Century: The Awakening of the Next Economic Powerhouse*, edited by L.J. Brahm, 403–13 (Singapore: John Wiley and Sons, 2001).

—— 'Government and Law', in *China's Century: The Awakening of the Next Economic Powerhouse*, edited by L.J. Brahm, 211–17 (Singapore and New York: John Wiley and Sons, 2001).

Bramsen, Christopher Bo. 'ASEM: A New Dimension in Asian-European Relations', in *China's Century: The Awakening of the Next Economic Powerhouse*, edited by Lawrence J. Brahm, 89–97 (Singapore: John Wiley and Sons, 2001).

Burstein, Daniel and Arne de Keijzer. *Big Dragon: China's Future – What It Means for Business, the Economy, and the Global Order* (New York: Simon and Schuster, 1998).

Buzan, Barry and Gerald Segal. 'Rethinking East Asian Security', *Survival* 36(2) (Summer 1994): 3–21.

Buzan, Barry and Ole Wæver, *Regions and Powers: The Structure of International Security* (Cambridge and New York: Cambridge University Press, 2003).

Cai, Kevin G. 'Is a Free Trade Zone Emerging in Northeast Asia in the Wake of the Asian Financial Crisis?' *Pacific Affairs* 74(1) (Spring 2001): 7–23.

Cai, Wenguo. 'China's Membership in the GATT/WTO: Historical and Legal Issues', in *China and the World Trade Organization: Requirements, Realities, and Resolution*, edited by Wenguo Cai, Murray G. Smith, and Xu Xianquan, 10–32 (Ottawa: Centre for Trade Policy and Law, 1996).

Calder, Kent E. *Pacific Defense: Arms, Energy and America's Future in Asia* (New York: William Morrow, 1996).

Caporaso, James A. 'International Relations Theory and Multilateralism: The Search for Foundations', *International Organization* 46(3) (Summer 1992): 599–632.

Carlson, Allen. 'Helping to Keep the Peace (Albeit Reluctantly): China's Recent Stance on Sovereignty and Multilateral Intervention', *Pacific Affairs* 77(1) (Spring 2004): 9–27.

Catley, Bob. 'The Bush Administration and Changing Geopolitics in the Asia-Pacific Region', *Contemporary Southeast Asia* 23(1) (April 2001): 149–67.

Cha, Victor D. 'Engaging China: The View from Korea', in *Engaging China: The Management of an Emerging Power*, edited by Alistair Iain Johnston and Robert S. Ross, 32–56 (New York and London: Routledge, 1999).

Chan, Gerald. *Chinese Perspectives on International Relations: A Framework for Analysis* (Basingstoke: Macmillan Press; New York: St. Martin's Press, 1999).

Chan, Steve. 'Chinese Perspectives on World Order', in *International Order and the Future of World Politics*, edited by T.V. Paul and John A. Hall, 197–212 (Cambridge and New York: Cambridge University Press, 1999).

Chang, Gene Hsin and Jack Hou. 'Structural Inflation and the 1994 "Monetary" Crisis in China', *Contemporary Economic Policy* 18(3) (July 1997): 73–81.

Chang, Gordon G. *The Coming Collapse of China* (New York: Random House, 2002).

Chen Jian. *Mao's China and the Cold War* (Chapel Hill, NC and London: University of North Carolina Press, 2001).

Cheng, Chu-yuan. 'Mainland China's Modernization and Economic Reform: Process, Consequences, and Prospects', in *Forces for Change in Contemporary China*, edited by Bih-jaw Lin and James T. Myers, 265–84 (Columbia, SC: University of South Carolina Press, 1993).

Cheng, Hang-Sheng. 'A Midcourse Assessment of China's Economic Reform', in *The China Reader: The Reform Era*, edited by Orville Schell and David Shambaugh, 311–21 (New York: Vintage Books, 1999).

Cheng, Joseph Y.S. and Zhang Wankun, 'Patterns and Dynamics of China's International Strategic Behaviour', in *Chinese Foreign Policy: Pragmatism and Strategic Behavior*, edited by Suisheng Zhao, 179–206 (Armonk, NY and London: M.E. Sharpe, 2004).

Chiang, Johnny Chi-Chen. 'Conceptualizing the APEC Way: International Cooperation in a Non-Institutionalized Regime', *Issues and Studies* 36(6) (November/December 2000): 177–204.

China Daily. 'Jiang Zemin's speech on Party's 80th Anniversary (part V)', 1 July 2001. www.chinadaily.com.cn/highlights/docs/2001–07–01/17467.html.

Choo, Yong Shik. 'Handling North Korea: Strategy and Issues', *SAIS Review* 23(1) (Winter–Spring 2003): 43–51.

Christensen, Thomas J. 'Chinese Realpolitik', *Foreign Affairs* 75(5) (September/October 1996): 37–52.

—— 'China, the US-Japan Alliance, and the Security Dilemma in East Asia', *International Security* 23(4) (Spring 1999): 49–80.

—— 'Posing Problems without Catching Up: China's Rise and Challenges for US Security Policy', *International Security* 25(4) (Spring 2001): 5–40.

Clarke, Henry L. 'An American View of Uzbekistan', *Central Asian Survey* 18(3) (1999): 373–83.

204

Coll, Steve. *Ghost Wars: The Secret History of the CIA, Afghanistan, and Bin Laden, From the Soviet Invasion to September 10, 2001* (New York: The Penguin Press, 2004).

Conable, Barber B., Jr. and David M. Lampton. 'China: The Coming Power', *Foreign Affairs* 71(5) (Winter 1992/3): 133–49.

Cooley, Alexander. 'Imperial Wreckage: Property Rights, Sovereignty, and Security in Post-Soviet Space', *International Security* 25(3) (Winter 2000/1): 100–27.

Cooper, Helene and Bob Davis. 'Barshefsky Drove Hard Bargain, but Lost to Politics', *The Wall Street Journal* (9 April 1999): A24.

—— 'Overruling Some Staff, Clinton Denies Zhu What He Came For', *The Wall Street Journal* (9 April 1999): A1, A6.

Craig Harris, Lillian. 'Xinjiang, Central Asia and the Implications for China's Policy in the Islamic World', *The China Quarterly* 133 (March 1993): 111–29.

Crone, Donald. 'Does Hegemony Matter? The Reorganization of the Pacific Political Economy', *World Politics* 45(4) (July 1993): 501–25.

Crossette, Barbara. 'Tough Sanctions Imposed on Taliban Government Split UN,' *The New York Times* (20 December 2000): A20.

Daniell, Mark. 'China in a World of Risk', in *China's Century: The Awakening of the Next Economic Powerhouse*, edited by Lawrence J. Brahm, 98–107 (Singapore and New York: John Wiley and Sons, 2001).

Dawn. 'Pakistan Bid to join Shanghai Five group', 4 January 2001. www.dawn.com/2001/01/04/top10.htm.

deLisle, Jacques. 'SARS, Greater China, and the Pathologies of Globalisation and Transition', *Orbis* 47(4) (Autumn 2003): 587–604.

Dent, Christopher M. 'The Asia-Europe Meeting and Inter-Regionalism: Towards a Theory of Maximum Utility', *Asian Survey* 44(2) (March/April 2004): 213–36.

Department of State Bulletin. 'United Nations Votes to Seat People's Republic of China and Expel Representatives of Republic of China', 65(1690) (15 November 1971): 548–56.

Dewitt, David B. 'Perspectives on Asian Peace and Security in the 21st Century', *Cancaps Papier* 28 (March 2002).

Di Yinqing and Zheng Gang. 'Why is the United States Anxious to Resume Talks with China on China's Entrance to the WTO?' *The Chinese Economy* 33(2) (March–April 2000): 6–12.

Dibb, Paul, David D. Hale and Peter Prince. 'The Strategic Implications of Asia's Economic Crisis', *Survival* 40(2) (Summer 1998): 5–26.

Dittmer, Lowell. 'Reform and Chinese Foreign Policy', in *Remaking the Chinese State: Strategies, Society, and Security*, edited by Chien-min Chao and Bruce J. Dickson, 171–89 (New York and London: Routledge, 2001).

—— 'Leadership Change and Chinese Political Development', in *The New Chinese Leadership: Challenges and Opportunities after the 16th Party Congress*, edited by Yun-han Chu, Chih-cheng Lo and Ramon H. Myers, 10–32 (Cambridge: Cambridge University Press, 2004).

Downs, Erica Strecker 'The Chinese Energy Security Debate', *The China Quarterly* 177 (March 2004): 21–41.

Downs, Erica Strecker and Phillip C. Saunders. 'Legitimacy and the Limits of Nationalism: China and the Diaoyu Islands', *International Security* 23(3) (Winter 1998/9): 114–46.

Dreyer, June Teufel, *The PLA and the Kosovo Conflict* (Carlisle Barracks, PA: US Army War College Strategic Studies Institute, 2000).

Duffield, John S. 'Why is There No APTO? Why is There No OSCAP?: Asia-Pacific Security Institutions in Comparative Perspective', *Contemporary Security Policy* 22(2) (August 2001): 69–95.

Dutta, Manoranjan. *Economic Regionalization in the Asia Pacific: Challenges to Economic Cooperation* (Northampton, MA: Edward Elgar, 1999).

Eckholm, Erik. 'A Quiet Roar: China's Leadership Feels Threatened by a Sect Seeking Peace', *New York Times* (4 November 1999): A10.

The Economist. 'China's Sackful of Surprises' (25 November 1995): 33.

—— 'The Best Things in Life' (2 December 2000): 42.

—— 'China's Confident Bow' (10 March, 2001): 37.

—— 'To Get Rich is Glorious' (19 January 2002): 33–4.

—— 'Something Rotten in the State of China' (16 February 2002): 37–8.

—— 'The Hungry Dragon' (21 February 2004): 59–60.

Economy, Elizabeth C. 'Reforming China', *Survival* 41(3) (Autumn 1999): 21–42.

—— 'The Impact of International Regimes on Chinese Foreign Policy-Making: Broadening Perspectives and Policies … But Only to a Point', in *The Making of Chinese Foreign and Security Policy in the Era of Reform*, edited by David M. Lampton, 230–53 (Stanford, CA: Stanford University Press, 2001).

—— *The River Runs Black: The Environmental Challenge to China's Future* (Ithaca, NY and London: Cornell University Press, 2004).

Elek, Andrew. 'Asia-Pacific Economic Cooperation (APEC)', in *Southeast Asian Affairs 1991*, 33–48 (Singapore: Institute of Southeast Asian Studies, 1991).

Evans, Paul. 'The New Multilateralism and the Conditional Engagement of China', in *Weaving the Net: Conditional Engagement with China*, edited by James Shinn, 249–70 (New York: Council on Foreign Relations, 1996).

Evans, Thammy. 'The PRC's Relationship with the ASEAN Regional Forum: Realpolitik, Regime Theory or a Continuation of the Sinic Zone of Influence System?' *Modern Asian Studies* 37(3) (2003): 737–63.

Falk, Richard A., Samuel S. Kim, and Saul H. Mendlovitz (eds). *The United Nations and Just World Order* (Boulder, CO, San Francisco, CA and Oxford: Westview Press, 1991).

Fang Yan, 'China Throws Itself into International Competition: Agriculture Faces a New Challenge,' *Economy and News*, 2 (1993). Reprinted in *China's Economic Reform: A Study with Documents*, edited by Christopher Howe, Y.Y. Kueh and Robert Ash, 278–90 (London and New York: RoutledgeCurzon, 2003).

Feeney, William. 'Chinese Policy in Multilateral Financial Institutions', in *China and the World: Chinese Foreign Policy in the Post-Mao Era*, edited by Samuel S. Kim, 266–92 (Boulder, CO and London: Westview Press, 1984).

Feng Chen. 'Order and Stability in Social Transition: Neoconservative Political Thought in Post-1989 China', *China Quarterly* 151 (September 1997): 593–613.

Fewsmith, Joseph. 'China and the WTO: The Politics behind the Agreement', *National Bureau of Asian Research NBR Report* (November 1999). www.nbr.org/publications/report.html.

—— 'The Political and Social Implications of China's Accession to the WTO', *The China Quarterly* 167 (September 2001): 573–91.

—— *China since Tiananmen: The Politics of Transition* (Cambridge and New York: Cambridge University Press, 2001).

—— 'China and the Politics of SARS,' *Current History* 102(665) (September 2003): 250–5.

Finkelstein, David M. 'China's "New Concept of Security"', in *The People's Liberation Army and China in Transition*, edited by Stephen J. Flanagan and Michael E. Marti, 197–209 (Washington, DC: National Defense University Press, 2003).

REFERENCES

Finkelstein, David and Michael McDevitt. 'Competition and Consensus: China's "New Concept of Security" and the United States Security Strategy for the East Asia-Pacific Region', *PacNet* No. 01 (8 January 1999). www.nyu.edu/globalbeat/asia/Finkelstein0 10999.html.

Finnegan, Michael J. 'Constructing Cooperation: Toward Multilateral Security Cooperation in Northeast Asia', *Asian Perspective* 23(1) (1999): 81–109.

Fishman, Ted C. 'The Chinese Century', *The New York Times,* 4 July 2004, 6.24.

Foot, Rosemary. 'Bush, China and Human Rights', *Survival* 45(2) (Summer 2003): 167–86.

Funabashi, Yoichi. 'Bridging Asia's Economics-Security Gap', *Survival* 38(4) (Winter 1996/7): 101–16.

Furtado, Xavier. 'Bridge over Troubled Waters: Strengthening the Role of Track II Security Mechanisms in the South China Seas', *Cancaps Papier* 19 (February 1999).

—— 'International Law and the Dispute Over the Spratly Islands: Whither UNCLOS?' *Contemporary Southeast Asia* 21(3) (December 1999): 386–404.

Gallagher, Michael G. 'China's Illusory Threat in the South China Sea', *International Security* 19(1) (Summer 1994): 169–94.

Gallant, Nicole and Richard Stubbs. 'APEC's Dilemmas: Institution-Building around the Pacific Rim', *Pacific Affairs* 70(2) (Summer 1997): 203–18.

Gang Lin. 'Leadership Transition, Intra-Party Democracy, and Institution Building in China', *Asian Survey* 44(2) (March/April 2004): 255–75.

Gartzke, Erik, Quan Li, and Charles Boehmer. 'Investing in the Peace: Economic Interdependence and International Conflict', *International Organization* 55(2) (Spring 2001): 391–438.

Garver, John W. 'China's Push through the South China Sea: The Interaction of Bureaucratic and National Interests', *China Quarterly* 132 (December 1992): 999–1028.

—— 'Sino-Russian Relations', in *China and the World: Chinese Foreign Policy Faces the New Millennium,* edited by Samuel S. Kim, 114–32 (Boulder, CO and Oxford: Westview Press, 1998).

Gerschenkron, Alexander. *Economic Backwardness in Historical Perspective: A Book of Essays* (Cambridge, MA: Harvard University Press, 1962).

Gilboy, George J. 'The Myth behind China's Miracle,' *Foreign Affairs* 83(4) (July/August 2004): 33–48.

Gill, Bates. 'Limited Engagement', *Foreign Affairs* 78(4) (July/August 1999): 65–76.

—— 'Two Steps Forward, Two Steps Back: The Dynamics of Chinese Nonproliferation and Arms Control Policy-Making in an Era of Reform', in *The Making of Chinese Foreign and Security Policy in the Era of Reform,* edited by David M. Lampton, 257–88 (Stanford, CA: Stanford University Press, 2001).

Gill, Bates and James Reilly. 'Sovereignty, Intervention, and Peacekeeping: The View from Beijing', *Survival* 42(3) (Autumn 2000): 41–59.

Gilpin, Robert. *War and Change in International Politics* (Cambridge: Cambridge University Press, 1981).

—— *The Political Economy of International Relations* (Princeton, NJ: Princeton University Press, 1987).

Glaser, Charles L. and Steve Fetter. 'National Missile Defense and the Future of US Nuclear Weapons Policy', *International Security* 26(1) (Summer 2001): 40–92.

Goldstone, Jack. 'The Coming Chinese Collapse', *Foreign Policy* 99 (Summer 1995): 35–52.

Goodman, David S.G. 'The Campaign to "Open Up the West": National, Provincial-level and Local Perspectives', *The China Quarterly* 178 (June 2004): 317–34.

Gourevitch, Peter. 'The Second Image Reversed: The International Sources of Domestic Politics', *International Organisation* 32(4) (Autumn 1998): 881–911.

Gray, Colin S. 'The Continued Primacy of Geography', *Orbis* 40(2) (Spring 1996): 247–59.

Green, Stephen. *China's Stockmarket: A Guide to its Progress, Players and Prospects* (London: The Economist/Profile Books, 2003).

Grieco, Joseph M. 'Anarchy and the Limits of Cooperation: A Realist Critique of the Newest Liberal Institutionalism', *International Organization* 42(3) (Summer 1998): 485–507.

—— 'Realism and Regionalism: American Power and German and Japanese Institutional Strategies During and After the Cold War', in *Unipolar Politics: Realism and State Strategies after the Cold War*, edited by Ethan B. Kapstein and Michael Mastanduno, 319–53 (New York: Columbia University Press, 1999).

Gries, Peter Hays. *China's New Nationalism: Pride, Politics and Diplomacy* (Berkeley, CA: University of California Press, 2004).

Gruber, Lloyd. *Ruling the World: Power Politics and the Rise of Supranational Institutions* (Princeton, NJ: Princeton University Press, 2000).

Gurtov, Mel and Byong-Moo Hwang. *China's Security: The New Roles of the Military* (Boulder, CO, and London: Lynne Rienner Publishers, 1998).

Haacke, Jürgen. 'The ASEANization of Regional Order in East Asia: A Failed Endeavour?' *Asian Perspective* 22(3) (1998): 7–47.

Haggard, Stephen. *The Political Economy of the Asian Financial Crisis* (Washington, DC: Institute for International Economics, 2000).

Hale, David. 'China's Growing Appetites,' *The National Interest* 76 (Summer 2004): 137–47.

Harris, Stuart. 'China's role in the WTO and APEC', in *China Rising: Nationalism and Interdependence*, edited by David S.G. Goodman and Gerald Segal, 134–55 (New York and London: Routledge, 1997).

—— 'China and the Pursuit of State Interests in a Globalizing World', *Pacifica Review* 13(1) (February 2001): 15–29.

Hartford, Kathleen. 'Cyberspace with Chinese Characteristics', *Current History* 99 (September 2000): 255–62.

Hays Gries, Peter and Thomas J. Christensen. 'Correspondence: Power and Resolve in US China Policy', *International Security* 26(2) (Fall 2001): 155–65.

Heisbourg, François. 'American Hegemony? Perceptions of the US Abroad', *Survival* 41(4) (Winter 1999/2000): 5–19.

Higgins, Andrew and Charles Hutzler. 'China Fails to Win Antiterror Spotlight', *The Wall Street Journal* (19 October 2001): A11, A13.

Higgott, Richard and Kim Nossal. 'Australia and the Search for a Security Community in the 1990s', *Security Communities*, edited by Emmanuel Adler and Michael Barnett, 265–94 (Cambridge, New York, and Melbourne: Cambridge University Press, 1998).

Hirschman, Albert O. *Exit, Voice, and Loyalty: Responses to Decline in Firms, Organizations, and States* (Cambridge, MA: Harvard University Press, 1972).

Holsti, Kalevi J. *The State, War, and the State of War* (Cambridge: Cambridge University Press, 1996).

Horseman, Stuart. 'Uzbekistan's Involvement in the Tajik Civil War, 1992–1997: Domestic Considerations', *Central Asian Survey* 18(1) (1999): 37–48.

Huang Weiding. 'Fighting Corruption Amidst Economic Reform', in *China's Century: The Awakening of the Next Economic Powerhouse*, edited by L.J. Brahm, 39–55 (Singapore and New York: John Wiley and Sons, 2001).

Huang, Yasheng. 'Sino–US Relations: The Economic Dimensions', in *In the Eyes of the Dragon: China Views the World*, edited by Yong Deng and Fei-ling Wang, 159–81 (Lanham, MD and Oxford: Rowman and Littlefield, 1999).

Hunter, Shireen T. *Central Asia Since Independence* (Westport, CT: Praeger Publishers, 1996).

Huntington, Samuel P. *The Clash of Civilizations and the Remaking of World Order*. New York: Simon and Schuster, 1996.

Hutzler, Charles. 'Is Central Asia Big Enough for U.S., China?', *The Wall Street Journal* (24 September 2001): A19.

Information Office of the State Council of the People's Republic of China. *China's National Defense in 2000* (Beijing: Information Office of the State Council of the People's Republic of China, 2000).

—— '"East Turkestan" Terrorist Forces Cannot Get Away with Impunity', *Beijing Review* (31 January 2002): 14–20.

Ispahani, Mahnaz Zehra. 'Alone Together: Regional Security Arrangements in Southern Africa and the Arabian Gulf', *International Security* 8(4) (Spring 1984): 152–75.

Jackson, John H. 'Managing the Trading System: The World Trade Organisation and the Post-Uruguay Round GATT Agenda', in *Managing the World Economy: Fifty Years after Bretton Woods*, edited by Peter B. Kenen, 131–51 (Washington, DC: Institute of International Economics, 1994).

Jacobson, Harold K. and Michael Oksenberg. *China's Participation in the IMF, the World Bank, and GATT* (Ann Arbor, MI: University of Michigan Press, 1990).

Jervis, Robert. *Perception and Misperception in International Politics* (Princeton, NJ: Princeton University Press, 1976).

—— 'Security Regimes', *International Organization* 36(2) (Spring 1982): 357–78.

Jian, Sanqiang. *Foreign Policy Restructuring as Adaptive Behavior: China's Independent Foreign Policy, 1982–1989* (New York and London: University Press of America, 1996).

Job, Brian L. 'Track 2 Diplomacy: Ideational Contribution to the Evolving Asian Security Order', in *Asian Security Order: Instrumental and Normative Features*, edited by Muthiah Alagappa, 241–79 (Stanford, CA: Stanford University Press, 2003).

Job, Brian, André Laliberté and Michael D. Wallace. 'Assessing the Risks of Conflict in the PRC–ROC Enduring Rivalry', *Pacific Affairs* 72(4) (Winter 1999–2000): 513–35.

Johnson, Chalmers. *MITI and the Japanese Miracle: The Growth of Industrial Policy, 1925–1975* (Stanford, CA: Stanford University Press, 1982).

—— 'What's Wrong with Chinese Political Studies?' *Asian Survey* 22(10) (October 1982): 919–33.

—— 'Political institutions and economic performance: the government-business relationship in Japan, South Korea, and Taiwan', in *The Political Economy of the New Asian Industrialism*, edited by Frederic C. Deyo, 136–64 (Ithaca, NY and London: Cornell University Press, 1987).

Johnson, Ian and Eduardo Lachica. 'China Hinders Its Own Bid for WTO, Adding New Trade Barriers as Old Ones Fall', *The Wall Street Journal* (20 May 1997): A15.

Johnston, Alastair Iain. *Cultural Realism: Strategic Culture and Grand Strategy in Chinese History* (Princeton, NJ: Princeton University Press, 1995).

—— 'China's Militarized Interstate Dispute Behaviour 1949–1992: A First Cut at the Data', *The China Quarterly* 153 (March 1998): 1–30.

—— 'The Myth of the Asian Way? Explaining the Evolution of the ASEAN Regional Forum', in *Imperfect Unions: Security Institutions over Time and Space*, edited by Helga Haftendorn, Robert O. Keohane, and Celeste A. Wallander, 287–324 (Oxford and New York: Oxford University Press, 1999).

Johnston, Alastair Iain and Paul Evans. 'China's Engagement with Multilateral Security Institutions', in *Engaging China: The Management of an Emerging Power*, edited by A.I. Johnston and R.S. Ross, 235–72 (New York and London: Routledge, 1999).

Jones Luong, Pauline and Erika Weinthal. 'New Friends, New Fears in Central Asia', *Foreign Affairs* 81(2) (March/April 2002): 61–70.

Jonson, Lena and Roy Allison. 'Central Asian Security: International and External Dynamics', in *Central Asian Security: The New International Context*, edited by Roy Allison and Lena Jonson, 1–23 (London: Royal Institute of International Affairs; Washington, DC: Brookings Institution, 2001).

Kahler, Miles. 'Legalization as Strategy: The Asia-Pacific Case', *International Organization* 54(3) (Summer 2000): 549–71.

Kahn, Joseph. 'World Trade Organization Admits China, Amid Doubts', *The New York Times* (11 November 2001): A16.

Kalyuzhnova, Yelena. *The Kazakhstani Economy: Independence and Transition* (New York: St Martin's Press, 1998).

Karniol, Robert. 'Why Asia Must Search for a Security Structure Formula', *Jane's International Defence Review* 2/2000 (February 2000): 38–43.

Kasenov, Oumirserik. 'Central Asia: National, Regional, and Global Aspects of Security', in *Security Dilemmas in Russia and Eurasia*, edited by Roy Allison and Christoph Bluth, 188–205 (London: Royal Institute of International Affairs, 1998).

Katzenstein, Peter J. 'Regionalism in Comparative Perspective', *Cooperation and Conflict* 31(2) (1996): 123–59.

Kawai, Masahiro. 'The East Asian Currency Crisis: Causes and Lessons', *Contemporary Economic Policy* 16(4) (April 1998): 157–72.

Kawasaki, Tsuyoshi. 'Formulating Canada's Grand Strategy in Asia', *International Journal* 56(1) (Winter 2000/1): 135–48.

Kennedy, Paul. *The Rise and Fall of Great Powers: Economic Change and Military Conflict From 1500 to 2000* (New York: Random House, 1987).

Kent, Ann. 'China, International Organizations, and Regimes: The ILO as a Case Study in Organizational Learning', *Pacific Affairs* 70(4) (Winter 1997/8): 517–32.

Keohane, Robert O. 'Lilliputians' Dilemmas: Small States in International Politics', *International Organization* 23(2) (Spring 1969): 291–310.

—— *After Hegemony: Cooperation and Discord in the World Political Economy* (Princeton, NJ: Princeton University Press, 1984).

—— 'International Institutions: Two Approaches', *International Studies Quarterly* 32(4) (December 1988): 379–96.

Keohane, Robert O. and Joseph S. Nye Jr., 'Power and Interdependence in the Information Age', *Foreign Affairs* 77(5) (September/October 1998): 81–94.

Kim, Samuel S. *China, the United Nations, and World Order* (Princeton, NJ: Princeton University Press, 1979).

—— 'China's International Organizational Behaviour' In *Chinese Foreign Policy: Theory and Practice*, edited by Thomas W. Robinson and David Shambaugh, 401–34 (Oxford: Clarendon Press, 1994).

—— 'China and the United Nations', in *China Joins the World: Progress and Prospects*, edited by Elizabeth Economy and Michael Oksenberg, 42–89 (New York: Council on Foreign Relations Press, 1999).

Kim, Taeho. 'A Reality Check: The "Rise of China" and its Military Capability toward 2010', *The Journal of East Asian Affairs* 12(2) (Summer/Fall 1998): 321–63.

Kireev, Genrikh. 'The Serpentine Path to the Shanghai G-5,' *International Affairs* (Moscow) 49(3) (2003): 85–92.

Kiyokatsu, Nishiguchi. 'Toward an East Asian Free Trade Area', *Japan Quarterly* (January–March 1993): 14–18.

Klintworth, Gary. 'China's Evolving Relationship with APEC', *International Journal* 50(3) (Summer 1995): 488–515.

Knudsen, Olav. 'What Promise for Regional Collective Security? A Comparison of the Baltic Sea Region and Northeast Asia', *Pacific Focus: Inha Journal of International Studies* 14(2) (Fall 1999): 5–42.

Krasner, Stephen D. 'Global Communications and National Power: Life on the Pareto Frontier', *World Politics* 43(3) (April 1991): 336–66.

Krauthammer, Charles. 'The Unipolar Moment', *Foreign Affairs* 70(1) (1990/1): 23–33.

Kristof, Nicholas D. 'The Rise of China', *Foreign Affairs* 72(5) (November/December 1993): 59–74.

Ku, Samuel C.Y. 'Southeast Asia and Cross-Strait Relations: the Policy of Separation of Politics and Economics', *Journal of Contemporary China* 7(19) (November 1998): 421–42.

Kupchan, Charles A. 'After Pax Americana: Benign Power, Regional Integration, and the Sources of Stable Multipolarity', *International Security* 23(2) (Fall 1998): 40–79.

Lake, David A. 'Beyond Anarchy: The Importance of Security Institutions', *International Security* 26(1) (Summer 2001): 129–60.

Lampton, David M. *Same Bed, Different Dreams: Managing US-China Relations 1989–2000* (Berkeley, CA and London: University of California Press, 2001).

Lanteigne, Marc. 'ASEAN Plus Three and the Changing Roles of Economic Institutions in the Post-Crisis Asia Pacific Region', in *Trading Arrangements in the Pacific Rim*, edited by Paul Davidson (University of British Columbia, Vancouver, Canada, Release 2001–1, January 2001).

—— 'Tipping the Balance: Theatre Missile Defense and the Evolving Security Relations in Northeast Asia', Working Paper #34 (Institute of International Relations, University of British Columbia, January 2001).

Lardy, Nicholas R. *China in the World Economy* (Washington, DC: Institute for International Economics, 1994).

—— 'China and the Asian Contagion', *Foreign Affairs* 77(4) (July/August 1998): 78–88.

—— 'China's Economic Growth in an International Context', *The Pacific Review* 12(2) (1999): 163–71.

—— *Integrating China into the World Economy* (Washington, DC: Brookings Institution Press, 2002).

Lasserre, Frédéric. *Le Dragon et la Mer: stratégies géopolitiques chinoises en Mer de Chine du Sud* [The Dragon and the Sea: China's Geopolitical Strategies in the South China Sea] (Montreal: Harmattan, 1996).

Lawrence, Susan V. and Shawn W. Crispin. 'Double-Edged Fury', *Far Eastern Economic Review* (20 May 1999): 10–13.

Lawrence, Susan V. and Bruce Gilley. 'Bitter Harvest', *Far Eastern Economic Review* (29 April 1999): 22–5.

Lawrence, Susan V. and David Murphy. 'Appearances Can Deceive', *Far Eastern Economic Review* (13 December 2001): 32–8.

Layne, Christopher. 'The Unipolar Illusion: Why New Great Powers Will Rise', *International Security* 17(4) (Spring 1993): 5–51.

Lee Lai To. 'China's Relations with ASEAN: Partners in the 21st Century?' *Pacifica Review* 13(1) (February 2001): 61–71.

Legro, Jeffrey W. and Andrew Moravcsik. 'Is Anybody Still a Realist?' *International Security* 24(2) (Fall 1999): 5–55.

Leifer, Michael. 'Chinese Economic Reform and Security Policy: The South China Sea Connection', *Survival* 37(2) (Summer 1995): 44–59.

—— *The ASEAN Regional Forum*, Adelphi Paper 302 (Oxford: Oxford University Press, 1996).

Levy, Jack S. *War in the Modern Great Power System, 1495–1975* (Lexington, KY: The University Press of Kentucky, 1983).

Lewis, John Wilson and Xue Litai. *China's Strategic Seapower: The Politics of Force Modernization in the Nuclear Age* (Stanford, CA: Stanford University Press, 1994).

Li, Cheng. *China's Leaders: The New Generation* (Lanham, MD and Oxford: Rowman and Littlefield Publishers, 2001).

Li Jingwen. *The Chinese Economy into the 21st Century: Forecasts and Policies* (Beijing: Foreign Languages Press, 2000).

Li Minsheng. 'Entrepreneurs from Non-Public Sector Hail Jiang Speech', *Beijing Review* (9 August 2001): 11–14.

Li, Xiao-Ming. 'China's Macroeconomic Stabilization Policies Following the Asian Financial Crisis', *Asian Survey* 40(6) (November/December 2000): 938–57.

Lievan, Anatol. *Chechnya: Tombstone of Russian Power* (New Haven, CT and London: Yale University Press, 1999).

Lim, Benito. 'Political Changes in China and Their Implications on the Philippines', in *Crisis and Transformation in Northeast Asia: Implications for the Philippines*, edited by Xavier A. Furtado, 59–73 (Manila: De La Salle University Press, 1999).

Lin, Justin Yifu. 'Economic Reform and Development Strategy in China', in *China's Entry to the WTO: Strategic Issues and Quantitative Assessments*, edited by Peter Drysdale and Ligang Song, 30–52 (London and New York: Routledge, 2000).

Lin, Justin Yifu, Fang Cai, and Zhou Li. *The China Miracle: Development Strategy and Economic Reform* (Hong Kong: The Chinese University Press, 1996).

Lincoln, Edward J. 'Japan's Financial Mess', *Foreign Affairs* 77(3) (May/June 1998): 57–66.

Lipson, Charles. 'International Cooperation in Economic and Security Affairs', *World Politics* 37 (October 1984): 1–23.

—— 'Why Are Some International Agreements Informal?' *International Organization* 45(4) (Autumn 1991): 495–538.

Lizée, Pierre. 'The Evolution of Great Power Involvement in Cambodia', in *Southeast Asia in the New World Order*, edited by David Wurfel and Bruce Burton, 221–43 (Basingstoke: Macmillan Press, 1996).

Lopez, George A. and David Cortright. 'Containing Iraq: Sanctions Worked', *Foreign Affairs* 83(4) (July/August 2004): 90–103.

Lu Aiguo. *China and the Global Economy since 1840* (Basingstoke: Macmillan Press, 2000).

Lu Jianren. 'China's Experience in Utilizing ODA and APEC Development Cooperation', in *APEC and Development Cooperation*, edited by Mohamed Ariff, 103–34 (Singapore: Institute of Southeast Asian Studies, 1998).

Lubin, Nancy. 'Pipe Dreams: Potential Impacts of Energy Exploitation', *Harvard International Review* 22(1) (Winter/Spring 2000): 66–9.

Luciani, Giacomo. 'Resources, Revenues, and Authoritarianism in the Arab World: Beyond the Rentier State?' in *Political Liberalization and Democratization in the Arab World. Volume 1: Theoretical Perspectives*, edited by Rex Brynen, Bahgat Korany and Paul Noble, 211–27 (Boulder, CO and London: Lynne Rienner, 1995).

Lutfi, Ahmad. 'Blowback: China and the Afghan Arabs', *Issues and Studies* 37(1) (January/February 2001): 160–214.

Maass, Citha D. 'The Afghanistan Conflict: external Involvement', *Central Asian Survey* 18(1) (1999): 65–78.

MacFarlane, S. Neil. 'Realism and Russian Strategy after the Collapse of the USSR', in *Unipolar Politics: Realism and State Strategies after the Cold War*, edited by Ethan B. Kapstein and Michael Mastanduno, 218–60 (New York: Columbia University Press, 1999).

—— 'The United States and Regionalism in Central Asia', *International Affairs* (London) 80(3) (2004): 447–61.

Magid, Alvin. 'Handle With Care: China's Policy for Multiculturalism and Minority Nationalities', *Asian Perspective* 22(1) (Spring 1998): 5–34.

Mahbubani, Kishore. 'The Pacific Way', *Foreign Affairs* 74(1) (January/February 1995): 100–11.

—— 'The Pacific Impulse', *Survival* 37(1) (Spring 1995): 105–20.

Mahmood, Afzaal. 'A New Strategic Alliance?' *Dawn* (2 July 2001). www.dawn.com/2001/07/02/op.htm#2.

Mann, James. *About Face: A History of America's Curious Relationship with China from Nixon to Clinton* (New York: Vintage Books, 2000).

Manning, Robert A. *The Asian Energy Factor: Myths and Dilemmas of Energy, Security, and the Pacific Future* (New York: Palgrave, 2000).

Manning, Robert A. and Paula Stern. 'The Myth of the Pacific Community', *Foreign Affairs* 73(6) (November/December 1994): 79–93.

Mao Zedong. *On Diplomacy* (Beijing: Foreign Languages Press, 1998).

Martin, Lisa L. 'Interests, Power, and Multilateralism', *International Organization* 46(4) (Autumn 1992): 765–92.

—— 'An Institutionalist View: International Institutions and State Strategies', in *International Order and the Future of World Politics*, edited by T.V. Paul and John A. Hall, 78–98 (Cambridge and New York: Cambridge University Press, 1999).

Mastanduno, Michael. 'Preserving the Unipolar Moment: Realist Theories and US Grand Strategy after the Cold War', *International Security* 21(4) (Spring 1997): 49–88.

Maynes, Charles William. 'America Discovers Central Asia', *Foreign Affairs* 82(2) (March/April 2003): 120–32.

McDevitt, Michael. 'Beijing's Bind', *The Washington Quarterly* 23(3) (Summer 2000): 177–86.

McVadon, Eric A. 'A Purple China Policy for the US', *Far Eastern Economic Review* (21 December 2000): 29.

Mead, Walter Russell. 'America's Sticky Power', *Foreign Policy* 141 (March/April 2004): 46–53.

Mearsheimer, John J. 'The False Promise of International Institutions', *International Security* 19 (Winter 1994/5): 5–49.

—— *The Tragedy of Great Power Politics* (New York and London: W.W. Norton, 2001).

Medeiros, Evan. 'China Debates Its "Peaceful Rise" Strategy', *YaleGlobal* (22 June 2004). http://www.yaleglobal.yale.edu/article.print?id=4118.

Medeiros, Evan and M. Taylor Fravel. 'China's New Diplomacy', *Foreign Affairs* 82(6) (November/December 2003): 22–35.

Melet, Yasmin. 'China's Political and Economic Relations with Kazakhstan and Kyrgyzstan', *Central Asian Survey* 17(2) (1998): 229–52.

Menon, Rajan. 'The New Great Game in Central Asia', *Survival* 45(2) (Summer 2003): 187–204.

Menon, Rajan and Hendrik Spruyt. 'The Limits of Neorealism: Understanding Security in Central Asia', *Review of International Studies* 25 (1999): 87–105.

Miles, James. 'Chinese Nationalism, US Policy and Asian Security', *Survival* 42(4) (Winter 2000–01): 51–71.

Miller, H. Lyman and Liu Xiaohong. 'The Foreign Policy Outlook of China's "Third Generation" Elite', in *The Making of Chinese Foreign and Security Policy in the Era of Reform*, edited by David M. Lampton, 123–50 (Stanford, CA: Stanford University Press, 2001).

Milner, Helen. 'International Theories of Cooperation among Nations', *World Politics* 44(3) (April 1992): 466–96.

Ming Liu, 'China and the North Korean Crisis: Facing Test and Transition,' *Pacific Affairs* 76(3) (Fall 2003): 347–73.

Montagnon, Peter. 'Disillusion Leads to Growing Spirit of Co-operation Among Asian Nations', *Financial Times* (21 July 2000): 12.

Moore, Thomas G. 'China and Globalization', *Asian Perspective* 23(4) (1999): 65–95.

Moore, Thomas G. and Dixia Yang. 'Empowered and Restrained: Chinese Foreign Policy in the Age of Interdependence', in *The Making of Chinese Foreign Policy in the Era of Reform*, edited by David M. Lampton, 191–229 (Stanford, CA: Stanford University Press, 2001).

Moravcsik, Andrew. 'Negotiating the Single European Act', in *The New European Community: Decisionmaking and Institutional Change*, edited by Robert O. Keohane and Stanley Hoffman, 41–84 (Boulder, CO and London: Westview Press, 1991).

Morgenthau, Hans J. *Politics among Nations: The Struggle for Power and Peace,* 4th edn (New York: Alfred A. Knopf, 1967).

Morphet, Sally. 'China as a Permanent Member of the Security Council: October 1971– December 1999', *Security Dialogue* 31(2) (June 2000): 151–66.

Mulvenon, James. 'Soldiers of Fortune, Soldiers of Misfortune: Commercialization and Divestiture of the Chinese Military-Business Complex, 1978–99', in *Remaking the Chinese State: Strategies, Society, and Security*, edited by Chien-min Chao and Bruce J. Dickson, 204–27 (London and New York: Routledge, 2001).

—— 'Your Guess Is As Good As Mine: PLA Budgets, Proposals and Discussions at the Second Session of the 10th National People's Congress,' *China Leadership Monitor* 11 (Summer 2004). www.chinaleadershipmonitor.org/20043/jm.pdf.

Murphy, David and Susan V. Lawrence. 'Beijing Hopes to Gain from U.S. Raids in Afghanistan', *Far Eastern Economic Review* (4 October 2001): 18, 20.

Murray, William S, III and Robert Antonellis. 'China's Space Program: the Dragon Eyes the Moon (and Us)', *Orbis* 47(4) (Fall 2003): 645–52.

Myers Jaffe, Amy and Steven W. Lewis. 'Beijing's Oil Diplomacy', *Survival* 44(1) (Spring 2002): 115–34.

Myers Jaffe, Amy and Robert A. Manning. 'The Shocks of a World of Cheap Oil', *Foreign Affairs* 79(1) (January/February 2000): 16–29.

Nathan, Andrew J. *China's Transition* (New York: Columbia University Press, 1997).

Nathan, Andrew J. and Bruce Gilley, *China's New Rulers: The Secret Files*, 2nd edn (New York: New York Review Books, 2003).

Nathan, Andrew J. and Robert S. Ross. *The Great Wall and the Empty Fortress: China's Search for Security* (New York and London: W.W. Norton, 1997).

Newton, Alastair and Robert Subbaraman. *China: Gigantic Possibilities, Present Realities* (New York: Lehman Brothers, 2002).

Nixon, Richard M. 'Asia after Viet Nam', *Foreign Affairs* 46(1) (October 1967): 111–25.

—— *Beyond Peace* (New York: Random House, 1994).

Nye, Joseph S., Jr. 'Comparing Common Markets: A Revised Neofunctional Model', in *Regional Integration: Theory and Research*, edited by Leon N. Lindberg and Stuart A. Scheingold, 192–231 (Cambridge, MA: Harvard University Press, 1971).

—— 'East Asian Security: The Case for Deep Engagement', *Foreign Affairs* 74(4) (July/August 1995): 90–102.

—— *The Paradox of American Power: Why the World's Superpower Cannot Go It Alone* (Oxford and New York: Oxford University Press, 2002).

—— *Soft Power: The Means to Success in World Politics* (New York: Public Affairs Books, 2004).

O'Hanlon, Michael. 'Star Wars Strikes Back', *Foreign Affairs* 78(6) (November/December 1999): 68–82.

—— 'Why China Cannot Conquer Taiwan', *International Security* 25(2) (2000): 51–86.

O'Neill, Mark. 'PLA sees Afghan Conflict as Threat to Border Stability', *South China Morning Post* (20 September 2001). Reprinted via *NAPSNet Daily Report* at www.nautilus.org/napsnet/dr/0109/SEP21.html#item3.

Oberdorfer, Don. *The Two Koreas: A Contemporary History* (Reading, MA: Addison-Wesley, 1997).

Okhotnikov, Sergei. 'China and Central Asia after the Beginning of the Antiterrorist Operation in Afghanistan', *Central Asia and the Caucasus* 5(17) (2002): 19–29.

Oksenberg, Michel. 'China's Confident Nationalism', *Foreign Affairs* 65(1) (Winter 1986): 501–23.

—— 'The China Problem' *Foreign Affairs* 70(3) (Summer 1991): 1–16.

Oksenberg, Michel and Elizabeth Economy. 'Introduction: China Joins the World', in *China Joins the World: Progress and Prospects*, edited by Michael Oksenberg and Elizabeth Economy, 1–41 (New York: Council on Foreign Relations Press, 1999).

Olcott, Martha Brill. 'Central Asia's Catapult to Independence', *Foreign Affairs* 71(3) (Summer 1992): 108–30.

Organski, A.F.K. *World Politics* (New York: Alfred A. Knopf, 1960).

Overholt, William H. 'Asia's Continuing Crisis', *Survival* 44(1) (Spring 2002): 97–114.

Pan, Philip P. and John Pomfret. 'Bin Laden's Chinese Connection', *Washington Post* (10 November 2001): A20.

Pang Zhongying. 'Globalization and China: China's Response to the Asian Economic Crisis', *Asian Perspective* 23(1) (1999): 111–31.

Park, Kyung-Ae. 'North Korea in 2003: Pendulum Swing between Crisis and Diplomacy', *Asian Survey* 44(1) (January/February 2004): 139–46.

Parrott, Stuart. 'China's Great Game', *Asia Inc.* 7(3) (October 1998): 40–43.

Paul, T.V. 'Nuclear Taboo and War Initiation in Regional Conflicts', *Journal of Conflict Resolution* 38(4) (December 1995): 696–717.

—— 'Power, Influence, and Nuclear Weapons: An Assessment', in *The Absolute Weapon Revisited: Nuclear Arms and the Emerging International Order*, edited by T.V. Paul, Richard J. Harknett, and James J. Wirtz, 19–45 (Ann Arbor, MI: University of Michigan Press, 2000).

Pearson, Margaret M. 'China's Integration into the International trade and Investment Regime', in *China Joins the World: Problems and Prospects*, edited by Elizabeth Economy and Michel Oksenberg, 161–205 (New York: Council on Foreign Relations Press, 1999).

—— 'China and Major Economic Institutions', in *Engaging China: The Management of an Emerging Power*, edited by Alastair Iain Johnston and Robert S. Ross, 207–34 (London and New York: Routledge, 1999).

—— 'The Case of China's Accession to the WTO', in *The Making of Chinese Foreign and Security Policy in the Age of Reform*, edited by David M. Lampton, 337–70 (Stanford, CA: Stanford University Press, 2001).

Peerenboom, Randall. *China's Long March toward Rule of Law* (Cambridge: Cambridge University Press, 2002).

Pei, Minxin. 'Rotten from Within: Decentralized Predation and Incapacitated State', in *The Nation State in Question*, edited by T.V. Paul, G. John Ikenberry and John A. Hall (Princeton, NJ: Princeton University Press, 2003): 321–49.

Pinkston, Daniel A. and Phillip C. Saunders. 'Seeing North Korea Clearly', *Survival* 45(3) (Autumn 2003): 79–102.

Powell, Robert. 'Anarchy in International Relations Theory: the Neorealist–Neoliberalist debate', *International Organization* 48(2) (Spring 1994): 313–44.

Prescott, Elizabeth M. 'SARS: A Warning,' *Survival* 45(3) (Autumn 2003): 201–26.

Puchala, Donald J. and Raymond F. Hopkins. 'International Regimes: Lessons from Inductive Analysis', in *International Regimes*, edited by Stephen D. Krasner, 61–91 (Ithaca, NY and London: Cornell University Press, 1983).

Qing, Dai and Lawrence R. Sullivan. 'The Three Gorges Dam and China's Energy Dilemma', *Journal of International Affairs* 53(1) (Fall 1999): 53–71.

Qureshi, Asif H. *The World Trade Organisation: Implementing International Trade Norms* (Manchester and New York: Manchester University Press, 1996).

Rachman, Gideon. 'Containing China', *The Washington Quarterly* 19(1) (1995): 129–39.

Raczka, Witt. 'Xinjiang and its Central Asian Borderlands', *Central Asian Survey* 17(3) (1998): 373–407.

Radelet, Steven and Jeffrey Sachs. 'Asia's Reemergence', *Foreign Affairs* 76(6) (November/ December 1997): 44–59.

Rapkin, David P. 'The United States, Japan and the Power to Block: The APEC and AMF Cases', *The Pacific Review* 14(3) (2001): 373–410.

Rasanayagam, Angelo. *Afghanistan: A Modern History* (London and New York: I.B. Tauris, 2003).

Rashid, Ahmed. 'The Taliban: Exporting Extremism', *Foreign Affairs* 78(6) (November/ December 1999): 22–35.

—— 'The Fires of Faith in Central Asia', *World Policy Journal* 18(1) (Spring 2001): 45–55.

—— *Taliban: Militant Islam, Oil and Fundamentalism in Central Asia* (New Haven, CT and London: Yale University Press, 2001).

—— *Jihad: The Rise of Militant Islam in Central Asia* (New Haven, CT and London: Yale University Press, 2002).

Richardson, Michael. 'China and US Clashing Anew in Pacific Forum: Differences on Security and Trade Begin to Disrupt Asian Meeting', *International Herald Tribune* (16 November 1995): 1, 8.

Ricks, Thomas E. and Susan B. Glasser, 'US Operated Secret Alliance with Uzbekistan,' *Washington Post* (14 October 2001): A01.

Roberts, Paul, *The End of Oil: On the Edge of a Perilous New World* (Boston, MA and New York: Houghton Mifflin, 2004).

Rogers, Steven. 'Beyond the Abu Sayyaf: The Lessons of Failure in the Philippines', *Foreign Affairs* 83(1) (January/February 2004): 15–20.

Rosecrance, Richard. 'Has Realism Become Cost-Benefit Analysis?' *International Security* 26(2) (Fall 2001): 132–54.

Rosen, Jeremy Brooks. 'China, Emerging Economies, and the World Trade Order', *Duke Law Journal* 46(6) (April 1997): 1519–64.

Rosendorff, B. Peter and Helen V. Milner. 'The Optimal Design of International Trade Institutions: Uncertainty and Escape', *International Organization* 55(4) (Autumn 2001): 829–57.

Rosenthal, Elisabeth. 'China, Russia, and Four Neighbors Seek Common Front on Terror', *The New York Times* (8 January 2002): A12.

Ross, Madelyn C. 'China's International Economic Behaviour', in *Chinese Foreign Policy: Theory and Practice*, edited by Thomas W. Robinson and David Shambaugh, 435–52 (Oxford and New York: Clarendon Press, 1994).

Ross, Michael L. 'Does Oil Hinder Democracy?' *World Politics* 53 (April 2001): 325–61.

Ross, Robert S. 'China and Southeast Asia: The Challenge of Economic Competition', in *Southeast Asia in the New World Order*, edited by David Wurfel and Bruce Burton, 142–64 (London: Macmillan Press, 1996).

—— 'Beijing as a Conservative Power', *Foreign Affairs* 76(2) (March/April 1997): 33–44.

—— 'The Geography of the Peace: East Asia in the Twenty-first Century', *International Security* 23(4) (Spring 1999): 81–118.

—— 'The Stability of Deterrence in the Taiwan Strait', *The National Interest* 65 (Fall 2001): 67–76.

Rostow, W.W. 'The Take-Off Into Self-Sustained Growth', in *The Economics of Underdevelopment*, edited by A. Agawala and S. Singh, 154–88 (New York: Oxford University Press, 1963).

Roy, Denny. 'Hegemon on the Horizon: China's Threat to East Asian Security', *International Security* 19(1) (Summer 1994): 149–68.

—— 'The 'China Threat' Issue: Major Arguments', *Asian Survey* 36(8) (August 1996): 758–71.

—— 'China's Reaction to American Predominance,' *Survival* 45(3) (Autumn 2003): 57–78.

Ruggie, John Gerard. 'Multilateralism: The Anatomy of an Institution', *International Organization* 46(3) (Summer 1992): 561–98.

Saeki, Kiichi, 'The Rise of China: Threats, Uncertainties, and Opportunities', *Asia-Pacific Review* 2(1) (1995): 203–10.

Scalapino, Robert A. 'Asia in a Global Context: Strategic Issues for the Soviet Union', in *The Soviet Far East Military Buildup: Nuclear Dilemmas and Asian Security*, edited by Richard H. Solomon and Masataka Kosaka, 21–39 (Dover, MA: Auburn House Publishing, 1986).

Scheff, David. *China Dawn: The Story of a Technology and Business Revolution* (New York: HarperCollins, 2002).

Schweller, Randall L. 'Bandwagoning for Profit: Bringing the Revisionist State Back In', *International Security* 19(1) (Summer 1994): 72–107.

Scobell, Andrew. 'Slow-Intensity Conflict in the South China Sea', *Foreign Policy Research Institute E-Notes* (16 August, 2000). www.nyu.edu/globalbeat/asia/FPRI081600.html.

—— *China's Use of Military Force: Beyond the Great Wall and the Long March* (Cambridge and New York: Cambridge University Press, 2003).

—— 'China and North Korea: The Limits of Influence', *Current History* 102(665) (September 2003): 274–8.

See Seng Tan and Kumar Ramakrishna, 'Interstate and Intrastate Dynamics in Southeast Asia's War on Terror', *SAIS Review* 24(1) (Winter/Spring 2004): 91–105.

Segal, Gerald. 'East Asia and the "Constrainment" of China', *International Security* 20(4) (Spring 1996): 107–35.

—— 'Does China Matter?' *Foreign Affairs* 78(5) (September/October 1999): 24–36.

Seki, Hiromoto. 'APEC: New Paradigm for Asia-Pacific Relations', *Asia-Pacific Review* 3(1) (Spring/Summer 1996): 131–6.

Sha Zukang. 'China's Perspective on Non-Proliferation', *Repairing the Regime: Preventing the Spread of Weapons of Mass Destruction*, edited by Joseph Cirincione, 127–31 (New York and London: Routledge, 2000).

217

Shambaugh, David. 'Growing Strong: China's Challenge to Asian Security', *Survival* 36(2) (Summer 1994): 43–59.

—— 'Containment or Engagement of China?' *International Security* 21(2) (Fall 1996): 180–209.

—— 'China's Military Views the World: Ambivalent Security', *International Security* 24(1) (Winter 1999/2000): 52–79.

—— 'Sino–American Strategic Relations: From Partners to Competitors', *Survival* 42(1) (Spring 2000): 97–115.

—— *Modernizing China's Military: Progress, Problems and Prospects* (Berkeley, CA and London: University of California Press, 2002).

Sheng Lijun. 'Bush's New China Policy: Air Collision, Arms Sales, and China–US Relations', *Pacific Focus: Inha Journal of International Studies* 14(2) (Fall 2001): 57–86.

—— *China's Dilemma: The Taiwan Issue* (Singapore: Institute of Southeast Asian Studies, 2001).

Shirk, Susan L. 'Chinese Views on Asia-Pacific Multilateral Security Cooperation', National Bureau of Asian Research *NBR Analysis*. http://www.nbr.org/publications/analysis/pdf/vol5no5.pdf.

—— *How China Opened its Door: The Political Success of the PRC's Foreign Trade and Investment Reforms* (Washington, DC: Brookings Institution, 1994).

Shumilin, Aleksandr. 'Pentagon Re-Targeting', *Izvestia*, 27 March 2001. Reprinted in *NAPSNet Daily Report* (28 March 2001): 6. www.nautilus.org/napsnet/dr/0103/MAR28.html#item19.

Singer, J. David. 'The Level-of-Analysis Problem in International Relations', *World Politics* 14(1) (October 1961): 76–92.

Skehan, Craig. 'Australia Dancing to US Tune, mocks China', *Sydney Morning Herald* (2 August 2001). www.smh.com.au/news/0108/02/world/world1.html.

Skehan, Craig and Hamish McDonald. 'Gang of Four Leaves China out in the Cold', *Sydney Morning Herald* (31 July 2001): 1. www.smh.com.au/news/0107/31/world/world1.html.

Smith, Gary. 'Multilateralism and Regional Security in Asia: The ASEAN Regional Forum (ARF) and APEC's Geopolitical Value', *Cancaps Papier* 13 (September 1996).

So, Alvin Y. 'China under the Shadow of the Asian Financial Crisis: Retreat from Economic and Political Liberalization?' *Asian Perspective* 23(2) (1999): 83–109.

Solomon, Richard H. *Chinese Negotiating Behavior: Pursuing Interests Though 'Old Friends'* (Washington, DC: United States Institute of Peace Press, 1999).

Song, Ligang. 'China', in *East Asia in Crisis: From Being a Miracle to Needing One?*, edited by Ross H. McLeod and Ross Garnaut, 105–19 (London and New York: Routledge, 1998).

Spanier, John. *Games Nations Play* (New York and Washington, DC: Praeger Publishers, 1972).

Starr, S. Frederick. 'Making Eurasia Stable', *Foreign Affairs* 75(1) (January/February 1996): 80–92.

Stein, Janice Gross. 'International Cooperation and Loss Avoidance: Framing the Problem', in *Choosing to Cooperate: How States Avoid Loss*, edited by Janice Gross Stein and Louis W. Pauly, 2–34 (Baltimore, MD: Johns Hopkins University Press, 1993).

Steinfeld, Edward S. 'The Asian Financial Crisis: Beijing's Year of Reckoning', *Washington Quarterly* 21(3) (Summer 1998): 37–51.

Stern, David. 'Central Asia Plan to Fight Terrorism', *Financial Times* (6 July 2000): 14.

Strange, Susan. 'The Persistent Myth of Lost Hegemony', *International Organization* 41(4) (Autumn 1987): 551–74.

Stubbs, Richard. 'ASEAN Plus Three: Emerging East Asian Regionalism', *Asian Survey* 42(3) (May/June 2002): 440–55.

Studwell, Joe. *The China Dream: The Quest for the Last Untapped Market on Earth* (New York: Atlantic Monthly Press, 2002).

Suettinger, Robert L. *Beyond Tiananmen: The Politics of US-China Relations 1989–2000* (Washington, DC: Brookings Institution Press, 2003).

Sun Zhuangzhi. 'China and Central Asia in the New International Climate', *The Times of Central Asia* 3(4) 99 (25 January 2001). www.times.kg/2001/N4/new-01.shtml.

Suny, Ronald Grigor. 'Provisional Stabilities: The Politics of Identities in Post-Soviet Eurasia', *International Security* 24(3) (Winter 1999/2000): 139–78.

Swaine, Michael D. and Alastair Iain Johnston. 'China and Arms Control Institutions', in *China Joins the World: Progress and Prospects*, edited by Michael Oksenberg and Elizabeth Economy, 90–135 (New York: Council on Foreign Relations Press, 1999).

Swaine, Michael D. and Ashley J. Tellis. *Interpreting China's Grand Strategy: Past, Present and Future* (Santa Monica, CA: Rand, 2000).

Taliaferro, Jeffrey W. 'Security Seeking Under Anarchy: Defensive Realism Revisited', *International Security* 25(3) (Winter 2000/1): 128–61.

Tammen, Ronald L., Douglas Lemke, Carole Alsharabati, Jacek Kugler, Allan C. Stam III, Mark Andrew Abdollahian, and A.F.K. Organski. *Power Transitions: Strategies for the 21st Century* (New York and London: Chatham House Publishers, Seven Bridges Press, 2000).

Tang, Shiping. 'Economic Integration in Central Asia: The Russian and Chinese Relationship', *Asian Survey* 40(2) (March/April 2000): 361–76.

Terrill, Ross. 'China and the World: Self-Reliance or Interdependence?' *Foreign Affairs* 55(7) (June 1977): 295–305.

—— *Mao: A Biography* (Stanford, CA: Stanford University Press, 1999).

—— *The New Chinese Empire and What It Means for the United States* (New York: Basic Books, 2003).

Titarenko, Mikhail and Vassilii Mikheev. 'The Asia-Pacific Region and Russia', *International Affairs* (Moscow) 47(3) (2001): 55–70.

Tow, William T. 'China and the International Strategic System', in *Chinese Foreign Policy: Theory and Practice*, edited by Thomas W. Robinson and David Shambaugh, 115–57 (Oxford: Clarendon Press, 1994).

Tow, William T. and Leisa Hay. 'Australia, the United States, and a "China Growing Strong": Managing Conflict Avoidance', *Australian Journal of International Affairs* 55(1) (2001): 37–54.

Troush, Sergei. 'China's Changing Oil Strategy and its Foreign Policy Implications', Brookings Center for Northeast Asian Policy Studies Working Paper (Fall 1999). www.brook.edu/fp/cnaps/papers/1999_troush.htm.

Tsai, Kellee S. *Back-Alley Banking: Private Entrepreneurs in China* (Ithaca, NY and London: Cornell University Press, 2002).

Tyler, Patrick E. 'China Pressing to Join Trade Club', *The New York Times* (14 November 1994): D1, D5.

—— 'The (Ab)normalization of US–Chinese Relations', *Foreign Affairs* 78(5) (September/October 1999): 93–122.

—— *A Great Wall: Six Presidents and China – An Investigative History* (New York: Public Affairs, 2000).

United Nations. *The United Nations and Cambodia, 1991–1995* (New York: Department of Public Information, United Nations, 1995).

Urayama, Kori. 'China Debates Missile Defence', *Survival* 46(2) (Summer 2004): 123–42.

Valencia, Mark J. *China and the South China Sea Disputes*, Adelphi Paper 298 (Oxford: Oxford University Press, 1995).

van Kamenade, Willem. *China, Hong Kong, Taiwan, Inc.: The Dynamics of a New Empire* (New York: Vintage Books, 1998).

Vasquez, John A. 'The Realist Paradigm and Degenerative versus Progressive Research Programs: An Appraisal of Neotraditional Research on Waltz's Balancing Proposition', *American Political Science Review* 91(4) (December 1997): 899–912.

Vatikiotis, Michael, Ben Dolven, and David Murphy. 'Terror Throws Us Together, For Now', *Far Eastern Economic Review* (1 November 2001): 36–40.

Waldron, Arthur. 'After Deng the Deluge: China's Next Leap Forward', *Foreign Affairs* 74(5) (September/October 1995): 148–53.

Walmsley, Terrie L. and Thomas W. Hertel. 'China's Accession to the WTO: Timing is Everything', *The World Economy* 24(8) (August 2001): 1019–45.

Walt, Stephen M. 'Beyond Bin Laden: Reshaping US Foreign Policy', *International Security* 26(3) (Winter 2001/2): 56–78.

Waltz, Kenneth N. *Theory of International Politics* (New York: Random House, 1979).

—— 'Structural Realism after the Cold War', *International Security* 25(1) (Summer 2000): 5–41.

Wanandi, Jusuf. 'ASEAN's China Strategy: Towards Deeper Engagement', *Survival* 38(3) (Autumn 1996): 117–28.

Wang, Fei-Ling. 'Self-Image and Strategic Intentions: National Confidence and Political Insecurity', in *In the Eyes of the Dragon: China Views the World*, edited by Yong Deng and Fei-Ling Wang, 21–45 (Lanham, MD and Oxford: Rowman and Littlefield, 1999).

Wang Hongwei, 'Pondering on Bush's "Axis of Evil" Remarks', *Beijing Review* (14 March 2002): 6–7.

Wang, Hongying. 'Multilateralism in Chinese Foreign Policy: The Limits of Socialization?' In *China's International Relations in the 21st Century*, edited by Weixing Hu, Gerald Chan and Daojiong Zha, 71–91 (Lanham, MD and Oxford: University Press of America, 2000).

Wang, Jianwei. 'Chinese Perspectives on Multilateral Security Cooperation', *Asian Perspective* 22(3) (1998): 103–32.

—— 'Managing Conflict: Chinese Perspectives on Multilateral Diplomacy and Collective Security', in *In the Eyes of the Dragon: China Views the World*, edited by Yong Deng and Fei-ling Wang, 73–96 (Lanham, MD and Oxford: Rowman and Littlefield Publishers, 1999).

Wang, Robert S. 'China's Evolving Strategic Doctrine', *Asian Survey* 24(10) (October 1984): 1040–55.

Ward, Adam. 'China and America: Trouble Ahead?' *Survival* 45(3) (Autumn 2003): 35–56.

Watts, Jonathan. 'China Admits First Rise in Poverty since 1978,' *The Guardian* (20 July 2004). www.guardian.co.uk/print/0,3858,4974418–103681,00.html.

Weisbrode, Kenneth. *Central Eurasia: Prize or Quicksand? Contending Views of Instability in Karabakh, Ferghana and Afghanistan*, Adelphi Paper 338 (New York: Oxford University Press, 2001).

Wendt, Alexander. 'Anarchy is what states make of it: the social construction of power politics', *International Organization* 46(2) (Spring 1992): 391–425.

Wilkinson, David. 'Unipolarity without Hegemony', *International Studies Review* 1(2) (Summer 1999): 141–72.

Willett, Susan. 'East Asia's Changing Defence Industry', *Survival* 39(3) (Autumn 1997): 107–34.

Wishnick, Elizabeth. 'Russia and China: Brothers Again?' *Asian Survey* 41(5) (September/October 2001): 797–821.

—— *Mending Fences: The Evolution of Moscow's China Policy from Brezhnev to Yeltsin* (Seattle, WA and London: University of Washington Press, 2001).

Wit, Joel S., Daniel B. Poneman and Robert L. Gallucci. *Going Critical: The First North Korean Nuclear Crisis* (Washington, DC: Brookings Institution Press, 2004).

Wonacott, Peter. 'China Begins Career as a WTO Member', *The Wall Street Journal* (11 December 2001): A14.

Wong, John and Sarah Chan, 'China-ASEAN Free Trade Agreement: Shaping Future Economic Relations,' *Asian Survey* 43(3) (May/June 2003): 507–26.

Wong, John and Zheng Yongnian. 'Nationalism and Its Dilemma: Chinese Responses to the Embassy Bombing', in *Reform, Legitimacy, and Dilemmas: China's Politics and Society*, edited by Wang Gongwu and Zeng Yongnian, 321–43 (Singapore: Singapore University Press and World Scientific Publishing, 2000).

Woods, Lawrence T. *Asia-Pacific Diplomacy: Nongovernmental Organizations and International Relations* (Vancouver: UBC Press, 1993).

—— 'Learning From NGO Proponents of Asia-Pacific Regionalism', *Asian Survey* 35(9) (September 1995): 812–27.

World Bank. *China 2020: Development Challenges in the New Century* (Washington, DC: The International Bank for Reconstruction and Development/World Bank, 1997).

Wu Baiyi, 'The Chinese Security concept and its Historical Evolution,' *Journal of Contemporary China* 10(27) (2001): 275–83.

X [George F. Kennan]. 'The Sources of Soviet Conduct', *Foreign Affairs* 25(4) (July 1947): 566–82.

Xiang, Lanxin. 'The China Debate and the Civilization Debate', *Issues and Studies* 34(10) (October 1998): 79–92.

Xiao Zan. '"Mini NATO" in Asia-Pacific Region Plan by the US and Australia', *Beijing Review* (13 September 2001): 10.

Xie Bai-san. *China's Economic Policies, Theories and Reforms since 1949* (Shanghai: Fudan University Press, 1991).

Xing, Guangcheng. 'Security Issues in China's Relations with Central Asian States', in *Ethnic Challenges Beyond Borders: Chinese and Russian Perspectives of the Central Asian Conundrum*, edited by Yongjin Zhang and Rouben Azizian, 203–17 (New York: St Martin's Press, 1998).

—— 'China and Central Asia', in *Central Asian Security: The New International Context*, edited by Roy Allison and Lena Jonson, 152–70 (London: Royal Institute of International Affairs; New York: Brookings, 2001).

Yahuda, Michael. 'Deng Xiaoping: The Statesman', *The China Quarterly* 135 (September 1993): 550–72.

—— 'China's Foreign Relations: The Long March, Future Uncertain', *The China Quarterly* 159 (September 1999): 650–9.

Yamazawa, Ippei. 'On Pacific Economic Integration' *The Economic Journal* 102 (November 1992): 1519–29.

Yang, Dali L. 'Rationalizing the Chinese State: The Political Economy of Government Reform', in *Remaking the Chinese State: Strategies, Society, and Security*, edited by Chien-min Chao and B.J. Dickson, 19–45 (London and New York: Routledge, 2001).

—— 'China in 2001: Economic Liberalization and Its Political Discontents', *Asian Survey* 41(1) (January/February 2002): 14–28.

Yi Ding. 'Upholding the Five Principles of Peaceful Coexistence', *Beijing Review* (26 February 1990): 13–16.

Ying, A. 'New Security Mechanism Needed for Asian-Pacific Region', *Beijing Review* (18 August 1997): 6–7.

Yong Deng. *Promoting Asia-Pacific Economic Cooperation* (New York: St Martin's Press; Basingstoke: Macmillan Press, 1997).

—— 'Research Note: The Chinese Conception of National Interests in International Relations', *The China Quarterly* 154 (June 1998): 308–29.

You Ji. *The Armed Forces of China* (London and New York: I.B. Tauris, 1999).

Yue, Chia Siow. 'Economic Cooperation and Integration in East Asia,' *Asia-Pacific Review* 11(1) (2004): 1–19.

Zacher, Mark W. 'The Territorial Integrity Norm: International Boundaries and the Use of Force', *International Organization* 55(2) (Spring 2001): 215–50.

Zerega, Blaise. 'What Would Mao Think?' *Red Herring* 83 (October 2000): 120–32.

Zhang Guochu. 'Employment after WTO Accession', *Beijing Review* (21 March 2002): 16–17.

Zhang, Yongjin. *China in International Society since 1949: Alienation and Beyond* (Oxford and New York: St Martin's Press, 1998).

Zhang Yunling. 'China and APEC: Interests, Opportunities, and Challenges', in *From APEC to Xanadu*, edited by Donald C. Hellmann and Kenneth B. Pyle, 195–202 (Armonk, NY: M.E. Sharpe, 1997).

Zhao, Suisheng. 'China's Periphery Policy and its Asian Neighbours', *Security Dialogue* 30(3) (September 1999): 335–46.

—— 'Military Coercion and Peaceful Offence: Beijing's Strategy of National Reunification with Taiwan', *Pacific Affairs* 72(4) (September 1999): 495–512.

—— 'Chinese Nationalism and Authoritarianism', in *China and Democracy: Reconsidering the Prospects for a Democratic China*, edited by Shuisheng Zhao, 253–70 (New York and London: Routledge, 2000).

—— *A Nation State by Construction: Dynamics of Modern Chinese Nationalism* (Stanford, CA: Stanford University Press, 2004).

Zheng, Yongnian. *Globalization and State Transformation in China* (Cambridge and New York: Cambridge University Press, 2004).

Zweig, David. 'China's Stalled "Fifth Wave": Zhu Rongji's Reform Package of 1998–2000', *Asian Survey* 41(2) (March/April 2001): 231–47.

INDEX

Printed in the United Kingdom by
Lightning Source UK Ltd., Milton Keynes
138623UK00001B/74/A